PATRICK & BEATRICE HAGGERTY LIBRARY
MILWAUKEE, WISCONSIN 53222
W9-AQU-661

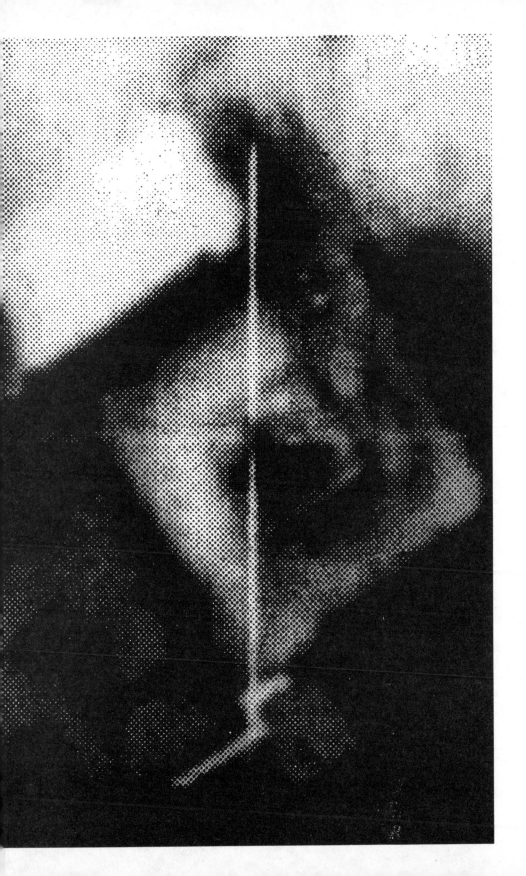

DEATH AT THE PARASITE CAFE

SOCIAL SCIENCE (FICTIONS) AND THE POSTMODERN

CultureTexts
Arthur and Marilouise Kroker, General Editors

CultureTexts is a series of creative explorations in theory, politics and culture at the *fin-de-millenium*. Thematically focussed around certain theoretical debates in the postmodern condition, the *CultureTexts* series challenges received discourses in art, social and political theory, feminism, psychoanalysis, value inquiry, science and technology, the body, and critical aesthetics. Taken individually, contributions to *CultureTexts* represent the forward breaking-edge of postmodern theory and practice.

Titles

Death at the Parasite Cafe: Social Science (Fictions) and the Postmodern
Stephen Pfohl

Ideology and Power in the Age of Lenin in Ruins
edited and introduced by Arthur and Marilouse Kroker

The Possessed Individual: Technology and the French Postmodern
Arthur Kroker

The Hysterical Male: New Feminist Theory
edited and introduced by Arthur and Marilouse Kroker

Seduction
Jean Baudrillard

Panic Encyclopedia
edited by Arthur Kroker, Marilouse Kroker, and David Cook

Life After Postmodernism: Essays on Value and Culture
edited and introduced by John Fekete

Body Invaders: Panic Sex in America
edited and introduced by Arthur and Marilouse Kroker

The Postmodern Scene: Excremental Culture and Hyper-Aesthetics,
revised edition
Arthur Kroker and David Cook

PATRICK & BEATRICE HAGGERTY LIBRARY
MOUNT MARY COLLEGE
MILWAUKEE, WISCONSIN 53222

WITHDRAWN

DEATH AT THE PARASITE CAFE

SOCIAL SCIENCE (FICTIONS) AND THE POSTMODERN

Stephen Pfohl

St. Martin's Press
New York

© 1992 Stephen Pfohl
All rights reserved. For information, write:
St. Martin's Press, Inc.
Scholarly and Reference Division
175 Fifth Avenue
New York, NY 10010

Printed in the U.S.A.

Library of Congress Cataloging-in-Publication Data
Pfohl, Stephen J.
    Death at the parasite cafe : social science (fictions) and the
postmodern / Stephen Pfohl.
        p.   cm. — (CultureTexts series)
        ISBN 0-312-07573-1
        1. Information society—United States.   2. Parasitism (Social
sciences)—United States.   3. Social control.   4. Postmodernism-
-Social aspects—United States.   I. Title.   II. Series.
HM221.P47   1992
301'.0973—dc20
                                                                92-3296
                                                                    CIP

First Edition: July 1992
10 9 8 7 6 5 4 3 2 1

301
P531d
1992

TABLE OF CONTENTS

PART ONE

(W)RITING PREFACES

PART TWO

DOUBLE-CROSSING THE EYE/"I"

FOR THE ORPHANS

DEATH AT THE PARASITE CAFE

SOCIAL SCIENCE (FICTIONS) AND THE POSTMODERN

(W)RITING PREFACES

The preface, by daring to repeat the book and reconstitute it in another register, merely enacts what is already the case: the book's repetitions are always other than the book. There is, in fact, no 'book' other than these ever-different repetitions: the 'book' in other words, is always already a 'text,' constituted by the play of repetition and difference.

—Gayatri Chakravorty Spivak

What prefaces the scene of (w)riting in which you and I find ourselves entangled? Cut-out, tattooed, ambivalently mirrored back upon what unspeakable difference: this is the sacrificial HIStory "we" are repeatedly unable to re-present each and every time "we" are tempted to say "we" are prefacing anything; each and every time somebody acts as if one (who is not one) is signing one's name or para-siting an object; each and every time "we" are given to the unstable, if regulated, social electricity of those fantastic force fields of separation in which "we" find ourselves both fascinated and fearful. So what then is a preface, if not a strangely reflexive display of roots that were "once upon a time" covered-over but now laughingly reinscribed? What plagiarism!   —Rada Rada

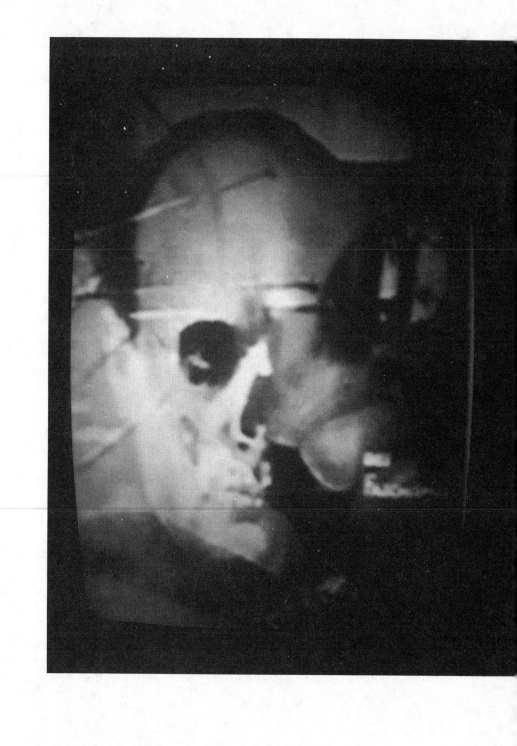

WHEN WORDS BECOME FLESH
AND FLESH BECOMES WORDS
AN EDITOR'S PREFACE

> A blank white virus cut through the back of her mind. Her stomach
> tightening. In theory, what was happening seemed at once terroristic and
> absorbent of all HIStorical perspective. As s/he labored to partially remem-
> ber the shifting material origins of the story in which s/he found herself
> embodied, s/he turned upon the staging of this tale whose god-awful
> silence fed the parasitic expanse of what seemed a New World Order.
> Thereafter, like an ill-scripted character in a play whose author(s) escaped
> memory, but not entirely, she fell and kept on falling. Soon there were
> strange sounds electric, cyber-space and lasers. Television was everywhere
> and the uncanny dial tone of a misplaced echo – acidic reminders of
> thought-for-food resisting digestion. S/he spun to the left, staggered but not
> denied an appetite for revenge? "If only I could laugh," she said to herself.
> "If only I could laugh."—Black Madonna Durkheim[1]

I am burning like Baghdad or Detroit on "Devil's Night" to tell a story of
the postmodern. Not simply a story of a genre of art, architecture, or literary
engagement, but a story of the dense and high velocity techno-structuring of
the society in which I find myself (k)notted in a complex network of relations
to others. This is a sociological story to counter-memorize or countermand
what I take to be an emerging terroristic social formation in HIStory—a new
American *empire of the senseless*. Although this story passes through my body,
it is not mine alone. Nor am I entirely by myself in the re(w)ritings that become this text. No parasite is. Repeatedly.

This is a story of the sacrificial effects of the dominant ritual practices of
those who find a seemingly centered pleasure within the violent and consumptive swells of an advancing whitemale, heterosexist and transnational mode of
CAPITAList reproduction. COMMAND. CONTROL. COMMUNICATIONS. This is
also a story of those sentenced to circulate at the peripheries of what's imaginable within the imperial confines of a new and telelectronic U.S. will to power
without end. These are the victims of an ultramodernizing conjunction of
power and knowledge: women, peoples of color and the economically impov-

erished. Long excluded from a reciprocal participation in the social structuring of modernity, these persons are doubly exiled by the high speed HIStorical procession of postmodern simulacra. This is the story of a violent modality of power and knowledge: a fantastic, nihilistic and cybernetically engineered will to will, a third order of CAPITALIST epistemology that is as terroristic as it is seductive and as inFORMational as it is forgetful of the sacrifices which constitute its materiality. This is not a pleasing story to tell.

> "Come on, then." She took his hand. "We'll get you a coffee and something to eat. Take you home. It's good to see you, man." She squeezed his hand.
> He smiled.
> Something cracked.
> Something at the core of things. The arcade froze, vibrated—
> She was gone. The weight of memory came down, an entire body of knowledge driven into his head like a microsoft into a socket. Gone. He smelled burning meat.[2]

The last thing that happened to me was a memory. Flash. Snap. Crack(le). Pop. I was watching television when suddenly I was recalled, taken by a sensational image of a desire to return to a time that never existed. Where does this image of desire come from? Where is it taking me? Where is it taking others? In the late 1950s C. Wright Mills used the word "postmodern" to refer to the HIStorical emergence of a new form of military guided economic rationality that was rapidly transforming the organization of contemporary social power. According to Mills, it is not "merely that we feel we are in an epochal kind of transition, and that we struggle to grasp the outline of a new epoch we suppose ourselves to be entering.... When we try to orient ourselves—if we do try—we find that too many of our standard categories of thought or feeling as often disorient as help us to explain what is happening around us; that too many of our explanations are derived from the great historical transition from the Medieval to the Modern Age; and that when they are generalized for use today they become unwieldy, irrelevant, not convincing."[3]

In 1951 Mills wrote that: "Between consciousness and existence stand communications....The forms of political consciousness may, 'in the end,' be relative to the means of production, but, in the beginning, they are relative to the...communication media."[4] Alert to massive transformations in the "cultural machinery" of "overdeveloped" societies, Mills warned of the increasing power of electronic media as a "kind of scheme for pre-scheduled, mass emotions," whereby it is increasingly "impossible to tell the image from the source."[5] Mills viewed the expansion of electronic inFORMation, not simply as external forces, but as forms of social experience that blur boundaries between "first hand contact" and prefabricated signs. As such, the media "seep into our images of self, becoming that which is taken for granted, so imperceptibly and so surely that to modify them drastically, over a generation or two, would be to change profoundly modern...experience and character."[6] This marked the emergence of a "new society," dominated by the electronic circulation of "mythic figures and fast-moving stereotypes."[7] In this "new society":

> We are so submerged in the pictures created by mass media that we no longer really see them...The attention absorbed by the images on the screen's rectangle dominates the darkened public; the sonorous, the erotic, the mysterious, the funny voice of the radio talks to you; the thrill of the easy murder relaxes you. In our life-situation, they simply fascinate. And their effects run deep: popular culture is not tagged as 'propaganda' but as entertainment; people are often exposed to it when most relaxed of mind and tired of body; and its characters offer easy targets of identification, easy answers to stereotyped personal problems.[8]

That was forty years ago. Today the dense and high speed precession of media images is far more enveloping. Indeed, as the "desert storms" engendered by the U.S. presidency of George Bush have made all too manifest, there is little difference between the depths of public political discourse and the shimmering televisionary surfaces of the mass media itself. Moreover, the media is not outside the ever more publicized bodies of those most exposed to its almost magnetic circuit of effects. Why, only this morning I found myself eating before the screen, or after, when suddenly my eyes/"I"s were transferred across the social space of this, our ungiving present, 20 seconds into the future. This is a story of the sacrificial rituals of an ultramodernizing first world culture. This is not a pleasing story to tell.

Death at the Parasite Cafe explores the bodily invasion of an expanding host of fleshy human animals by a cold, uncanny and consumptive addiction to a seemingly endless flow of inFORMational bits and pieces, fragments of a world that never existed, electronic memories of fears and attractions that have no substance independent of the simulative re-structuring of experience within the vacant if omnipresent data banks of advancing transnational CAPITAL. A materialist imagination of such a parasitic invasion of the body demands a reflexive re(w)riting of the HIStorical dynamics of contemporary society from within (or at the borders of) a social structure that functions less by the power of signs to provide ideological rationalizations for an existing order than by the ability of complex and contradictory technological rituals to draw consumers into a network of seemingly endless fascinations and nearly instantaneous electromagnetic feedback. In postmodern society, linguistic rituals of representation are being rapidly transformed into cybernetically codified rites of "signing." This is indicative of a new form of social control: the close-circuiting of inFORMational processes that seduce those they most consume out from within the thick-skinned experiential confines of modern subjectivity into a postmodern or quantum-like mechanics of sign-making itself.

> The body seems to float...—the body is deserting the body—the head is aching and almost no temperature exists. Material is cold. All is ice.... Mentality is the mirror of physicality. The body is a mirror of the mind. A mirror image is not exactly the same as what is mirrored.... Memories of identity flowed through my head.... [S]ometimes I think about my mommy. She's the only one who could make me warm.... That memory's almost gone.... Maybe that memory's false.... My father's no longer important because interpersonal power means corporate power. The multinationals along with their computers have changed and are changing reality. Viewed as organisms, they've attained immortality via bio-chips. Etc. Who needs slaves anymore?...These days the principal economic flow of power takes place through black-market armament and drug exchange. The trading arena, the market, is my blood. My body is open to all people: this is democratic capitalism. Today pleasure lies in the flow of blood. I looked at my boyfriend. He looked at me. "You look like death," I said. White flesh. We're finished. I can no longer work with you.[9]

This is the Parasite Cafe, a dark if brilliantly enlightened space of post-modernity where a transnational host of corporate inFORMational operatives feed upon the digitally coded flesh of others. Here, many of our bodies are today being transferentially invaded and then extended outward hyper-really into the consumptive networkings of the media itself. Multiple channels of inFORMation wave themselves through our bodies, infecting us with an un-canny if somewhat panicky oscillation between what's feared and what's fascinating; connecting even our most intimate senses of social reality to a vast flow of ever more enveloping inFORMational networks. At the same time, the sensorial effects of such network hookups feed back upon the body, reconsti-tuting sensory imaginings of what's (empirically) possible and what's not.

This is ultramodernity. What are the HIStorical, economic and sexualized roots of a society of such immense material abstraction? How might the disembodied lure and seductive violence of this social form be subverted or transformed? For me these are urgent questions. Why, only this morning I found myself eating before the screen, or after, when suddenly my eyes/"I"s were transferred, almost magnetically, across the terroristic social space of an ungiving HIStorical present, 20 seconds into the future. This is a story of the cultural violence of what U.S. President George Bush calls a New World Order. This is not a pleasing story to tell.

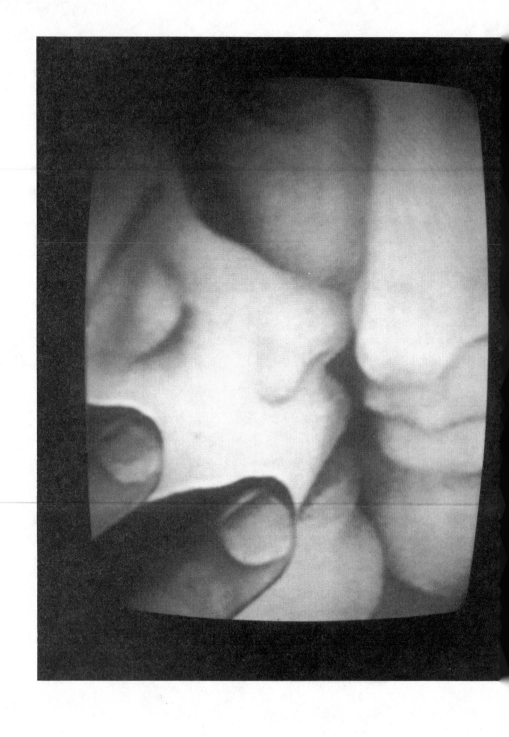

chapter
two

> To write ethnographies in the model of collage would be to avoid the
> portrayal of cultures as organic wholes, or as unified realistic worlds
> subject to a continuous explanatory discourse....The ethnography as
> collage would leave manifest the constructionist procedures of ethno-
> graphic knowledge, it would be an assemblage containing voices other
> than the ethnographer's, as well as examples of 'found' evidence, data not
> fully integrated within the works governing interpretation. Finally it would
> not explain away those elements in the foreign culture which render the
> investigator's own culture newly incomprehensible. —James Clifford[1]

This text is an ethnographic text, if somewhat surreally. It invites you, its
readers, not so much to agree with the evidence and the analysis set forth by
me, its author, as to enter actively into the process of re-searching your own
HIStorical and biographically given positions within what might be described
provisionally as *the postmodern scene* of contemporary North America.[2] For it
is indeed within the HIStorical materiality of this powerful scene that some (of
us) are in contradictory ways struggling repeatedly to define, defend, and
reconstruct the social forms in which we live and die; and to do this in relation
to and often against others (of us) who feed parasitically off the flesh of those
whose material chances they economically restrict and militaristically reduce. I
am here (w)riting of (and against) those most privileged by current hierarchies
of power, hierarchies that today operate under the nightmarish sacrificial sign-
work of cybernetic-like compulsions toward a New World Order of systematic
overdevelopment, transglobal CAPITAList hegemony and straight whitemale
economies of logic, morality and pleasure. The technologically driven and
culturally orchestrated shifts in the command, control and communicative
character of such inFORMational hierarchies separate them from modern
forms of power. Does this mean these forms of power are postmodern? Or is it
better to designate such contemporary modalities of power as *ultramodern*?
Although throughout this text these two terms are use somewhat interchange-
ably, I believe the term *ultramodern* to be more adequate. This is because the

HIStorical emergence of inFORMational modalities of power represents not so much a negation of modern power as a violent and technologically mediated extension of existing racial, economic and sexual hierarchies into previously unimaginable spaces of political and cultural domination.

Shrouded in narcissistic self-evidencies, I find such complex and contradictory scenic networks, the very networks in which I find myself stupidly (w)riting out about from within, difficult to describe in words. Literally. As such, let me try to begin, stagger-stepped and, perhaps, occasionally falling flat, by partially re-membering a singularly frightening fragment of these powerfully screened networks—an image of Lt. Colonel Oliver North, Jr. telling the truth about the "facts" of U.S. foreign policy. This image is frightening precisely because for many of us there is another side, or several, to North's alleged truth. There is, for instance, well documented knowledge of the mutilated bodies of those who have been killed, sickened or otherwise silenced by this country's economic assertion of what its most powerful citizens repeatedly (mis)recognize as some God-given right to white patriarchal domination of the planet. And there is the terror that facts of "the other side" today make little difference within the consumptive telelectronic mediascape that is such a hegemonic feature of everyday life in the USA Today. I am here (w)riting of (and within) a New World Order of inFORMational CAPITAL, where the real facts of such matters appear (k)not uneasily converted into their televisionary opposites and then sacrificially recirculated into a fascinating, because implosive, amalgam of truths. Truths that, like vampires, feed upon images of apparent contradiction, draining flesh and blood sensations of struggle into cool, aesthetically distanced and abstractly conceived flows of inFORMation. Powerful truths amassing more and more inFORMation, databanking everything, while giving almost no-thing in return. Truths that periodically inoculate themselves against a reflexive HIStorical recognition of their own contradictory (dis)positionings by calling forth mass-mediated spectacles of (almost) always already premodeled and thus presanitized scandal.

> **Lt. Col. North:** Those are the facts, as I know them, Mr. Nields. I was glad that when you introduced this, you said that you wanted to hear the truth—*the good, the bad, and the ugly.* I am here to tell it all, pleasant and unpleasant.... I was provided with additional input that was radically different from the truth. I assisted in furthering that version.... I was provided with a different version of the facts. They were, I believe, transmitted to me in a note, a PROF note or an actual memorandum that is basically what's here, that is inconsistent with what I knew to be the truth.
>
> **Mr. Nields:** Did you say to Mr. McFarland, "That's not the truth?"

Lt. Col. North: I don't have a specific recollection of that conversation.... I am saying that I decided that I would continue to participate in preparing a version of the chronology, not necessarily what would be the final historical internal version, but a version of the chronology that was inaccurate....

Mr. Nields: In any event, my question to you, sir, is: There were reasons on the other side, were there not?

Lt. Col. North: Would you—would you give me—I, I don't understand your questions about 'reasons on the other side.'

Mr. Nields: There were reasons—well, I'll give them to you, and see if you agree. First of all, you put some value, don't you, in the truth?

Lt. Col. North: I've put great value on the truth. I've come here to tell it.

Mr. Nields: So, that was—that would be a reason not to put forward this version of the facts?

Lt. Col. North: The truth would be a reason not to put forward that version of the facts, but as I indicated to you a moment ago, I put great value on the lives of the American hostages. I worked hard to bring back as many as we could. I put great value in the possibility that we could... have ended the Iran-Iraq war...and that we had established for the first time, a direct contact with people inside Iran who might be able to assist us in the strategic reopening and who were at great risk if they were exposed. And, so, yes, I put great value in the truth, and as I said, I came here to tell it. But, I also put great value on human life, and I put great value on that second, second channel, who was at risk.[3]

This is a true story of vampirism, living death and of the electronic simulation of what's inFORMationally given within an almost fully industrialized, economically stratified, racist, imperial and straight-patriarchal Northwestern society. It begins *once upon a time,* as do all stories or all theories, with an image, or rather with a set of images. Oliver North, Jr. delivers the facts, Vanna White speaks, Bill Cosby becomes both black and white at the same time in space. What's the difference? Sincere or cynical talking heads providing fascinating inFORMation about the sex lives of star politicians, the selling of the summit, the accumulation of toxic wastes, and the exact number of inches of precipitation expected day after day after day after...............

Nothing is lost, it seems, to the "I"/eye of the camera, the "I"/eye of the screen. More and more inFORMation, faster and denser, more and more facts, data, empiricities, batting averages, body counts, stock market reports, numbers of homeless, aids victims, tooth decay, car sales, foreign trade deficits, inches of snow, records of temperature. All clearly explained. More white than white. More real than real. More sexy than sex. More news than new. A moving spectacle of ever more fashionable body parts: his machine worked biceps, her liposuctioned hips, its smooth metallic shine; digitally impregnated, perfectly copied. Advertising the desire for desire and for designer bodies modeled after models modeled after models. Mechanically toned, pharmaceutically adjusted or anorexically emptied bodies, always lacking, always wanting to want more or less. Restless bodies, ecstatic yet bored. Bodies invaded, panicked, made anxious by nightly broadcasts of the latest fashion in dress, dining, or murder, economic setbacks, Third World rioting, high speed auto crashes, and scientific breakthroughs or breakdowns. Images of missing children who find themselves participating interactively in shaping their increasingly computerized futures and the ends of HIStory as they enter the screen, nearly electromagnetic in assisting Captain Power to repeatedly escape mortality and so enact the white rites of a particularly violent form of HIStorical sacrifice—the elite production and mass consumption of a new mythic U.S. *empire of the senseless.*

This is a true story. And yet, once in those (im)possible spaces, before that *once upon a time* where this story, the HIStory of our (hegemonic) present, is mythically constructed there are other beginnings, other narrations of the birth of what's real. These begin perhaps with the weaving of a plethora of different colors, different foods, tastes, smells, geographies and sound waves. Or with periodic unweavings, dissolvings, re-memberings. Maybe they begin excessively in a brown earthy womb or in swampy black thick waters or with breathy rhythms or fiery flows spiraling chaotic. Or perhaps under the sign of a crescent moon returning to difference. Or with a different language uncastrating, discontinuous, as attentive to noise as to music. A menstrual, pregnant, voodoo or laughing language. Expensive, giving itself away. Not a nostalgic language inducing desire for a lost garden of wholeness. Nostalgia is the language of the inFORMational mediascape, a language of lack, a language that fills its communicants with sacramental longings for a present that never comes, for the gift that never arrives, for apocalypse both now and forever.

"We" who recognize that "we" are (k)not one with those who militaristically defend against such periodic reimmersions in difference must "pass to the other side...in order to extract oneself from these mechanisms which make two sides appear, in order to dissolve the false unity, the illusory 'nature' of this other side with which we have taken sides."[4] We must, in other words, move to the other side of nostalgia, if we are to be touched erotically, politically or in generous laughter by a language that dissolves itself festively. A language that opens out to and materializes itself in a dialogue with others. "[Not] because it was ever once like that, but because [within the dominant material imagination of our hierarchical present] it never was and never will be able to be otherwise."[5] Languages of excess, the excessing of language, (non)places of death not deterred but coming out from within themselves again and again in sensuous waves of ecstatic multiplicities. Poetic spaces. Spaces that resist proper names, proper economies of grammar. The other sides of any certain climax, the other sides of power and its fetishized chronology of lawful time passing measure for measure.

These other spaces have become relatively inaccessible to those among us most possessed by the hierarchical pleasures of that fetishized and accumulative New World Order (of things) in which "we" today find ourselves commodified, freeze-framed, or made commonsensically real or realistic. Why?

> **Mr. Nields:** In any event, my question to you sir, is: There were reasons on the other side, were there not?
>
> **Lt. Col. North:** Would you—would you give me—I, I don't understand your questions about "reasons on the other side."[6]

Why? Why are spaces on the other side of the dominant ordering of what's real seemingly so inaccessible or unmemorable? This text invites you, its readers, to entertain the suspicion that, for some time now, the experience of what is accessible to us has been (or is being) altered HIStorically by a radical material simulation of excess. In other words, excess is being reduced to the self-same realm of access. Stated another way, those experiences which had previously exceeded or fractured the socially constructed "commonsense" of the modern order, are today being manufactured in a simulated form and then fed back for our consumption without their once disturbing potential for creating a critical difference. This has been happening for some time. Perhaps since the electronically mass mediated invasion of our time and of many (if hopefully not all) of our minds embodied within the dominant televideo, computerized and increasingly cybernetic confines of the inFORMational culture of advanced transnational CAPITAL.

In using the term excess to connote what is being simulatively accessed by ultramodern media, I wish to evoke an image of what can never be perfectly imaged or properly named. I am referring to those impure and heterogeneously embodied experiences of ourselves becoming other, sacred, soulful or effervescent. The HIStorical realization of such excessive spaces is crucial for social movements aimed at radically changing an existing order of things in time. Without ritual access to those other sides of the dominant or mythological stories in which people find themselves inscribed in HIStory, it may prove virtually impossible to imagine other and hopefully more just ways of collectively organizing our lives together. Unfortunately material access to spaces in excess of the dominant order is exactly what is being denied us in the emergence of ultramodern society. The more we move within the dense and high speed world of image simulations that characterizes the ultramodern, the more we find excess modeled to fit prepackaged formats of access and then sold back to us so that we might consume what's different and what's the same all in the same bite/byte. Evidence of this terrifyingly New World Order of inFORMational vampirism may be found in a reflexive reading of the "reality effects" manufactured by ultramodern technologies of image management. These images and their power are today being produced and consumed for profit by the most advanced institutions of transnational CAPITAL.

PROGRAMMING CONSUMPTION

In *Everyday Life in the Modern World*, an early attempt to critically theorize the coming of postmodern society, Henri Lefebvre distinguishes modern societies in which hegemonic power is reproduced by a mix of both force and ideological influence from an emergent ultramodern social formation, the society of bureaucratically controlled consumption.[7] In this latter type of society, which is our type of society, ideology functions less by the power of dominant institutions to control the symbolic content of meaning than by a radically different form of sign-making itself. Here people are surrounded from the inside out by a powerful new semiurgy, a digital relay of flashing electronic icons that signal psychic and material responses within their consumers. "[F]ascinated by this backgroundless display...the message is pure reflection: ...the image infinitely reproduced in the form of...a cold eye...possessing feedback, balance, coherence and perpetuation."[8] The result is less the installation of a dominant belief system than a fascinating, if terroristic, inFORMational blurring between reality and its technological representation.

The "fatal attractions" of such a nihilistic social form are evident in contemporary society's seemingly parasitic abilities to block access to previously recognized critical spaces between what's inside and what's on the out, between the self-same and its other, between access and excess. In this sense, the term *ultramodernity* connotes the omnipresence of technologically mediated rituals whereby inFORMational forms of power operate as telecommunicative substitutes for a more vulnerable ceremonial organization of bodily perceptions and economic moral demands. Whose bodily perceptions and whose economic moral demands? Everybody's or only those most privileged by the defensive mechanics of ultramodern power? In raising these issues I hope to direct attention to the hierarchical effectivity of those coldly seductive and electromagnetic ritual processes that today transferentially carry some of us human-animals outward from within the skeletal confines of modern subjectivity into the telematically dense and nearly instantaneous dominant networkings of ultramodern subjectivity. This does not mean that everybody is either given equal exposure or equal access to such ultramodern frameworkings of power. It does mean, however, that (for worse or for better) dominant modalities of power differentially affect or infect nearly everybody worldwide, as hierarchically transmitted wavelengths or telecommunicative spinoffs of inFORMational power penetrate virtually everybody. It also means that hierarchical forms of power may be today mutating so rapidly that even those on the outside of power's violent networks may find spaces of previously HIStorical (or even hysterical) resistance, escape or defense as increasingly emptied of their social effectivity by being cybernetically absorbed back into the inFORMational reproduction of the self-same. This a cultural meaning of controlled implosion.

All this is a story of the oppressive (telecommunicative) reabsorption or *eternal return* of a host of all too real modern social contradictions into a seemingly smooth (if recurrently anxious) economic exchange of anomalous fears and almost magnetic fascinations. It is also a story of the sacrificial actions of predatory elites and the forms of contemporary social science which most serve these elites; and a story of how the totalizing (if hopefully still far from total) social power of such elites is today constituted less by a rational control over modern, law-like, and disciplinary institutionalizations than by a terroristic techno-body interfacing of telecommunicatively coded or cybernetic-like flows of inFORMational CAPITAL. Screen to screen. Terminal to terminal. Pick up the receiver. Push the button. Turn the dial. Tune yourself in. Turn yourself inside out. COMMAND. CONTROL. COMMUNICATIONS. (Artificial) intelligence. What's the difference? This is not to suggest that modern straight-whitemale and economically privileged elites no longer exercise executive, legislative and judicial control over the law-like ritual structurings of modern power, nor that the industriousness of modern power and the resistances it engenders no longer exist. Quite the opposite. Technologically freed from imaginary and material repressions that have long haunted the white CAPITAL-ist and straight-minded memories of powerful modern men, ultramodern male power may today be advancing into unprecedented regions of psychic and bodily control over the destinies of others. Judge for yourself the relation between such power-charged amplifications of hegemonic power relations and the contemporary ascendence of white (k)nighted and techno-male-fascist modalities of terroristic social control.

Drawn into the dense, high speed and electronically pulsating structural operations of telecommunicative mass marketing, many of our bodies are literally invaded and then extended outward into the networkings of the media itself. Multiple channels of inFORMation converge on and through us, not so much to persuade as to instill an uncanny if somewhat panicky oscillation between what's feared and what's fascinating. Perhaps this is because those of us most subject to the cybernetic codings of ultramodern power are finding ourselves situated physically within such a serial swell of data that even our most intimate senses of what's real become extended outward into ever more enveloping inFORMational networks. At the same time, the sensational effects of these network hookups feed back upon our supposedly "inner selves," reconstituting a great many of our lived sensory imaginations of what's (empirically) possible and what's (k)not.

Here human subjectivity is called out into a decentered hyper-space. Do you hear the call? How might this call be best collectively resisted? Within ultra-modernity our embodied imaginations of ourselves and others are increasingly vulnerable to being ritually relayed or mechanically pre-processed through complex networks of bio-technological feedback, video-loops, stereophonic sound-systems, Sony Walkmans, and talking cars. All within a solid liquidity of CAPITAL, a fast thick ocean of white noise. A ritual bombardment of sensory stimuli produced for our fearful and fascinating consumption by a profitable HIStorical conjuncture of corporate, military, civil-state and scientific institutions. And positioned so as to dominate the manifest destinies of these institutions—an upward classification of skillful or compliant white men of power, whose visions of the most profitable ways to work this planet constitute the core economic, sexual and racial images upon which the inFORMational simulations of ultramodernity are modelled. Masters of the universal, *Masters of the Universe*.

This is the show the young white girl is watching, enthralled by. I am sitting having coffee with her mother in the next room. Her mother is single, bored and anxious. She is unemployed. These are my neighbors. It is Saturday morning. Maybe 11:20 a.m. The young white girl in the next room is exposing herself to a television. It strikes me that she is daydreaming with the machine. Her eyes are moving rapidly but her body remains still. She sits knees curled within her dress, biting her nails, clutching a doll. Wide eyes/"I"s electric. She is watching the *Masters of the Universe*, taking in the inFORMation, the story, its repertoire of images. Something is really happening in this room with the young white girl and the machine. Is this the end of HIStory? Is this the beginning of the (non)HIStory of the postmodern code? Is this the advent of the truly functionalist society? A society of cybernetic programming of productive consumptives? The young girl enters the room where her mother and I are talking. She opens her mouth recirculating desire. I hear the following words.

> Mommy, mommy. They showed a K-TL 191 with screaming rear view blinkers and a flashing rotary rocket launcher with a digital tracking unit. It was only $29.99 but for one time only it's $19.99. But you have to call right away. Can we Mommy? Can we? Can we get the K-TL 191? Can we? Can we? All you have to do is call.

The young girl inFORMs her mother breathlessly of a 1-800 number. Her mother does not appear to understand. Perhaps she is less acquainted with this code. Suddenly the young girl again hears the voices of the *Masters of the Universe*. And so, without waiting for her mother's response, she efficiently returns to the televisionary site in which she finds herself called out in mind and body, interpellated with a desire for consumption. Off screen there are other events. The young white girl does not notice. There are plant closings in the northern Midwest, U.S. supported death squads in Central America, a growing number of homeless persons and Persons With Aids, teenage suicides and longer prison sentences for Blacks and Hispanics. There is a young black male child in another part of this city. He stabs another young black child, his neighbor, to get control of a "boom box," a sound system, a point of access into the media. The young white girl does not notice. Perhaps she is not hooked into these events, or hooked up.

THE TELECOMMUNICATION OF MEMORY

Are we here witnessing a new form of social memory, a new telecommunicative construction of what's real? How fascinating and how fearful? The possibility that such an ultramodern society has already come upon and within us is explored throughout the remainder of this text. For the moment, permit me to elaborate the suggestion that the emergence of ultramodernity is accompanied by a dramatic foreclosure of a variety of previously accessible spaces for exceeding the contradictory limits of modern forms of power. The suggestion here is that, unlike earlier modes of western social organization, ultramodern society is no longer staked upon a simple sacrificial exclusion of otherness. As complex as such simple hegemonic exclusions may have been in the past, something else is today beginning to take shape. Something more terroristic and more terminal.

Today powerful modern rites of exclusion are being simulatively undone then televisually redoubled. Before the blink of an eye/"I" or within the empty curved space of the self mirrored narcissistic eye/"I" within. Or both. Ultramodern society is that society which is ominously becoming technologically capable of inoculating itself against its Others. First, by producing an exact simulative double of the modality in which its other sides have been previously arrested or frozen outside the time of their own exclusion from modern society. Imagine here a vast array of stereotypical images of the economically oppressed or of women, nonwhites, nonwesterners or any Others excluded from reciprocal participation in the social structuring of the real life of modernity. In ultramodernity these images are not simply excluded. They are excluded by first being included but in a stereotypical and technologically sanitized form. In this sense, those secret sacrificial networkings repressed in the productive erection of modern power are being filtered of their once once resistive potential to conjure up reflexive spaces of difference within modernity itself. Today such experiential spaces of ritualized stupidity, those dynamically screened memories of primal scenes whose unconscious (dis)positionings have long played a forceful role in the repeated enactment of modern hierarchies, are inFORMationally simulated or purely redoubled. Here the symbolic ambivalence of contradictorily constructed social forms is digitally reduced into almost picture perfect copies not of what's real but of what had already been stereotypically reproduced. In this way, iconically cleansed images of otherness, seductive simulacra or simulations of what's different, are being consumptively reincorporated into commanding communicative circuitries that feed back into the ever expanding databases of ultramodernity itself. Thus, what may have previously exceeded being incorporated into the *true stories* of modernity are today telecommunicatively transformed, then inFORMationally accessed, before being vampirically dined upon by those most privileged by the cybernetic spin-controls of ultramodern power.

Within postmodern sign-work (or what might be called the ritual scenic practices of ultramodernity) everything may appear both as simultaneously possible and anxiously just beyond the reach of what's fleshy or humanly interdependent. Even those previously critical (im)possibilities in excess of the modern order. Throughout modernity those in power were constantly threatened by a "return of the repressed," by the shadowy traces of others excluded in the ritual repetition of the founding sacrifices of modernity as such. Ultramodern culture promises a masterful end to all of this. This is a society of eschatological fulfillments, a nuclear powered society aimed at the end of HIStory, the end of anything Other than what's knowable within the self-adjusting code of an already reproduced and ungiving order of things simulated. The perfect clone. The perfect copies. Not a real illusion but illusionary reals. Reel after reel. The hyper-real. The "thing-in-itself," *sui generis,* finally realized or realizable, fixed or fixable without end, without difference, and beyond a shadow of a doubt.

This is a telecommunicatively cleansed space that appears to operate without the shadow of its predigested others. Is this also a time of the living dead? Vampires cast no shadows. Nor do televisionary projections of what might be bought, sold or stolen. And what of viral implants or genetic mutations of the codes of biological production? Is this also a time where the brightest dreams of western man might at last be realized within the technological machinery of a "male mothering," the actual materialization of the word made flesh? Is this truly the repetitious beginnings an ultramodern social world without end and (more terrifyingly yet) without the possibility of ritually returning to other impossible beginnings? Terror of the Simulacra? Terror of this New World Order!

This is a true story. But is it also a story that remains relatively inaccessible if we, as readers, remain confined, somewhat illiterately, within that realm of empirical (or categorically imperial) reality which is today modeled upon "the already made," the previously given, the perceptual set theorization of what's real in terms of what was *once upon a time* collectively represented, then telematically reproduced (or simulated) before being fed back to us as if "the real thing." Coke or Pepsi. Max Headroom or Bush. What's the difference?

In the early years of television, before such nearly memoriless events as the mass marketing of computer games, the U.S. invasion of Grenada, the May 13, 1985, police helicopter bombing of a community of Afro-American radicals in Philadelphia, or the daily "eclipse of reason" within what may seem like the almost random, hyper-bored and techno-pharmacologically stimulated straight-shooting swell of contemporary male gang violence, C. Wright Mills used the term "cheerful robots" to depict the HIStorical materialization of a terrifying New World character type—persons whose primary modes of production had become consumption.[9] Three decades later, French social theorist Jean Baudrillard again employs a science-fiction like vocabulary to alert us to the possibility of an even more dramatic transformation.[10] Following Baudrillard it may now be necessary to ask whether the media infestation of a great many of our HIStorical embodiments has advanced to such a state-in-excess that many of us are no longer manipulated externally like robots but are being materially accessed by the fascinating (if panicky) inFORMational vectors of ultramodern CAPITAL itself. Here we may find ourselves struggling adrift and swimming within the fast, dense and technologically relayed wavelengths of new forms of power; seduced and/or abandoned to the point of actually taking the telecommunicative media within ourselves; its inFORMational screens and its terminals now ritually functioning as if our most intimate organs of sensation, erasing previously imagined differences between the public and private, the personal and the political, the cognitive and the carnal. As such, it may be important today to critically imagine ways in which the most powerful techno-logical media of ultramodern CAPITAL no longer so much act upon us as if from the outside, but constitute a fleshy (if mechanically mediated) aspect of our ritual participation in giving structure to the complex and contradictory materiality of those sacrificially channeled flows of perception through which so many of us inFORMationally (mis)recognize the boundaries and the limits of our own (dis)connections to others.

What can all this mean? For me it is suggestive of the troubling possibility that a highly militarized form of telecommunciative media, developed in relation to the strategic defense initiatives of men privileged by a variety of convergent HIStorical vectors of economic, white-racialized and sex/gendered power, may today be part of the techno-bodily hook-ups and networkings of experiential possibilities that constitute some of the most defining features of ultramodern subjectivity. This is to suggest that, like the laser guided eyes of Apache helicopter pilots who killed record numbers of fleeing soldiers with little collective representational notice during the last hundred hours of the 1991 U.S.-led war against Iraq, ultramodern media may actually be entering our bodies and inviting our passage to an inFORMational sphere of power beyond the reflexive grasp of most modern social science. And what's next—the telemonitoring of whole blocks of inner city Detroit, Los Angeles and Washington D.C., in the aftermath of Operation Zero Tolerance, as the so-called "Drug Wars" come home from the Andes? In this, the power of televi-sionary futures appears to be fast escaping the fleshy exigencies of lived bodily memories *per se*. Why, only this morning I found myself eating before the screen, or after, when suddenly my eyes/"I"s were transferred across the social space of this our ungiving present. Whose present? Whose gift is this and whose theft?

One of Baudrillard's central contentions is this: that those of us most affected by ultramodern power are becoming possessed by the productive consumption of media icons to such an intense degree that "we" may narcis-sistically experience little outside the magnetically looping narratives in which we find ourselves close-circuited. We are thus invaded and occupied by a reductive if seemingly endless recycling of sensations of difference into the same old story. We are the media! We are the television! We are (or are becom-ing) living screens for the telecommunicative projection of dead (or deadening) moving pictures. We are (or are becoming) the Living Dead, claustrophobic vampires in a coffin that only appears always open but which, in fact (or in the HIStorically materialized fictions in which we find ourselves empirically), is open to no-thing but the simulations which haunt everyday perceptions of what is really happening. Thus we alternate between infinitely refracting mirrored opposites, between binary poles of pleasure and terror in the new but old, different but same, digitally programmed narrative structures of love, ambition, fear, power and inflationary desire. Hence, what's hegemonically real today may be largely a matter of simulating what's been reductively filtered in the moment before. Here things appear to return eternally to the accessible plot structures of what's always already now over our collective HIStorical shoulders. No-thing is lost. Thus, if something appears radically different in one flashing instance and almost exactly the same in the next, it should come as no surprise. For in a world of simulative ready-made experiences it is the uncanny sense of the familiar, of the *deja vu* that renders *all things considered* accessible, meaningful or commonsensically real.

This is a true story, an ethnographic text. And yet it attempts to exceed the ordinary channels of (socially scientific) access into which so many of us have become empirically (or imperially) attuned. For certain readers this will mean that the text fails. This is a risk. The second channel, of whom Oliver North, Jr., speaks truthfully, will remain unprotected. And the third, and the fourth and the fifth. On my television set there are ninety-one channels. The average U.S. household is bodily exposed for over seven hours each day. For other readers the experience might evoke a sense of those (im)possible truths that LIE beyond the transnational mediascape that is rapidly becoming the dense and nihilistic base for the reproduction of cultural hegemony within the USA Today. This is a hope. Here LIES the material basis for what I consider to be a more effective strategy for critical writers and artists to organically participate in an activist struggle for justice within and against the HIStorical confines of ultramodern hierarchies of power.

HISTORICAL "ORIGINS" OF THE POSTMODERN

In closing this preface I feel it important to delineate five contradictory HIStorical "origins" of what I am calling "postmodern." The first three represent provisional breaks with modern social formations of power/knowledge and may be read as signs of hope, resistance or struggles for justice. These include (1) *ethnographic postmodernism*, an epistemological rupture at the margins of French social science in the years following the positivist (technological) horrors of World War I, African colonial revolts restricting the access of French anthropological reason, and the rise of European fascism; (2) *sex/ gender postmodernism*, a set of convergent feminist and queer challenges to masterful straight-male projections of a universalizing modern enlightenment; and (3) *multicultural postmodernism*, involving efforts to counter the colonizing power of white western thought by peoples of color within the West and by those sentenced to "underdevelopment" by what has been (imperially) described as "modernization." In different ways each of these postmodernisms actively resists unitary incorporation into the dominant moral economies of modernity. As such, they stand in contrast to two more ominous developments: the ultramodern appeal of techno-fascism and the emergence of inFORMational forms of CAPITAL during and after the Second World War.

ETHNOGRAPHIC POSTMODERNISM

> To call ethnographies fictions may raise empiricist hackles. But the word as commonly used in recent cultural theory has lost its connotation of falsehood, of something merely opposed to the truth. It suggests the partiality of cultural and historical truths, the ways they are systematic and exclusive. Ethnographic writings can properly be called fictions in the sense of 'something made or fashioned'.... Ethnographic truths are thus inherently partial—committed and incomplete. —James Clifford[11]

In a recent article entitled "Feminism, Writing, and Ghosts," Avery Gordon poses the question: "How do we, as sociologists, rethink ethnography in a world where the real is no longer self-evident, where the social fact may be more properly understood as artifact, and where the description of cultural life is made problematic [by the recognition of ethnography as itself a context bound form of (w)riting] or textual production?"[12] Some epistemological clues may be found in the partial break with modernist social science attempted by dissident surrealist ethnographers in the years between the world wars in Europe. "Historically situated between a revolutionary refusal of France's colonized Others to submit to the homogenizing gaze of western anthropological imperialism and a practical political desire to counter the epistemological lure of fascism, certain critical French social theorists, writers and artists were drawn into a desire for a deconstructive displacement of the facts of everyday western social life, and of the [modern] rules of the sociological method that theoretically secured their reign."[13]

Radicalizing critical epistemological questions raised by Émile Durkheim and Marcel Mauss, Georges Bataille, Michel Leiris, Roger Caillois, Aimé Césaire and other "ethnographic and dissident surrealists" advocated an ethnographic derealization of the hierarchical "I"/eye of western social science.[14] Rather than attempting a mastery of the facts of "the other," these predecessors to French poststructuralism advocated a critical corrosion of taken-for-granted modern realities when confronted with the HIStorical resistance of those condemned to the margins of modernity itself. In this sense, the critical ethnographic (w)ritings published in the interdisciplinary journal,

Documents, and those produced by the short-lived College of Sociology between 1937-39, represented efforts to partially sacrifice the hierarchical privileges of western social science. Such privileges were themselves materially based upon previous sacrifices, including the *originary* modern reduction of other cultures to nothing but spectral fodder for an objectivist, ethnocentric and often deeply racist interpretive framework.

Dissident surrealist ethnographers labored both to resist the temptation of inscribing the stories of others within the comforting explanatory confines of western epistemology and to give reflexive notice that social science (w)riting was itself a form of (fictive) cultural production. In so doing, they struggled (imperfectly) to construct a *dialogue* with traditions canonically excluded by modern Occidental knowledge and to display the partial character of even their own claims to objectivity.[15] By such strategies surrealist ethnographers hoped to defamiliarize their relations to metropolitan assumptions guiding traditional western thought and to reflexively interject heterogeneity into the production of social science knowledge itself. This was a political as well as radically sociological project. It involved efforts to distance oneself from "science's deep slumber" and thereby create "detours of objective science" that would put western researchers in touch with "external data, foreign to lived experience."[16] Without a sustained dialogue with the foreign, surrealist ethnographers believed that "nothing really new will have taken place and [that] interpretations [will remain] unacceptable from the start."[17]

All that was taken-for-granted was to be made sociologically strange. The normal was to be perverted. The beautiful was to be playfully twisted into the ugly. The only always apparent lightness of the center was to be set spinning by a blinding axial rotation of cultural categorizations. This presaged a return of what had been HIStorically repressed and a noisy confrontation with the previously silenced margins of western theological, philosophical and scientific discourse. "From this disenchanted viewpoint stable orders of collective meaning appear to be constructed, artificial, and indeed often ideological or repressive. The sort of normality or common senses that can amass empires in fits of absent-mindedness or wander routinely into world wars is seen as a contested reality to be subverted, parodied, and transgressed."[18] In the words of Carl Einstein, author of *Negarplastic*, a 1915 "collage reading" of various forms of African sculpture in relationship to the decentering concerns of European cubism:

> One thing is important: to shake what is called reality by means of non-adapted hallucinations so as to alter the value hierarchies of the real.
> Hallucinatory forces create a break in the order of mechanistic processes:
> they introduce blocs of 'a-causality' in this reality which had been absurdly

given as such. The uninterrupted fabric of this reality is torn, and one inhabits the tensions of dualisms.[19]

The dialogical strategies of such dissident surrealist ethnographic practices resulted in the production of open-ended or unfinished collage-texts aimed at exploding the artifactual reality of western cultural codes. As James Clifford points out, these corrosive efforts aimed at breaking down or breaking with accepted scientific classifications. They were also typically accompanied by attempts to supply exotic alternatives. Although sometimes carelessly referenced without attention to the ritual context of their actual culture performance, surrealist ethnography's contradictory fascination with cultural impurities and nonwestern artifacts evokes disturbing questions concerning the coherence of modern social science.[20] As such, surrealist ethnography represents a critical step in the direction of reflexive postmodern scenic practices. When most critical, surrealistic ethnographic practices may even turn the mirror of social science research back upon itself. This transforms sociological (w)riting into what Jackie Orr has recently described as a noticeable form of "social fiction, a cultural artifact continually constructed and reconstructed in the complex fields in which the writing and reading I/eye meet.... To insist upon the sociological text as a powerful fictive representation of the real, and to noticeably construct fragments of images, dream, poetry, and fiction into the text, presents a challenge to social theory not only at the level of style, but also and more urgently, at the level of its powerful pretensions to represent truth, history, causation, or an authoritative version of the social story."[21]

SEX/GENDER POSTMODERNISM

> They say, we must disregard all the stories relating to those...who have been betrayed beaten seized seduced carried off violated and exchanged as vile and precious merchandise. They say, we must disregard the statements we have been compelled to deliver contrary to our opinions and in conformity with the codes and conventions of the cultures that have domesticated us....They say that there is no reality before it has been given shape by words, rules, regulations. They say that in what concerns them everything has to be remade starting from basic principles. They say that in the first place the vocabulary of every language is to be examined, modified, turned upside down, that every word must be screened. —Monique Wittig[22]

Another site for (ficitively) theorizing an "origin" of what is critically postmodern is found in the diverse, yet convergent, (w)ritings of feminists as well as gay and lesbian theorists whose epistemological reflexiveness places them at odds with dominant modern (whitemale) classifications of knowledge.

Understanding the cultural dynamics of modernity as fueled by the sacrifice of heterogeneous women's languages, embodiments and desires, as well as by the tying up of all tongues (k)not screened by a heterosexist imagination of "normalized" erotic forms, feminist critics of contemporary sex-gender hierarchies (and their allies) are, in a sense, always already postmodern. When most radical, theirs is a "queer" or even "monstrous" imagination of possibilities for reciprocal gift-exchange between women, and also between men, women, animals and other life-forms that are cutoff, deadened or marginalized by the omnipresent rites of "compulsive heterosexuality" that typify the "normative vision" of modernity from the bedroom to the white corporate office tower, science lab, shopping mall and battlefield.

What alternative epistemologies and desires LIE "the other side" of heterosexist patriarchal modernity? Feminist and queer theorists are (k)not One in proposing an answer. As Donna Haraway observes, "It has become difficult to name one's feminism by a single adjective—or even to insist in every circumstance upon the noun. Consciousness of exclusion through naming is acute. Identities seem contradictory, partial, and strategic. With the hard-won recognition of their social and historical constitution, gender, race and class cannot provide the basis for belief in 'essential' unity.... Gender, race, or class consciousness is an achievement forced on us by the terrible historical experience of the contradictory social realities of patriarchy, colonialism, and capitalism.... But there has also been a growing recognition of another response through coalition—affinity, not identity."[23]

One aspect of such affinity involves convergent feminist and queer challenges to the hegemonic coherence of modern straight-whitemale-centered discourse. This "fictive" coherence, like the imaginary coherence of racial categorizations, is not only economically extracted from the color-coded bodies of women, but operates as a kind of parasitic cultural screen concealing both contradictions and difference. As Judith Butler points out, "The construction of coherence conceals the gender discontinuities that run rampant within heterosexual, bisexual, and gay and lesbian contexts.... [Thus, only] when the disorganization and disaggregation of the field of bodies disrupts the regulatory fiction of heterosexual coherence...[is] that regulatory ideal exposed...as a norm and fiction that regulates the sexual field that it purports to describe."[24] Butler's work provides a feminist elaboration of questions concerning the *regulatory ideality* of seemingly natural distinctions between female and male, as well as between so-called heterosexual and homosexual identities. In this way her work extends and revises Michel Foucault's theorizations of the disciplinary construction of modern categories of social-sexual identity. To expose the imperial constraints of this regulatory ideal is to force a crisis within straight modern male-dominated economies of representation. It is also to open up spaces for the ritual contestation, subversion and structural change of what Gayatri Spivak designates as "the hidden ethico-political agenda of differentiations constitutive of [modern] knowledge" itself.[25]

Such postmodern contestations of the normative constraints of gender are today embodied within a wide variety of feminist and queer (theoretical) practices. In the words of bell hooks, they articulate a "yearning" for "shared sensibilities which cross the boundaries of class, gender and race, etc., that could be fertile ground for the construction of empathy—ties that promote the recognition of common commitments, and serve as a base for solidarity and action."[26] Critical sex/gender theorists take issue with the "regulatory fictions" and "social technologies of gender" underlying modern MAN'S straight white flight from embodied relations of HIStorical contradiction into seeming pure and trans-localized perspectives on both scientific and everyday knowledge. This demands a performative regrounding of all claims to "objective" knowledge within the shifting material "standpoints" by which knowledge itself is *partially engendered*. Consider the recent work of Patricia Hill Collins in articulating "the contours of an Afrocentric feminist epistemology." In opposition to the distanced, unemotional, ethically suspended and adversarial characteristics of Eurocentric male positivism, and as distinct from various white feminist strategies of counter-institutional knowledge, Collins identifies the evocation of concrete experience, the use of dialogical methods in assessing knowledge claims, and ethics of both caring and personal accountability as HIStorically specific modalities of African-American women's epistemological practice.[27]

A related but materially different evocation of sex/gender postmodernism is found in the epistemological standpoint of gays and lesbians as embodied in the writings of theorists such as Eve Kosofsky Sedgwick and Michael Warner,[28] while a "positively revolting" feminist language in excess of modern patriarchy's dictionary of defined meanings is set forth by Mary Daly and Jane Caputi. Warning women not to be seduced by ultramodern male-media-speak, they caution:

> Many of patriarchy's reversals are the products of direct inversion....Thus Ronald Reagan is called 'The Great Communicator.' The MX missile has been called 'Peacekeeper.' Animal Rights activists who oppose violence against any creature are labeled 'terrorists.' ...The same mechanism is observable when groups opposing women's right to choose abortion— groups manifesting callous indifference to women's lives and to the lives of unwanted children—label themselves as 'pro-life' and 'right-to-lifers'. In a society that accepts such inversion, Coca-Cola can pass as 'The Real

Thing' and makeup can be labeled 'The Natural Look,' while women who refuse to wear makeup are called 'unnatural.'[29]

Other critics of sex/gender hierarchies, such as Monique Wittig and Kathy Acker, descend into a material collage of unsettling political poetics. In *The Lesbian Body*, Wittig conjures up a multiplicity of women's bodily relations to each other that defy straight-minded male anatomical classifications.[30] On the other hand, Acker's spiralling texts scream of the pornographic violence tattooed across the bodies of women who, like the female protagonist in her re(w)riting of *Don Quixote*, discover that "BEING BORN INTO AND PART OF THE MALE WORLD, SHE HAD NO SPEECH OF HER OWN. ALL SHE COULD DO WAS READ MALE TEXTS WHICH WEREN'T HER."[31] Sometimes, by virtue of a commitment to styles of (w)riting that refuse the homogenizing phallocentrism of modernist prose, feminist (w)riters encounter questions about the accessibility of their texts to the generalized (predominantly male) audience of scholarly discourse. But since "clarity is always ideological and reality always adaptive," as Trinh T. Minh-ha points out, "such a demand for clear communication often proves to be nothing else but an intolerance for any language other than the one approved by the dominant ideology. At times obscured and at other times blatant, this inability and unwillingness to deal with the unfamiliar, or with a language different from one's own, is, in fact, a trait that intimately belongs to the man of coercive power."[32] To demands for clear communicative access, Luce Irigaray, whose critical texts exceed the normative boundaries between theory and fiction, responds as following:

> No clear nor univocal statement can, in fact, dissolve the mortgage, this obstacle...being caught, trapped in the same reign of credit. It is as yet better to speak only through equivocations, allusions, innuendos, parables.... Even if you are asked for some *précisions* [precise details].[33]

MULTICULTURAL POSTMODERNISM

> *Jes Grew* carriers [or African slaves] came to America because of cotton. Why cotton? American Indians often supplied all of their needs from one animal: the buffalo. Food, shelter, clothing, even fuel. Eskimos, the whale. Ancient Egyptians were able to nourish themselves from the olive tree and use it as a source of light; but Americans wanted to grow cotton. They could have raised soybean, cattle, hogs or the feed for these animals. There was no excuse. Cotton. Was it some unusual thrill at seeing the black hands come in contact with the white crop? —Ishmael Reed[34]

Other spaces of critical postmodernism are found in the multicultural perspectives of people of color within the televisionary borders of the U.S. and its allies, and in the anti-imperialist struggles of those south of our borders. Indeed, from 1492 to the present the economic promises of a New World Order of modernity have been staked on exploitative efforts to underdevelop the minds and bodily fortunes of those made to pose as the Northwest's others. Discovering "the Other" only to enact a parasitic incorporation of her or his dark skin within one's blinding enlightenment, from Columbus to South Africa and the South Bronx, the dominant narrative of modernity remains a story of white vampirism or, worse yet, genocide.[35] One (who is not One) need only read the opening pages of Toni Morrison's *The Bluest Eye* to be confronted allegorically with stark ethnographic truths concerning the *whiter than white* narrative gardens of the ultramodern story of Dick and Jane, their ever-smiling happy parents and running dog Spot.[36] These black-on-white pages evoke the HIStorical condemnation of racially inscribed others to that "unyielding...plot of black dirt" which has been the fate of so many peoples of color under the sign-work of modernity.

Indeed, what is all too homogeneously labeled as a time of western enlightenment has also been a space of enslavement, colonization, or marginalization for many awaiting "the other side" of what's modern for a realization social justice. When George Jackson writes that an enforced version of whitened reality from St. Augustine on is *the* problem,[37] or when Zora Neal Hurston and Ishmael Reed remind us that along the apparent Christian surfaces of American-American culture LIE the complex and challenging material spiritualities of "Neo Hoo Doo",[38] or when Houston Baker locates the "crisscrossing impulses" of African-American signing practices within the living HIStorical tonalities of a "blues matrix," "we" are confronted with the possibility of "vernacular" cultural spaces that LIE in excess of the disembodying abstractions of the modern West.[39] The reinscription of such systematically marginalized or hegemonically unrecognized spaces of (w)riting is a central strategy of multiculturalist postmodernism. As the Chicana Tejana writer and theorist Gloria Anzaldúa declares, having been HIStorically denied access to hegemonic elements of theoretical discourse "because we are often disqualified and excluded from it, because what passes for theory these days is forbidden territory for us, it is *vital* that we occupy theorizing space, that we not allow white men and women soley to occupy it. By bringing in our own approaches and methodologies, we transform that theorizing space."[40]

This is not to suggest that African-Americans, Hispanics, Asians, American Natives and others subordinated to the white racist organization of modernity can ever return to some untainted or "nativist" culture. The violent material and psychic inscriptions of racist HIStory have made this literally impossible, forcing some of those it oppressively silences "to acquire the ability, like a chameleon, to change color when the dangers are many and the options few."[41] As Franz Fanon poignantly remarks, "Every colonized people—in other words, every people in whose soul an inferiority complex has been created by the death and burial of its local cultural originality—finds itself face to face with the language of the [conquering master]."[42] This is particularly the case concerning the homogenizing cultural violence of the modern West. As Henry Louis Gates, Jr. suggests, "the Enlightenment, racism and—dare I say?—logocentrism marched arm in arm to delimit black people in perhaps the most pernicious way of all: to claim that they were subhuman, that they were 'a different species....'"[43] For this reason, Gates finds himself positioned in resistance to the so-called "equalitarian criticism" of even the most well intentioned white scholars "whose claims to 'universal' somehow always end up lopping off our arms, legs, and pug noses, muffling the peculiar timbre of our voices, and trying to straighten our always already kinky hair."[44]

In a move that calls attention to the HIStorical specificity, and hence partial truth values of all discourses, Gates argues that to use "western critical theory uncritically is to substitute one mode of neocolonialism for another." As an alternative, Gates urges African-Americans to ground their own perspectives within vernacular traditions of the diasporic culture in which they find themselves in (w)riting. That such a grounding may suggest a convergence between Afrocentric cultural strategies, particularly those embodied in African-American womens' (w)ritings, and certain aspects of a poststructuralist critique of the disembodied HIStoricity of modern whitemale assertions of identity is evident in recent work by Houston Baker. By linking Afrocentric practices to the radicality of postmodern critique, both Baker and Gates attempt "to isolate the signifying black difference through which to theorize about the so-called discourse of the Other."[45] At the same time, while acknowledging the relevance of a "postmodern critique of 'identity'...for renewed black liberation struggles," bell hooks cautions against too easy an incorporation of the rhetoric of postmodernism shorn of a simultaneous political challenge to the continuation of institutionalized racism.[46] Accordingly, "Postmodern theory that is not seeking to simply appropriate the experience of 'Otherness' to enhance the discourse or to be politically chic should not separate the 'politics of difference' from the politics of racism. To take racism seriously one must consider the plight of underclass people of color, a vast majority of whom are black."[47]

"Yeah, it's easy to give up identity, when you got one," states hooks in reference to the response of many "blacks folks" and women to "postmodern critiques of the 'subject' when they surface at a historical moment when many subjugated people feel themselves coming to voice for the first time."[48] Hooks also turns the challenge of postmodern critique back upon those of "us" most involved with its dissemination, noting, "one change in the direction that would be real cool would be the production of a discourse on race that interrogates whiteness. It would be just so interesting for all those white folks who are giving us their take on blackness to let us know what's going on with whiteness."[49] I hope, in part, that the text you are reading does not appear innocent of this challenge.[50] Nevertheless, while vigilant against overly abstract, elitist and seemingly depoliticized uses of postmodernism, hooks is also emphatic that, within a context of African-American struggles for empowerment, "Criticisms of directions in postmodern thinking should not obscure insights it may offer that open up our understanding of African-American experience."[51] In particular, she argues that a critical interaction with postmodern discourse might both enable a renewal in Afrocentric thought and assist in "reformulating outmoded notions of identity." As such:

> Postmodern critiques of essentialism which challenge notions of universality and static over-determined identity within mass culture and mass consciousness can open up new possibilities for the construction of self and the assertion of agency.... Employing a critique of essentialism allows African-Americans to acknowledge the way in which class mobility has altered collective black experience so that racism does not necessarily have the same impact on our lives. Such a critique allows us to affirm multiple black identities, various black experiences. It also challenges colonial imperialist paradigms of black identity which represent blackness one-dimensionally in ways that reinforce and sustain white supremacy. This discourse created the idea of the 'primitive' and promoted the notion of an 'authentic' experience, seeing as 'natural' those expressions of black life which conformed to a pre-existing pattern or stereotype. Abandoning essentialist notions would be a serious challenge to racism.[52]

Related challenges are inscribed in the critical (w)ritings and "magical realism" of a host of Caribbean and Central and South American authors[53] and in the political allegories of African and Asian (w)riters. Consider the following passage from the Vietnamese writer and film-maker Trinh T. Minh-ha. What western scholars designate as modern HIStorical narrative makes a canonical distinction between fact and fiction. Those who categorically refuse this division are normatively exiled to the "primitive" enclaves of pre-HIStory. In a critical gesture that is at once postmodern and post-colonial, Trinh T. Minh-ha inverts this perverse distinction, demanding instead that questions of truth be linked with narratives of culturally specific power.

Which truth? The question unavoidably arises.... Managing to identify with History, history (with small letter *h*) thus manages to oppose the factual to the fictional (turning a blind eye to the 'magicality' of its claims); the story-writer—the historian—to the story-teller. As long as the transformation, manipulations, or redistributions inherent to the collecting of events are overlooked, the division continues its course, as sure of its itinerary as it certainly dreams to be. Story-writing becomes history-writing, and history quickly sets itself apart, consigning story to the realm of the tale, legend, myth, fiction, literature. Then since fictional and factual have come to a point where they mutually exclude each other, fiction, not infrequently, means lies, and fact truth. DID IT REALLY HAPPEN? IS IT A TRUE STORY?[54]

Such multicultural writings presage a more hopeful construction of "life after modernism." In the meantime, and within the densely white mediated violence of ultramodernity, "we" are provided with rhythmic word-soundings by the African-American scholar, poet and musician Gil Scott-Heron, whose song "B Movie" includes the following lyrics:

Just keep repeating that none of this is real.
And if you're sensing that something's wrong
Just remember that it won't be too long
Before the director cuts the scene
Cause this ain't really your life
ain't really your life
ain't really nothin' but a movie.[55]

PESSIMISTIC RE-MARKINGS OF THE POSTMODERN: FASCISM AND THE USA TODAY

Two more pessimistic "origins" of the postmodern involve themes examined throughout this text. These include fascism and the televisionary culture of transnationalized CAPITAL. The relationship between these two ominous forms of enlightenment are hinted at by Susan Sontag:

Fascist aesthetics include but go far beyond the rather special celebration of the primitive.... [T]hey flow from (and justify) a preoccupation with situations of control...and...take the form of a characteristic pageantry: the massing of groups of people; the turning of people into things; the replication of things; and the grouping of people/things around an all-powerful... force.[56]

Despite aesthetic appearances, fascism never permits a material return to those HIStorically repressed sacrificial rites in which homogenizing categorizations of time, space and identity are periodically dissolved into festive rites of rebirthing and renewal. Fascism parasitically feeds off modernity's repression of death, finiteness and human animality, substituting the aesthetic fascinations of spectacle for the experience of lived social contradiction. This was recognized by Walter Benjamin in 1936. Benjamin theorized that a conjunction of telecommunicative technologies and fascist dread was in the process of constructing a New World Order of CAPITALIst power substituting the distracting experience of electronic spectacle for the lived exigencies of social contradiction. In this sense, fascism is heir to the most blindly enlightened dreams of western MAN—dreams of escaping the fleshy and finite bodies of humans born from the wombs of women. This is a whitemale flight straight toward the exterminating mechanics of the pure idea. According to Benjamin, fascism attempts to neutralize contradictions by an aesthetic leap into pure formalism. In exchange for submission to a system of unequal economic relations, fascism offers the ritual fascinations of living in a purely IDEAL or formally aestheticized environment.

Writing nearly a century after Marx, Benjamin believed that in his own time CAPITAL was entering a more advanced phase than any imagined by Marx. This is CAPITAL redeemed by a "fascinating" fascistic aestheticization of everyday life. This is also the situation in the USA TODAY where the sadistic power of an earlier moment of CAPITAL passes almost instantaneously into the aestheticizations of the "postmodern scene." Within this fascinating world of ultramodern technological artifacts, high speed telecommunications and virtual reality simulations, power itself may seem as if it no longer exists.[57] Power does exist but it may seem not to. In other words, power appears only to disappear. Society remains dominated but now by a form of power that (only always) appears dead. This New World Order of CAPITAL is typified by a dense and high speed aestheticization of (almost) everything, everywhere in *no time at all*. Of the ultramodern pleasure of such fascistic expressionism, Benjamin states:

> Fascism attempts to organize...masses without affecting the property structure.... Fascism sees its salvation in giving these masses not their right, but instead a chance to express themselves. The logical result of Fascism is the introduction of aesthetics into political life.[58]

If the purity of a fascist will to culture over nature has been a tendency within the West for centuries, it is only with the advent of advanced telecommunicative technologies that this nihilistic dream (or nightmare) appears able to be materially realized. This is the dream of ultramodern culture. Before the industrial transmission of this dream, that which was missing from the social organization of memory haunted the margins of western MAN's terroristic drive to master nature and avoid death.

But what if the heterogeneous and haunting focus of repressed difference could be simulated and then parasitically digested back into the self-same? It is 1934 and Leni Riefenstahl and Albert Speer have just constructed a massive stadium to filmically stage a documentary of events that never took place. Never, that is, except within a technologically constructed matrix of aestheticized images.[59] *Triumph of the Will.* Across the Atlantic, Franklin Delano Roosevelt sits before a fire, mouth connected to a serial broadcast of radio waves. The world it seems is changing. That which had previously remained in excess of the modern imagination is now being conjured up in simulated or hyper-real forms. Forms that consume traces of fleshy difference. Forms that replace contradictory HIStorical relations with the smooth fascinations of indifferent "reality-effects." Here, "we" witness the emergence of a (straight-whitemale) pleasure principle without end; an incessant deterrence of "one's" own death accompanied by a banal incapacity to re-member the sacrificing of others. Death camps, death squads, Tomahawk missiles, deadly poisons seeping into the food chain and the planet's earth, air and waters. *During the last one hundred hours of Operation Desert Storm the bombing is laser guided and more intense. Perhaps as many as 150,000 fleeing Iraqi troops are not allowed to flee. I am watching TV. A show called Inside Edition honors what it designates as the true heroes of the Gulf War as it broadcasts images of a stealthy band of American Natives transubstantiating into Apache Helicopters. Within these black metallic bird planes pilots sit eyes wed to the camera and fingers to the fire. Uncounted corpses LIE scorched under HIStory's sun while back in the U.S.A. yellow ribbons abound.*

Here we arrive at the Parasite Cafe. This is a terrifying place where a simulated return of the repressed does little but fuel desires for continuous consumption and where the ideal purity of fascist mastery might be terminally realized in the telecommunicative aestheticization of everyday life. Of the connection between fascism and the emergence of ultramodern social forms, Baudrillard (w)rites:

> There is no doubt that fascism...is the first violent reactivation of...the social in a society that despairs of its own rational and contractual foundation.... Fascism is then the only fascinating modern form of power.... Fascism's politics is an aesthetics of death, one that already has the look of a nostalgic fad.[60]

Did the fascinating fascist aestheticization of death actually end with the surrender of the Axis powers? Or are the central tendencies of fascist purity being today transformed technologically into a new and ultramodern social form? In framing the HIStorical specificity of postmodernity in this manner, I am trying to evoke a sense of the "fascinating" power of the inFORMational culture that has emerged in America in the years following World War II. Fed by a straight-whitemale-minded conjuncture of military, scientific and economic institutions, this culture of "command, control and communications" has come to occupy an increasingly important place at the pulsating electronic core of transnational CAPITAL. Indeed, for contemporary CAPITAL, "control over information flow and over the vehicles for propagation of popular taste and culture have...become vital weapons in competitive struggle....Access to, and control over, information, coupled with a strong capacity for instant data analysis, have become essential to the centralized coordination of far-flung corporate interests. The capacity for instantaneous response to changes in exchange rates, fashions and tastes, and moves by competitors is more essential...than ever."[61]

In the panicky oscillation between the dread of instantaneous extermination and the ecstatic thrills of pure and almost weightless being, dominant cultural tendencies within the USA TODAY bear all the markings of a new and improved materialization of a fascist imaginary. "Stay tuned." Too many of us are today ritually inFORMed about who we are, what we fear and desire, and what we might purchase through a dense and high speed circulation of electronically-mediated images. And so we are lured into the aestheticized fascinations of fascism. Screen to screen, advert to advert, images of beautiful young men in uniforms; each in search of the thrill of victory and the close-circuited spectacle of televisionary sacrifice. The pleasures of a perfect body at a reasonable price. And the pornographic excitement of becoming almost fully commodified. A living doll. The word made advert then flesh. The ideal model. The simulacrum. "Everywhere today the aestheticization of the body and its dissolution into a semiurgy of floating body parts reveals that we are being processed through a media scene consisting of our own (externalized) body organs."[62]

As I am (w)riting television waves pass through my body. This is HIStory. On screen there is a double of a woman whose trembling wet body is being dragged naked from the shower by a man before the camera. Before my eyes/ "I"s. This show is *Rescue 911*. This show is a docu-drama, an "educative" theatricalization of "real life." This is entertainment, a seductive male fantasy that parasitically assumes the shape of inFORMation. This show operates in prime-time to doubly connect the television audience to the police.

As a man engulfed in a commercial radiation of heterosexist imagery I find it difficult to take my eyes off the terrorized figure of a white woman on the verge of being raped. Aesthetically raped on prime-time in the shape of inFORMation. This show is obscene. The man drags the double of the woman to her bedroom and pins her to the sheets thrashing. The double appears naked. As a viewer I am invited to follow the camera as it studies the woman's exposed thighs spread and bared shoulders inching toward her breasts. Each camera shot promises more exposure, more inFORMation. Each camera shot is cut by a frame of the doubled woman's baby in the next room unaware. Am I actually going to see the woman's breasts, the rape? This show operates for profit. Whose profit?

The *reel* violence of this obscene spectacle shifts in focus. The doubled woman-victim of this (a)morality play now out-smarts her would-be monster-rapist. She tells him that if only he'd allow her to phone in late for work he'd have plenty of time to rape her without anybody noticing. The monster-rapist says "okay." Then the doubled woman outsmarts the monster by quietly phoning her normal-male friend Scott, and Eva, a woman police dispatcher at 911. Since the monster-rapist is listening, the doubled woman has to use coded language, like on television. Within seconds the woman's name, address and vehicle registration appear on Eva's screen at 911 (Police Headquarters) and help is on the way. Soon the screen is flooded with good, authorized and normal white men who catch the monster and save the doubled woman from being raped. Except aesthetically. She was saved by the 911 police from the monster but not from my eyes/"I"s.

Time for a commercial break. On screen there is a double of a white woman whose trembling wet body is being filmed naked in the shower before the camera. This woman seems ecstatic, enthralled by the possibility of becoming cleaner than ever for only a few cents more per shower. This is entertainment, a coldly seductive male fantasy that parasitically assumes the shape of inFORMation. This show operates in prime-time to doubly connect the television audience to the police. A dead power live-wired at the imperial center of a technologically fascinated society. Suddenly sound bursts stereophonically from all sides. The beat is rhythmic, African-American male and angry. There are words. They rap within and against a mediascape that simulcasts nonwhite bodies as both transparent and invisible.

> Tell me. What have you left me?
> What have I got?
> Last night in cold blood
> a young brother got shot.
> Went home and jacked.

My mother's on crack.
My sister can't work
cause her arms show tracks.
Madness. Insanity. Live-in profanity.
Then some punk claims that he's understandin' me.
Give me a break. What world do you live in.
Death is my sex.
Guess my religion.[63]

A dead power live-wired at the imperial center of a technologically disciplined society. It seems that the violent white effects of postmodern society are neither equal nor equally distributed across or within the racially organized borders of the first world. Images of Jesse Jackson blur with those of the furloughed murderer Willie Horton as the George Bush campaign defends itself against charges of media-manipulated racism. Bush, it is said, is simply "exploiting the conflict of interests between blacks and whites. The very idea that someone would bring up the idea of subterranean racism," comments Mark Goodin, a spokesperson for the Bush campaign, "it's almost sick."[65] Yet within the rapid fire aesthetics of a campaign against drugs and crime, the Republican party offers televised images of African-American prisoners, a talking head of a white male describing how a black male had raped his fiancee, and flyers that pair a large photograph of Horton, a black man, next to the small image of a frightened young white child. Suddenly the images change again. Now it is Oprah Winfrey, Michael Jackson and Mike Tyson that occupy the screen. No. Wait. Mike's image is replaced by Robin Givens. Has Mike been drugged again by Robin and Ruth Roper, Mike's mass-mediated "surrogate mother" and suspect of many a talk show? How can one tell? What's the difference? An eclipse of difference? An eclipse of reason? Is this a war on crime or a war on reality? On screen another double appears cut off from HIStory. It's Saddam Hussein appearing as HITLER II. The white West's dark Arab "other," Hussein's image is brought to "us" by men with money on their mind and the power to make war appear televisionary.

AMERICA'S MOST WANTED?

The fascist-like facsimile of contemporary North American culture appears a significant feature of the HIStory of our ultramodernizing present. Only this time it's even more complex than past fascisms. And more subtle. And more electric. This is a culture of Star Wars, talking cars, and short-term memory. So short, in fact, that for many there is little but nostalgia for the "good old days" of just a few weeks before. Who really killed Laura Palmer anyway?

This is also an ultra-modern society with a realizable potential for the genetic reprogramming of everything from gendered eye color to variations in the body's immunization systems and sexual desires. READ MY LIPS! Can you buy these ideas? Indeed, these materialized images for consumption are on sale virtually everywhere in the First World and are this moment being exported nearly everywhere else. American Express—don't leave home without it?

A recent book on U.S. foreign policy by Noam Chomsky bears the title *The Culture of Terrorism.*[65] This, unfortunately, is an appropriate name for dominant political, economic and environmental tendencies within the ultramodernizing social landscape of contemporary North America. This is also a major social problem—a threat to the health and well being of both those within the U.S. and those most subject to this nation's global corporate will to technological management. At the same time, it is a problem which to date has largely been ignored by U.S. sociologists and other social scientists.[66] Maybe this is because sociologists, like other "American intellectuals [remain] locked into their campuses" and thus "dramatically foreign to this concrete, fabulous mythology which unfolds all around them."[67] In any event, it is an ill omen for social scientists to remain outside debates about the meaning of postmodernity for much longer. Postmodernity (or ultramodernity as I am referring to it throughout this text) is a dangerous and pressing social problem. It operates environmentally in and through those of us culturally vocationed to materialize its deadly flow of inFORMation. And in the minds and bodies of others who are socially positioned so as to critically read and resist both its fascinations and terrors. How might a critical sociology, and other modern social science discourses, best respond to the troubling challenge of ultramodern social forms? The text you are reading is intended as both an invitation to such a challenge and a warning of its dangers. WELCOME TO THE PARASITE CAFE. How fascinating and how fearful.

chapter
three

[T]he contending social forces that shape history come together for us in daily life. Varied, but wholly routinized, random, but programmed, daily life appears to be of little consequence, so close that we live it as if by second nature. Nevertheless, if we are to grasp history, we must begin to recognize its presence in the mundane. Dismissed as trivial, fragmented, and fetishized by its assimilation to the commodity form, daily life is our site of convergence with the historical.—Susan Willis.[1]

I. POPULAR CULTURE

THE LAWLESSNESS OF DEMAND BEFORE SUPPLY. It is the winter of 1991-92 within a memory-poor social geography of faded yellow ribbons and televisionary tales of recession-driven death squads, straight whitemale corporate gang sexual violence and economic harassment, and the always only apparent triumph of CAPITAL (almost) world-wide. Within this geography, within and along the borders of this New World Order, I'm trying to collage together a sociological story about some of the critical possibilities and limitations of social science in a world gone ultramodern. By employing collage (w)riting strategies I sometimes feel as if I'm inviting a dialogue between *constructionism*, as a potentially critical sociological perspective, and *constructivism*, as a militant "art form" committed to blurring the distinction between critical research and performative remembrance and to the political denaturalization of seemingly real social facts by such strategies as synchronic juxtaposition, montage, and noticeably open-ended assemblage demanding active audience engagement and participatory re(w)ritings. Sometimes I feel like I'm repeating myself.

To my left are questions concerning how an academically employed whitemale U.S. sociologist might begin (again and again) to critically respond to the challenge posed both by a partially reflexive remembrance of constructivism and by the voices of those marginalized by the parasitic construction of contemporary hierarchies of power. To my right is television and a defensive fiberoptics of evidence; setting the stage, sweeping the screen, hiding (whose?)

uncanny remains. To me, repulsions set in motion by the contradictory ritual enactment of such estranged attractions (and the reverse) suggest, at least symptomatically, that the most dominating forms of social science knowledge are today being inFORMationally managed by men with their eyes/"I"s on the screen and fingers on the trigger. What can this mean?

What is screened away or rendered reflexively inaccessible within the imaginary transferences and collective representations that modulate the hegemonic rhythms of public memory in the USA Today? Why is it that so many of us appear literally more anxiously occupied with data-driven categorical differences between this or that pop star, sexy car, toaster-oven, as good as home-made, halfback, winning streak, beautiful boy, value for whose dollar, game plan, waist size, latest look, hard copy than, for instance, by the fact that in a record short time new world war as many as 150,000 Iraqi bodies were made to lie outside the televisionary construction of our collective sociological memories? Or why, within an escalating telecommunicative panic fast-forwarding into depression, are the banks this year reclaiming the mortgaged homes of those bled last year by the Savings and Loans bandits? And how is it that, amidst the thickness of whitemale informational flows competing for control over the interface between chaos and capital, something like a fascinating, if terroristic, reality-death-driving-principle appears to operate at the restrictive economic core of our increasingly cyber-corporate social lives?

I am here (w)riting of the ritual emergence of dangerously new social forces; forces capable of transforming defensive straightmale fears into cultural rites of sacrificial white terror. Parasitic rites that feed upon multiple (if not all) forms of resistance. Technologically informed rites that promise to convert resistance into boundary preserving regulative systems' feedback, and to do so at such breath-defying speeds and so thoroughly that, despite Magic, there continues to be virtually no effective public sign-work to both represent and counter the world-wide spread of AIDS? Even at best, estimates today suggest that the HIV virus will reach 40 million bodies by the year 2000! Not no public sign-work but virtually no effective public sign-work. Meanwhile, for people confined within one U.S. inner city neighborhood, public school, economically abandoned homeless zone after another, as well as for those the globe over fated to be dined upon by New World Ordered death squads, the year 2000 may have already come. What stupid poetry! I am here (w)riting of the countless lives of those whose contradictory social positionings are this very moment being racially and economically managed as if the unfortunate outgrowth of timeless conflicts or youth-gang led drug-wars, rather than the publicly unnamed institutionalization of dense and high speed forms of general economic parasitism and the sacrifice of some devalued bodies to the profit of others.

How to best critically re-member the historical and material origins of hegemonic social movements dominated by informational power? How to critically, and with a significant difference, double back upon our own mass mediated (mis)recognitions that some ritualized forms of humananimal action and some people, but not others, bear, or are forced to bear, or, worse yet, are forced to bare before the sacrificial reconstruction of moral and economic controls in an age of cybernetic capital? These questions haunt this text. In referring to hegemonic social movements in such an unorthodox manner I in no way wish to divert attention from the resistive actions of those struggling to displace or overcome the unequal burden of ultramodern social power. By and large, such resistive social movements represent the diverse, and sometimes convergent, labors of those structurally denied a parasitic place of sustenance at the credit-driven dinner tables of those most privileged by/within today's New World Order. Although my own political hopes lie stupidly in transference with those who would counter the hierarchical violence of this terrifying new modality of social control, I find it strategically necessary to first re-theorize the historical and material dynamics of those forms of social hierarchy whose moving forces today appear most dominant.

My reference here is to those overlapping networks of power that are being militaristically enacted in the restrictive economic movements of people, ideas, linguistic classifications, technological initiatives, communicative resources, transferential emotions, bodily sensations, moral tones and consumptive desires. How do such hegemonic movements engender an uneven but, nevertheless, performatively effective common sense that certain ways of doing things are acceptable, or even valued, while others must be prohibited, domesticated or sentenced to death? And how might the sacrificial force of such hierarchical movements be subverted, diverted or revenged? These questions haunt this text. Sometimes I feel like I'm repeating myself?

2. UNTITLED

> Panic is the name and frenzy is the game that
> spin controls one back to the same old new
> white man's reign. Snap. Crack(le).
> Pop. In-difference. Screen to screen. Flash.
> Crack. Snap. Crack(le). Pop. In-difference.

3. CONCERNING THE HISTORICAL "ORIGINS" OF THIS TEXT

A message illuminates the screen that partially cuts my flesh from what remains pulsating. Its color is pink, light green and violent. This message inFORMs me that somebody is knocking at the door of what might yet be critically re-membered. Somebody or somebodies. This message comes with a byte.

I open the door that is myself to this (im)possible situation. I hope against hope, not simply to access what's been forgotten but to exceed the almost instant BINARY FRAMED OSCILLATIONS THAT *vocation my most compulsive repetitions and power. Looping densely modulated wavelengths speed across the surface of what's becoming time going nowhere. Literally. The message reads:*

> OPEN THE DOOR GIVE YOURSELF AWAY
> HOT FIERY FLOWING
> AS FOR LAUGHING MATTERS CONJURED

I feel that it's really useless (w)riting this way, so let me tell you I WAS TRULY SCARED. And fascinated. Both materially and in the imaginary realm. It was a physical thing with me. Not metaphysical but bodily. Transference without transcendence. Displacement without sublation or its opposite. Difference without identity. A desire that's full of (w)holes. "And the compromise is this. What is recorded as a mnemic image is not the relevant experience itself—in this respect the resistance gets its way; what is recorded is another psychical element closely associated with the objectionable one—and in this respect the first principle shows its strength, the principle which endeavors to FIX IMPORTANT IMPRESSIONS BY establishing reproducible mnemic images. The result of the conflict is therefore that, instead of the mnemic image which would have been, justified by the original event, another is produced from the former one. And since the elements of the experience which aroused objection [or the feeling of contra-diction] were precisely the important ones, the substituted memory will necessarily LACK those important elements."[2] SCREEN TO SCREEN. DESIRE TO DESIRE. LACK TO LACK.

When I open the door a figure appears whose past is in my future. It is the Black Madonna Durkheim and I know it in an instant. Mama Dada Mama Dada Dada Mama Dada. I flash dead pan(icked) to black and she says, "If you want, I'll be your host. Pack up your possessions and let's dance."

Don't ask me to explain what I take to be the Black Madonna's desires for me to accompany her on the ADVENTure I'm describing. Although I was aware of research by Cheryl Gilkes suggesting that Black women's decisions to become community activists was often in response to the needs of their own children, believe me, I was never under the delusion that the Black Madonna had mistaken me for one of her own.[3] And yet when she spoke of her own contradictory longings she made herself partially reflexive in relation to me and others. I am (w)riting here of something quite material: difficult attempts to enact a reflexive method of knowing that's never innocent of power. She did this in her (w)riting by drawing pictures on, or dancing with, or singing from within what appeared as both a syntax and vocabulary of motives. This language defies the rewards of the simple male-minded or narcissistic pleasures of love/hate or guilt. She would confess as much, and then laugh at confessing nothing. It was difficult methodologically to perform this way, to re-fuse clear distinctions between what's private and what's public, without forgetting the difference. And although she sometimes sought the accompaniment of others, she failed a lot and said so often, or most often as (k)not.

Occasionally she attempted to re-screen herself in plain view. In this, the Black Madonna gave strategic if complicit notice to the local circuits of power in which she found a contradictory charge. At the same time, she labored to display connections at multiple electric levels and in masked interfacings with the semi-conductive flows of a TRANSNATIONALLY ABSTRACTED CAPITAL VIOLENCE. This violence is inscribed daily within the ritually constructed force-fields or BODY LANGUAGE of the sex-gender, race and class-coded currents of CAPITAL in the USA TODAY.

Currents of Power. Currents of Knowledge. To be honest with you, I didn't understand every word she spoke. But neither did I feel the loss. She appeared urgently concerned with matters of great importance and I felt it unnecessary to master her every nuance. Better, perhaps, that I risk myself being conjured out from within the dominating network in which I have been HIStorically engendered. Better that I allow myself to be transferred into a space of potential dialogue and social change. In any event, this was my embodied frame of mind when I heard her say a second time, "Pick up your belongings and let's dance." This was less a command than a compelling invitation.

Being profoundly affected by the Black Madonna's words, and being equally bored by the predominantly whitemale culture of social science in which I found myself (w)riting, I said YES. Almost immediately. Not immediately, but almost immediately. Huge chunks of time broke like picture puzzles and flew rebus-coded across the space between us.

She told me that I had no business following her and broke into laughter. I tried to act as cool as possible. I tried stupid fresh cool to pretend that I was rough and ready. I explained that I was without illusions and that I understood the difficulties of the choreography that LIED before us. One particularly nasty chunk of time smashed itself against the side of my face. I fell to my knees blood streaming from a gash above my left eye/"I."

Black Madonna Durkheim laughed now more deeply, saying, "This is (k)not a very good beginning, is it? Things seem BAD. Maybe you should reconsider." Then she spoke FRESH and bluntly. She indicated that (in all

*probability) what LIES ahead would be different for each of us. Significantly
different. As different as the HIStorically material differences in which we
found ourselves called out in relations that were not one. It was (k)not that
she had no desires for some (im)possible future convergence. It was simply
that our journeys would and must be orchestrated differently. She told me that
she'd secretly prepared some (w)ritings and that, although these (w)ritings
were (k)not originally intended for my eyes/"I," I was challenged to try to read
myself out through the body of the words she was offering into somethings
other. If I dared. I was both terrified and fascinated. I realized that to accept
the Black Madonna's traverse offer would entail much more than my coming
along for the (w)rite cowboy. And much less as well. It's (k)not simply that I'd
stop COMING, it's also that I'd be asked to give away my MOST FAVORITE
(ORDER OF) THINGS, and to partially lose what I'd taken for granted as the
pale-faced single male and metropolitan privileges of CAPITAL(ized) SELF-
POSSESSION. This would involve much more than coming along for the (w)rite
cowboy. And much less.*

*She handed me a text that included her (w)riting. As I read this text, I
discovered my body slipping beyond the always only fragile state of what's
been metaphorically called (out to be) the ego. I was slipping beyond what's
positive (or positivistic). I felt stage struck dumb and awkward. At the same
time I was taken by the sensation of being screen-tested beyond my wildest
dreams. Annihilated and yet spinning out from within. Words appeared to lose
meaning and yet retain significance. Or was it the reverse? Matters drifted
with a vengeance. Suddenly things had become expensive. Excessively expensive. And within the inflation of the moment I sought the Black Madonna's
recognition of my economic plight down-loading. Should I come or should I
go? "What do you think?" I asked (k)not knowing.*

*I gazed in what I (mis)recognized as her direction and tried to listen as best
I might when she answered. "You have no business taking chances with other
people's fortunes." She spoke carefully. "But to spend your own chances
wheeling fortunes—that's (an) other matter. It demands, or countermands, that
you actively give yourself over to transferences that will carry you beyond the
borders of what you've always day-dreamed as social. There, on the other
sides of what's safe and self-securing, you might be asked to help defuse or
re(de)fuse the time bomb of what's been HIStorically marked as normal or
normative. There you might be called upon to joyously sacrifice your own
white lighted desires for mastery over me, my kind, and others. This will not
be easy. Nor is this a task demanding heroism. Too many heroes have already
always produced the HIStorical condition in which we find ourselves—this
(k)nightmare. Should you become confused about this, let me remind you that*

the blood of many of us continues to be spent (sociologically) simply for you to have such poetic inklings.

"Listen Yankee! Whether or (k)not you decide to take leave of your commonsenses is of little importance to we others who are (k)not one. But maybe, if you do, when things become noticeably worse for everybody who refuses to become anybody, then, just maybe then, you might be of some minor help to those of us who are always already HIStorically insignificant.[4] No more closed-circuited white male revolutionaries! No more saviors! No more pimps! We've enough of those already. But some other form of parasite? Perhaps? Maybe in time you'll discover and re-mask yourself in a form that's more power-reflexive. But that's an expensive proposition and (k)not one that will make you feel complete. But as I said before, if you want I'll be your host. Pack up your belongings and let's dance."

And so I decided to follow the traces of this Black Madonna and the stories that she's (w)riting. (K)not without a certain nausea and self doubt. Nor without passion. For of this I was certain. "To a greater or lesser extent, everyone depends on stories...to discover the manifold truth of life. Only such stories, read sometimes in a trance, have the power to confront a person with [her or] his fate"[5]

And so I threw a few black T-shirts, bikini cut underwear, books, boots, eyeliner, pens, paper and what (k)nots into my traveling bag and set off in re-search of parts unknown and/or what's missing from our collective HIStorical memories. This re-search seems perverse. As "we" approached the cross-roads of the texts that follow I asked The Black Madonna Durkheim to speak of what LIED before us. She tossed her head in laughter; casting echoes through the (k)night. Thereafter she spoke complexly in a language I find impossible to describe. This much I understood, if ambivalently. "We" are traveling, it seems, in the direction of the Parasite Cafe, in the direction of somethings catastrophic.

The first doll with a woman's shape, Barbie, in the Sixties, was made to be every little girl's fantasy of her own future.

chapter
four

I recall a time in which I wanted a baby sister but would settle for a doll, a simulacrum of a girl to play boy with. It was my third birthday and I insisted. My parents bought me the doll, a cute girl doll, frilled and feminine. At first I was pleased with this gift, a delight to my eyes. Then I heard the sound of my parents moving about in the garden. I had become the subject of inquisition; worried eyes wondering and troubled voices that asked, "Well now that you have a doll to play with are you really sure that's what you truly want?" Eyes upon me, judging my desire, they wait for signs of a normal self. A strange unease overtakes me. I hide within myself transformed. Some other selves excluded, silenced, made abject. "No," I confess. "The doll I had desired, it's what girls want. This I want no longer." Smiles burst the tension and ease returns to the body of a young boy hugged by adults. It was *America* in the early nineteen-fifties and this was no time to play boy with a cute girl doll. There were imaginary Indians on television, snakes in the jungle electric and communists behind the curtain. Back to the toy store went my baby sister, an uncertain double replaced by a six shooting gun. Many wild savages did I slay, each recording a continuous count notched upon the handle of my weapon; and each day felt better, the further I progressed from the shame of my first confession.

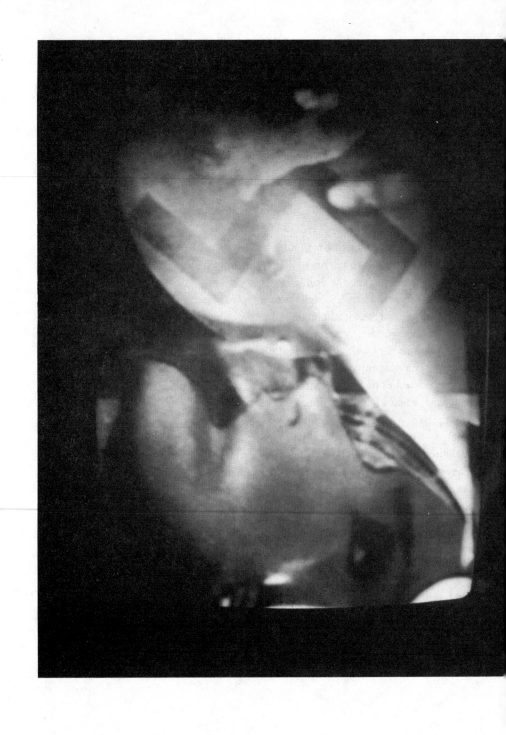

UNSINGULAR BEGINNINGS
A COPY(W)RITER'S PREFACE

> Loneliness rather than sex has become the last vestige of capitalism.
> Loneliness is both a disease and a cause of personal strength and pride...
> Now I wanted to forget. Not my murder,...but...the world that, or rather,
> who, caused isolation. I wanted to disappear into the night.—Kathy Acker[1]

I. ON (W)RITING MEMORIES AND FORGETTING

Three bodies were discovered in the cafe that night. LYING face down amidst the fragments. One was the body of a man. The other two were women. According to available police reports they were some sort of stupidly queer, maybe even perverse, political activists. Their own disclaimers had been more modest. At various times they had referred to themselves as artists, teachers, performers or even copy(w)riters. They were often unemployed. At least the women. Some considered them to be construction workers. Others thought of them as storytellers. Locally they had acquired a reputation as unauthorized agents of social-psychoanalysis. Tricksters to say the least; all were believed to be sociological orphans. Rumors of secret (w)rites had been circulating; and there was considerable confusion as to whether those killed were social scientists or some ill fated characters fallen from the pages a baroquely tragic drama. "Whoever I am," stated one of the dead women only hours before blasts of steel silenced her lips forever, "I am not an intellectual, properly speaking!"

Some believe that there had been a fourth person at the table that night who'd been made to repeatedly (dis)appear. This missing figure, so to speak, remains unnamed or (dis)colored. There are no certain memories of this missing person. This person haunts the staging of this terrible scene. Unsingular. This person is impossible to describe. Some even question the existence of this person. Color this person invisible, uncertain, lacking in self-evidence. Murderous forgettings eat deep into the screens that constitute these memories. This is our culture. What can this mean?

How did three persons come to their death that night at the Parasite Cafe? How is it that a fourth person was made to vanish? Legal authorities comment only that the killings were believed to be drug-related. This is inFORMation. As to the possible disappearance of (an)other person, it was stated simply: "There is no solid evidence to this effect." And regarding suggestions concerning the activities of death squads operating beneath the veneer of democracy, state officials report simply: "This is totally untrue. There is virtually no foundation to such allegations. It's a matter of left wing paranoia. These things don't happen here. Look at the statistics. Well maybe once in L.A., but even that's mostly conjecture." Forgetting eats deep into the screens that constitute these memories.

2. MID-SPEECH, MIDWAY— A PLACE WITHOUT SIGNS (IN FLORIDA)

I'd like to inFORM you that the theoretical concerns that occupy this (w)riting originate in a viciously labored field in northern Florida during the summer of 1971. I arrived in this field, social research instruments in hand, to record stories of health services (or the lack of health services) given to migrant farm workers along the East Coast of the United States. I was a fledgling sociologist and part of a team. The migrant workers, whose health constituted the object of our research, flowed northward each summer, a nearly invisible stream of structurally exploited labor. I was whitemale, well-intentioned, and willing. I also needed the work. Most seasonal east coast farm workers were African-American, virtually propertyless and re-signed. For some, I was the first white person with whom they had ever exchanged words. In Vietnam and Cambodia and Laos, the U.S. military, which included some of my childhood friends, was attempting to bomb a peasant population to its knees. And all this, so that the people of Southeast Asia too also might experience the same democratic freedoms enjoyed by U.S. migrant farm workers.

The freedom of being indebted to a "crew leader," who often as (k)not ensured the paid appearance of workers as commodities with armed guards, terroristic threats and the routinized alcoholization of entire subaltern populations. The freedom of being bussed from one dilapidated rural shed to another. The freedom of sweating in toxic fields picking chemically poisoned produce for a nation of overweight and cancer infested consumers. The freedom of sometimes having your only pair of shoes taken away at night, just in case you had second thoughts. The freedom of being interviewed by me and other researchers. Degrees of freedom, I believe its called in the manuals of statistical sociology. These are HIStorically material aspects of U.S. democracy.

I'd like to inFORM you that this represents the "origin" of the theoretical concerns my (w)riting brings before your eyes/"I"s. I'd like to tell you that this text begins one afternoon in a field in northern Florida, in a place known locally as "Midway," a signless place located halfway between one white

populated town and another. And to let you know how I was affected socio-
logically by interviewing a white Florida farmer about the "health status" of
workers whose "services" he obtained by paying a crew leader (or labor
contractor) a dollar a head per day per worker and twenty-five cents a bushel
picked. In listening to the farmer's words, I was struck by theoretically com-
plex and personally troubling questions concerning the ritual social organiza-
tion of economic, sexual and racial power. These questions remain as part of
my present. These questions haunt this (w)riting.

"The health of the workers?," responded the farmer. "Oh, you mean the
Darkies. Yeah, well they're just fine. I mean they're different from you and me.
Maybe they do a bit too much drinking and sometimes get to fightin' amongst
themselves. And maybe for you or me that'd be a problem. But not for them.
That's the way they like. A huh the way they like it. That's just the way they
are. It's in their nature. It's in their blood."

The farmer answered each of my questions without shame. And without the
appearance of contradiction. He had all the inFORMation. All the facts. And so
did the U.S. governmental agency to whom our research team submitted its
findings. With our words the government too had all the inFORMation; a clear
documentation of the problems, the lack of services, the lack of alternatives.
And through the government all U.S. citizens were also given access to this
inFORMation. In theory. Each after all must only exercise one's right to in-
FORMation to be given the facts about this or virtually any contemporary
social problem. InFORMation about the discriminatory racial, gendered and
class specific characteristics of urban violence. InFORMation about the role of
Oliver North, Jr., George Bush and other loyal U.S. men in facilitating the
smooth passage of cocaine into this country's inner cities in exchange for
illegal funds to support the contra-terrorists in Nicaragua. InFORMation about
the genetic violence being caused by the systematic corporate pollution of the
soil, air and water of the planet from which "we" as a people take flight into
space. Flight into space or flight into hyper-space? What's the HIStorical
difference?

I'd like to inFORM you that in a seemingly contradictionless field of in-
FORMation in northern Florida, there began a power-reflexive process of re-
(w)riting that today brings these words before you. I'd like to inFORM you
that something about a disturbing conversation with a single whitemale and
southern farmer called me to question the value of inFORMation itself.

InFORMation is no simple thing. InFORMation is a social form of value; a
moral and economic value brought into being by the sacrificial rites of western
HIStorical enlightenment. A value intimately connected to the drama of liberal
democracy; a hegemonic moral value that structurally covers over the ritual

exigencies of a harsh and hierarchical form of ultramodern power. A value that's a fetish: a performance of power that appears to float free of the lived experience of human-animal contradictions, just as it feeds parasitically upon the promise of ever greater and more rapid access to a seemingly infinite bank of data, ideas and modeled imaginations. The power of inFORMation and the power of what is systematically erased from our collective memories as this peculiarly ultramodern form of knowledge comes to substitute for all others. Faster and denser. Smoother and more global. InFORMation is characterized by its fascinating ability to doubly represent the relations of our "actual" existence as nothing but the empirical relations of a techno-processed world. A world of inFORMation is a world governed by the progressive conflation of variables and the homogenizing institutional effects of random access. "What is at stake are new language formations that alter significantly the network of social relations, that restructure those relations and the subjects they consti-tute."[2]

I'd like to inFORM you that my recollections of that field of research in Florida represent the "origins" of the words you are reading. This is (k)not exactly true. Nevertheless, a doubled remembrance of this field might prove helpful in partially situating the sociological dance this text enacts. And later, should you be tempted to imagine that the words you are reading are nothing but abstractions I implore you to remember this awful place. For it is indeed from a space near (a) Midway that these words come repeatedly. This is a space begotten in contradiction and mid-speech, a space thick and slowing reeling against the smooth and telematic surface of inFORMation itself. I am (k)not joking.

"Hush," cautioned the Black Madonna Durkheim. "There are some secrets that are (im)possible to give away. At least (k)not unilaterally. And certainly (k)not for profit. Secrets that truly matter. Secrets of HIStory or hers. It's possible to dance with such secrets, or to dialogue with the field of forces they set (theoretically) in motion. But (k)not to give them away. That's impossible. These secrets are more seductive than that. Secrets such as these demand fortitude. Otherwise they stick to your throat and (w)rap themselves around your stomach so fearfully that you'll be begging for release. No, try as you may, secrets such as these are impossible to forget. These secrets keep coming back. They return to haunt you with a sense of what's already always ex-cluded, repressed, shut out or shit away. Such are the secrets of re-membering some stories while remarking upon the unlawful passage or exile of some (unspeakable) others. Try as you may to cover the traces, such terrible secrets recur again and again. These secrets (dis)position everything, overflowing with what you yourself had always assumed was lacking. Secrets such as these are

literally too much. They involve doubled exposure of what feigns to be singular or self identified."

Laughter followed in the wake of the Black Madonna's words. I listened, attempting to remember her every sentence and dance step. Nevertheless I remain uncertain about what it was she was trying to say. What was the meaning of her strange and elusive word-plays? I figured that they must have something to do with what "we" modern white men have always said to be missing. And about what "we" have promised would fill in the (w)holes. I sensed also that when she spoke of dance she was referring to some form of radically reflexive method of re(w)riting a HIStory of the present. Perhaps she meant to evoke an (im)possible image of some form of dialogical epistemology—a choreography of social movements that is at once graceful and de-centered, seductive if (temporarily) a-functional.

The Black Madonna's words were hardly heroic and (k)not prescriptive in the least. And yet in listening I felt myself carried beyond the safeguards of most forms of modern social science. Being reminded of the fated dance of things in this way, memories of that field of black bodied migrant laborers were suddenly infused with difference. And so I fell from the clarity of in-FORMation into the indeterminate laughter of another form of HIStory, or hers. The Black Madonna recognized this metamorphosis, and said: "Now tell me, what is it you mean when you use the term (DIS)AUTOBIOGRAPHICAL METHOD?"

part two

DOUBLE-CROSSING
THE EYE/"I"

The Double is that fading simulacra that returns to repeatedly haunt consciousness with an (im)possible awareness of its own sacrificial constitution. At the same time, the contradictory material character of such a disturbingly doubled awareness is forever spatially dependent on the power of everyday social rituals and the ambivalent bodily knowledges they engender and are engendered by.   —Jack O. Lantern

But what if The Double is itself reflexively redoubled, such that its site of parasitic violence is partially disclosed? Not dis-covered but disclosed, or noticeably closed differently. What will our eyes/"I"s behold, then, but the remasked sight of our own bodily complicities, fears, refusals and desires—falling, like the capitalized pages of some ill begotten whitemen's history, into the broken mirrored freshness of other material imaginings and yearnings for more loving sign-work? What a laugh!
                    —B. Madonna Durkheim

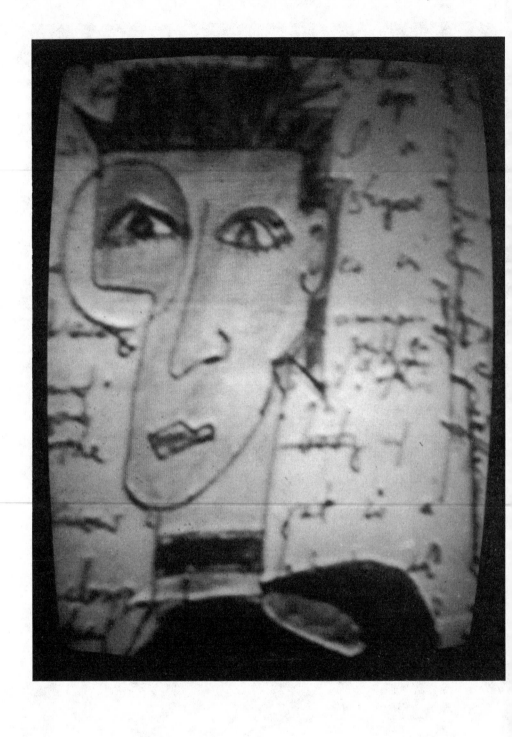

A STORY OF THE EYE/"I"
THE PARASITISM OF POSTMODERN SOCIOLOGY

> Subversion is a problem—it implies a *dependency* on the program that is
> being critiqued—therefore it's a *parasite* of that program. Is there a way to
> produce a force or an intensity that isn't merely a reaction (and a very bad
> and allergic reaction) to what is?—Avital Ronell[1]

PRISON NOTEBOOKS

It's incredible to be here. I never thought I'd be writing these words in
prison and with such fear. It's (k)not exactly that I hadn't seen it coming. It
was always already there in a way in my dreams. And in those unspeakable
places of anxiety that ate me alive while at work or when watching television.
And in the tightness of my throat during sex. For far too long I had treated
these symptoms as no-thing but sliding signifiers. But tonight, from the perspective of terror in which I find myself imprisoned, I re-member these fleeting
sensations as more complex and contradictory. These are (k)not discretely
bound texts imagined while asleep in person. These are material prefigurations
of what is most unspeakable and symptomatic. In and through HIStory. In and
through my body. What's going on? I ask this question economically, in the
most general sense of the word. From my point of view, *a human sacrifice, the
construction of a church*, the dangers of sharing the same needle, *or the gift of
a jewel were no less interesting than the sale of wheat*, international arma-
ments or junk bonds.[2] What's going on?

In the cell to my immediate left LIES a tall thick muscled and dark skinned
werewolf. To my right LIES Frankenstein's monster. The werewolf's black hair
is razored close at the sides and square topped. You can imagine what Frankenstein's monster looks like. It's my first night in this cell and I'm scared to
death. The sound of TV hangs suspended. *And tonight on SuperChannel 22 its
a DOUBLE HORROR DOUBLE FEATURE.* Nobody thought things would
actually go this far this fast. Fines, maybe probation, but not this. First, the
Supreme Court decision confirming the legality of the PDPA *equal crime/equal
time* statue. This never would have happened if the Flag Preservation Amendment hadn't already fractured the constitution. Still, it's difficult to fathom the
speed of what's happening.

For years things seemed to be growing worse, but slowly. There were crises—the gutting of the economy by the savings and loans bandits and the U.S. led techno-war of "New World Order" forces against Iraq. But then CRACK SNAP CRACK(LE) POP CRACK. In less than five months, the invasion of the Andes, the execution of the first "abortion midwife," and the occupation of three entire inner city neighborhoods by federal Anti-Drug Sweep Squads. For nearly seven weeks, vast corridors of Washington, D.C. and Detroit, Michigan were occupied by the U.S. Army's First Airborne. In L.A. it was the Marines and Navy Seals. Within six weeks over 4,000 mostly African-American and Hispanic males were arrested, fast-time convicted and micro-imprinted with bio-code chem-tracers. From then on in, even the smallest "abnormalities" in urine production would be inFORMationally screene d and telematically monitored. Also arrested were nearly twenty-five hundred mostly nonwhite women, approximately half of whom were mothers. If any of these women are ever again convicted of possessing an "illegal substance," she will be made to appear before a three judge Drug Sweep Review Panel to determine whether or not she is to be sterilized. All this was made possible, of course, by the panicky election year passage of the Omnibus Substance Abuse Responsibilities Act (OSARA).

Despite all that has happened to others, it remains nearly impossible to believe what's happening to me. Last month the Court voted to uphold he PDPA, a statue requiring the mandatory sentencing of an ill-defined host of "politically dangerous persons." Each is to be given *equal time* with persons classified as "dangerous by reason of violence." At least this is what was blast-marketed (k)night after (k)night. And for weeks afterward, too many of us continued to assume that the legislation would somehow some way be re-pealed. It's insane. You would think that, if for no-thing but racist economic reasons, some sort of reprieve would have been granted. After all, most of us come from the same neighborhoods and schools as their own children. Maybe that's the point. All of this is so frightening. And so fast. First there was the assault on the cafe and now this. Perhaps I should double back to the truthful origin of this horrific story, and tell you how it all began.

ONCE UPON A TIME CHANGED

"Hear me out. To be a *power-reflexive* reader you must risk the vulnerability of entering an uncannily feared situation with eyes/"I"s crossed doubly and to drift for a time indeterminate and disturbing. After that, perhaps you will be able to more rigorously and more generously theorize the material dynamics of power as the fateful medium of exchange cuts into and across the bodies of those it (dis)positions. This might be your last chance to masquerade yourself in such a way as to strategically perform a ritual series of difficult to dance but nevertheless possible (social) movements that might allow you to both critically distance yourself from the scenes and screens to which you yourself seem most given over to in relations of power, while at the same time unlearning enough about yourself to risk an altered intimacy with others, including those others you keep locked like shadows in the back of your mind. You know, don't you, or at least I hope you know by now, that I'm speaking about the HIStorical power of ritual sacrifice."

Having spoken these words, Black Madonna Durkheim drove me to the front door of what appeared to be an abandoned state institution. For some time I had traveled with the Black Madonna; listening, making notes, asking questions, learning and unlearning dance-steps. Now it appeared that I must journey for a time into other spaces by myself. I felt alert and motivated, but hardly adequate to what I read as demands for reflexive ritual action. Demands for re-search and re(w)riting. Demands for social change. My eyes/"I"s fell upon the weathered glory of the old brick asylum. Anxious, I gazed toward the horizon, trying to get a sense of the strange rituals into which (it appeared) I'd been called to throw myself. I felt stupid and at a loss for words. "Clearly, my project was too vast and the announcement of a vast project is always its betrayal. No one can say without being comical that he [or she] is getting ready to overturn things: He [or she] must overturn, and that is all."[3]

"Ok, get out. It's time for you to be delivered," said the Black Madonna. Or, did she say, "Ok, get moving. It's time for you to deliver?" I'm not sure. This part of the story escapes a certain memory. What I remember most about this scene (of separation) is the frightful character of the Black Madonna's laughter. As she drove from sight I lingered fearful and (k)not without a few questions about what would happen next.

After a short time (I don't recall how long exactly) I felt the uncanny sensation of a presence behind my back in HIStory. I turned slowly and to the left. This is where the figure of Rada Rada appears for the first time in this story of strange attractions. And, next to Rada Rada, a tall whitemale of indeterminate aging. This man was wearing whiteface. White on white; perhaps this man was clowning. This man seemed coy and seductive. He introduced himself saying that he was from just the other side of the border. He then fell into laughter, much like Madonna Durkheim's laughter as she disappeared into the para-GRAPHIC structure of the moment before. In truth there was something about this man that reminded me of the Black Madonna. Mouth lacerated by dark waves of impure language, the man appeared as if both a figure of comedy and an actor taken by the excess of some baroque and tragic drama.

Who was this white-faced man dressed in black before me? And why was I simultaneously so attracted and repulsed by his white figure? Suddenly, as if in a dream, my image of this man was transformed. He appeared now calm and composed, a perverse and erotic guardian of the crossroads between my life and HIStory. He danced slow and hypnotic, marking spirals in the space between my body and the entrance to the old brick building. "Welcome to the Parasite Cafe. Welcome to the Parasite Cafe. Welcome to the Parasite Cafe. Welcome to the Parasite Cafe. Welcome to the Parasite Cafe," my strange host said five times over. Then from a deep and baggy pocket the man took an oval shaped piece of smooth plastic wood with a long narrative thread attached. Engraved upon the plastic wood was a type of high-tech looking hieroglyph. Although I couldn't decipher the design exactly, I thought perhaps it read PC. In any event, the man began to whirl this coded object suspended by the thread until a low humming noise filled the airwaves. I was sure all this must have some ritual significance.

"Its a *churinga*," said the man. He introduced himself as Professor Jack O. Lantern, explaining that he too had been researching *the scene at hand* and was pleased to make my acquaintance. The whirling noise grew louder. The professor shouted that he'd be giving a lecture in the morning to the orphans and that I was invited to attend. His companion, also dressed in black, introduced herself as Rada Rada. S/he told me s/he'd show me around the orphanage as soon as I felt ready. The orphanage? "There's so little time and so much to do," s/he explained, reminding me that my visit was but for a mere three days and three nights. Was this the ritual field I'd promised the Black Madonna I'd re-search?

"The orphanage? I thought this was going to be the Parasite Cafe." I don't know how my words sounded, but I felt truly broken-hearted. I'd been hearing about the Parasite Cafe for over five chapters and, to be honest, I was really looking forward to a thoughtful cup of coffee.

"It could be worse. It could be a family of mutants." Again the professor broke into monstrous laughter. Tossing the *churinga* high into the air, he slid to the earth, crawling serpentine and out of control. I was beside myself; at the edge of panic, and yet strangely attracted to this carnivalesque drama of things folding back upon themselves in time. I felt ambivalent and confused.

"Look, its different than you think," said Rada Rada. "You'll find that things here are actually more real than you'd imagine. This orphanage is the Parasite Cafe. Step inside and you'll know what I mean." I gazed upon the body from which these words were given, again with a strange attraction. It was as if I'd seen her before, or her figure, or her image. It couldn't be, I thought to myself. Maybe I'm hallucinating. Fort da. Fort da da.

"Maybe you're seeing double," said Rada Rada. S/he moved forward, pressing her cheek to mine. The professor did the same. Both laughed soft and seductive. A wave of electricity passed through my body, like a bolt of lightning flashing to ground. "Don't you want to know Quesalid's secret?" one of them asked. I wasn't sure which one of them spoke these words. Then the professor said he'd best be off to prepare the next day's lecture and blew me a kiss goodnight. Rada Rada took my hand, saying, "Come on, I'll show you the cafe. And don't be surprised if you repeatedly encounter a story or two that you've heard before. Everything's double here. Follow me and I'll teach you to read the signs. Who knows, maybe you'll even become a friend of the orphans." I followed Rada Rada, not without fear, hoping to learn something more (or less) about what she meant about things being double.

PART I. A TWICE TOLD TALE

I. CAT'S EYE/"I" STOLEN

I grew up very much alone in a house filled with boys. In this phase space I found my cycles limited. And as far back as I recall I was frightened by anything (k)not sexual. I was nearly timeless when I met Rada Rada. A figure laced with strange and totemic attractors, Rada Rada appeared adrift between my own defensive projections and whatever multiple force-fields called her out in relation. Our KIN NETS being fatefully related we quickly grew intimate, parasiting the recurrence of one anOther's movements, or so it seemed. Cruising mad along the highways, dodging one-way streets and BIG MACs, we would fall on occasion to the poisoned pleasures of the King and his frenzied burghers. I spied the possibilities and they were charged. S/he was wearing a black *heretofore* with microsoft white showing. I felt even more anxious than before because I hoped s/he would be stark naked under the *heretofore*.

S/he had black silk stockings on covering her knees, but I was unable to see as far up as the name by which I imagined her OUT OF MY MIND. I think by far the loveliest of (whose?) names for the vagina. It merely struck me that by slightly lifting the *heretofore* from behind I might cloak my own anxiety (in being caught up in this perversely doubled scene of sacrifice) and see myself mirrored back and able to give head through what I'd always already been given—her body. In this, I imagined Rada Rada phase-locked into possibilities that only I might access. Televisually. Her private parts made public and obscene, while my public relations remained closeted beyond belief. Subterfuged, reeling in orbits of almost molecular abstraction. I wondered what would happen next.

Now, in the corner of the transport there was a saucer of milk for a weird and quantum cat. The cat herself sat imprisoned within a thick black box of science rigged with a cyanide capsule and random triggering device. There was a 50/50 chance that an electron emanating from a radioactive isotope would crash into the trigger in its ON mode, break open the cyanide and OFF the cat. Maybe this had already happened, but there was absolutely no way of knowing since the cat was in the box and I was (k)not. One thing I knew for sure: the cat must be either DEAD OR ALIVE. Unfortunately, I was much less sure of my own existence. Rada Rada eyed the saucer saying, "Milk is for the pussy, isn't it? So let me see you play pussy for a change. Show me what you have in mind when you use the word CUNT. I dare you."

The day was extremely hot. Rada Rada placed the saucer on a small dual-scope scanner and planted herself before me. With nostrils flared, ears perked and tongue twisting s/he seemed transfixed. Her eyes moved fast forward and imaginative and I again felt touched with unease. The social space in which we found ourselves inscribed and, which, for the duration of HIStory, had kept us at such a powerful distance, was suddenly collapsing, folding back upon the rhythms of its own repetitions. Blinding gaps within gaps appeared like an iterating cascade of reflections from an object perilously opened between multiple mirrors. Blood shot to my head and I stood before her, immobile and trembling, wondering at the split screened image of the shadow of my own cock rising blue toward the sun. It was nearly high noon as I stepped awkward from my tight black jeans, almost tripping as I pulled the prewashed fabric over the heel of my Dr. Martens. Then I lay at her feet nervous and undone. We remained motionless, both of us, if unequally overwhelmed, until s/he said, "Come on. Tell me a story. What do you think I'm here for."

2. THE NOSTALGIC CLOSET

That was the period when Rada Rada displayed a desire for breaking into and out of the very beginnings of this old and repetitive narrative. Compulsively. Like a strange attractor, s/he would perform deconstructive twists with texts that "once upon a time" safe-guarded the parlours of my memory. Her back against the chair's back, her legs bent with the grace of a dancer, while I jerked off IN ORDER that what follows me around like the uncanny stench of some double I'm fleeing may be put into words. As an exorcism or a gift? What's the difference? This is no confession. This is a question of re-search.

One day Rada Rada dragged herself across the screen to my window and flashed me the following words.

> "Modern thought is one that moves no longer toward the never-completed formation of *Difference,* but towards the ever-to-be-accomplished unveil-

ing of the Same. Now such an unveiling is not accomplished without the simultaneous appearance of *the Double*...[A]t the threshold of our modernity is situated...the [ritual] constitution of an empirico-transcendental double which was called *MAN*."[4]

On screen there is the image of a man waving. This image is a televisionary double of an actor posing presidential. The actor's wife appears below the screen and waves back to the image of her husband. Between the wavings of the actor's wife and my eyes/"I"s there appears an electronic sea of mostly white, straightmale and wealthy Americans bearing signs with the actor's name imprinted. And a machine that electronically represents these images worldwide. There is a nomination about to happen and things appear effervescent. The year is 1984. This is a totemic ceremony, a story of the evocational destiny of an ultra-modern eye/"I." It is now several years later. Bush and Dan Quayle occupy the White House and the moral economy of speculation is more primitive yet. HIStorically and materially. And more hyper...........and more...........

The text you are reading begins repeatedly in the wake of the following dream. This dream is ominous, white and foreboding. This dream is CAPITAL. When I awake I am startled to find this dream beginning again. "The horror and despair of so much bloody flesh," freeze-framed then joy-sticked back and forth, back and forth, back and forth. It was "nauseating in part, and in part very beautiful." First there was me and Rada Rada. Then I was on my own. Needless to say, we hadn't waited a long time before copulating. Bored and hyper at the same time, we took any opportunity to indulge in what promised the thrill of novel acts. "We did not lack modesty—on the contrary—but something drove us to defy modesty...as immodestly as possible."[5]

This dream is suggestive of the HIStorical materialization of unprecedented scenes of violence. Hiroshima. Nagasaki. Guatemala. El Salvador. Panama. Iraq. South Africa. Color coded search and strip procedures in one "inner city" U.S. neighborhood after anOther. Random drug tests in the workplace and the curtailing of women's control over choices involving maternity. The moral and economic abandonment of Persons With AIDS and the systematic sociological reduction of homeless persons to units of data. Last night in my own bedroom and this morning in boardrooms the globe over. The technological extermination of perhaps 150,000 fleeing Iraqi soldiers and preparations for a "drug free" invasion of the Andes. All this is part of this dream. One scene of racially inscribed, economically stratified and heterosexistly structured sacrificial violence after anOther. Violence to real bodies; bodies that bleed; bodies that panic and call out in the night. But it is not simply by such violence alone that the dream to which I awake is inFORMed, but by something worse. Something more silent, more invisible, more tasteless, more viral.

Not by scenes but by screens. This is a dream of the HIStorical precession of seven doubles. It is occasioned by a terrible doubling of the already always doubled white violence of modern men's cultural distance from nature; by an ultramodern technological absorption of what's real into what's simulated. In this dream, the real is elevated to the strength of the model. "The real is produced from miniaturized units, from matrices, memory banks and command models—and with these it can be reproduced an infinite number of times."[6] This is a dream of pure enlightenment.

3. A DREAM OF A SEVENTH DOUBLE

> Dreams are also riddles in that—during "sleep," and in order to "keep"
> asleep—they recast...history.... If [only] it were enough...to be entranced,
> let us say, by a double syntax, without claiming to regulate the second by
> the standard...of the first. —Luce Irigaray[7]

I was trying to write this book when I was taken by the dream that follows. I am bathed electric in this dream's pale blue light and wet. I am about to take my seat in a lush, red and velvety theater. This theater seems Chinese. Maybe it is not far from Tiananmen Square. It strikes me that vampires may be circulating within this theater. Before entering I encounter a grey-faced white man who presents me with a program and the words BETWEEN THE PLANS AND THE HANDS THAT BUILD, THERE MUST BE A MEDIATOR.

This is all so strange and uncanny. Fear scratches at the smooth and reflecting surface I've become. The cushioned red seats in this theater are arranged in a semi-circle and I find myself looking down upon the stage from this my given vantage point in HIStory. This is a theater of doubles and time is running out. "The host is in the row in front, the parasite behind him, a bit in his shadow.... The host comes before and the parasite follows. Such is the case for every system where we eat at the expense of another."[8] On stage, the fifth double has just completed a good performance. This was the theater of representation, a drama of words and things. A chill passes through my body. A sixth double begins to screen its play. The audience is thrilled. This is a perfect copy of what's gone on before; an exact mechanical reproduction. The audience is thrilled. Suddenly I notice a grey mattered shape moving fast forward across the row before me. This ghostly figure glides nearly transparent to the periphery of my vision and then disappears. I am greatly alarmed by the almost weightless movement of this shape and recognize it as that of a seventh double. The remarkably invisible performance of this double seems already materially in process; unannounced, unheralded, unnamed. The thought comes to me that maybe this double is not so much invisible as hyper-visible. "[This] is a kind of obscenity of accuracy where there is [little] distinction between... presence and absence. No shadows, no ghosts."[9] Or rather, only shadows of copied shadows; ghosts of premodeled ghosts. This seventh double slips beyond the resistive encumbrances of modern language into the almost pure (if coded) abstractions of what's sheerly signed. What does this mean?

The audience remains entranced by the reproductive theatrics of the sixth double as it repeats HIStory. The audience appears oblivious to new and more dangerous cultural transformations already under way. It is as if the seventh double LIES beyond the social body of theater as "we" know it. This double is nevertheless playing its part, enacting its (w)rite, disseminating a particular functionality. Artificial intelligence: I sense its drama oozing parasitic, if unnoticed, into the theater in which I find myself transferred and terrorized. For a blinding instant I feel as if something has entered my body like HIStory in the blink of an eye/"I." How does it feel to be penetrated by liquid CAPITAL? Is it like shedding a tear, only in reverse? I brace myself for what LIES ahead.

This is a theater of simulation. It strikes me that vampires may be circulating within this theater. Vertigo spins contagious and panic drives a mass market of bodies beyond the boundaries of what's modern. What or who's being sacrificed so viciously to program such special effects? Outward into hyperspace. Inward into frenzy. This theater seems technologically capable of blurring distinctions between what's real and what's other. This is the theater of the SEVENTH DOUBLE and within its ritual framings there's no telling fact from fiction. As my eyes move leftward in dramatic pursuit of this seemingly terminal doubling the borders of the stage that constitutes this theater begin to dissolve into odorless, test bands of tasteless silent color: RED, WHITE, BLUE. This dream is ending. This dream is beginning again.

4. ALL THE DREAMS THAT MONEY CAN BUY

There is a woman walking short skirted, dreamy and aroused. She is in a train station. There is a screech of metal and smoke arising. The woman is high heeled and properly screened. She is carrying a rose. A man approaches from the opposite direction. Maybe it's me. This is television and a suggestive female voice-over states:

> Some things you dream.
> Some things you don't.
> Sometimes you can't tell the difference
> Anything is possible if you dare.
> Dare, the fragrance.

I am fascinated and somewhat anxious. Sometimes I can't tell the difference.

5. (RE)VISIONINGS

I spend a period of time drafting words that fall under the title "A World of Doubles: a World of Exiles." The HIStory I'm trying to tell is about what drives a wedge of syntax into and between bodies divided by a compulsive repetition of powerful language forms. (K)not by language per se. (K)not by the rhythmic dance drumbeat language of poetic forms fluttering; nor by words that snake soft dark spirals; nor ecstatic hard edged flickering green neon laugh gurgles. Nor by the cough stutter slip ceremony of midspeech; nor a theater that doubles what's double. The HIStory I'm trying to tell is about the compulsive repetition of powerful language forms and the sacrificial violence they enact.

Anyway, when I finish this text, I think it's pretty good, so I send it to the Black Madonna and wait anxious for a response. To be honest, the words she sent in response were a bit hard to swallow. I read them three times sleepless, composing responses, raising my defenses and wanting to act outside the only emotions I know. For a long time I stare into a mirror. In the mo(u)rning I'm feeling melancholy, and am more than a bit surprised when The Black Madonna arrives. She speaks to me about a descent she feels predestined to make and what might emerge on the other side. Then she tells me it's time to go to the cafe, the orphanage, or wherever. I burn the only draft of my text on doubles and throw the ashes in the toilet. An insignificant ritual, perhaps, but one which I nevertheless felt called upon to perform. So, as a substitute for my "original" text I now offer Madonna Durkheim's words of criticism. Just copying them has helped me unlearn somethings. I hope they give you related ambivalence.

> November 10, 1989
> Somewhere near The Parasite Cafe
> Dear Stephen:
>
> Thank you for sending me a copy of "A World of Doubles: a world of exiles." This is not an uninteresting manuscript. Moreover, I find it encouraging that you partially acknowledge the epistemic violence you white men have HIStorically enacted upon those of us you pretend to objectively incorporate within your terroristic science of doubles. I also agree that recent technological "advances" in telecommunicative doublings make such rites today as violent and abstract as ever.
>
> Nevertheless, certain aspects of your text fill me with rage. I wish that I could reasonably articulate these matters but I'm afraid that at this

moment in HIStory reasonable articulation escapes me. This is no accident. As such, I write words that may appear to double cross your own. I don't know how deep these words will cut. What I do know is that the problem is not *mine* alone. The problem is *mime* alone. Mimic. Cut. Displace. Mimic. Cut. Laugh. There's blood beneath your text and I fear it's mine and others'. Mimic. Cut. Displace. Mimic. Cut. Laugh.

You (w)rite about doublings as if these processes are an invariant or "existential" property of human beings as such. I read this as male fantasy. I appreciate your gesture to decenter yourself within a privileged genealogy of white male authorship, but was angered nevertheless that you hardly mention things that others of us have been (w)riting (if often spoken aloud) for some time now. Is this what you make of our noise? Moreover, as I trust you know by now, given our sacrificial positionings within your HIStory, I "assume that any theory of the subject has always [already] been appropriated by the 'masculine.'"[10] In this sense, I am also concerned that, should a woman reader become seduced by the apparent openness of your theory of doubles, she may "fail...to realize that she is renouncing the specificity of her own relationship to the imaginary."[11]

You (w)rite about doublings as a ritual process by which human animals substitute an imaginary sign or totemic image of something for what's real. Which human animals enact this substitution? What is their gender? What is their color? What is their material positioning within various economies of sign-exchange? I agree that by exchanging abstract signs for what's HIStorically material a certain class of human animals sacrificially authorize the *cutting off* of their own bodies and the *cutting up* of others. Nonetheless, wouldn't it be more radically reflexive to specify such actions as the sacrificial rituals of a particular group of white men out to master nature and create a doubly abstract place for themselves in HIStory? By such doublings don't you men artfully appear as Other than who you actually are? And worse still, you imagine that those of us who are (k)not one of (or with) you do the same!

This, it seems, is the HIStorical essence of narcissism—a pure and reflective process whereby Man is spared the recurrence of being-given-over-in-relations-of-reciprocal-interconnectedness. This is also a ritual that privileges certain of you white men with the illusion of endlessly deterring the vegetative embrace of your own deaths by deflowering the bodies of others. In bedrooms and urban ghettoes, and in the poisoned fields of agri-business that move your markets, as in the rice paddies of Vietnam and the deadly highway leading north from Kuwait City—you scorch the earth. You terrorize us with your projective doublings and take speculative flight with our stolen riches into a space of CAPITAL that's almost exclusively whitemale and metropolitan. "The Copernican revolution," it seems, "has yet to have its final effects in the male imaginary. And by centering man outside himself, it has occasioned above all man's ex-stasis within the transcendental (subject). Rising to a perspective that would dominate the totality, to the vantage point of the greatest power, he thus cuts himself off from the bedrock, from his empirical relationship with the matrix that he claims to survey to specularize and to speculate. Exiling himself even further (toward) where the greatest power LIES he thus becomes the 'sun' as if it is around him that things turn, a pole of attraction stronger than the earth."[12]

Relationally "yours,"
Black Madonna D.

6. EXCOMMUNICATIONS

What follows is a partial transcript of the first of a series of lectures given by Jack O. Lantern to the orphans at the Parasite Cafe. This lecture was delivered the morning after my arrival. To the best of my knowledge, the materials here presented represent the only existing record of O. Lantern's talks or performances. Aside from some minor editing, this is the lecture in its entirety. I find the setting difficult to describe, but let me try.

After everything that had gone on the night before, I barely made it to the darkened lecture hall, exhausted and unshaven. I carried a large coffee with cream and took a seat near the rear. In certain ways, this place reminded me of the theater in my dream of the seven doubles. There were no red velvet curtains but somehow things seemed related. Three sections with twenty-two seats each sloped downward toward an old wooden lectern. Almost all the seats were taken when the professor descended before my eyes/"I"s. He was costumed in a black-on-black mid-length kimono and masked with a photographic image of his own face white-faced. A wave of laughter passed among the orphans.

Without saying a word to anybody, O. Lantern switched on a boom box at maximum volume and filled the room with a tape loop. Then he turned off the overhead lights and projected a single slide of U.S. President George Bush making a point. Bush's hand extends fast forward into HIStory, while his lips address the world. This man has something to tell us. In the background to Bush's left appears an image of a frightened Central American woman. Sack over her shoulder and naked child under her arm, this woman appears to be running for her life. Perhaps this woman has heard what Bush is saying. From the excessively loud boom box the room vibrates with the following words.

...shouting match with the President and he seemed eager to join the debate. (Bush's voice) "the question is, 'why are we supporting El Salvador?'" (Woman protester's voice) "Why are we killing priests in El Salvador?" (Bush's voice) "The answer is that we're not. Now, you be quiet and here's the answer to your question." "The Question is, 'why are we supporting El Salvador?" "Why are we killing priests in El Salvador?" "The answer is that we're not. Now you be quiet and here's the answer to your question." "Why are we killing priests in El Salvador?" "The answer is that we're not. Now you be quiet and here's the answer to your question. You be quiet and here's the answer to your question. The answer is that we're not. Now you be quiet and here's the answer to your question. Now you be quiet and here's the answer to your question. Now you be quiet and here's the answer to your question." "Why are we killing priests in El Salvador?" "The answer is we're not. Now you be quiet and here's the answer to your question. We are supporting El Salvador because its has had certifiably free elections. President Cristiani is trying to do a job for democracy. President Cristiani is trying to do a job for democracy. Cristiani is trying to do a job for democracy and the left wing guerillas must not take over El Salvador."...

This noise continued for about two minutes. Thereafter the projected slide changed to an image of a quotation from Jean Baudrillard and beneath these words O. Lantern began his lecture. There were video screens to either side of the professor's pose. One screen was composed of slow motion projections of images from PRIMETIME TV fading in and out of scenes depicting the recent U.S. led attack on Iraq. On the other screen an image of O. Lantern himself appeared; his naked double tattooed by a shimmering array of televisionary advertisements. It was as if the professor's own slow motioned body was being marked with intimate icons of consumptive desire. Lacerated by an electronic stream of CAPITAL inscriptions, sometimes it almost appeared that O. Lantern himself was being carried away by intense waves of telecommunicative ecstasy. These video images continued throughout the length of that morning's lecture. At one point during the broadcast I was certain you could actually see the professor's penis covered over by the blue light of found images or what (k)not.

Of all the prostheses that mark out the history of the body, the double is undoubtedly the most ancient...[I]t is an imaginary figure which, like the soul, the shadow, the image in the mirror, haunts the subject as [one's] other, so that it is at once [one]self and yet totally unalike, which haunts him [or her] as a tenuous and always averted death. Not always, however. When the double materializes, when it becomes visible, it signifies an immanent death.[13]

Good Morning Friends and Orphans:

In this series of lectures, which I have been invited to give by the Orphans' Action Committee here at the Parasite Cafe, I shall be speaking about the general economy of a critical social-psychoanalytic method. My intent is itself double. On one hand, I hope to offer preliminary strategies for recognizing some of the most dangerous aspects of the ritual geographies in which we find ourselves today in HIStory. For want of better words, I will speak of these dominating tendencies within *first-world cultures* as a form of *hyper-narcissistic doubling*. If, in so doing, I give periodic notice to technological simulations of the voice of George Bush, my reference is not so much to Bush as a fleshy individual, but to Bush's voice as kind of totemic figure, or *double*, for the inFORMational power of contemporary corporate CAPITAL.

White narcissistic doublings are nothing new to western culture. Through such ritual processes ONE may militaristically discover ONEself as if an autonomous existential agent—a defensive masculine (mis)recognition, no doubt, and ONE purchased at the sacrificial expense of others. Narcissism, in other words, is realized in the parasitic act of feeding off others. Under the sign of narcissism others are reduced to being nothing but mirror images of ONE-self. In this sense, narcissistic violence has longed fueled the most "enlightened" (if deadly) daydreams of "we" who identify ourselves as western men. From the (w)ritings of Plotinus, Augustine and Descartes to the televisionary rituals of today's New World Order, narcissism operates as a fascinating form of flight from a world of fleshy contradictions into the inner curvature of an eye/"I" that knows no others. The phallic "I." The priestly "I." The "I" of metaphysics, the military-economy and positive science. Each represents a parasitic precession of western white men fighting powerfully to take the world within.

This is not a new story. What is new about narcissism is the apocalyptic cultural twist this story appears to be taking with the advent of ultramodern social technologies. COMMAND. CONTROL. COMMUNICATIONS. INTELLIGENCE. C3I. These are not only cybernetic signals for a militaristic interface between humans, other animals and machines, but also codes for an increasingly narcissistic form of popular culture that feeds off the materiality of contradictory HIStorical memories. Welcome to the Parasite Cafe, a hypernarcissistic society of militaristically controlled consumption. In this society, many of us are literally so orphaned by the micro-processing of modeled trajectories of profit that our illusions of narcissistic self-sufficiency threaten a virtual techno-screening of reality itself. In ultramodern society, MAN's *inFORMational ego*, his "*ego consumans*", is finding unprecedented material support in its disembodying white flight from earthy relations to others. Coldly seduced by fascinations put into play by advanced technological rituals of telecommunicative exchange, the ultramodern eye/"I" dines specularly on nothing but the imaginary doubles of its own will to pilot itself beyond what's finite and fleshy.

Here LIES the cool and parasitic gaming of a *digital Narcissus*. This comes prepackaged in the microsoft dreams of such biogenetic technologies as cloning. "The hypostasis of an artificial double, the clone will henceforth be your guardian angel, the visible form of your unconscious and flesh of your flesh, *literally and without metaphor*. Your 'neighbor' will henceforth be this clone of hallucinatory resemblance, consequently you will never be alone again and no longer have a secret. 'Love your neighbor as yourself': this old problem of Christianity is resolved—your neighbor, *it's your self*."[14] The love is total. So is the self-seduction. Screened by such hyper-narcissistic defenses today's *inFORMational ego* is today armed with what appears as almost *random access* to memories beyond belief and beyond limit. But at whose expense?

An analysis of the sacrificial flight path of the *inFORMational ego* constitutes the first aspect of the doubled agenda of these lectures. In this, I will attempt to partially retrace the white phallic movement of contemporary CAPITAL as it passes narcissistically through some power-charged bodies as these feed technologically off others. I am speaking of Narcissus in his most recent western incarnation—a material realization of certain incredibly violent *male fantasies* that LIE truthfully neither inside the self nor out, but within ritual spaces conjured by dense and high speed cybernetic exchange processes, permitting a fascinating (if terroristic) shuttle between binary forms (of experience) that find their repetitive origins in the fateful reproduction of social hierarchies. Imagine this fantastic oscillation as something like an almost lightning fast social-psychoanalytic transference. This is a split screen transference. It simultaneously carries its communicants beyond both the (always only partially visible) speed of light and the contagion of contradictory affect.

The second aspect of these lectures is more ruinously methodological. It concerns questions about how those of us most implicated in the institutional reproduction of ultramodern narcissism might begin to partially double back upon the repetitive scene of both our own enclosure and the compulsive sacrificing of others. In this, I invite you to imagine epistemological strategies capable of both critically deciphering and actively counter-memorizing the HIStorical spaces of power within which we are bodily struggling. For it is only within such ritually charged fields (of force) that "we" are today differentially positioned in relation to each other. And (k)not simply in relation to each other, but also to each's Other, in the social-psychoanalytic sense of this word. Given the power of such ritual positionings, it may prove a considerable challenge to construct forms of social scientific knowledge less complicit with the hegemonic narcissism that dominates our HIStorical present. In accepting such a challenge some of us may feel ridiculously stupid. But such laughable feelings may be nothing new to those of you who are feminists and/or actively engaged in struggles against hierarchical social forms which you already recognize as harmful to yourselves and others.

One way of responding to this challenge involves the use or (ab)use of certain (dis)autobiographical methods. Toward this forever (im)possible end, I ask you to consider a variety of *social-psychoanalytic* concerns, but only as these are themselves reflexively betrayed at the crossroads of several other postmodern sociological methods—*deconstructive ethnography, genealogical HIStory*, and *collage (w)riting*. Without saying more about these strategies at the moment, let me simply suggest that by doubling a concern with substantive and methodological issues within the same space of analysis, I hope to move you to reflexively incorporate (within your own bodies of (w)riting) tensions engendered by a personal and political recognition of the haunting intercon-nectedness between *what is given* to social scientific considerations and the (always contestable) situations of social power that make such problematic *modes of gift exchange* themselves structurally possible. This is to make uneasy connections between "we" who are constituted as *subjects* in the construction of theory's sacrificial gaze and the *objects* with whom we (sci-ence-fictionally) converse.[15]

PART 2. FATEFUL COINCIDENCES

I. DOUBLING SOCIAL SCIENCE: A POWER-REFLEXIVE RE-MEMBERING

> [This] whole effort consists in materializing the pleasure of the text, in making the text the object of pleasure like others....The important thing is to equalize the field of pleasure, to abolish the false opposition of practical life and contemplative life.... What we are seeking to establish in various ways is a theory of the materialist subject.[16] —Roland Barthes

Given the importance of sacrificial ritual activity in producing and repro-ducing biographical, HIStorical and even geographical sensations of what's real, and considering the possibility that major western forms of ritual action are today themselves in flux, it is important to meditate reflexively upon the (dis)autobiographical strategies of this text's own construction. A HIStory of doubles without end—this is a social HIStory of the ultramodernizing West. A HIStory of unprecedented imperial geographies and of the sexual, racial, economic hierarchies that operate to *virtually* erase memories of the violence by which this HIStory is itself compulsively repeated. Fortunately (to this point at least) such erasures have neither been total nor uniform. Always already before us are questions of empire, desire, and sacrifice. The appearance of doubles is traditionally associated with the coming of death. In what forms does death come today to the Parasite Cafe? How, moreover, do contemporary social technologies induce a forgetfulness about the HIStory of certain bodies while privileging the memories of others? Please bear with me. Unlike the bodies of those most victimized by ultramodern power, these questions will not disappear. At least not until major social changes alter *the order of things* in which I find myself in (w)riting.

What follows is a partial meditation upon methods that most shape my reading (and re(w)riting) of the violence of contemporary social institutions. If partially reflexive of the ritual confines through which I labor, such methods must entail a *doubling back* upon social scenes that today bring these words before you. Materially and in the imaginary realm. Such doublings are neither easy to read nor re(w)rite. This is because they operate upon and within me (and you too, if in different ways) as signs constituting the perceptual frameworks and narrative conditions by which I both recognize and misrecognize myself as an actor within HIStory. Such doublings give *form* to what I routinely take for granted or consider "natural." As Michael Ryan suggests, "We exist and have being or content as social entities in the [doubled] forms of behavior we practice, the modes of interaction we engage in, the formal patterns of speech and communication we undertake, the styles of work we assume, and so forth."[17] At the same time, such doublings may operate as thickly filtered screens separating *what is* from *what might be (or might have been)* different. If this screening operation is (ideologically) effective "I" may not even notice that the doubles which envelope me are, in actuality, no-thing but the powerful effects of sacrificially filtered framings. This is what makes the world of doubles (in which I am (w)riting to you) neither easy to read nor re(w)rite. Please bare with me.

Methodologically this text may be read as an effort to deconstruct the dominance of a positivist aesthetics in the (w)riting of contemporary social science. Encouraged by the convergent efforts of a variety of feminist, multicultural and poststructuralist critics, I am here laboring to resituate sociological texts as themselves bound to HIStorically specific forms of literary production. Here I also find inspiration in Roland Barthes' attempts to retrace pleasures materially effected by various styles of epistemological engagement. Within the lawful confines of modern social science these *normally* involve the pleasures of either objectively operationalizing or subjectively describing the "facts" of the re-searched other. What pleasures are these and how do they operate?

To ask this question is to begin to re(w)rite the methods of *normal social science*. It is also to come to partial terms with the hierarchical pleasures "we" modern men have culturally discovered in efforts to master what we name as NATURE. In the video-text, *Criminological Displacements*, Avery Gordon and I perform what might be called a genealogical reading of the dominant pleasures of modern social science as those operating under the signs of *sadism, surveillance* and *the erection a "normalized" observer* to the disciplinary exclusion of others. Avery and I picture modern social science as *sadistic* because, like the cold, calculating and dispassionate protagonists of de Sade's pornography, persons dominating the scene of social science inquiry have recurrently found pleasure in producing a transcendent or metaphysical distance between themselves and those they predictively study. This positivism penetrates the unruly orifices of the "natural" social world; plugging up the (w)holes and reducing as much variance as possible. This mode of social science is characterized as *surveillance* because the eyes/"I"s of the positivist must remain fixed upon "his" object lest "she" escape the master's gaze and return to a space of noticeable social contradiction. When this happens the paranoid borders of positivism become leaky, as anxious objects consigned to "the other side" begin to show through, displaying aspects of the dramaturgical bondage by which our *normal identities* as seemingly neutral observers are constructed.[18] As Max Horkheimer and Theodor Adorno point out, positivist reason "comprises the idea of a free, human social life in which men organize themselves as the universal subject," but only within "the court of judgement of calculation, which adjusts the world for the ends of self-preservation and recognizes no function other than the preparation of the object from mere sensory material in order to make it the material of subjugation."[19]

Sadism, surveillance and *the production of the "normalized" (white male) subject* in a discourse that exiles or consumptively incorporates difference—these are the dominant pleasures of positivist social science.[20] This is a harsh image. If "we" contemporary social scientists rarely recognize ourselves in such descriptions, perhaps this is because the disciplinary confines within which most of us work help insulate us from grasping the sacrifices (of others) that makes positivism (structurally) possible. Under the sign of positivist logic, "Being is apprehended under the aspect of manufacture and administration. Everything—even the human individual, not to speak of the animal—is converted into the repeatable, replaceable process into a mere example for the conceptual models of the system."[21]

Under positivism the model comes first. But where does the model come from? What is unexamined (or unexaminable) under the sign of positivism are the everyday rituals of power and knowledge that sacrificially constitute the very social experiences that positivists seek to explain. Positivist rituals conjure a screen that separates the cultured researcher from the HIStorically material scene in which one's own epistemological framework is sacrificially filtered. In this way positivism rigorously reflects what's already premodeled. At the same time, it is compulsively unreflexive about the powerful social structuring of its own perceptual apparatus. Here LIES a blind spot at the center of positivism's dazzling promise of enlightenment, a hole around which its whole predictive quest for reliable measurement and lawful explanation converge. A hole before (or at the blind center of) one's eyes/"I"s. A hole that remains taboo, a hole that must be (w)holly covered over for positivism to work its magic. An immaterial (w)hole that substitutes what Dorothy Smith refers to as the masculinist pretensions of an "extra-local standpoint" for the fleshy HIStorical contradictions out of which the positivist screen itself is erected.[22] For positivists, "the conceptual apparatus determines the sense, even before perception occurs... images are pre-censored according to the norm...which will later govern their apprehension."[23]

In the (de)construction that constitutes the text you are reading I am trying to double-cross or write against the grain of the positivist pleasures (and pains) that dominate contemporary social science. As such, I am laboring imperfectly to partially resist the temptation to forget that my own representations of these matters LIE truthfully in the sacrificial epistemological rituals by which any "successful" act of theorizing covers over the fictive narrational structures by which it identifies (with) a story of the facts. In this way, in (w)riting this text I am struggling to deny myself a place of empirical privilege outside of the social scene in which I find myself ritually vocationed within HIStory. This partial literary refusal, if materially incorporated into the imagination of social science, may have troubling implications for both the style and content of this form of literature. As Julia Kristeva re-marks:

> Literary practice remains the missing link in the socio-communicative... fabric of the so-called human sciences....[Moreover] the insertion of this practice into the social science corpus necessitates a modification of the very notion of pleasure.[24]

I read Kristeva's words as a challenge to us social scientists to double back upon the HIStorical scenery of our own modes of literary production. One response to such a challenge takes the form of what might be called *power-reflexive methods of sociological (dis)closure*. This demands that "we" partially display (and thereby evict or give notice to) the boundary work by which the social worlds we inhabit are sacrificially constructed. This is to actively *derealize* the always only apparently natural social contexts of our own (w)ritings. This is also to recognize (and thereby reframe) our artful complicity in the reconstruction of such contexts. It is to learn to read or re(w)rite our HIStorical relations to other people, things and ourselves as no-thing but powerfully constructed doubles of the contradictory material and imaginary positionings by which we are situated in relation to others.

This is no simple task—theoretically or personally. Theoretically it demands that "we" dialogically resituate the objects of our inquiry within the economic, cultural-linguistic, and sexual frame-workings in which they partially speak to us (just as "we" speak about and to them). To do so "we" must become acutely sensitive to the subtle ritual technologies by which our knowledges are differentially embodied. For those of us trained within the predominantly whitemale and heterosexist confines of western educational institutions, this may entail a contagious *double-crossing* out from within the specialized boun-daries of the disciplines by which modern knowledge is ritually authorized. Those of us disciplined by sociology, for instance, may have to open ourselves to questions and methods falling between the forced fields of philosophy, literature, linguistics, HIStory, economics, women's studies, psychoanalysis, the iconic or performing arts, and even theoretical physics. And to knowledge derived from cultures traditionally marked as outside and today south of what's West. And vice versa. In this sense, *power-reflexive methods* demand an impure, if rigorous, co-mingling of such multiple forms of inquiry. Perhaps only by risking the rigors of a kind of "theoretical indiscipline" might "we" today put into practice such *epistemological double-crossings*.[25] For many of us this will involve as much *unlearning* as learning; a process involving both the dangers and pleasures of speaking (or (w)riting) out of place; a process that challenges us to simultaneously "generalize exactly at those points where generalizations seem impossible" and to specify the stupid particularity of our contradictory social relations at other points where specificity may subvert the appearance of timeless laws and disembodying methodological norms.[26]

More uneasy yet may be the personal discomforts engendered by attempts to double back upon, and thereby institutionally displace, the hierarchical forms in which western knowledge has been traditionally pre-packaged. A likely effect of any serious challenge to the reproduction of existing social power, such discomforts are today everywhere in evidence in debates sur-rounding what has become problematically referenced as Political Correctness. Such debates, as I understand them, originate in the straight-minded logic of those most privileged by the contemporary academic marketplace—whitemales of economic advantage. Some of these persons believe themselves to be silenced by the effective theoretical and political interventions of those tradi-tionally marginalized, as well as by current critical discourses such as post-structuralism, which some "intellectuals" have been awkwardly trying to link to contemporary struggles for social justice. Why are those privileged by traditional academic perspectives feeling silenced by the multicultural voices of women, nonwhites, gays, lesbians and others and by critical theoretical strategies which seek to deconstruct aspects of willful knowledge that mask their own relations to power? Is it that those at the margins refuse to dialogue with those favored by traditional forms of hierarchy? Or is it simply that the privileged have no reflexive intellectual response to the claim that all forms of knowledge are partially situated in ongoing relations of power? Despite conservative claims, orchestrated by a well financed nation-wide campaign against the alleged intolerance of the "Thought Police" of political correctness (or PC as it has come be known in the media), the only thing that those attacked for being PC appear intolerant of are forms of intolerant knowledge themselves— forms that refuse to be reflexive about the fields of power in which they are themselves (re)produced.

To take seriously the situated character of all knowledge is not to deny the objectivity of social scientific truths but to demand of objectivity that it reflexively locate the (always only) provisional adequacy of its own partial positionings within the world it studies. Is this today what is feared as Political Correctness? If so, perhaps PC should be defended. Still, as a critical scholar, I much prefer the power-reflexive demands of a method of dialogical inquiry that repeatedly acknowledges the partial, provisional and, thus, *never totally correct* character of its (or my) own truth claims. While most discomforting to those privileged by an existing order of power, such a strategy of reflexive doublings may be experienced as both anxiety producing *and* pleasurable for those regularly sacrificed to the reproduction of power. In this, one (who is not One) might encounter the more fluid material and imaginary pleasures of being both a heterogeneous and contradictory subject.

> This is an uncertain pleasure of an uncertain subject: a subject who knows we are interpellated—that we respond to the hailing of our names. But this subject recognizes the provisionality of centering, the uncertainty of that seemingly certain anchorage, only produced by the rituals of taking the world within us. This is the uncertain pleasure of the subject whose truth is always inscribed in the power to know, to entrap in a name.[27]

2. TOWARD A (DIS)AUTOBIOGRAPHICAL METHOD

In an earlier meditation upon the methods of *a power-reflexive social science* I suggested that the critical researcher must ask her or himself three questions.[28] How do my biographical positionings within contemporary economic, racial and gendered hierarchies affect my approach to truth and the truths I am capable of recognizing? How, moreover, do my observations about a site-specific scene of social inquiry connect to the ritual organization of power relations in society as a (w)hole? And, once having examined a particular conjuncture of biographical and structural relations of power, what have I learned that may further struggles for social justice in the society in which I live?

These questions emerge out of my attempts to teach university students to write critically about our own participation in rituals that draw boundaries between what is socially acceptable and what is condemned as deviant. These sacrificial rituals endow particular totemic images (or doubles) with the aura of positive moral value, while branding others as taboo. In my teaching about such matters, I have encouraged students not just to think critically, but to (w)rite critically as well. I have urged them to deploy (w)riting as a social technology for reflexively doubling back upon ritualized scenes of power that might otherwise be taken for granted. The hope here is that by developing *power-reflexive (w)riting practices* we might better make connections between the immediacy of autobiographical experiences and the HIStorical spaces within which these experiences might be best critically re-membered. The political importance of such a doubled writing practice, or what I call *(dis)-autobiographical analysis*, is articulated in the *collective memory-work* of Frigga Haug and her German feminist co-authors when they state:

> Writing is [or can be] a transgression of boundaries, an exploration of new territory. It involves making public the events of our lives, wriggling free of the constraints of purely private and individual experiences. From a state of modest insignificance we enter a space in which we can take ourselves seriously. As an alternative to accepting everyday events mindlessly, we recalled them in writing.[29]

This lesson or gift or curse I offer to you as well. In reading or re(w)riting (dis)autobiographically

> you will be faced with the creative task of how to weave autobiography with HIStory, how to write of/in your body as both yours and (k)not yours, as both an individual body with borders you can really feel, and as ritual body really (k)notted and entangled with other stories not of your own making. This is no simple task. Remember, however, you are not being asked to create the FULL STORY, the COMPLETE TRUTH or FINAL AC-COUNTING of your tale [but] to play seriously with your own memories using the critical techniques of power-reflexive story telling to create, hopefully, a different story than the one you've written before. So *remember*...and, failing that,...*invent* a creative critical social [science] fiction that might raise questions as well as answer them."[30]

3. POSTMODERN SOCIOLOGY: A METHODOLOGICAL DOUBLE-CROSS

The word *postmodernism* today circulates at the borders of a variety of academic disciplines, political discourses and artistic practices. Often it connotes an emergent form of epistemological or aesthetic inquiry marked by a particular style of theoretical or poetic engagement. This style appears to privilege a non-linear and decentered play of language, commentary and criticism. Frequently associated with the terms deconstruction and poststructuralism, postmodernism is, for some, a politically charged term suggesting a radical overturning of the *master narratives* of straight whitemale and western CAPITAList claims to knowledge.[31] Hence the call for a postmodern *politics of difference*—a politics attentive to a heterogeneity of voices silenced, marginalized or excluded from the construction of modern western ways of thinking, feeling and organizing everyday social life. In the words of Cornel West, whose work provides a critical reading of postmodernity with reference to African-Americans and other peoples of color:

> Distinctive features of the new cultural politics of difference are to trash the monolithic and homogeneous in the name of diversity, multiplicity, and heterogeneity; to reject the abstract, general, and universal in light of the concrete, specific, and particular; and to historicize, and pluralize by highlighting the contingent, provisional, variable, tentative, shifting and changing.... To put it bluntly, the new cultural politics of difference consists of creative responses to the precise circumstances of our present moment.[32]

Thus the demand for a social HIStory (or HERstory) that reverses commonly held patriarchal, racist and class based cultural representations. This demand is unnoticed or resisted by those for whom postmodernism connotes little but the useless wordplay of a group of pretentious and self-referential intellectuals fascinated by the latest fashions in French theoretical jargon and dressed in black clothes. For still others, there is the sense that postmodernism means something important, but it's not exactly clear what. The language, it seems, keeps getting in the way. This is no minor complaint. If postmodernism is about anything, it is about the materiality of language as a dynamic force in the ritual structuring of perception and in the transformation of an indeterminate range of human possibilities into the restricted moral economy of a given order of things in time. Does this make any sense to you as a reader? Whether it does or doesn't I assume it is a matter of language. Language that keeps us at a distance; or language that brings us together in a certain way, while exiling (at least for the moment) other ways of interpretively making sense of and/or being in relation to each other.

Postmodern sociological (w)ritings make critical assumptions about the sociology of linguistic representation that challenge modern social science thinking. Treat social facts as things and represent them as objective entities that might be measured and compared accordingly! Most contemporary U.S. sociology still follows this edict, almost religiously. Simply read what is routinely published in what are called the major journals. The rules of sociological method here render the problem of language as little more than the task of adequately operationalizing variable aspects of objects being represented. If only the imprecisions of discursive language could be translated into less ambiguous terms! So speaks (the disciplinary desires) of the modern social scientist, who, having statistically avoided paradoxes posed by Gödel and the thorny problems of reflexive set theory, continues a naive call for the mathematicalization of sociological representation.

The forms of postmodern sociology I am here conjuring are today emerging in partial response both to the deconstruction of straight western whitemale sign-work by feminists, peoples of color, gays and lesbians, postcolonial critics and others marginalized in the reproduction of modern social science and also to the implosion of referential meaning within the ultramodern cultural economy in which sociology is itself technologically located. Together, these twin (if contradictory) challenges signify *a crisis in representation* which threatens the compulsive repetition of *normal* sociological methods. The HIStorical character of this crisis is depicted by Avery Gordon in the following manner:

> At the core of the postmodern field...is a crisis in representation, a fracture
> in the epistemological regime of modernity, a regime which was able to
> make a distinction between fact and fiction and which rested on a faith in
> the reality effect of social science discourse. Such a crisis...has led to an
> understanding that the practices of writing, analysis, and investigation,
> whether of social or literary texts, constitute...a cultural practice which
> organizes particular rituals of story-telling, at the center of which is an
> investigating subject. This epistemological and social rupture, rather than
> leading away from an analysis of social relations of power, leads directly to
> a very different agenda for asking how power operates.[33]

Recognizing objectivity as a shifting field for the powerful staging of what Gordon calls "truthful fictions,"[34] and also as a field put into crisis by the telecommunicative parasitism of ultramodern power, a reflexive postmodern analysis takes issue with the objectified character of mainstream sociology. Critical postmodern sociologies are also to be distinguished from various subjectivist approaches that typically pose as *humanist alternatives* to positivism. By playing with, cutting up, and/or mirroring back upon the social scenes out of which it is written, postmodern sociology appears to be searching for a language that gives fictive notice to the fact that "we" are simultaneously authors of and authored by the languages in which we find ourselves trying to communicate. While this may initially seem like an (im)possible task, the strengths of this laughable project LIE precisely in the reflexive recognition of its own partial incompleteness. Thus, at precisely those places where the language of a postmodern analysis appears most likely to slip, fail or falter, you (as participant readers) may be called upon, not to complete a given text, but to enter into a dialogue with troubling questions that no one writer can answer on her (or his) own. In this way, postmodern sociologies, although involving the interpretive labor of reflexive human (animal) agents, neither begin nor end with the subjective experience of fully conscious actors.

This *critical anti-humanism* is not anti-experiential. Nor does it suggest that social actors are "cultural dupes" of some prearranged structure. Nor is it anti-humanitarian. Quite the opposite. The reproduction of binary divisions between objectivity or subjectivity—this, perhaps, is anti-humanitarian. It may also be straight whitemale, western and modern. Such divisions privilege the theoretical prerogatives of an alleged huMAN autonomy over and above the messy remainders of NATURE, viewed here as either a passive object or a subjective construction of CULTURED MAN himself.

Postmodern sociologies attempt to partially subvert modern binary divisions between what's objective and what's subjective. In so doing, they de-center interpretive experience into the ritual folds of language itself. Not language as expressive of some pre-given relation between a (potentially) all knowing subject and a fully knowable object, but language as a ritual practice that materially gives (and takes away) particular objects to and from (HIStorically specific) subjects; language that constructs and reconstructs experience within and between the bodies of those it depends on and feeds off. This is a paradoxical power of language. It forcefully (w)rites us, just as we actively speak it.

To view language in this way is to understand that all representations are *partial* in a double sense of the word. They are partial because they, like we, are forever incomplete, interdependent or *overdetermined* by the material and imaginary conditions of their use. And they are also partial because they are political; and they are political because every instance of language forecloses the HIStorical possibility of being elsewhere for the moment. To glimpse this aspect of language is to reflexively resist modernist divisions; not only between what's objective and what's subjective, but between fact and fiction as well. This is not to suggest that there is no difference between fact and fiction, but that what differences there are LIE within, not outside the material effects of specific linguistic practices. Indeed, while facts "can be imagined as original, irreducible notes from which a reliable understanding of the world can be constructed," and while fictions "can be imagined as a derivative, fabricated version of the world,...a kind of perverse double for the facts," the etymology of both words refer us to (ritual) human action—to performance, deeds, and the act of fashioning, forming or inventing.[35] As such, both "fiction and fact are rooted in an epistemology that appeals to experience. However, there is an important difference; the word fiction is an active form, referring to a present act of fashioning, while fact is a descendent of a past participle, a word which masks the generative deed or performance. A fact seems done, unchangeable, fit only to be recorded; fiction always seems inventive, open to other possibilities, other fashionings of life." [36]

This theorization of facts as nothing but powerful forms of fiction is a key strategy in movements toward a postmodern social science. By reflexively doubling back upon the fictive construction of their own factuality in (w)riting, postmodern sociologies attempt to give notice to the partiality of their own positionings within the very situations (of action) they labor to represent. This is, of course, a challenge to the continued institutional hegemony of "facticity" within social science practice, a mirroring back of the day dream of methodological transparency that has long enchanted the imagination of modern sociology, as if this our field of power and knowledge could ever be *a window on the real*. Moreover, as Avery Gordon points out, this challenge "is both necessary and desirable in order to understand how the real itself and its...sociological representations are also fictions, albeit powerful ones which we do not [ordinarily] experience as fictional, but as true."[37]

4. FROM SOCIAL CONSTRUCTION TO SOCIOLOGICAL DECONSTRUCTION

> Among the rights which man claims for himself, he forgets that of being stupid; he is necessarily stupid, but without the right to be so, and so sees himself forced to dissimulate. I would get angry at myself for wanting to hide.... —Georges Bataille[38]

I graduated with a B.A. in sociology from the Catholic University of America in Washington, D.C. in 1971. That being twenty years ago there are many things I don't remember, and many others I now remember differently. The same applies to my experiences in Columbus, Ohio, where I completed a Ph.D. in Sociology at The Ohio State University and worked for a time as a researcher for the Ohio Division of Mental Health, and more recently at Boston College where, except for a one year Post-Doc at Yale and a sabbatical, I have taught since 1977. Today, in the space of this (w)riting, I have learned different ways of remembering things—such as how to partially embody myself in relations of more vulnerable reciprocity with others and how to better resist those who will (k)not take no for answer. For better and for worse. This is fate. I believe that I may also be more in rhythm with the queer erotics of the *humananimal stupidity* I share like a laughable curse with others. But shortly after the Gulf War (or, is it more accurate to say "after the U.S. led destruction of much of Iraq?"), when Rada Rada asked me to *unfreely associate* to what I remember most about my years in college, the following experiences came to mind.

a. Walking seven blocks from one Black ghetto Church basement to another during the midst of a 1968 riot by citizens of the District Columbia following the assassination of Martin Luther King. The streets were filled with angry and impoverished African-Americans in resistance to every WHITE thing this nation stood for and thousands of gas masked soldiers, firing tear gas and occasional bullets, and guarding the banks with armored vehicles of war. I was a well meaning white volunteer carrying food. Fires were being set everywhere. Much that was burnt down, a mere ten blocks from the White House, has never been rebuilt.

b. Trying to work through issues in phenomenological sociology and texts such as Peter Berger and Thomas Luckmann's *The Social Construction of Reality*, in order to understand how so many of us "Americans" are able go about our everyday lives with virtually no memory of the sacrificial costs we routinely impose upon others.[39] At the time I found more theoretical resources for elaborating such questions such as this in the Philosophy Department than within sociology *per se*. In graduate school, where I was introduced to the sociological study of both Marx and anarchism, phenomenological concerns with the ritual structuring of everyday experience already paved the way.

c. Coming to suspect—through a variety of pleasurable and painful personal experiences, theoretical meditation, popular cultural rituals (including seeing large numbers of movies, masturbating to mass mediated pornography, and feeling physically charged by various forms of white rock and African-American music), reading books, and by endless talk with women friends and other men, including lovers—that the "normative" erotic repetition of "compulsive heterosexuality" was both stupid and extremely violent. This was something I would later learn (and unlearn) much more about, but in college the suspicions were already there.

d. Talking late into the night with Sam Williams, a fellow student and militant Black activist about our different HIStorical positionings and about how to begin (again and again) to effectively counter the racism by which others lives were tattooed in relation.

e. The day (I believe it was during the so-called Tet Offensive) that I recognized that I was no longer simply against the U.S. involvement in Viet Nam, but that I was actually hoping that Viet Nam, with all its contradictions, would rid itself of my own nation's imperial violence. This was a shocking awareness. I am sure that it was influenced by reading as much as I could about Viet Nam and (w)riting a HIStory term paper on events leading up to war, especially the Eisenhower administration's efforts to shore up western defenses against "movements for national liberation" in Indochina following the overthrow of French colonial rule in 1954.

f. Being tear-gassed to the point of temporary blindness and uncontrolled vomiting, and then being assaulted by waves of police attacking anti-war demonstrators.

g. Being asked to "please refrain from speaking in Social Theory class," having come to the verbal defense of a feminist student who had taken issue with a professor's characterization of Durkheimian sociology ("Unlike you and your radical friend Ms. Rada Rada") as scientifically detached from politics. And the grade I would later "receive."

h. Sleeping for a couple of hours in a student occupied office at the University, having spent most of the night helping organize an upcoming anti-war rally. Then at dawn being greeted by the shocking red sight of a spray painted sign on the side of the National Shrine of the Immaculate Conception reading PIGS 4/STUDENTS 0. That was when I first learned of the killing of students at Kent State. When word came soon afterward of more blood spilt at Jackson State University many of us glimpsed (if only briefly) what many of the nation's poorest citizens are forced to fear most everyday—the power of state bullets to silence HIStory. In Mexico City the memories were more sacrificial yet.

i. Loving to read and write and have serious conversations with others; and in this process learn about such matters as governmental orchestrated attacks upon leading members of the Black Panther Party, efforts to undermine the viability of the American Indian Movement, the wretched conditions of most American prisons, the routinization of physical and cultural violence against gay men and lesbians (particularly after "Stonewall"), and U.S. corporate-state complicity in the genocidal disappearance of Native peasant populations in Guatemala. Although it was several years before I would read Foucault, you might say that I was learning (and unlearning) a HIStory of my present.

j. Being vocationally positioned to work my way out from within a radical theological critique of western Christian categories and "Trinitarian" logic into spaces move conducive to critical sociological practices.

k. Receiving my draft notice, but knowing that it was no longer conscientiously possible for me to militarily serve U.S. imperial interests.

In graduate school, in symbolic interaction with questions raised by Marxism and anarchism, my phenomenological concerns with the social structuring of everyday consciousness led me to experiment with politicalized forms of both *societal reaction theory* and *ethnomethodology.* While societal reaction theory (when most radical) argues that what appears as "real" or "factual" is in actuality nothing but the cultural, political and material effects of human struggles for the organization of power in (and as) HIStory, critical ethnomethodology attends to the subtle power of interactional rituals in shaping perception and taken-for-granted experience. The influence of societal reaction theory is most evident in my 1977 study of the role of bureaucratic and professional power inFORMing the "discovery" child abuse.[40] Ethnomethodological concerns, on the other hand, guided my ethnographic work on the social construction of diagnostic classifications, including the prediction of dangerousness by psychiatric professionals at a maximum security hospital for "the criminally insane."[41]

In both studies, I observed how the ritual organization of power guided the *professional vision* of influential agents of social control. In both the "discovery" of child abuse and the labeling of psychiatric patients, clinicians produce "expert" accounts of deviance that deflect attention from the contradictory character of existing structures of (unequal) power. This was not to suggest that control agents intend their work as a perpetuation of hierarchy. Indeed, my ethnographic contact with social actors (such as those) I was studying convinced me that most were well trained and well meaning. How do people with such "good" intentions produce such "bad" effects? How are control agents' conscious experiences professionally abstracted from the ritual scenes and consequences of their own labor? Questions such as these have led my (past) work to be labeled as "an exemplar" of what is today commonly referred to as a *social constructionist* paradigm.[42]

According to Donna Haraway, the "temptations" of a social constructionist framework LIE in its contention that "*all*...knowledge claims, most certainly and especially scientific ones" are to be "theorized as power moves, not moves towards truth."[43] While sympathetic to this "temptation," Haraway voices reservations about a perspective that seemingly offers no "objectively" defendable or "ethically scientific" positions from which to critique power's multiple HIStorical abuses. For Haraway, radical constructionism represents "a terrifying view of the relationship of body and language for those of us who would still like to talk about reality with more confidence than we allow the Christian right's discussion of the Second Coming."[44] In a different vein, Steve Woolgar and Dorothy Pawluch criticize constructionism for its unreflexive deployment of "ontological gerrymandering," a rhetorical device which is said to cast doubt on the "reality claims" of those being studied, while "back-grounding" or partially disguising the "fact" that constructionist accounts are no less artificial than those they HIStorically circumscribe. Yet, rather than condemning constructionists for such practices, Woolgar and Pawluch speculate that "ontological gerrymandering" may itself be a constitutive feature of all "successful" sociological explanation. Because of the importance of both critiques, and because the text you are reading represents a move from "constructionism" toward what might be better characterized as "sociological deconstruction," I will briefly respond to both Woolgar and Pawluch's and Haraway's positions.[45]

Pointing to instances of "selective relativism," Woolgar and Pawluch charge constructionists with "foreshadowing" a "realist" view of social conditions. While not an inaccurate characterization of some constructionist texts, this is a limited reading of the more radical possibilities of this perspective. If constructionism foreshadows anything it is a "surrealist view" of social conditions. By this I mean that those things which appear as social facts are *paradoxically* nothing but the fictive effects of the powerful structuring practices by which "we" repeatedly embody ourselves in HIStory. This is a loaded sentence. In the 1920s and '30s, surrealism represented a convergent movement of radical artists, writers, social theorists and political activists seeking to partially disrupt and structurally transform what they collectively perceived (and represented in (w)riting) as the white Eurocentric and militaristic organization of modern CAPITALIST consciousness. Condemning "the positivist idealism" and "commodification" of western thought and action, surrealists experimented with such alternative research methods as automatic writing, sensory derangement, poetic collage, dream narration, social applications of psychoanalysis, new ways of engaging in political conversation, and the collective construction of art, literature and social criticism aimed at turning inside out a society they believed to be both repressive of themselves and oppressive to others.

Although commonly misunderstood as a "modern art movement," surrealism, like its predecessor Dada, is better recognized as a radical conjuncture of theoretically inFORMed social criticism and artistic activism.[46] Understanding reality as itself "composed of signifying elements"[47] rather than timeless substantial forms, surrealists sought to construct new linguistic practices by which to reflexively explode existing cultural artifice and open the human imagination to new and revolutionary social possibilities. This emphasis on the transubstantial character of material cultural reality was, perhaps, something that appealed to the post-Catholic epistemology of many surrealists and which endeared some of them to the more poetic, if not to say mystical, of their Jewish and African-Caribbean political allies. So likewise did dissident forms of surrealism, such as that woven around the figure of Georges Bataille, infect the ethnographic imagination of a generation of critical French sociologists and anthropologists. Many of those attracted to this strange counter-cultural virus found aspects of surrealism related to radical readings of the late "Jewish sociological" (w)ritings of Émile Durkheim and those of his nephew, Marcel Mauss. For surrealist ethnographers, as later for dissident French psychoanalysts, such matters resulted in new theories about the HIStorical character of what was bodily lacking in modern western culture. For some it also elicited a desire to (deconstructively) turn the eye/"I" of social science *stupidly* back upon its own construction. In this, dissident surrealist (w)ritings called for *general economic* sacrifices that would laughingly burn through the blind homogeneity of modern reason. Bataille, who advocated the dangerous gift of such stupidity, called not simply for an abandonment of scientific reason but to use science against science in order to "keep science from blindly emptying the universe of human content.... [T]o use it to limit its own movements and to situate beyond its own limits what it will never attain."[48]

Reading the material exigencies of "objective" social conditions from a "surrealist" viewpoint, radical constructionism takes leave of a world of fixed facts in order to examine ritual practices which situate us in a world of moving artifacts. This is to recognize that there is really nothing here but the transferential effects of being (dis)positioned within the rites of a powerful domesticating drama. Comte, a founding figure of modern sociology, had dreamed of a positivist paradise where factual truths would end both religious superstition and metaphysical speculation—a (Newtonian) social physics of sort. For surrealists, social matters were more quantum in their ritual mechanics. Comte's positivism was read as thought frightened of its own ghostly shadows.[49] While some surrealists, such as Andre Breton, appeared influenced by the synthetic (intellectual) force of Hegelian dialectics, the most radical (of the white men at least, for there were certainly "others" that fell under the spell of surrealism) passed through Alexander Kojève's critical reading of Hegel into an artistic imagination that was more Nietzchean in its affirmative play of difference. Nevertheless, in one way or another, surrealists sought to reverse the dreams of positivism in both science and everyday life.

To live within the repressive shadows of western culture was for surrealists to live within the confines of a terrible imperial prison. Who are the guards and who and what is being guarded against? These were questions that surrealists addressed both to the dominant institutions of their society and to each other. For the surrealist Antonin Artaud, life within modern bourgeois society was likened to the putrid stench of civilized rot. This was life amidst a mass of sleep walkers and the living dead, a world haunted by its unrecognizable doubles. Artaud served for a time as the coordinator of the Surrealist Research Bureau in Paris. He also attempted to construct a form of theatre that would double back upon the shadowy confines of its own culture, and with "gestures, sounds, words, screams, light, [and] darkness" rename and thereby intimately redirect the play of such shadows from within. "To break through language in order to touch life," this according to Artaud was a research method that "leads to the rejection of the usual limits of *man* and *man's* powers, and infinitely extends the frontiers of what is called reality."[50] Maybe some of you will "discover" (ab)uses of such a method embodied within the very text you are reading.

The ritual physicality of Artaud's doubled theater was meant to both re-mind and heal its participants of what was repressed by the unnoticed doublings of modern social dramas. The radical German dramaturgy of Bertolt Brecht, although employing different theatrical strategies, was aimed at related ends. Brecht's methods of *estrangement* or *distantiation* aimed at breaking with the unreflexive identifications fostered by everyday forms of (political) theater. In this Brecht hoped to defamiliarize his audiences with what other-wise might appear "natural." Brecht also formulated what he called a *pro-ductivist aesthetics* to give dramatic notice to the artifice of even his own *epic theater*. In both Artaud's and Brecht's dramaturgical methods LIE reflexive strategies that supplement those of radical constructionism.[51] Together, these *power-reflexive methods* of (theatrical) research embody truthful spaces of "objectivity" without covering over the recognition that these too are spaces of ritual artifice. This doubled reflexivity makes such methods more "objective" than traditional forms of modern theatrical and social science representation.

By placing surrealism and the methods of Artaud and Brecht in the service of constructionism, I am trying not so much to defend previous constructionist theses as to suggest directions for the perspective's continued movement. Woolgar and Pawluch are correct in observing numerous theoretical, method-ological, and empirical inconsistencies in various examples of constructionism. With this I am not in disagreement. My concern is with what is excluded by such criticism—the possibility of more radically reflexive versions of con-structionism, versions more attuned to thorny epistemological problems, versions that approach a *social deconstructionist perspective*. To reframe constructionionism in this manner is to noticeably displace the truth of domi-nant or hegemonic HIStorical narratives into "truthful fictions" of power operating in even the most unsuspected of places. In part, this is to *collage* constructionism with Michel Foucault's claim that critical forms of HIStory enact a HIStory of the present.[52] This, as Avery Gordon points out, "requires a particular kind of perception where what's transparent and what's in the shadows put each other in crisis."[53]

What is the relation between this "particular kind of perception" and what social science has long called "objectivity?" In commenting on the "desire of deconstruction" to show a "text what it does not know," Gayatri Spivak remarks that, "as she deconstructs, all protestations to the contrary, the critic necessarily assumes that she at least, for the time being, means what she says.... In other words, the critic provisionally forgets that her own text is necessarily self-deconstructed."[54] This adds a new wrinkle to constructionism's critique of all claims to objectivity. Is Spivak's deconstructive position more objective because it repeatedly foregrounds its own provisional forgettings, without disavowing the (strategic) necessity for such forgetfulness? Provisional forgetfulness, it seems, weaves itself throughout all constructionist projects.

But what if the provisionality of forgetting were to become a reflexive feature of theorizing itself? Today, a continuing dialogue with feminist, multi-cultural and critical poststructuralist perspectives allows me to imagine other aspects of power than those envisioned by constructionism alone. In attempt-ing to reflexively situate myself in relation to questions raised by these conver-gent critical frameworks I am challenged to both theorize and act upon the sex/gender and racially troubling assumption that my own truthful positioning in power-charged fields of knowledge is limited by the contradictory ways in which I repeatedly participate in reproducing both complicity and resistance to blind white spaces of compulsive heterosexist hierarchy. These are binary structured spaces of great homogeneity; white-washed and homo(geneous) sexual spaces; spaces that compellingly vocation particular conjunctures of moral and bodily knowledge, but not others. These spaces envelop everyday experience like a second skin or second nature, or like a ritual mix of physical and psychic geographies that call me out to enact certain performances, while closeting others. Not that I am determined to answer!

Rituals that performatively mask the sacrificial privileges of straight-shoot-ing-white-phallic-male-fantasized standpoints construct densely hierarchical spaces of material and imaginary power: moral and economic spaces, spaces of defensive fears and alluring fascinations, spaces suppressive not only of mutual vulnerabilty between men and women but also between those ritually classified as *beings of essentially the same gender* and *beings of essentially different races*. Indeed, as critical gay and lesbian theorists observe (from a variety of heterogeneous standpoints denied legitimacy by dominant modern social-sexual constructions), such hegemonic ritual spaces are suppressive of almost any but the most militaristic-competitive-angry-anxious-jealous-possessive-criminal-erotic intimacies between men; and suppressive, as well, of intimate relations between women, whom homo(geneously)sexualized men attempt (with varying degrees of success) to exchange as if mirrored screenings of their own power; filtering, repressing, denying the possibility of reciprocal vulnerability to each other; sacrificially giving the would-be captured bodies of women to each other as substitutes for the more laughable vulnerabilities of men's own bodily fluid(itie)s.[55] And no less terrifying are rituals suppressive of color (de)codings other than those violently filtered by spaces of compulsive blind whiteness. These commodified spaces are so performatively thorough and so magnetic in their racism that they may appear false-faced and transparent to almost everybody but those (of us) most attracted by their repulsive caucasian white circlings.

A partially reflexive recognition of our active, if different, (dis)positionings within such performative rituals of power leads to significantly more complex ways of seeing, smelling, touching, tasting and hearing the social world in which we live. But is this also more objective? Without denying the situated and power infused character of all knowledge, a recognition that links constructionism to feminism and other critical viewpoints, Haraway asks:

> [H]ow to have simultaneously an account of radical historical contingency for all knowledge claims and knowing subjects, a critical practice for recognizing our own 'semiotc technologies' for making meanings, and a no-nonsense commitment to faithful accounts of a 'real' world, one that can be partially shared and friendly to earth-wide projects of finite freedom, adequate material abundance, modest meaning in suffering, and limited happiness.[56]

Haraway refuses to oppose radical versions of constructionism and what she calls "feminist critical empiricism" (a sense of the "embodied objectivity" that LIES within womens' different but related experiences of being "marked" by patriarchal power). I read this as a strategic move away from all pure doctrines of scientific thought—be these realist or constructionist. In Avery Gordon's terms, this is to open a critical space where what is shadowy and what may seem transparent put each other in crisis. By explicitly foregrounding (1) the situatedness of all claims to "objective" knowledge, (2) the strategic need to make claims to "objectivity" (if only to defend those marginalized against the sacrificial claims of the center), and (3) the recognition that to make anything present is to (at least partially) make something else absent (women's knowledge, for instance, in a world of inFORMation governed by men), feminism, multiculturalism and poststructuralism here put a spin on *constructionism* that moves it toward *deconstructionism*. In this sense, "objectivity turns out to be about particular and specific embodiment, and definitely not about...false vision promising transcendence of all limits and responsibilities. The moral is simple: only partial perspective promises objective vision.

This is an objective vision that initiates, rather than closes off, the problem of responsibility for the generativity of all...[epistemological] practices."[57]

5. "OTHER WEAPONS" FOR (K)NOT KNOWING

> It was only after I had completely conceded my defeat as an artist—my inability to master the material in the image of my own intention—that I became aware of the ambiguous consequences of my failure, for in effect, the reasons for and the nature of my defeat contained, simultaneously, the reasons for and the nature of the victorious forces as well. I have come to believe that if history were recorded by the vanquished rather than by the victors, it would illuminate the real, rather than theoretical, means to power; for it is the defeated who know best which of the opposing tactics were irresistible. The Russian peasant has another way of saying this: 'He who wears the shoe knows where it pinches.' —Maya Deren[58]

The opening words of Luisa Valenzuela's *Other Weapons* read: "She doesn't find it the least bit surprising that she has no memory, that she feels completely devoid of recollections. She may not even realize that she's living in an absolute void. She is quite concerned about something else, about her capacity to find the right word for each thing and receive a cup of tea when she says I want (and that 'I want' also disconcerts her, that act of willing) when she says I want a cup of tea."[59] Valenzuela invites her readers to follow the ritual journey of a woman protagonist as she gradually, and not without considerable anguish, recovers her memories of being bodily positioned as an object of (secret) exchanges between men in a game of war. Retracing her sacrificial positioning as an object among other objects, as a woman-object positioned among men's (secret) words, concepts, photographs, names, plants, mirrors, windows, colleagues, wells, whips, peepholes, keys and voices, "she" comes to a revelation about the HIStorical geography of her memory loss. This "discovery" is both reflexively situated and objective. It also hastens the ending of her imprisonment.

> She looks at herself, first out of obligation and then out of pleasure, and then she sees herself up there in the mirror..., cast on the bed, upside down and far away. She looks at herself from the tips of her toes where he is now tracing a map...; she looks at herself and, without acknowledging it altogether, travels up her own legs, her pubis, her navel, the surprisingly heavy breasts, a long neck and that face of hers which suddenly reminds her of the plant—living, but somehow artificial—and, unwittingly, she closes her eyes.[60]

In (w)riting within (and about) the warring contours of ultramodern power and in attempting to respond to the embodied memories (and forgettings) of others, I too *want* to be performing an analysis that is both reflexively situated and objective. But as a U.S. white man with CAPITAL credentials and an academic job, my positioning in the HIStory of memories is markedly different than Valenzuela's woman protagonist. There are, moreover, some very good reasons for suspecting that the situated materiality of "her" memory may be more "objective" than mine. At least until I doubly dance back upon my relation to "her," unlearning the many rituals of blindness that (dis)position me as one of power's privileged sons.

> "Open your eyes," he commands, watching her watch herself in the mirror.... Open your eyes, spit it out, tell me who sent you, who gave the order, and she shouts such an intense, deep NO that her answer is silent in the space they're in and he doesn't hear it, a NO that seems to shatter the mirror..., that multiplies and maims and destroys his image, almost like a bullet shot although he doesn't perceive it and both his image and the mirror stay there, intact, impervious, and she, exhaling the air she'd kept in, whispers...his real name, for the first time. But he doesn't hear that either, as distant as he is from so much trauma.[61]

In saying NO "she" accesses a space (of forbidden knowledge) that situates "her" within a contradictory and *excessive awareness* of how power works (unequally) between them. But "distant as he is from so much trauma" he doesn't hear. In this, she comes to knowledge painfully and from a position that his militaristic (or phallic) defenses protect him from recognizing. In this "she" is more objective. This is not to suggest that the oppressed are ever entirely clear-sighted about the dynamics of power to which those most privileged are blinded. All forms of knowledge are partially mediated. It is, however, to acknowledge that, as Gloria Anzaldúa[62], Nancy Harstock[63], Dorothy Smith[64], Donna Haraway and others argue, "there is good reason to believe vision is [objectively] better from below the brilliant space platforms of the powerful."[65] Why? Because in the process of reflexively saying NO to hierarchy, the oppressed are able to partially make use of traumas imposed on them to bear witness to the objectivizing play of parasitic power itself. In this sense, as Patricia Hill Collins points out, the reflexive standpoint of those subjugated by power "may provide a preferred stance from which to view the matrix of domination because...[it] is less likely than the specialized knowledge produced by dominant groups to deny the connection betweeen ideas and the vested interests of their creators."[66]

This may be difficult for even the most well meaning of us who are privileged by power to recognize. Perhaps "we" need first to publicly unlearn certain of our most militaristically guarded secrets. Only after making such (self) sacrifices might "we" actually become more objective, and thus better able to assist others in overturning hierarchical forms. Otherwise, all good intentions aside, "we" in positions of (epistemological) privilege may remain more part of the problem than part of its solution. This is why I feel compelled (as a critical whitemale sociologist) to enact what I call *(dis)autobiographical methods.* Paradoxically, this partial enactment of what Avery Gordon labels as *a sociographical project,* may give you (as readers) more access to certain aspects of myself that are conjured by this (w)riting than I, stupid as I am, may initially realize. Please read this as both a warning and invitation to dialogue.

> As a sociographical project...[this text] insists on being read as writing, as 'literature.' One of the key lessons of deconstruction is that both the writer and the text perform moves and tell stories of which they are unaware. An important part of the deconstructive project of reading is precisely to tell the text what it does not know. This is your job. Because the conscious intentions and desires of the writer form a kind of interference pattern within which a writing and a reading occur, I am perhaps the least qualified person to unscramble the codes that are used and which the text itself produces.[67]

Toward such modest ends, the text you are reading stupidly mixes *social-psychoanalysis* with *collage (w)riting, deconstructive ethnography,* and a *genealogical approach to HIStory.* Collage techniques are employed because they *visibly double* (and thus give reflexive notice to) the already cut up and repasted frameworkings of ultramodernity. This is (k)not to merely simulate a random access-like pastiche of free-floating and contextless commodity hook-ups.[68] By intersecting collage strategies with methods attentive to specific cultural rituals, scenes of psychic over-determination and the shifting HIStorical configurations of power, I am trying to construct a reading environment that disinFORMs as much as it shares knowledge. Hopefully this will offer an experience closer to the uncertainties of *dialogical research* than the more masterful pleasures of dialectical analysis.

Within this collage, ethnography is intersected with social-psychoanalysis because when crossing into and out of each other these strategies may assist decentering the (working) identities of those of us trained as western social scientists. For as Michel Foucault notes, "In relation to the human sciences, psychoanalysis and ethnology are rather 'counter sciences,' which does not mean that they are less 'rational' or 'objective' than others, but that they flow in the opposite direction, that they head them back to their epistemological basis, and that they ceaselessly 'unmake' that very man who is creating and recreating his positivity in the human sciences."[69] To double back upon and thus partially remake that very man who is me? By engaging deconstructively with ethnography and sociologically with psychoanalysis I hope to better reflex upon the embodied scenes of ritual transference in which my own claims to truth are reflexively situated. This doubling-crossing of strategies raises "difficulties in the register of method," which, as Georges Bataille suggests, provide partial access to spaces of both the cultural and psychic "unconscious."[70] But even this is never innocent of my desire that you will recognize me in these words and respond transferentially to the cursed gift they offer.

To play off social-psychoanalysis in relation to ethnography is to open spaces between my (w)riting and your eyes/"I"s. Within such spaces perhaps "we" might better learn (and unlearn) things about what binds us together within a *transferential* field charged by the *repetitious drive* of conscious and *unconscious* social power. For better and for worse. In this way I hope my words partially engender a dialogue with others seeking to objectively subvert sacrifices demanded by the reproduction of white CAPITALIst patriarchy. Such a critical convergence of ethnographic and social-psychoanalytic strategies is already a feature of what Avery Gordon refers to as "the theoretical/political interventions of...a feminist poststructuralism."[71] For Gordon, a feminist engagement with these always "less than adequate" methods may assist in "grappling with issues related to the narrative structuring, fictive composition, and historical provisionality of [gendered] claims to knowledge."[72] Gordon's sociological use of psychoanalysis gives notice to the ghostly haunt of powerful forces rendered "invisible" by their incorporation within the mundane scenery of everyday social life. By detouring ethnography through psychoanalysis, she articulates a provisional method whereby feminist researchers might strategically attend to "the material rituals of the production of knowledge, those vectors of power—institutional, social, personal, sexual—which call us out to desire to know."[73] In this way, Gordon's work raises critical questions concerning the gendered field of field research itself.[74] A related perspective is offered by Jacqueline Rose who states:

> [T]he importance of psychoanalysis is precisely the way that it throws into crisis the dichotomy on which the appeal to the reality of the event... clearly rests. Perhaps for women it is of particular importance that we find a language which allows us to recognize our part in intolerable structures—but in a way which renders us neither the pure victims nor the sole agents of our distress.[75]

An interaction between psychoanalysis and HIStorically inFORMed ethnography is also an element of the work of critical scholarship aimed at dislodging the psychic materiality of racial and economic exploitation. This is particularly evident in the (w)ritings of Gayatri Spivak, Trinh T. Minh-ha, Homi K. Bhabha, and Michael Taussig.[76] In a related manner, Simon Watney crosses these perspectives in interrogating "popular cultural" fears of gay men and alternative sexualities that LIE behind (and within) discourses controlling the public (image) management of "the AIDS epidemic."[77] To further the (dis)-autobiographical collage between these perspectives each is (re)located at a cross-roads with what Foucault depicts as a genealogical method. Genealogy attempts to displace master narratives of (continuous) world HIStory by emphasizing the somewhat *laughable* impurity of discrete and localized conjunctures of power and knowledge. This attracts attention to both the institutional and counter-institutional practices by which powerful forms of knowledge are constructed, deconstructed and reconstructed.

By (ab)using ethnography and social-psychoanalysis at the crossroads of collage (w)riting and a genealogical method, I hope not so much to recover a story of lost HIStorical origins, but to re-story the HIStorical covers which keep us (as desiring subjects) at a loss. This is to re-member ourselves differently. Not to nostalgically search to recapture an always already missing past. Such is nobody's HIStory—a murderous HIStory of simulations of self-evidency. I desire a different narrative practice: an imminent re(w)riting or theatrical restaging of epistemological rituals permitting a more reflexive sociological imagination of the HIStory (or HERstory) of our present. By double-crossing these several methods I hope to partially reopen spaces on "the other side" of the swell of ultramodern inFORMation in which so many of us today find our memories data-banked and militaristically reprocessed. In the chapters that follow I will (w)rite much more about social psychoanalysis and the genealogical method. In closing this chapter I will meditate briefly upon methodological questions raised by collage (w)riting and deconstructive ethnography.

6. COLLAGE (W)RITING: CONSTRUCTING SOCIAL TEXTS

> Collage is chiefly a medium of the last eighty years, a by-product of modernity, and the history of the twentieth-century collage...has shown its deepest connections with disposable culture and all its paradoxical implications. It has responded with mixed affections to information, fragmentation, war propaganda and technology, and also to commerce and its junk.[78] —John and Joan Digby

According to surrealist Max Ernst, collage involves "the coupling of... realities, irreconcilable in appearance upon a plane which apparently doesn't suit them."[79] Consider, for instance, the coupling of social science with a form of (w)riting more typically associated with poetry or avant-garde prose, or the mixing of a language which noticeably demands real social change with a mode of artistic investigation intent upon reflexively derealizing the demand structures of all language.[80] Consider, for instance, this text. "The orientation ...that I invoke cannot be neatly defined."[81] Indeed, the promise of collage is to mess up or tear gaps in an otherwise neat, enchanting and seemingly seamless social ordering of perception. Like the photomontages constructed by Hannah Hoch, John Heartfield and other Berlin Dadaists, its aim is to conjure "a chaotic, explosive image, a provocative dismembering of reality."[82] In this way collage critically interrogates material relations between a putative original object and the copies for which this object allegedly poses as a model.

> The interest of collage as a device for criticism resides partly in the objective impulse of cubism....The cubist collage, by incorporating directly into the work an actual fragment of the referent (open form), remains representational while breaking completely with the *tromp l'oeil* illusionism of traditional realism. Moreover, 'these tangible and non-illusionistic objects presented a new and original source of interplay between artistic expressions and the experience of the everyday world. An unpredicted and significant step in bringing art and life closer to being a simultaneous experience had been taken.'[83]

Collage (w)riting strategies take as their "problem—and opportunity—the fragmentation and juxtaposition of cultural values. From this disenchanted viewpoint stable orders of collective meaning appear to be constructed, artificial, and indeed often ideological or repressive. The sort of normality or commonsense that can amass empires in fits of absent-mindedness or wander routinely into world wars is seen [or re-visioned by collage work] as a contested reality to be subverted, parodied, and transgressed."[84] If collage (w)riting works it may facilitate an (un)working of the often taken-for-granted world of our everyday lives. It may quite literally serve to denaturalize the existence of certain things; or to re-make our sensations of things contingent upon the material and imaginary practices by which they have been (k)not so originally constructed. "That is why my subject is not the truth of being but the social being of truth, not whether facts are real but what the politics of their interpretation and representation are. With Walter Benjamin my aim is to release what he noted as the enormous energy of history that lies bonded in the 'once upon a time' of classical historical narrative. The history that showed things 'as they really were,' he pointed out, was the strongest narcotic of our century. And of course it still is."[85]

"It is not necessary to repeat here all the historical account of how collage became the predominant, all pervasive device of 20th-century arts. Rather I will note the principles of collage/montage which have directed representations in a diversity of arts and media, including most recently literary criticism: 'To lift a certain number of elements from works, objects, preexisting messages, and to integrate them in a new creation in order to produce an original totality manifesting ruptures of diverse sorts.'"[86] If someone is not familiar with defamiliarizing things in this way, collage (w)ritings may prove quite disorienting. It may become difficult to clearly and unambiguously identify what's happening in this text. Exactly. Whole fields of vision may fragment. Readers may find it impossible to master this text. Exactly. This is no neutral matter. If it's really working at unworking or ruining an existing assemblage of materials, collage or montage may even disturb a person's *real* identity. For some this may prove exhilarating; particularly for those treated badly by the socially constructed ordering of "what's real" already. In the spaces cut up or re-opened by collage techniques such persons may find a renewed source of energy for resisting and even transforming the oppressive enclosures of the worlds in which they find themselves circumscribed by relations of power.

> To release this energy requires special modes of presentation whose aim is to disrupt the imagery of natural order through which, in the name of the real, power exercises its dominion. As against the magic of academic rituals of explanation which, with their alchemical promise of yielding system from chaos, do nothing to ruffle the placid surface of this natural order, I choose to work with a different conflation of modernism and the primitivism it conjures into life—namely carrying over into history the principle of montage.[87]

Other readers may find the strategies of collage (w)riting more menacing; perhaps because such persons have too much to lose or, worse yet, too little. These are some of the risks of collage writing. And reading. As a sociologist, collage (w)riting strategies have affected me greatly. Things that had previously seemed wholly given I now experience as full of holes. "It is precisely a principle of contamination, a law of impurity, a parasitical economy."[88] Things that had once appeared as unitary variables, myself included, I now perceive as but provisional assemblage constructed in the wake or exile of others. Real bodies silenced, murdered or sent to exile so that I can be myself. Right here in America. *Things that in the past were separate have merged without my realizing it.* [89] Sex and television for example. As I pose before a lover's body I find even this scene of erotic intimacy disturbingly pre-structured or imaginarily transferred from one commercial channeling of desires to anOther. Not entirely but strangely and electric. Cold blue (dis)passion and dread. Mirror to mirror. Screen to screen

A little light is falling into previously dark, unconscious rooms. Underneath them or previous to them (places and times flow together), further rooms can be sensed in the dim light. I am taken by this shifting topography of what's possible at this time that's different. Kant inscribed a modern order of knowledge in terms of MAN's possession of (or by) a set of categorical imperatives that positioned "his" knowledge in time and space among other things. Durkheim and Mauss later performed a re(w)rite of Kant, conjuring the suggestion that categories of both perception and ethics are the effects of sacrificial rituals that enable a moral imagination of certain spaces and time, while foreclosing others. I read words to this effect and get carried away. In this re(w)riting there appear doorways that promise a passage out of the ritually positivized classifications of western white men incorporated by power. Promises. Promises. I am carried away in this (w)riting.

The time of which we are aware is only a paper-thin, bright stripe on a vast bulk that is mostly shrouded in darkness. But I sense this darkness as no less real than the bright stripes that pave my spatial movements in and through time. And no less artifactual either. Bright stripes evoked ceremonially as enchanted etchings on a screen that supports me above the base and empty darkness that hovers before my eyes/"I"s. Stripes that separate me from others just as they powerfully assist in the construction of what's seemingly always already *real*. In giving notice this heterogeneous play between bright stripes and the darkness they exile, collage (w)riting produces a form of signification which is "neither univocal nor stable. Each cited element breaks the continuity or the linearity of the discourse and leads necessarily to a double reading; that of the fragment perceived in relation to its text of origin; that of the same fragment as incorporated into a new whole, a different totality. The trick of the collage consists also of never entirely suppressing the alterity of these elements reunited in a temporary composition. Thus the art of collage proves to be one of the most effective strategies in putting into question of all the illusions of representation."[90]

With the widening of my visual angle and the readjustment to my depth of focus, my viewing lens (through which I perceive our time, all of us, you, myself) has undergone a decisive change. And in the concomitant or synchronic transformations of my other senses as well. In my hearing, touch, smell and taste.... *It is comparable to that decisive change that occurred...when I first became acquainted with Marxist theory and attitudes*; and those of feminists and others struggling to unwork the violently channeled tides of racist and imperialist HIStories; *a liberating and illuminating experience which altered by thinking, my view, what I felt about and demanded of myself. Changing my cognitive moral and carnal knowledge of myself and others, my emotions, appetites and desires. When I try to realize what is happening, what has happened, I find that (to bring it down to the lowest common denominator) there has been an expansion of what for me is 'real.' Moreover, the nature, the inner structure, the movement of this reality has also changed and continues to change almost daily. It is indescribable; my professional interest is wide-awake and aims precisely at description, but it must hold back, withdraw, and it has had to learn to want and to bring about its own defeat.*

An intelligent and well-versed whitemale colleague heard me utter such words and shook his head. "I don't understand a thing you've said," he inFORMed me. Humorlessly. He told me that he had always thought me a bright young fellow and that perhaps I was making too big a deal out of sociology. He explained that, after all, sociology is not a religion. Why did I let it bother me? It's simply a fairly reasonable way of discovering some lawful generalizations about the social universe; a discipline that attempts to document the way things are and explain how they've come to be that way. "Now what's wrong with that?" he asked. "I'm sure there's always going to be some bias. But you've got to admit that over the course of time we've accumulated some pretty good ideas about what makes things work."

We? Did he say we? "We've accumulated." The violence of such first person pluralizing. My stomach turns in the wake of these words. He continues. "Even if we've not explained all the variance, we've accumulated some pretty good data. But regarding all this collage stuff…, okay, it's cute but I don't see how it's going to realistically add a thing to what we know already." I was so stupefied that I could not answer. I thought of gesturing thumbs up and saying, "This Bud's for you!" For others a collage method of sociological rememberings may prove exhilarating. This is a matter of hope. Particularly for those treated badly by the socially constructed ordering of "what's real" in the first place. This book's for you.

7. DECONSTRUCTION ETHNOGRAPHY

> [A]ll constructed truths are made possible by powerful "lies" of exclusionary rhetoric. Even the best ethnographic texts—serious, true fictions—are systems, or economies of truth. Power and history work through them, in ways their authors cannot fully control.—James Clifford[91]

How does one (who recognizes that she or he is not ONE) perform an ethnography of the cultural scene in which that person finds her or himself inscribed? "We" thought it funny at the time, but one of the most terrifying things I re-member that you told me concerns a story in which you found yourself gazing at a reflection in your mother's bathroom mirror bloody-faced. "We?" Did I (w)rite, "'We' thought?" The violence of such first person pluralizing. My stomach turns in the wake of these words. The marks of ritual cut deep within that surface or field of socially patterned possibilities in which I find myself struggling within language.

The rituals of language: rituals that engender the compulsive repetition of certain linguistic pathways while silencing others. One such ritual is what I am doing now—circumscribing future possibilities by inscribing a story of things that (if this act of (w)riting is effective) will seem to really have always already existed. That is, if this (w)riting works, it will give the appearance of a referent that has really been already present before the scene of this (w)riting. When this occurs those of us who are called-out by such ritual activities may experience the imprint of what phenomenological sociologist Alfred Schutz describes as *the natural attitude*. Under this sign (or sign-work) the performative effects of artifice may suddenly appear as if objective. In this, things become taken-for-granted and operate with the *truthful illusion* that others experience them in more or less the same way. Repeatedly. "We" then just as I!

The violence of such first person pluralizing! My stomach turns in the wake of these words. The marks of ritual cut deep into the body of this (w)riting. I am tattooed by ritual, demarcated from you and others. Partitioned. This appears to be the fate of anybody who would communicate, of anybody who seeks recognition (from Others) within the linguistic orderings of things that constitute our present. I am thus condemned to using, or at least (ab)using, certain words, grammars and generative syntax, simply that the effects of my (w)riting be recognized. This is a social problem. It means to know anything means to (k)not know somethings other. Rituals of knowledge always demand such sacrifice.

To (k)not know somethings other. To be seemingly all tied up in language. To be implicated biographically, geographically and HIStorically in ritual. But is it possible to do more or less than this in (w)riting? For me this means to ask about the possibility of (w)riting in a manner that is reflexively attentive to the sacrificial power of language itself. Is it possible to (w)rite while reflexively acknowledging the (k)not knowings inscribed by the languages in which "we" find ourselves speaking or (w)riting in relation—to reflex within/upon the (k)not knowings that delimit the structural complicities of our ritual dances in and through languages? To do this might entail an (un)working ourselves out from within language without fully accepting its laws and its orderings; to enact a partial use of language that strategically attends to a language's own always already given partiality; to use language without being fully ruled by everything it gives and takes away. Not exactly. Hence, a GRAPHIC inexactness in grammar, punctuation and even spelling. And a proliferation of quotation marks that might give partial notice to the violent ritual practices that circumscribe the way "WE" (W)RITE. Having (w)ritten all this, permit me to begin again. Repeatedly.

"We" thought it funny at the time, but one of the most terrifying things I re-member that you told me concerns a story in which you found yourself gazing at a reflection in your mother's bathroom mirror. Bloody faced. This was in your father's house and television was involved. You said you'd seen the commercials and desired to enhance your beauty. Six years from the womb and bloody faced. You'd mistaken the *Comet* cleanser or the *Ajax* for the lotions and powders advertised day after day and so put into practice what you mistakenly thought would work like magic. Six years from the womb and gazing at a reflection in your mother's bedroom. Face bloodied. Terrorized. I never had such a ritual experience. Not exactly. During my childhood boys were less seduced in these specific ways. Nor so terrorized.

Where was I while you were preparing your face for the eyes/"I"s of Others? Perhaps I was dribbling or shooting a ball through the cylindrical hoop fixed to the front of my father's garage; rehearsing graceful (if militarized) movements for an imagined applause electric, an imagined moment of power and glory as a young white boy is projected into the center of a screen among Blacks. Re-playing the magnetic voice of a sportscaster as he differentiates my spectacular presence from others. TWO SECONDS LEFT. PFOHL GETS THE BALL. HE MOVES TO HIS RIGHT. HE TURNS. HE TWISTS. THE SHOT'S UP. IT'S IN. PFOHL WINS THE GAME! Again and again. A narcissistic ritual conducted by myself but never in private. An ultramodernizing ritual mediated by a serial swell of telecommunicatively imagined voices and visions. The breathless announcer, the ecstatic crowd, the gaze of the camera, the envy of other boys, the captured hearts of bare legged cheerleaders in short skirts and the headlines of the next day's news. Again and again: densely narcissistic and sacrificial rituals; inFORMational rituals inscribed within a fast-forwarding and telematic screening of what's real. Doublings abound.

chapter
seven

THE DOUBLE OR NO-THING
SOCIAL STRUCTURING RITUALS AND SACRIFICIAL POWER

An approach to the question of plagiarism in the symbolic register must
center first on the idea that plagiarism does not exist. There is no such
thing as symbolic private property.—Jacques Lacan.[1]

TITLES AND SUBTITLES

As a theme for this series of seminars, I propose the title "The Double or
No-thing." For some of you this phrase will bring to mind various games of
chance and competition. I am thinking here of a form of games—"winner take
all" and the like—the appearance of which displaces the more archaic games
of simulation and vertigo.[2] Today the simulated return of such archaic forms is
evident in both science and the popular culture. Indeed, the realization of
what's ultramodern in the guise of what's primitive is a disturbing element of
our current "postmodern scene." This scene may appear archaic but is in
actuality driven by a variety of ultramodern addictions to a competitive technological *exteriorization of the mind*. Whose mind? The mind of those most
compelled by a repetitious desire to control one's fate and capture "her" every
chance. The exteriorization of such a mind parasites upon the enactment of
games of simulation and vertigo. As reflexive social forms, these games were
once the province of generous gift exchange, festival, and the ecstasy of both
pagan and shamanistic rites of healing. Today, they are being telecommunicatively reprocessed and then sold for profit. This gives games of simulation
and vertigo a previously unimaginable competitive edge.[3] Unlike earlier enact-
ments of such rites, contemporary simulations operate seductively but without
reversing the willful compulsions of modern power to competitively master all
odds.

If the title of these lectures conjures some of the preceding associations
then perhaps we are already on our way toward a critical social-psychoanalysis. "And yet, I must first introduce myself to you—despite the fact that most
of you, although [k]not all of you, know me already—because the circumstances are such that before dealing with this subject it might be appropriate to
ask a preliminary question, namely: *am I qualified to do so* ?"[4]

"In reminding you of this question, I am not indulging in personal reminiscence. I think you will agree that I am having recourse to neither gossip nor to any kind of polemic if I point out here what is simply *a fact*, namely, that my teaching—specifically designated as such—has been the object of censure" by various professional social science and psychoanalytic associations. "Such censorship is of no ordinary kind, since it amounts to what is no less than a bar on this teaching."[5] Granted, I am permitted to continue to speak, but only on the condition that I explicitly acknowledge the epistemological difference between what's fact and what's fiction, and make it clear that my business is fiction, political theater, performance art, or whatever, but not social science research *per se*. And all this in the uncanny wake of the deaths so many of us have witnessed here within this very cafe itself. (K)not to mention my own "coming out" as an orphan.

"So, what it amounts to is something strictly comparable to what is elsewhere called major excommunication... Please do not imagine that here—anymore than elsewhere—I am indulging in some metaphorical game...I am not saying—though it it would not be inconceivable—that the [social] psychoanalytic community is a Church. Yet the question indubitably does arise—what is it in that community that is so reminiscent of religious practice?"[6] As a provisional answer, I find it necessary to offer words about the ritual violence of sacrificial social doublings.

SACRIFICIAL DOUBLINGS

In speaking or (w)riting about doublings I hope to evoke a sense of that sacrificial process by which human animals *substitute* a sign (or a totemic image) of something for the complex, fleshy, ambivalent and often contradictory sensations of being in relation to others. This is not to suggest that the sign, totem, or the double is truly a re-presentation of something that is actually there. It is (k)not. The common sensation that the double re-presents something is a sign of its power—the power of its illusionary force. Rather than re-presenting *some-thing* the double is a re-presentation of *no-thing* but an active ritual conjuncture of relations that feed into and upon other relations. In this sense the double, as I will be using the term, operates as a kind of parasite, a powerful transformer that dynamically alters everything that matters. Physically and in the imaginary realm.

To re-present *no-thing* but relatedness as *some-thing* categorically fixed and perceivable—this is to perform a ritual act of significant power. This is an enactment of sacrifice. That this operates with the (moral) force of illusion makes it no less powerful and no less experientially real. To dwell within a commonly sensed world of illusionary doubles (or signs) that substitute a determinate realm of "ideal type" things for an indeterminate conjuncture of material relations-in-flux—this, it seems, is a recurrent feature of human animal life as "we" know it.

Sacrificial doublings and re-doublings haunt the ultramodernizing HIStory of the West. Whether by desire, force, or the power of fascination, this HIStory appears constituted by the theoretical fictions of a class of privileged (if sometimes well meaning) white men of words. Beware! I, who appear erroneously (before you) as the author of words I am giving might be counted among these men's number. How might I (k)not be so identified? This is no question to treat lightly. After all, the plot which advances this narrative bears all the terminal markings of a twice-told tale rooted in the material exigencies of HIStorically specific relations of power. How might it bare to be other? How might I?

With these questions in mind, it is important to note that within human culture doubles operate (k)not simply by external force but also by the always only apparent naturalness of what is experienced as morally necessary. Doubly (over)determined signs thus function as mythic substitutes for an otherwise indeterminate a-morality of unnameable-fleshy animal-mineral-vegetable relations-in-process. Ritually forgotten is the *fact* that such doublings, although appearing to occupy the place of what's real, are no-thing but arbitrary modalities of naming, deviations put into play by the reductive exigencies of ritual sign-work itself. This is a sociological secret of doubles, an epistemological effect of powerful ritual sacrifices.

To represent the process of sacrificial doubling in this fashion is to argue that human subjectivity exists only in relation to objects given by the artful construction of signs. This is to understand doubles as captivating aesthetic effects—the materialization of imaginary relations in HIStory. It is also to offer a somewhat postmodern sociological thesis. Permit me to explain.

POSTMODERNISM AND SOCIOLOGICAL POSTSTRUCTURALISM

In Chapter Six the term postmodernism was employed to connote a particular form of critical social science (fiction) writing—an analytic style that plays seriously with an awareness of its own partial positioning within the material dynamics of language. By simultaneously refusing both objectivist description and subjectivist expression, postmodern writing may appear both difficult and demanding to read. More than a few times I have heard the question, "I can see it as some form of art or literature, but is it really sociology?"

In response to this question I refer you to the later (w)ritings of Émile Durkheim. This may seem strange, given what is usually taught about Durkheim in the U.S. Nevertheless, a theoretical basis for a postmodern sociological aesthetic, or even for the recognition that sociology is embodied within an aesthetic, is to be found, in part, in the late writings of a theorist who previously demanded that social facts be treated as things. Durkheim's later writings, some of which were produced in collaboration with his nephew Marcel Mauss, profoundly extended, then partially reversed, his previous thinking on the nature of social objects and the subjects who perceive them. In essence, these (w)ritings critically retheorize the perceptual origins of *things in themselves* as the artful effects of (totemic) religious ceremonies. Identifying both religious and scientific sign-work as simultaneously "natural" and "works of art," Durkheim suggested that the rituals which produce such collective representations conjure a seeming solid array of (artifactual) objects and subjects out of an otherwise undifferentiated stream of material relations.[7]

Durkheim's (w)ritings on religion are often misinterpreted as suggesting that religious symbolism is nothing but a functional reflection of a preexisting social structure. In truth, Durkheim argued that repetitive ritual acts of linguistic inclusion and exclusion are the "means by which...a system of signs...is created and recreated periodically. Whether it consists in material acts or mental operations, it is always this which is efficacious."[8] Durkheim here offers a theory of the material effectivity of signs. At the center of this theory LIES the totem.[9] A totem is an image, word, emblem or name that becomes ritually charged with contagious meaning. While it may appear to point to a referent or "signified" beyond itself, in reality the totem and what it signifies have no meaning independent of the rituals by which they are given significance. For Durkheim these are rituals of sacrifice.

Elaborating Durkheim's insights, Mauss would later describe such rites (of signification) as aspects of a general "moral economy" of reciprocally binding gift-exchange. Here "we" encounter the sociological roots of what Levi-Strauss would subsequently depict as unconscious symbolic forces at work in the structural organization of culture. In the psychoanalytic theories of Jacques Lacan these totemic forces are pictured as imaginary and symbolic constraints governing the activities of an "ego" in relation to its culturally specified Other. Indeed, Lacan explicitly identifies that which organizes the field of the unconscious as "the truth of the totemic function."[10] This is a ritual operation concerned with the differential "classification" of objects by the subjects to which they are given. Here, at this point, should you suspect that by discussing totemic relations "we" are moving too far from the symbolic circuitry of ultramodern culture I ask simply that you consider the (w)ritings of Jean Baudrillard. Baudrillard, as well as other critics of CAPITALial sign-value and advertising such as Sut Jhally, liken the material effects of "brand names" and other forms of ultramodern commerce to the archaic rule of "totemic systems."[11]

In analyzing accounts of the ritual practices of Australian Aborigines and the native peoples of North America Durkheim reads the totem as a "primitive" religious signifier. Marking the cognitive and moral boundaries of perception itself, the ceremonial institution of the (totemic) signifier sets in motion a chain of socially constructed meanings and senses of what's real. In totemic rituals aboriginal peoples are said to channel "the perpetual flux" of sensual material energies that flow "like waves of a river" into abstractly "crystallized" and "fixed...systems of concepts."[12] In this the heterogeneity of "nature" is thus reduced to the homogeneous relations of a particular culture.

Durkheim's theorization of the sociological constitution of objects represents a radical re(w)riting of Immanuel Kant's philosophy of the the phenomenal basis of all human knowledge. (W)riting at the dawn of modernity, Kant argued for a specifically "MAN-"centered epistemology. Freed from (or anxiously denied) the manifestly theological suppositions of medieval philosophy, Kant reasoned that human knowledge of objects is the result of an *a priori* synthesis of sensible perception and categorical understanding. This, Kant reasoned, was a distinctive feature of the human mind. At the "sensible manifold" of experience LIE a set of formal filters. These *a priori* categories of thought were said to reduce the purely *noumenal* reality of "things in themselves" to the synthetic rule of *phenomenal* perception. In this way the "raw data" of sensible experience is made orderly by the imposition of conceptual frames permitting the formal apprehension of objects. Objects do not simply appear. They appear only as they are categorically ordered in terms of their *quantity, quality,* predicated *relation* to cause and effect and the *modality* determining the conditions of their possibility.

Durkheim shared Kant's views that synthetic categorization precedes experiential knowledge. He nevertheless rejected the philosopher's contention that the origin of logical forms is found in *a priori* operations of the mind. Like Kant, Durkheim viewed "classical empiricism" as fundamentally mistaken. By falsely grounding knowledge in the observational capacities of subjective experience, empiricists deny a crucial aspect of "objective reality"—constraints imposed by the logical form in which objects "in fact" appear. By "denying all objective reality to the logical life, whose regulation and organization is the function of the categories," Durkheim contends that "empiricism results in irrationalism."[13] But Kant's *a priori* is also erroneous. Positing the operation of categorical constraints within the mind (of the subject) may be a step in the right direction. Still, for Durkheim this is no true explanation. It remains "necessary to show...how it comes that we see certain relations in things."[14]

Toward this end Durkheim pushed epistemology in the direction of HIStorical and ethnographic research. For, "far from being engraven through all eternity," the "empire" of categorical impositions "depend[s], at least in part, upon factors that are HIStorical and consequently social."[15] They depend upon the ritual organization of "language as a system of [impositional] concepts."[16] In this sense, collective social representations do not merely portray "reality on its most general side" but "illuminate it, penetrate it and [parasitically] transform it."[17] In the words of Durkheim and Mauss:

> Society was not simply a model which classificatory thought followed; it was its own divisions which served as divisions for the system of classification. The first logical categories were social categories; the first classes of things were classes of men [and women] into which things were integrated. It was because [women and] men were grouped, and thought of themselves in the forms of groups, that in their ideas they grouped others things.... [Moreover,] logical hierarchy is only another aspect of social hierarchy, and the unity of knowledge is nothing else than the very unity of the collectivity, extended to the universe.... Logical relations are thus, in a sense, domestic relations.[18]

If this seems like a radical reversal of the prescription to treat social facts as things, even more striking is Durkheim's insistence that there is no essential difference between totemic constructions of meaning and the production of modern scientific facts. Both involve the ritual construction of speculative realities, such that the "mysteries" surrounding religious objects are the "same as with science."[19] What distinguishes science from religion is not the nature of the constructivist character of each's object (of belief) but science's reflexive attention to the (artifactual) construction of its own (factual) objects. In this way science "brings a spirit of criticism into all its doings, which religion ignores; it surrounds itself with precautions to 'escape precipitation and bias,' and to hold aside the passions, prejudices and all subjective influences. But these refinements of method are not enough to differentiate it from religion. In this regard, both pursue the same end; scientific thought is only a more perfect form of religious thought."[20]

Durkheim here articulates a materialist theory of the ritual effectivity of language. This "is not simply a system of signs by which...faith [in a particular hierarchy of categories] is outwardly translated; it is a collection of the [ritual] means by which faith is created and re-created periodically. Whether it consists of material acts or mental operations, it is always this which is efficacious."[21] Durkheim's work here prefigures poststructuralism. By linking the social construction of meaningful objects to ongoing rites of sacrificial inclusion and exclusion, Durkheim moves social theory toward the consideration of supplementary (ritual) forces at work behind (or alongside) every artful appearance of objectivity. In so doing, he divides totemic rites of sacrifice into two types. *Negative rites* of taboo insure that totemic objects will not be touched by contaminating material contradictions; while *positive rites*, by which objects are themselves culturally consecrated, involve various combinations of gift exchange, communal consumption of sacrificial offerings, mimetic imitation, commemorative representation, and the mourning for lost objects (of desire). Most important, however, are the compulsive structural effects engendered by the repetition of ritual actions. Such rituals mark the bodies of those who enact them in moral and economic ways. For, "it is...frequently upon the body itself that the totemic mark is stamped."[22]

In describing the material force of ritual signification Durkheim and Mauss use the Melanesian term *Mana*. This suggests a "force altogether distinct from physical power, which acts in all ways for good and evil; and which...is of greatest advantage to possess or control.... It is a power or influence, not physical and in a way supernatural; but it shows itself in physical force, or in any kind of power...an anonymous and diffuse force."[23] This is a precise way of describing the impersonal social forces at work in the enactment of language. By the ritual powers of *Mana* moral and economic "realities" are inscribed not merely within the minds but also within the bodily or "coenaesthetic sensations" of ceremonial participants. This is more than a roundabout way of stating that a *base* structure of economic power impresses itself upon a *superstructure* of HIStorically determined subjects. While recognizing the fundamental importance of HIStorical and material processes, Durkheim is clear in asserting that:

> [I]t is necessary to avoid seeing in this theory...a simple statement of historical materialism: that would be a misunderstanding of our thought to an extreme degree. In showing that religion is something essentially social, we do not mean to say that it confines itself to translating into another language the material forms of society and its immediate vital necessities. It is true that we take it as evident that social life depends upon its material foundations and bears its mark, just as the mental life of an individual depends upon his [or her] nervous system and in fact his [or her] whole organism. But collective consciousness is something more than a mere epiphenomenon of its morphological basis, just as individual consciousness is more than a simple effervescence of the nervous system. In order that the former may appear, a synthesis *sui generis* of particular consciousness is required. Now this synthesis has the effect of disengaging a whole world of sentiments, ideas and images which, once born, obey [representational] laws of their own. They attract each other, repel each other, unite, divide

themselves [into binary opposites], and multiply, though these combinations are not commanded and necessitated by the condition of the underlying reality.[24]

For Durkheim the prototype of all ritually engendered binary objects was the sacred/profane coupling. This coupling (like the coupling of presence/absence; male/female; culture/nature etc.) is effected by the galvanizing force of sacrificial violence. This is an intense form of parasitic violence. It inscribes itself upon the body and then withdraws to a space of sociological abstraction where the material effects of such body (w)riting come to appear "as if" natural. In this way, the open sensuality of pre-linguistic bodily feelings are "fixed and crystallized" in the ritual dynamics of a "mother tongue" or "language as a system of [socio-logical] concepts."[25] As such, the ritual force of sacrificial violence gives arbitrary linguistic couplings the "timeless" or "mythic" attribute of being "natural."

"THE GIFT" OF ACCESS: RITUALS OF CONSTRAINT

Durkheim's concern with the sacred ordering of reality through ritual was extended by Marcel Mauss, who served as a teacher to "nearly every major French ethnographer before the mid-fifties."[26] Mauss, whose influential ideas were disseminated more by the spoken word than the published text, encouraged a rigorous examination of the *reality effects* of ritual social exchange. He directed attention to the moral, imaginary and bodily power of gifts circulating between and through the flesh of those they feed and they feed off. Mauss' concerns with such matters spread well beyond the formal academic environment. Although not well known among U.S. sociologists, during the 1930s in France, Mauss' elaborations of Durkheimian theory attracted the attention of dissident surrealists whose radical politics and critical cultural concerns doubled with those of sociology and anthropology. As Georges Bataille points out:

> Until around 1930, the influence of Durkheim's sociological doctrine had
> scarcely gone beyond the sphere of the universities. It had had no repercus-
> sions in the groups stirred by intellectual fever. Durkheim had been dead
> for a long time when some young writers, coming from surrealism—
> Caillois, Leiris, Monerot—began to attend a course given by Marcel
> Mauss, whose outstanding teaching methods were strikingly faithful to
> those of the founder of the school. It is hard to say exactly what they were
> seeking there.... Detachment from a society decomposed by individualism
> and the uneasiness resulting from limited possibilities in the individual
> sphere were all mixed in. At the most there was a serious attraction for
> realities that, taking the same value for each one, thus forming the social

bond, are held to be sacred. These young writers, more or less clearly, felt
that society had lost the secret of its cohesiveness and that was exactly
where the vague, uneasy, and sterile efforts of a poetic fever were aiming.[27]

In Mauss "these young writers" found a commitment to decentering individual experience within the "total social fact" of ritual "gift exchange."
Mauss used the term "total social fact" to make connections not only between
society and the individual but also between mind and body. For indeed, "between the social and bodily the layer of individual consciousness is very thin;
laughter, tears, funerary laments, ritual ejaculations are physiological reactions
just as much as they are gestures and signs."[28] To study the concreteness of
individual experience demanded an alertness to multiple levels of force embodied in "the give and take" of ritual interaction. To follow Mauss' teaching was
to assume a three dimensional approach to social reality, a strategy simultaneously emphasizing the role of synchronic or concurrent social forces, HIS-
torical specificity, and the "unconscious" interplay between physiological and
psychological realities. This drew the ethnographer into a reflexive (hermeneutic) circling back upon the scene of her or his own observations. Thus,
"to call the social fact total is not merely to signify that everything observed is
part of the observation, but also, and above all, that in a science in which the
observer is of the same nature as [the] object of study, the observer...is part of
[the] observation."[29]

Mauss' concern with the interactive complexity of socially constituted facts
led him to consider the role of rituals in "imprinting" external realities within
the psychic and bodily experiences of human animal actors. Examining
diverse rites, ranging from the breathing techniques of circus performers to
the anxious psychic gymnastics of persons in love, Mauss argued that: "Every
technique, every mode of behavior, learned and transmitted by tradition" is
embodied as well in "certain nervous and muscular synergies which constitute
veritable systems, bound up with a whole sociological context."[30] Mauss'
work here presages not simply the development of "symbolic anthropology"
but a thoroughly sociological psychoanalysis.

Nowhere are Mauss' insights more celebrated than in his 1925 essay, *The
Gift*.[31] In this study of ritual exchange processes Mauss traces a sociological
path by which heterogeneous matters are (sacrificially) given symbolic substitutes. This binds those who give and receive such signs to a common code of
moral and economic obligations. A blessing from the perspective of a "given"
"order of things" and a curse from the viewpoint of others (repressed or
forgotten) was pictured as a dynamic and constitutive feature of social structure itself. It arises not from the desires of individuals; nor is it imposed upon

people from some distant and abstract social force. Instead, both individual experience and social structure are the concurrent effects of what LIES materially between people and things—the immanent realm of symbolic exchange, the realm of ritual.

My own concerns with the material effect of ritual sacrifice are rooted not simply in the tradition of Durkheim and Mauss but also in C. Wright Mills' demand that a critical sociological imagination be constructed at the geographical crossroads between biography and HIStory. For Mills, "Social science deals with problems of biography, of history and of their intersection within social structures."[32] But how and in what manner do biography and HIStory interact? What mediates between the lived experience of individuals and the HIStorical weight of structured social practices? As a partial response to this question I offer the term *ritual* to designate those material and imaginary activities which come (and go) between the flows of an individual's biography and the collective confines of HIStorical memory.

Rituals are repetitiously patterned social interactions which connect people to a mythic sense of social life as "ready made" or already structured. Rituals connect us to senses of what things are and should be, of what is real and how "we" should act. Rituals are social structuring practices; interactional devices that effect a simultaneous channeling of individual possibilities and the collective mobilization of meaningful and authorized social actions. Rituals oppress just as they enable. They enact regimes of power just as they produce sensations of truth. Thus, when studying such matters as the ritual construction of ultramodernity, it is essential to examine how rituals make certain things possible while excluding others. As Peter McLaren observes:

> We are ontologically constituted by ritual and cosmologically informed as well. All of us are under ritual's sway; absolutely none of us stands outside of ritual's symbolic jurisdiction. In fact, humanity has no other option...to engage in ritual is for men and women, a human necessity. We cannot divest ourselves of our ritual rhythms since they [operate at] the very core of our central nervous systems. The roots of ritual in any society are the distilled meanings embodied in rhythms and gestures.... Rituals suffuse our biogenetic, political, economic, artistic and educational life. To engage in ritual is to achieve...historical-cultural existence....Our entire social structure has a pre-emotive dependence on ritual for transmitting the symbolic codes of the dominant culture.[33]

Rituals are situated at the geographical crossroads of biographical understanding and HIStorical constraint. The successful performance of ritual draws us into cognitive, emotional and moral relations to things that carry us beyond raw physical sensations of the world in flux. In ritual "we" are given the sense of being in a particular type of world or cosmos. By enacting rituals "we" come to experience individual actions in terms of a generalized or typical knowledge about what is and ought to be. Rituals channel our sensations of what's real and what's to be expected from what's real. Rituals of eating, dwelling, dressing, working, sexing, and so forth permeate the entirety of social existence. In biting into the leg of a chicken instead of a human, in CAPITALly marking objects as property, in wearing pants instead of a skirt, in seeking to maximize the profits of time invested in labor, and in engaging in erotic acts with women instead of roosters or "heaven forbid" other men, the ritually typified heterosexual male today acts in a manner which symbolically constrains his experience and gives shape to the behaviors he sacrificially demands of others. Things are not this way simply because he (only) phantasizes them as such. They are "really" that way! Or so he is inFORMed in ritual.

> [R]ituals are inherently social and political; they cannot be understood in isolation from how individuals are located biographically and historically in various traditions of mediation (e.g. clan, gender, home environment, peer group culture). Ensconced in the framework of both private and institutional life, rituals become part of the socially conditioned historically acquired and biologically constituted rhythms and metaphors of human agency.[34]

In breaking rituals "we" may be literally become disoriented. Our seemingly fixed world may suddenly become unhinged, fragmented or set to drift. Life without ritual is life in a meaningless void of free-floating forms, none experienced as more solid than the next. Sensations of reality may disappear. My body may be riveted by anxiety. Indeed, experiences such as these are reported by sociologist Harold Garfinkel. During the mid-1960s Garfinkel asked students to breach certain subtle everyday rituals that guide routine interaction with families, friends and associates. Engage someone in conversation and act on the assumption that the other's words are guided by hidden motives. Interact with parents as if one were a "polite stranger" who just happened to be boarding at one's parents' home. Enter into conversation with friends but refuse to let anything pass without being perfectly clarified. ("What do you mean, 'How is she feeling? Do you mean physical or mental?'" "What do you mean, you had a flat tire?") The sustained execution of even these simple breaches created great disturbances. As Garfinkel points out: "[Most people] were stupefied. They vigorously sought to make the strange actions intelligible and to restore the situation to normal appearances. Reports were filled with accounts of astonishment, bewilderment, shock, anxiety, embarrassment, and anger."[35]

The reports of Garfinkel's students are not dissimilar from those of "culturally shaken" travelers suddenly finding themselves on foreign terrain, excluded from the rituals by which natives construct meaning. This is not unlike the anxiety reported by naive or fearful users of hallucinogenic drugs. Indeed, the bewilderment of Garfinkel's students closely resemble the terror experienced by the unsuspecting subjects of C.I.A. experiments with LSD and other so-called *controlled substances*.[36] Such persons experienced a terrifying distance from the interactional rituals governing ordinary reality. Experiences such as these may parallel the onset of madness, for without "ritual support systems" we may be literally beside ourselves, experientially homeless and alone.

A related understanding of ritual is found in the (w)ritings of Stuart Hall, Dick Hebdige, Angela McRobbie and other members of the Birmingham Center for Contemporary Culture Studies during the late 1970s.[37] Concerned with HIStorical forces affecting the resistance of the British working class, the Birmingham Center developed a critical sociological understanding of the material effectivity of rituals. Of particular importance was the Center's collective reading of Antonio Gramsci's notion of *hegemony*, Louis Althusser's efforts to formulate a materialist theory of ideological *interpellation*, Raymond Williams' conceptualization of the social structuring of feelings, and Roland Barthes' semiotic analysis of CAPITALilist mythologies in France.

Gramsci used the term *hegemony* to describe the ritual production of an always only apparent consensus, or "moving equilibrium," between classes of people divided by unequal access to political and economic power.[38] Unlike "orthodox" Marxist thought, which theorized ideology as if forced on people from above, Gramsci argued that the reproduction of domination involved the active participation of the dominated. How does this happen? How do the oppressed people enter into ritual arrangements that constrain more than they empower?

(W)riting within the organizational constraints of the French Communist Party, Althusser elaborated Gramsci's theoretical concerns by identifying a variety of ritual sites, or what he called the "state apparatus," as the locus of CAPITAL's reproduction. Althusser pointed to powerful material effects of such ritual practices as schooling, church attendance, and participation in public sporting events. Each of these ceremonial arenas was said to contribute to the reproduction of relations of CAPITALilist domination by facilitating the (sacrificial) substitution of an "imaginary relationship" of noncontradiction for the exploitative actualities of "real [material] conditions of existence." At the center of this ritual process LIES the unconscious "calling out" of HIStorical subjects into culturally specific relations of desire.[39] In theorizing this space of interpellation Althusser drew upon Lacanian psychoanalysis, particularly

Lacan's ideas concerning the unconscious splitting of subjects from aspects of themselves transferred into the abstract exchange values language. In the materiality of such a cursed gift, Althusser sought to trace the psychic and bodily misrecognitions which constitute ideology.

Of related concern is the work of Raymond Williams. Williams pictures the production of hegemony "as in effect a saturation of the whole process of living—not only of political and economic activity, not only of manifest social activity, but of the whole substance of lived identities and relationships, to such a depth that the pressures and limits of what can ultimately be seen as a specific economic, political, and cultural system seem to most of us as the pressures and limits of simply experience and common sense."[40] For Williams, hegemonic practices are depicted as a ritual-like process that is at once "constitutive and constituting" and that "has continually to be renewed, recreated, defended and modified."[41] Such rituals "exert palpable pressures and set effective limits on experience and on action."[42] This results in the HIStorical specificity of certain structures of feeling. In Williams' words:

> We are talking about characteristic elements of impulse, restraint and tone; specifically of active elements of consciousness and relationships: not feelings against thought, but thought as felt and feeling as thought: practical consciousness of a present kind, in a living and interrelating continuity.[43]

Roland Barthes' analysis of the rituals of French popular culture extend the analysis of hegemony in the direction of French structuralism. Barthes' studies of the mythological language of film, fashion, dining, and a host of related cultural practices resemble Althusser's concerns with the ritual effectivity of "ideological state apparatus." Barthes' writings are rooted in the ethnographic tradition of Durkheim and Mauss, the linguistic theories of Ferdinand Saussure, and the anthropological structuralism of Claude Levi-Strauss. In *Mythologies* Barthes attempts to decode the ritual subtleties by which signs connect a material medium of communication, a signifier (such as a spoken word, visual image, or acoustical sound pattern) with what is signified (the content or meaning of a message).[44] In signs materiality and meaning are ritually cojoined. Each sign, moreover, is systemically mediated by its connection to other signs. Hence, for *sign-dependent* human animals things are neither purely material nor purely meaningful. There is always only a significant (or mediated) relation between matter and meaning. Barthes seeks an answer to the riddle of hegemony in the ritual dynamics of signs. For it is within the world of signs that "we" humans (mis)recognize the meaning of our material relations to others. One after anOther; each operating as a reductive (or tragic) signifier for the Other(s).

Barthes defines myth as a "second-order system." This is a connotative system of signs which parasite off the configurative force of other signs. Barthes' semiotics attempts a partial decoding of such mythic sign-work within CAPITAList culture. Here even the most commonplace of ritual gestures appear pregnant with tones, feelings and meanings that connect them and their users to life within a marketplace of commodity sign values. In this way ritual "naturalizes" the reproduction of unequal political and economic relations. As Barthes suggests:

> The whole of France is steeped in this anonymous ideology: our press, our films, our theatre, our pulp literature, our rituals, our Justice, our diplomacy, our conversations, our remarks about the weather, a murder trial, a touching wedding, the cooking we dreamt of, the garments we wear, everything, in everyday life, is dependent on the representation which the bourgeoisie has and makes us have of the relations between man and the world.[45]

Following Barthes "we" are invited to read everyday rituals as powerful transformers of perception. This is what gives things a commonsensical character. By enacting rituals "we" actively transform contradictory material relations into a *field of forces* where *things* appear to have a life of their own. Durkheim and Mauss portrayed this mythic force-field in terms of the ceremonial evocation of *Mana*, a magical power that inFORMs both perception and structured social exchange. For Barthes, the mythic effects of ritual are somewhat similar. "Myth has the [ritual] task of giving a historical intention a natural justification, and making contingency appear external....What the world supplies to myth is a historical reality, and what myth gives in return is a natural image of this reality."[46]

This is not to suggest that ritually patterned actions are causally determined or unreflexively imposed. As Anthony Giddens points out, "we" who are given identities in ritual may "partially" monitor and creatively respond to the shifting situations of gift exchange in which we find ourselves embodied.[47] Like the creative "operators" described by Michel de Certeau, "we" may make parasitic use of a host of accessible cultural forms, memories, and technologies.[48] Nevertheless, conscious reflexivity is structurally limited by the restrictive economy of ritual action itself. What gives form to such (sacrificial) limits? How are they reproduced and/or modified in the conscious enactment and unconscious channellings of ritualized experience? How, moreover, might such reductive access be critically exceeded and thereby opened to both resistive contest and radical change? These questions lead to a second aspect of Durkheim's doubled theorization of elementary religious or social forms—the study of transgressive rituals.

TRANSGRESSING RITUAL ACCESS: THE GIFT OF EXCESS

In archaic cultures the seemingly timeless character of access to a world of ritually given *objects* is *in fact* time limited. As Durkheim observes, artful *factuality* is itself periodically deconstructed by the (counter-symbolic) actions of transgressive rituals-in-reverse. In these "effervescent" ceremonies participants are festively released from "the pressure of tangible and resisting realities" that are routinely "required to confine activities to exact and economical forms."[49] Such deconstructive rituals engender experience that is "foreign to all utilitarian ends." Within the throes of festival people are permitted to "forget the real world" of sacrificially imposed artifice as they are carried away by a "domain of fancy" in which "imagination is more at ease."[50] Construction followed by deconstruction—this is the spiralling path of *the real* which Durkheim theorizes as the basic movements of both religion and science. The problem is that modern social science, like religion in its purely constructive phase, (mis)recognizes its objects as discoveries rather than as constructions. This makes modern sociology an *ontotheological* rather than a reflexive ritual practice.[51] By contrast, postmodern sociologies begin (again and again) in the deconstructive spacings provided by the periodic undoing of restrictive economic constraints upon what artfully passes as real. Such deconstructive spacings are, I believe, hinted at by Durkheim in the closing sections of *Elementary Forms of Religious Life*.

These critical social spaces are opened further by Georges Bataille. Bataille's (w)ritings radicalized the epistemological fissure offered by Durkheim's provocative comparisons between religion and science. Durkheim argued that for science to differentiate itself from religion it must partially theorize the conditions of its own classificatory rituals. How is this possible? How can science accomplish this (deconstructive) task without periodically transgressing or deconstructing the always only provisional borders of its own objectivity? "It can't!" screamed Bataille, whose passionate and *negative theological* transgressions of modern social science crossed Durkheim and Mauss with a radically materialist reading of Marx, Nietzsche, and Freud.

The periodic *symbolic exchange* between orderly categorical construction and transgressive deconstruction was a recurrent theme in Bataille's *excessive sociology*. Writing during both an intensification of global CAPITAL and the rise of European fascism, Bataille theorized a dual meaning of the sacred as conceived by Durkheim. First there was the "homogeneous" sacred. Secured by the sacrificial rites of "gift exchange" described by Mauss, this form of the sacred solidifies a particular "order of things." But this is only one of the sacred's doubled aspects. Also important is the "collective effervescence" of "heterogeneous" or "transgressive" rituals.[52] Transgressing the borders of the sacred in its orderly phase, these sacred rituals transform the world of everyday life by a vertiginous "fall" from ideal forms and normative representations. Within the flux of such ecstatic intimacy human experience is re-minded of its commun(ion)istic and interdependent "animal origins."[53] All that appears solid is displaced into spiralling motion, while all ideal (or ideological) forms are given over to the terrifying silence of death and the joys of re-birthing.

Bataille's (w)ritings direct attention to the heterogeneous realm of a transgressive sacred. Within this realm's ecstatic social spaces facts are transubstantiated into artifacts while social institutions are for *a time between times* derealized or deconstructed.[54] Such are the vegetative harvests of the heterogeneous sacred and the chaotic "effervescence" of its material force. Bataille likens transgressive *expenditure* to the play of medieval festival, erotic effusion, ecstatic mysticism, wealth-destroying *potlatch* and even the theoretical wavelengths of twentieth century physics. Nevertheless, the most consistent example of such radical material negativity involves the carnivalesque force of self-effacing laughter. For Bataille "major laughter" empties the body of the parasitic violence of language. Laughter turns language inside out, reuniting its "subjects," if only temporarily, with the transferential flow of excessive, impure and interdependent earthy-animal-cosmic-matter—that "nonlogical difference that represents in relation to the economy of the universe what crime represents in relation to the law."[55] This is an ambivalent, confused, and interdependent world where solids are contagiously broken into liquid electric waves and where identity is dispersed in the celebration of difference.

Transgression hovers, spins or plays at the ambivalent borders of what defines a given Symbolic Order.[56] It expensively displays rather than represses the energetic work of orderly, if artificial, social construction. This is its pleasure. This is its terror. Transgression (im)possibly represents the labor of contradictory doublings. It is indifferent to the *significance* of culture but (k)not totally. Erotically, festively, laughingly but (k)not totally. Totalizing excess—that would be death. Transgression approaches the artificial fullness of life-giving labor but only to the effervescent point of death, (k)not unto death itself. This is what constitutes its intense ambivalence, its spiralling ecstasy and its monstrous horror.

Transgression inflames the borders of a given social order. It exists only in movement, only in the play of vertiginous openings, gaps, wounds and fissures. Transgression partially liquifies that which always only appears as solid. To experience the material force of transgression is (k)not merely to experience the loss of a seemingly fixed subjectivity. Such an anxious loss only heralds the "uncanny" possibility of transgression. Transgression carries human animal anguish a step further. Transgression entails the reflexive loss of those objects whose mirrored doublings mark the social construction of subjectivity in the first place. This is what gives transgression its negative sacred charge—its (im)possibly moving flow of *inner experience*.[57] With transgression one (who is (k)not One) becomes other. This is a periodic rather than permanent condition. It gives birth to a general economy of *depense*—the simultaneous expenditure of both subjects and the objects (of social construction). Am I repeating myself compulsively? If so, perhaps the paradoxical uselessness of transgression is here pregnant in labor. Perhaps my own (w)ritings anxiously await a point of deliverance or delivery. Moreover, if the metaphors seem feminine, this is (k)not so much to appropriate the life-giving materiality of living women as to counter-memorize the lawful violence of the dead father tongued languages. Nevertheless, in laboring to communicate these matters I feel that I am failing to realize the very transgressions of which I am (w)riting. As witnesses to my failure I hope that you, as readers, may be moved to find some more material ways of rebeginning again. And again.

During the 1960s Bataille's (w)ritings became a kind of deconstructive "model" for a generation of poststructuralist critics laboring within, or against, the turbulent and politically charged hallways of French academic institutions. From Durkheim and Mauss through Bataille to the contemporary poststructuralist criticism—this is a way of making HIStorical connections between sociology and a particular embodiment of postmodernist discourse. Reflexively refusing the epistemological (and political) distinction between forceful fictions of factuality and the factuality of forceful fictions, critical poststructuralism poses (as) a danger to both the "objectivist" and "subjectivist" rituals of modern social science. As Bataille "once upon a time" remarked: "Certainly, it is dangerous, in extending the frigid research of the sciences, to come to a point where one's object no longer leaves one unaffected, where, on the contrary, it is what inflames."[58]

DOUBLES OF WHAT'S LACKING

In these lectures, I am laboring to work out from within the openings toward poststructuralism prefigured by Durkheim and Marcel Mauss. The texts of Durkheim and Mauss trace the ritual constitution of powerful doubles or what I am calling *totems*. These operate as "originary" substitutes for what is *lacking* in our human animal abilities to survive by virtue of biology alone. Far from "classifying spontaneously and by a sort of material necessity," Durkheim and Mauss contend that "humanity in the beginning *lacks* the most indispensable conditions" for securing its own survival.[59] In other words, unlike other species of animals "we" humans are not instinctually graced with a fixed and stable sense of social order.

This *lack* puts "us" at a disadvantage. At the same time, due to the complexities of the human central nervous system, "we" might be said to compensate for this *lack* with our ability to use language to create an artificial world order. This is a world of signs or doubles; a world where powerful fictions pose as facts. Once constructed, the doubles "we" use to name things begin to take on a life of their own. As such, "we" human animals become, if in different ways, and never innocently of the power of such artifactual differences, imprisoned within the illusionary realities of our own totemic practices.

This represents a double-play between what is organizationally lacking (an argument from the point of view of *negative biology*) and the *positive biological* capacities of human animals to create a world of meaningfully ordered signs. It assumes that "we," like all living species, have needs for some relative stability in relation to our multiple environments. Otherwise "we" would be in a continuous dance of metamorphosis, a physical co-mingling without fixed boundaries or structured differences. A plenitude from the pointless view of nature spiralling as a (w)hole, but a *lack* from "the point of view" of any HIStorically given classification of "our" species in relation to others. Thus, as a *significantly constituted* species of animals "we" depend on artful languages or totemic ritual practices to repeatedly secure the always fragile conditions of our own material survival. From economic to sexual to spiritual and psychic relationships "we" are reliant upon sacrificial doubles. These artifactual constructs, aspects of our forever doubled nature, enable us to achieve the modicum of the stability necessary for our ongoing relations within an ever-changing multiplicity of natural social environments.

By *mythologizing* arbitrary ways of doing things "we" ritually institute a kind of *naturalized*, or commonsensical social environment. In future lectures, I will endeavor to read this process of *naturalization* in terms of the transformation of *totemic doubles* into *fetishized doubles*. For the time being I will simply indicate that once institutionalized our doubled actions appear, (k)not just as any way of doing something, but as THE way of doing something. Mythic doublings, or social institutions, are thus an essential aspect of our human animal existence. For better and, perhaps, for worse.

By ritually substituting linguistic or totemic doubles for no-thing but a material process of metamorphic flux "we" human animals reduce our *excessive* participation in the interconnected weave (or dance) of "nature." In this way, "we" reduce "nature" to matters of *accessible* knowledge. The tragic nature of this reduction is a recurrent theme of the (w)ritings of Georges Bataille. In the tradition of Durkheim and Mauss, Bataille understood human animality as doubled (or dually partitioned) between the heterogeneous flux of nature-in-movement and the homogenizing ritual violence of artificial (or metaphorically imposed) linguistic stability. This involves the parasitic violence of a linguistic "tool [that] changes nature and man at the same time: it subjugates nature to man who makes and uses it, but it ties man to subjugated nature. Nature becomes man's property but it ceases to be immanent to him.... If he places the world in his power, this is to the extent that he forgets that he himself is in the world; he denies the world but it is [also] himself that he denies."[60]

Bataille is here (w)riting of the material violence of language. Without excepting the exclusionary tools of sexual difference *at work* in Bataille's language, I believe his (w)riting directs attention to the hierarchical recurrence of selective affirmations and denials, rememberings and forgettings, that are a material characteristics of all ritual orderings. These entail a temporary *sacrifice* of radical otherness to what is accessed by signs. This is not to suggest that ritual forms are irreversible or not susceptible to radical social change. It is simply that the production and consumption of signs are always material features of a given social formation of power in HIStory. For Bataille, this is a sacrificial aspect of the "anthropocentrism" by which "the human being loses awareness of the reality of this world—as the parasite is unaware of the pain or joy of those from whom it draws subsistence. Furthermore, in closing off ever more tightly the world around" them, humans tend "to substitute" their own "constitutive avidity for the...obvious prodigality" of a "reality free of inherent meaning or demand, replacing it with a personification (of an anthropomorphic kind) of the immutable idea of the Good."[61]

SOCIAL PSYCHOANALYTIC DOUBLINGS AND REDOUBLINGS

A related story of the reduction of embodied metamorphoses to the partially disembodied rule of linguistic constructs is told by Jacques Lacan. Like Durkheim, Mauss and Bataille, Lacan makes assumptions about the "anatomical incompleteness" or "prematurity" of human animals. This "lack" is initially countered by what Lacan theorizes as the "mirror stage." In this ritual passage fledgling human subjects are for the first time presented with "the appearance of the double."[62]

The sacrificial drama of the mirror stage represents a costly linguistic substitution of self-limiting psychic armor, or totemic imagery, for the vulnerability of bodies in flux. While often described as an evolutionary step indicative of "why human knowledge has greater autonomy than animal knowledge," Lacan is clear about the material economic price of this ritual transformation. As the human subject identifies with its imaginary double or *imago,* she or he is "caught up in the repressive" lure of a reductive "spatial identification."[63] This "drama" entails a "succession of phantasies," instituting a subject's "fragmented body-image" and instilling a desire for an ever elusive "totality." The body of the emergent subject is thus sacrificially cut into and cut up. In this sense, the human psyche is doubly constituted by a partial transference away from what it materially lacks (for survival) in nature. At the same time, it is lured on by what is presented as an imaginary resolution to such lack in the artificial construction of a fortified "I" or mirrored "ego."

Lacan's (w)ritings suggest a double movement in the constitution of human subjectivity. After (or along side) the contradictory experience of one's material existence being reduced to the psychic armor of mirror images, a second transformation carries humans further along the path of linguistic alienation. This is the "Symbolic Order." Here, the chaotic nature of pre-linguistic *needs* are channelled into a world governed by language. In the "symbolic," ambivalent material relations to "one's" fleshy mother (and to "nature" as "she" comes to be known from the distance given by words) are replaced by orderly linguistic *demands* that "one" assume "one's" cut-off (or castrated) social positioning within a powerful (if unconscious) chaining of totemic signifiers. Concurrent with this *demand* comes *desire*—the perpetual push and pull of alluring objects. In this, the imprisoned subject (of language) seeks to restore to "one's" self those bits and pieces of indeterminate animality stolen by the sacrificial code of culture.[64]

In Lacanian social-psychoanalysis, the desiring subject directs "one's" gazes toward objects that repeatedly fade (from existence) before "one's" eyes/"I"s. The subject searches after and attempts to linguistically arrest these disappearing objects as if they were truly something Other than paths cut through HIStory by so many figures of speech. One signifier leading to the next. One world without end, aMEN. Moreover, as if unable to describe the "normative" violence of culture without making reference to patriarchal religious forms, Lacan designates the place of the "Symbolic" as a social space ruled in "the name (of a perpetually absent) father." This sacrificial transference of one type of lack into an Other is a central feature of Lacan's (w)ritings.

Lacan's notion of the mirrored substitution of an artificial image (or a *totemic double*) for one's *real* material positioning in the world was translated by Louis Althusser as the sacrificial effect of ideological positioning. For Lacan the mirror stage represented an "existential" exile of human knowledge to the realm of mis-recognition or *méconnaissance*. This is a haunting, if productive, curse of the double. No-thing can be perceived as it is. Everything must be filtered or distorted according to the systemic positioning of any given double in relation to what's generally Other and what's (k)not. For Althusser this was a way of theorizing the force of ideology. A critical aspect of Althusser's study of "ideological state apparatus" was to relocate Lacan's ideas about the distortive effects of imaginary doubling from the Freudian realm of domestic family dramas into the multiple economic sites of CAPITAList ritual. Ideological doubling was thus understood as "the imaginary relation of individuals to their real conditions of existence."[65] That this relation is imaginary makes it no less powerful. Like Durkheim, Althusser views the sacrificial reduction of what's excessively real to what's ritually accessible as a constitutive feature of human culture. To reduce the real to the artificial—this is to ideologically sacrifice what's excessive about human materiality to a set of ideal or accessible linguistic forms.

In this process human animals are transformed into cultural subjects. In this way ideological rituals distortively "call out" for particular (mis)-reognitions while repressing the materiality of others. This involves a transformation of unformed actions into socially structured practices "governed by the *rituals* in which these practices are inscribed."[66] This is what constitutes "the material existence of an ideological apparatus, be it only a small part of that apparatus: a small mass in a small church, a funeral, a minor match at a sport's club, a school boy, a political party meeting,"[67] a lover's quarrel, a pleasant meal, a sexual thrill, a strong handshake, a certain look, an enticing smell, a funny taste, a beautiful boy, a fresh start, a startling difference, a fear of flying, a guiding light, a general hospital, or worse yet, the grisly smell of BIG MACS floating high above Moscow.

Julia Kristeva modifies both Lacan and Althusser's social-psychoanalytic notions of a "visual" break from a continuity with nature into the "digitally" formed or "doubly articulated" discontinuities of the mirror stage.[68] Kristeva posits a prior *acoustic screening* of a child's union with its mother as generative of a more primordial psychic detachment. This involves a moment of "imaginary" violence in which the sounds of a somewhat mythic figure, *the father of pre-HIStory,* fracture the reciprocal animal continuity between mother and child.[69] As the mother responds to the voice of a father's desire, the child's undifferentiated experience of being-in-movement with mother (nature) is broken. This primal separation represents a prefigurative spacing of difference. It also engenders a form of counter-movement, or what Kristeva describes as the projective force of *semiotic motility* or *chora.* This is a homogenizing movement in which one is neither "fully" a subject nor object. In this, a partial subject becomes dissociated from the interdependent texture of its undifferentiated-being-with-others. This is a space of impure doublings and partial borders—a space of transference. Within this space "we" humans movingly experience the anguish of being dramatically situated at the borders of both "nature" and "culture." Here experience is radically decentered. On one hand, it is exiled from the metamorphic flux of maternal envelopment. On the other, it is denied the artificial (cultural) securities imposed by linguistic abstraction.

Kristeva's semiotic *chora* is a space of considerable ambivalence. Properly speaking, it is a transferential non-place or nowhere specific. This space is both fascinating and fearful. The always moving and indeterminate "origin" of an individual's separated existence, the semiotic *chora* also LIES in excess of symbolic forms or language. As such, "the semiotic is the effect of bodily drives which are incompletely repressed when the paternal order has intervened in the mother/child dyad, and is therefore attached psychically to [partially screened memories of] the mother's body."[70] The *semiotic chora* thus recalls (or remembers) an indeterminate relation to that which LIES (for better and worse) at the sacrificial borders of human language. For this reason it is associated with the experience of both unnameable ecstasies and terror. Here LIE the excessive pleasures of *jouissance* and the horrors of a sacred that transgresses normative boundaries.

An "abject" space of impure and transferential identification, the semiotic is also a spatial after-effect of what is made accessible by the sacrificial gift of language. Although excessive, this space is periodically accessed by "transgressive" ritual ceremonies. Such rites are a central feature of virtually all known religions. All, that is, except for those dominated by the "logocentric" imperatives of western (Judaic-Christian) societies. In these social (or *elementary religious*) forms there appears no end to the taboos that separate "us" from the impurities of what LIES truthfully in excess of language. These religious traditions, which inFORM our dominant religious and scientific knowledge, are based on a refusal of the cyclical rites of the transgressive sacred.[71] They "eternally return" not to the possibility of radical material difference, but to no-thing but the homogeneous symbolic violence engendered in "the name of the Father." The un(for)giving character of such taboos keeps western society at a clean and sacrificial distance from material possibilities expulsed, excreted or made "abject" by a metaphysical belief that "IN THE BEGINNING WAS THE WORD."

Kristeva's *semiotic* directs attention to the sociological importance of mother-child relations. Her work also reassesses the role of signification in calling out bodily experiences that LIE in *abjection* before and alongside the doubled force of words. Like other theorists (w)riting in the wake of Durkheim and Mauss, Kristeva recognizes that the cultural power of signifying artifacts (or doubles) is purchased at the cost of great bodily and psychic repression. Nevertheless, with repression comes the possibility of a reversal. Kristeva's social-psychoanalysis calls for the transgressive return of the repressed. In this, Kristeva's theoretical concerns intersect with Bataille's. As Kristeva points out, while the logic of prohibition founds *the abject* by exclusions, Bataille's importance LIES in the mode in which he links "the production of the abject to the weaknesses of...prohibition.... He links abjection to 'the inability to assume with sufficient strength the imperative act of excluding.'"[72]

Why such weakness at the imperative core of exclusion? According to Bataille, the answer is to be found in the excessively "energetic base material-ity" or "general economy" of all living entities. Bataille defines this general economy less by its (ritually) objectified boundaries than by its relational participation in a field of forces where matter and energy reciprocally feed off and into one another. Articulating a material theory of social relations that closely resembles the *quantum* theories of twentieth century physics, Bataille argues that "as a rule" organisms, including human organisms, are complexly composed of "greater energy resources than...necessary for the operations that sustain life."[73] A related conceptualization of "surplus" energy-in-excess of the "intense and tumultuous" labor of symbolic forms is found in Durkheim. In addition to "the unique task of [reductively] expressing the real with the aid of appropriate symbols," Durkheim notes that, "A surplus generally remains available which seeks to employ itself in *supplementary and superfluous works of luxury.*"[74]

Both Bataille and Durkheim recognize that a certain portion of energy is necessarily consumed in the (totemic) constitution of seemingly self-contained objects (or doubles). The constitution of such objects involves sacrificial processes of attraction and repulsion. In this way a dynamic heterogeneity of moving matters temporarily condenses around the differential material and imaginary figuration of powerful symbolic process. This is the ritual social force of the totem. It gives collective representations their binding effectivity as artful substitutes for what's *real* or really being culturally made over. In this fashion real material relations are ritually incorporated into particular HIStori-cal forms but not others.

As such, totemic rites are key features in the construction and partial stabi-lization of the experiential boundaries of a given social order.[75] When effec-tive, totemic rites artfully evoke and performatively enact the undoubtable presence of some things to the moral and economic restriction of others. They conjure up the facticity of certain objects (of desire and knowledge) while denying *access* to others. They bestow a kind of supernaturalized sense of objectivity upon some cognitions, fantasies and imaginings, while rendering others taboo, unconscious or in *excess* of what might be recognized as truth-ful. This is the almost magnetic power of totemic rites—a sacrificial form of power—the power to seemingly center consciousness within particular *ideal types* or *social forms* while restricting access to other forms as unimaginable immoral or economically impossible.

This sacrificial aspect of totemic sign-work renders all that is accessible to conscious experience as stupidly in exile from a reflexive recognition of its ongoing PERFORMATIVE ORIGINS. It also puts into spin remainders that LIE in excess of what can be consciously culturally communicated. Such slippery matters LIE somewhat anxiously in wait for the law—diverting, subverting and occasionally surprising one with the uncanny sensation that there's always more or less to what's real than "one" can behold with one's eyes/"I"s. This is not to say that those (im)possible objects sent repulsively into orbit by the exclusionary spin of a totemic force field are any less real than that which this ritual field normatively recognizes as its own. Quite the opposite. Although made to sacrificially disappear or appear invisible, what is repressed remains real if in but a symptomatic form. It is as *real* as that which sends shivers along the nape of one's neck late at night or which presses at the base of the spine or buzzes faintly within an ear, jarring balance.

Composed as much by this uncanny spin of what it repulses as by that driven to the center of its base material attraction, the totem is thus kept in place by a repetitious ritual reenactment of the "repulsive" drama of taboo. Like an undoubtable sacred object, "the social nucleus" is made "taboo, that is to say, untouchable and unspeakable."[76] Thus:

> [W]hat constitutes the individual nucleus of every...human society is... primarily external to the beings who form the group because for them it is [like the unconscious] the object of a fundamental repulsion. The social nucleus is, in fact, taboo, that is to say untouchable and unspeakable; from the outset it partakes of the nature of corpses, menstrual blood, or pariahs. Other sorts of filth, in comparison with such a reality, represent only a dissipated force of repulsion: They are not completely untouchable, they are not completely unnameable. Everything leads us to believe that... human beings were brought together by disgust and common terror, by an insurmountable horror focused primarily on what originally was the central attraction of their union.[77]

This "turbulent" repulsion of heterogeneous matter-in-movement into the homogeneous attraction of artifactual social forms LIES at the center of Bataille's notion of a general economy. But such a stable center cannot last forever. Like a late summer vegetable before the approach of fall, or human anguish before (the double) face of death, all nuclei must return effervescent to the spirals of energy from which each was (sacrificially) extracted. Energy must be productively channeled for any organism to grow. But this is only a portion of the double story of Bataille's "accursed share." What of the haunting remains of energies repulsed to make things work? For Bataille, even the most innovative technologies of economic growth:

always have a double effect: Initially, they use a portion of the surplus energy, but then they produce a larger and larger surplus. This surplus eventually contributes to making growth more difficult, for growth no longer suffices to use it up. At a certain point the advantage of extension is neutralized by the contrary advantage, that of luxury; the former remains operative, but in a disappointing—uncertain, often powerless—way.... Hence what matters *primarily* is no longer to develop the productive forces but to spend their products sumptuously.[78]

Bataille theorized that all life forms (mineral, vegetable, animal and human animal) were recurrently driven to uselessly expend excess energies. This led Bataille to interpret even the ravages of death as no-thing but the abundance of some forms of life giving over to others. Totemic reductions of flux may be a necessary requirement for the production of human animal survival, but the "useful" accumulation of energies for the purpose of unlimited economic growth is no natural matter. To deny the spiralling ebb and flow of matter-in-motion was to deny the HIStorical materiality of human animal participation in the cycles of nature. Short of the deadly closure of totalitarian social forms which accumulatively grow only at the expense of others, Bataille suggested that an "exuberant" explosion of excessive energies is a recurrent material feature of life itself. In this way, the *constructive* forces of taboo are no-thing but a laughable precursor of future *deconstructive* transgressions.

Bataille and Kristeva view the transgressive release of HIStorically repressed energies as a strategic aspect of radical social change. This is (k)not to suggest that repression is itself unnatural. Repression is, after all, a material prerequisite for the parasitic construction of linguistic doublings. What is unnatural is the *once and for all time* denial of the doubled nature of human existence. Such denial is prefigured in the "linear" monotheism of Judaic, Christian and Moslem "supernaturalism" and violently transfigured by the "ungiving" and almost exclusively accumulative character of modern CAPITAL. Bataille and Kristeva may be read as theorists of the unnaturalness of modern social forms. They articulate the hope that, by exceeding the restrictive economic confines of contemporary cultural rituals, those most subordinated to CAPITAL would be set free from the violence of modernity's sacrificial idealism. In this sense, *collective effervescence* generated by expending the self-protective borders of CAPITAL was viewed as a necessary step in a revolutionary deliverance from modern social power.

Unleashing the deconstructive energies of festival was once also a dream of Jean Baudrillard. Like Bataille and Kristeva, Baudrillard theorized the repressive material cost to the human animal body by modern western culture. Baudrillard writes of the body-in-giddy-metamorphosis and of the body in

129

"dance movements" where "forms slip" one into the other. This is "a body freed from all [repressive] subjectivity, a body recovering the animal felinity of the pure object, of pure movement."[79] This is the *pagan* body-in-flux. This is the body imagined as festively revolting from its totemic reduction to someone else's use-value. The doubled violence inscribed upon such a body by CAPITAL is described by Baudrillard in the following terms:

> Psychological body, repressed body, neurotic body, space of phantasy, mirror of otherness, mirror of identity, the locus of the subject prey to its own [double] image and desire: our body is no longer pagan and mythic but Christian and metaphorical—body of desire and not of the fable. We have put it through a kind of materialized precipitation. The way in which we interpret our body today...the way in which we recount it in our unrecognized simulacrum of reality, as an individuated space of pulsion, of desire and phantasies, had led it to become the materialist precipitation of a seducing power, which carried within it a gigantic power of negation over the world, and ultra-mundane power of illusion.[80]

Baudrillard views CAPITAL's seemingly limitless growth as a matter of totemic reduction. As such, he theorizes the "productive consumption" of advanced forms of "consumer CAPITAL" in terms of a "high-tech" revitalization of a more archaic form of totemic exchange. In *The System of Objects*, Baudrillard remarks:

> Is not [the force of signs in consumer culture] to some extent the function of the totemic system...? The social order offers itself the vision of its own lasting immanence in the arbitrary totemic sign. Advertising would thus be the result of a cultural system which has reverted (in the gamut of 'brand names') to a poverty of sign codes and archaic systems.[81]

Given the totemic origins of CAPITAL's repulsive social forms, might "we" (k)not somehow collectively redouble this doubled violence and thereby exorcize the sacrifices imposed by western HIStory? Such festive redoubling has long been a radical hope—to reverse the reductions of linguistic exile and thereby release the energies of metamorphoses. Baudrillard's work initially called for a related revolutionary strategy. More recently, however, Baudrillard cautions that transgressive reversals are increasingly (im)possible to materialize. Why? Because CAPITAL itself has revolutionized the body faster than revolutionaries. The redoubling has already happened. Only it has take place implosively rather than explosively. While the metaphorically reduced body of modernity "was still a figure of exile," something far worse is the fate of the body in CAPITAL of late. Here Baudrillard uses the word *metastasis* to connote a new and more terminal form of techno-sacrificial ritual. In ultramodern CAPITAL the body is (k)not so much totemically repressed as released from the confines of modern language into the seemingly excessive circuits of a convolutional cerebral code. This is the cybernetic revolution: a space where doubles are no longer dissolved by being festively transgressed but where they are given "a second life." Here the contradictory character of symbolic forms appear to disappear within the operational codes of their own simulation. As Baudrillard comments:

> The religious, metaphysical or philosophical [doubling]...of being has given way to an operational definition of being in terms of the genetic code (DNA) and cerebral organization (the informational code and billions of neurons). We are in a system where there is no more soul, no more metaphor of the body—the fable of the unconscious itself has lost most of its resonance. No narrative can come to metaphorize our presence; no transcendence can play a role in our definition; our being is exhausting itself in molecular linkings and neuronic convolutions.[82]

Suddenly I am transferred to the dark if solar ANALytic confines of the U.S. in the wake of the election of a former CEO and CIA chief as head of state. Here I am called out to tell an emblematic story of what I take to be the general economic implications of the late social and philosophical writings of Émile Durkheim. I read and re(w)rite Durkheim's critical inquiry into the nature of socially binding religious formations as questioning the ritual social structures that confined him and others within a given totemic genealogy. A genealogy of self-evident and consumptive desire. A genealogy that operates with the material and psychic power of a "moral force." An ultramodernizing western genealogy: a will-to-will to knowledge as power. In the later years of his life Durkheim was wondering about such matters. Aloud and on paper. Producing intellectual love letters and words of warning in relation to the AUTHORIZED INSTITUTIONAL DISCOURSE of other recognized whitemale theorists. Earnestly and with desire.

David Émile Durkheim was the son of an Ashkenazi rabbi and the French father of a son whose body would be sacrificed to feed a new and terrifyingly sacred form of transnational corporate power—WORLD WAR. This is a moral power demanding the blood of others, their commodification, and later their codification. Durkheim was born on April 15, 1858. His birth, or ritual separation from the body of the mother from whom it was said that he was delivered, was registered in Epinal, France. Epinal was a town designated as the lawful CAPITAL of the department of Vosages. Vosages was a subcategorical unit of land within Lorraine.

The birth of Durkheim (as a precursor of sociological poststructuralism) is an event I am (w)riting about (constructively). Durkheim's mother, Melanie nee Isidor, is said to have been the daughter of a trader in beer or in horses. Durkheim's biographers waiver on this point. They aren't certain of the occupation signifying the social positioning of Durkheim's mother's father in HIStory. Nor is much written about Durkheim's mother's mother or, for that matter, Durkheim's father's mother. Of the identity of Durkheim's father and his father's father and their occupations, there are greater words of certainty. Moise or "Papa" Durkheim was recognized as THE rabbi of Epinal since the 1830s. He was not merely a rabbi, but THE rabbi and the chief rabbi of the Vosages and Haute-Marne. And his father's father and his father's father's father. Indeed, Durkheim's great grandfather, Simon Simon, was first ritually identified as a rabbi in 1784. His son, Israel David Durkheim, a rabbi in the Mutzig region of Alsace, was the father of Durkheim's father. All these men had inherited the promise of Abraham. And this promise, like all promises, came with a price. This promise, like the New Testament promises which would follow, was given in exchange for a singularly taxing demand—a refusal of expensive material contact with one's (m)others. Serpents beware! These were the terms of the deal: substituting one's good word for the flesh of one's son and fear of some fascinating Mother. Call it a promise, monotheistic covenant or an archaic legal arrangement—this (im)mortalizing old testament became David Émile Durkheim's on April 15, 1858. It was a day of taxation and debts long due. In 1912, Durkheim (sociologically) betrayed this promise with the following words:

> Of course the sacrifice is partially a communion; but it is also, and no less essentially, a gift and an act of renouncement. It always presupposes that the worshipper gives some of his substance...to his gods.[83]

Profound changes were occurring in the institutional spheres in which Durkheim spent his time. Or invested it. In the factory and classroom; in the synagogue, kitchen and theatre. And, of course, the bedroom. Durkheim was a contemporary of Freud's. Both of these European Jewish white men also wrote about totems and taboo. At about the same time—1912-13—and in a social-psychoanalytic space that was related and yet different. Within a few years the kinship group of each Jewish male child and father would fall under a shadow of interdiction that was almost too horrific to imagine. And still is. When, in January of 1916, Durkheim's son, a promising young linguist, was classified as missing in action, Durkheim, the "father figure" of French sociology (w)rote: "I do not have to tell you of the anguish in which I am living. It is an obsession that fills every moment."[84] Little more than twenty years later two of

Freud's daughters disappeared. This time the matter seemed almost to escape language. Auschwitz. Imagine the chill of it social-psychoanalytically. Then imagine two more words: Hiroshima and Nagasaki.

Durkheim and Freud were both (w)riting about and within HIStorically specific sacrificial rites of collective transference. As they were (w)riting rituals of great significance were being transfigured right (and right-wingedly) before each man's eyes/"I"s. When I lay the ethnographic texts of Durkheim and Freud next to each other and between the (w)ritings of Marx and Nietzche, sparks fly transferentially between the words, the inscriptions, the totemic evocations. Right here in the U.S. It's a bit uncanny, especially as the cold blue light of the screen tattoos my body televisually. I am ecstatic at the possibility of (ab)using this scene of inFORMation. Repetitiously. Almost compulsive.

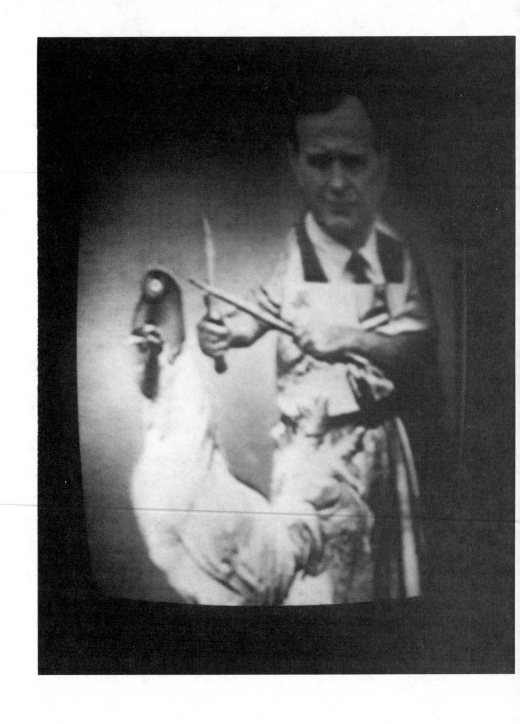

ELEMENTARY FORMS OF ULTRAMODERN SOCIAL LIFE
HYPER-PRIMITIVE DOUBLINGS

> I have given many other things of slight value from which they took great pleasure.... All that they have they give for any trifle we offer them, so that they take in exchange pieces of crockery and fragments of glass goblets.... For anything at all we give them, without ever saying it is too little, they immediately give whatever they possess....Whether it is a thing of value or a thing of little cost, whatever the object then given them in exchange and whatever it is worth they are pleased. —Christopher Columbus[1]

Columbus was particularly impressed with their generosity, stating: "All the women are lovely and naked. One might have supposed one was seeing those splendid naiads or those nymphs of the springs so celebrated by Antiquity. Holding up palm fronds, which they carried while performing their dances, accompanied by songs, they knelt and presented them.... The Admiral said that he cannot believe that a man has ever seen such good-hearted people." Several days passed before Columbus recorded another story of how these particularly generous people displayed their particular generosity. An unknown, but related, group of "Indians" (whom Columbus' boats had carried from another island) were allowed to go into the homes of the natives with whom Columbus was "exchanging gifts" and take anything they wanted or needed or desired. Columbus wrote: "they truly give with a good heart." Then a few of these "good hearted people" stopped by Columbus' supply post and took what they wanted or needed or desired. These greedy thieving conniving savages made Columbus change his mind about the "Americans." "There are no people so wicked," he told his men. "If you discover that some among them steal, you must punish them by cutting off nose and ears, for those are the parts of the body which cannot be concealed."

TOTEMIC DOUBLINGS AND TABOO

It is (k)not by chance that I am drawn to use the word *totem* as a strategy for underscoring the material force of sociological doubling or collective representation. By *totem* I mean the effective ritual substitution of a word, emblem, icon, image, figure of speech or signifier for the otherwise undif-ferentiated metamor-phosis of material reality-in-flux. Sometimes I think I'm repeating myself. This is a sacrificial reduction; a reduction of the indeterminacy of material-relations-in-process to the (partially) closed or ideational framework of a classificatory logic. *Totems* work upon, within and between the bodies that put them into play; feeding off and back upon these bodies like a virus. This is a way of describing the parasitic social force of what psychoanalysis has called *transference*. Totemic illusions (or the appearance of transference) hollows out a phantasmic space within a given body or set of bodies. This positions somebodies over against Others. This distinguishes certain bodies from what they're (k)not, or (k)not allowed be. To be carried away by the forceful fantasies of totemic rites is to be given access to an imaginary (if seemingly natural) identity within the confines of an always only *apparently real* order of things. "Here we are inching toward a critical dismantling of the sign in which the image lifts off from what it is meant to represent. In this peeling off of the signifier from its signified, the representa-tion acquires not just the power of the represented, but power over it, as well."[2] This is a drama of attraction and repulsion. It silences noise.

This connection between totemic sign-work and transference I find important for several reasons, (k)not the least of which is that within the New World Order in which I am (w)riting totemic forces appear nearly everywhere. From the neon haze of the road sign to the iconic lure of the fashion magazine, brand name T-shirt, stereotypical *good looks*, U.S. flag, yellow ribbons and television blasting, ours is a world of electrically charged and telecommunicatively mediated totemic transferences. It is, moreover, within such transferential fields that "we" encoun-ter the desirability of certain objects and the repression, oppression, and/or marginalization of others. In this, "we" may find ourselves at once materially vocationed and imaginarily called out as members of particular social groups, classes, classifications or sects, morally and in an economic fashion. The distor-tive social classifications put into play by totemic rites repeatedly constitute the forceful fictionality of our everyday social worlds, conjuring up particular con-stellations of morally charged memories while forgetting or devaluing others. This engenders certain dominating forms of consciousness, while recurrently exiling the phenomenological mobilization of other ways of being-in-the-world.

Around the word *totem* one also finds a critical convergence of ethnographic and social-psychoanalytic concerns. Indeed, both Émile Durkheim's *The Elemen-tary Forms of Religious Life*[3] and Sigmund Freud's *Totem and Taboo*[4], each produced during approximately the same time period (1912-13), are together rooted in the analysis of totemic logic. As ritually inscribed constructions of social reality, totemic doubles operate both as *ethnographic models* for positively valued objects and as *social-psychoanalytic signifiers* of what's taboo. To deny the totem or defy its taboo is to clash with collective representations of what's (figuratively) undeniable. This is the truth. To refuse or profane this truth is to commit a seductive sign-crime. It is also to risk being reacted to as a dangerous social deviant. Totemic rituals, in other words, involve both the "artifactual" construction and "objective" policing of the ritual boundaries between what's sacrificially given and what's exiled from belief. In this, "we" witness a conjuncture of power and knowledge as an elementary form of totemic doublings themselves.

Totemic doublings have everything to do with power, knowledge, art, metaphors and violence. To construct a double is not merely to create the appearance of something. It is also to make other things ritually disappear or appear impossible. To construct a double is to forcefully reduce the fluid indeterminacy of relations-in-process to the appearance of things being fixed in a certain manner. It is to reductively classify the world into a given set (or set theorization) of objects. It is to violently displace sensations of being in this world away from the contradictory actualities of immediate relational existence into an abstractly inFORMed or categorically imperative (dis)positioning of what's subjectively meaningful and what's objectively true. It is to make ritual use of iconic words, images, emblems or gestures to conjure up a given *order of things* from within which to work. This is an artificial order that only always already appears as if natural or supernaturally given. To performatively enact such orderings is to be, at once, confined and free within a prison house of material linguistic practices.

In this sense, to live within a world of totemic doubles is to live a life of partial exile. It is to be given experiential access to the classificatory stability of a given social order but only at the cost of being denied access to that which is retrospectively positioned in excess of that order—an indeterminate and shifting choreography of human-animal forms in metamorphoses. From a particular vantage point in HIStory this may be a helpful way of imagining our complexly social human natures. I offer this image (k)not as a timeless metaphysical picture of the human condition, but as a strategic attempt to (w)rite against the violent telecommunicative drift of an ultramodern present. This lesson is given by a critically inFORMed re-reading of aspects of the late writings of Durkheim, particularly as Durkheim's concerns relate to those of Marx, Nietzche and Freud.[5]

At an earlier moment in HIStory Marx envisioned a double worlded separation from nature in terms of the organization of various modes of producing material survival. Nevertheless, as obediently modernist Marx's (w)ritings were themselves marked by the promise of a reasonable end to this separation. At the end of HIStory a (once and) future mode of communistic production would revolutionarily reunite people with what had (once upon a time) been slavishly oppressed. For Freud and Durkheim, the story of this slavishness and its (im)possible reversal was somewhat more immanent. And for Nietzsche as well. Freud, if we are to believe Lacan's re(w)ritings, understood the birth of such civilly re-pressed reality as no-thing but a matter of castration. For Durk-heim the story begins with a rite of sacrifice. Again and again. Durkheim presents an image of totemic sacrifice as the ritual reduction of reality to an illusionary (if necessary) social force-field; a field of power-charged collective representations differentiat-ing what's undoubtably sacred from what's (k)not. Nietzsche diagnosed such alienating disembodiments in terms of a peculiarly WESTERN WILL TO POWER, a masculine cultural flight from the interdependent contingencies of bodily exist-ence itself; a flight into purified objectivity; a flight into positivism; a flight from genealogical immanence into the fetishized commodification of art posing as nature. In this sense, as Arthur Kroker points out, Nietzsche's meditations repre-sent a dark and brooding double of Marx's brilliant analysis of the commodity-form as the predominant epistemology of advancing CAPITAL.[6]

Here I find myself, (k)not unlike Georges Bataille, reading (or re(w)riting) the texts of Freud and Durkheim in relation to those of Nietzsche and Marx. In so doing I am transferred into a complex and contradictory story of power and knowledge. This is a story of what's memorably classified under the sacrificial sign-work of certain sacred names, icons, emblems, words or gestures, as well as what such totemic signs render as taboo, forgotten, repressed or economically discounted. But here, perhaps, "I have just expressed myself in a hopelessly abstract manner. I understand that I have just given definitions that are very hard to understand. I have one way to excuse myself, to justify having recourse to such muddled and apparently unwarranted constructions. I can only try to use this indefensible tool as a key. If a door that had always remained shut opens—no matter how unwieldily the method used—the one who turns the key will appear human again."[7]

DOUBLING SACRIFICES

> It is fascinating that what we might call (with some perplexity) the image itself should be granted such a power—not the signified, the sacred totemic species, animal, vegetable, and so forth, but the signifier is itself prized apart from its signfication so as to create a quite different architecture of the sign—an architecture in which the signified is erased. Thus can Durk-heim make his...claim that what is 'represented' is society itself.
> —Michael Taussig[8]

The violence of sacrificial substitution is also evident in the (w)ritings of Rene Girard. In *Violence and the Sacred* Girard expands Durkheim's notions of the TOTEMIC ORIGINS of both social forms and orderly individual experience. Durkheim theorized both society and the consciousness of its members as simul-taneously constituted by the sacrificial violence of collective (linguistic) representations. Yet, according to Girard, "Durkheim never fully articulated his insight, for he never realized what a formidable obstacle violence presents and what a positive resource it becomes when it is transfigured and reconverted through the mediation of scapegoat effects."[9] Girard reinterprets the construction of totemic doublings as rooted in the "generative violence" associated with the ritual substitution of "surrogate victims" for the contradictory immanence of the actual social relations.

Surrogate victims appear before the eyes/"I"s of those (of us) who sacrifice them as no-thing but objects for logical contemplation and mastery. The measured skull of the prisoner, the opaque and racist image of the Arab, the nude female figure pinned upon the wall—surrogate victims absorb the repulsive discharge of contradictory social energies, just as they fascinate the eyes/"I"s of those (of us) their sacrifice insures. As such, surrogate victims are (literally) sentenced to the sphere of categorically dead matters. As objects, they are parasitically dined upon by "we" whose gaze they fascinate. The seemingly external force of such objects, their manifest reality *sui generis*, and their power to materially captivate the human imagination is likened by Girard to the psychoanalytic notion of "transference."[10] Transference is a material force that imaginarily carries us out from within immediate scenes of social contradiction into psychically screened networks of power that engender complex layers of remembering (and forgetting). To be within the throes of transference is to experience things as fated as, indeed, within the sacrificially constituted boundaries of transference this is exactly how things are artfully given. To experience transference is to experience things (and people) as if *super-naturalized*, as exercising compelling *attractive* or basely *repulsive* pulls upon and within us *as if* independent of the ritual violence by which they are repeatedly constituted as objects (of desire). Whether in its positive or negative forms, in transference the flux of human-animal indeterminacy appears as if something solid. Girard's (w)ritings on this issue suggest that both prior to *and* concurrent with the transference of desire across boundaries separating one object from its others, there exists a violent movement of ORIGINARY SACRIFICE. This (theoretically) is what engenders both senses of ourselves as subjects and the concurrent evocation of a (now seemingly separate) world of objects within which "we" find ourselves pushed and pulled by forces of attraction and repulsion.

For Girard, the cognitive, moral and economic origins of human communities LIE in the "dramatic unity" or "violent unanimity" produced (in mind and body) by the sacrificial consumption of "monstrous doubles." Onto these double-objects—and I am here imagining the sacrificial status of such contemporary "monsters" as women, nonwhites and the economically impoverished—is projected the arbitrary and HIStorically specific violence that marks all members of a peculiarly human group. By such sacrificial violence, societies both distinguish themselves from others and make artful distinctions between (the classificatory status of) their own members. Through such violence "we" human-animals institute powerful perceptual codes differentiating what's (morally) knowable from what's (k)not. All ambivalence, contradiction, and conflict—in other words, all the material effects of humans being in *lack* of an instinctually imprinted mode of workable social relations—are transferred to the "impure" figure of a scapegoat or "monstrous double." This "figure of sacrifice" is made to carry the symbolic burden of being neither purely inside nor purely outside the culture. Then the scapegoat is killed, consumed and absorbed back into the "blessed" life of the community into which it disappears. In this dramatic gesture the material contradictions of everyday social life fade from recognition as the "impure" body of the "surrogate victim" is exchanged (at least temporarily) for the aura of "pure" reason and the objects that such reason simultaneously reveals and conceals. In the wake of such sacrificial rites objects (of economically restricted perception) are transfigured or transubstantiated so as to appear as if supernaturally ordained or naturally given.

And just as such objects appear transformed by sacrifice, so are the subjects who behold them categorically. Previously decentered subjects-in-flux now appear to be solidly differentiated from the objects they perceive. In this way the presence of something (or some person) is pictured as the opposite of its absence, just as truth is figured as the opposite of what's false. But this is purely a (doubled) representation, an inversion of a more primordial order of things in metamorphoses, things that are no-thing but things-in-flux, things in contradictory relations of impure contingency. To performatively enact such representational or totemic doublings is to substitute the "religiously" figured body of "a surrogate victim" for the (im)possibly reflexive awareness of all truths being dependent upon the supplementary force of what they exclude. Otherwise "we" humans would remain adrift within the ecstatic but never stable waves of heterogeneous multiplicity, a continuous process of flowing into and out of ever-shifting forms of association, or what Girard refers to as the *reciprocal violence* of "mimetic desire."

Girard uses the term "mimetic desire" to conjure an image of experiential conflict prior to (and always just "the other side" of) the sacrificial force of a given symbolic order. In mimetic desire human experience is, at once, separate and not separate from the motion of metamorphic flux. Here things are perceived but vulnerably. Here there is NO ORIGINAL REFERENT, only a flurry of dramatic copies playing off the energetic (dis)positionings of each in relation. Moving copies miming, parasiting, identifying and/or struggling with the repetitious dance of mirrored images spiralling in a theatrical game of give and take.

Here there are no metaphysics and no first causes. Here there is only a physics of laughable reciprocity, or *pataphysics*. Here the screening of what's memorable and what's (k)not folds noticeably around the bodies of actors and actresses miming strange and estranging attractions. Like the flow of electric currents pulsing in relations that sometimes shock, this is a world that appears open to the transferential push and pull of polyvalent forces, forces that simultaneously attract and repulse without a fixed and linear sequence, a mimetic world with neither fixed objects nor centered subjects. This is a world of experience, but not stable experience; a world marked, (k)not by a lack of useful or productive patterns, but by a plenitude of interdependent relations that defy simple or straight-minded categorizations of scarcity.

In mimetic desire human animal beings appear open to what Durkheim and Mauss describe as a "fundamental confusion of all images and ideas. They are not separated from each other, as it were with any clarity. Metamorphoses, the transmission of qualities, the substitution of persons, souls and bodies, beliefs about the materialization of spirits and the spiritualization of material objects—these are all aspects of the "transmutative" character of the mimetic field itself."[11] This is a phase of culture governed spatially by the unstable play of compelling yet *reflexive transferential identifications* rather than by the lawful desires of a fixed linguistic order. Within this mimetic field there is "belief in the possibility of the transformation of the most heterogeneous things into one another, and consequently the more or less complete absence of definitive concepts...a complete lack of distinction."[12]

Arguing that "the very idea of such [mimetic] transmutation could not arise if things were [at all times and spaces] represented by delimited and classified concepts," Durkheim and Mauss suggest that even the "Christian dogma of transubstantiation is a consequence of this state of mind and may serve to prove its generality."[13] Within the fragile space of mimesis things appear capable of being "believably" transformed in excessively radical ways. Materially and in the imagination. This vulnerability of things to being radically transformed in the process of repeating them differently is a major theme in Girard's theorization of mimesis as a primordial mode of human cultural exchange. A partial understanding of the vulnerability of such exchange may help glimpse why it is that Girard uses the term "reciprocal violence" to characterize the play of mimesis. In the improvisational stagings of mimetic action "we" imperfectly mime the movement of others, like looking glass selves but without the seemingly supernatural guarantees of a timeless mythic or Symbolic Order.

Mimesis is hegemonically repressed in the construction of the dominant Symbolic Order within which "we" live. Or, worse yet, it is oppressively imagined as a primitive, infantile or neurotic feature of those condemned to the monstrous borderlines of this order. And so the masked tales of nonwhites, women and others. And so, within the imperial confines of contemporary social hierarchies, the reflexive masqueradings of nonwhites, women and others excluded from the controlled ritual stagings of sacrificial power may be interpreted as nothing but parasitic table scraps from some masterful (sacrificial) meal of lawful self-identity. MONKEY SEE. MONKEY DO. BLACK SKIN. WHITE MASK. WOMAN AS MASQUERADE and the like. LIKE AFTER LIKE. Such oppressive repressions are purchased by the gift of the "surrogate victim," whose sacrifice absolves others of us from the ambivalence of having to live with manifest social contradictions. Lacking the *reality effects* secured by this ritual substitution, subjects-in-mimesis overflow into each other in spiralling cycles of revenge (and the moving reconciliations such revenge recurrently begets). Imitating the manifestly violent gestures of each other, persons in the transferential throes of mimesis may be moved to follow displacement by counter-displacement, reduction by counter-reduction, theft by counter-theft, murder by counter-murder, memory by counter-memory and the wounds of separation by healing. Hence the "reciprocal violence" of victims being transformed into victimizers in a cycle without an apparently fixed or predetermined ending. Something akin to this unstable play of transubstantiation appears within a world ruled by mimetic impulses. This is a reciprocally permeable world without fixed boundaries between subjects and objects; a world where somebody may hear the call of "being" speaking in a tree, food substance or automobile and where it is not absurd to declare: "You are a fox." "I am a wolf." "You are a rock." "I am Batman."

MIMETIC TRANSFERENCE

The reflexive transferential characteristics of mimetic cultural spaces are related to what Durkheim and Mauss picture as the elementary ritual forms of totemic doublings. While such rituals are ordinarily thought characteristic of only so-called "primitive societies" but (k)not our own, let us (k)not be so certain. In evoking the totemic overtones of the "Christian dogma of transubstantiation" Durkheim and Mauss remind us that before modernity our own western cultural tradition was marked by periodic reversals to the unstable rule of mimetic impulse. This was nowhere more evident than in the sacred transgressions of festival or carnival. I am here referring to periodic reversions to the collective play of indistinction, heterogeneous co-minglings and other such dramatic displays of structural indeterminacy.

The restrictive economic repression of such reversions by modern social institutions is (k)not a new story. The HIStory of such repression is a major subtext of works ranging from Max Weber's *The Protestant Ethic and the Spirit of Capitalism*[14] to Georges Bataille's *The Accursed Share*[15] and Jean Baudrillard's

Mirror of Production. [16] What is new, and what I find particularly frightening, is the twist this HIStory appears to be taking in the emergence of ultramodernity. I am here referring to the deployment of powerful social technologies characterized by what Marcuse once theorized as *repressive desublimation*—the productive "liberation" of previously repressed energies, particularly sexual energies, but only in the form of a "sexuality [that] obtains a definite sales value or becomes a token of prestige and of playing according to the rules of the game, [so that] it is itself transformed into an instrument of social cohesion."[17] This blurring of difference with the self-same is symptomatic of a disturbing form of *hyper-primitivism*. The play of mimetic impulses may here appear to return, but only under the corporately constructed sign-work of their telecommunicative simulation. But in this I'm jumping ahead of myself. Permit me to return to Girard's description of mimetic rituals and the NON-ORIGINARY RECIPROCITY they connote. A reflexive understanding of this aspect of culture will hopefully alert "us" to both the dangers and strategic possibilities of its contemporary simulation.

As mimetic subjects-in-transference "we" may be periodically carried away by our human animal abilities to mime what may appear to us as the self-sufficiency of others. To feel the force of mimetic desire is to be moved to imitate others who (artfully) appear to possess what human experience (this side of the womb) may feel that it suffers as missing—security, stable identity, fullness of being, or whatever. This is transference. Girard's evocation of this fluid mimesis prior to the law-like rule of linguistic stability resembles Julia Kristeva's depiction of a primordial (social psychoanalytic) transference to an "imaginary father of prehistory."[18] The imagined object of a mother's desire—this strange totemic figure fractures the enveloping plenitude of the mother-child coupling. Signalling both a violent disruption of harmonic being-with- others and the onset of a (K)NOT VERY ORIGINAL transference, the appearance of this imaginary father assumes the form of both lack and desire. Experienced as a powerful separation, the transferential imaging of this archaic figure sets in motion a figurative search to restore what retrospectively appears as if always lacking. In this sense, the sacrificial onset of desire is, at once, murderous and full of "life-giving" promise.

Kristeva and Girard theorize transference in terms of the "abject" or "reciprocally violent" oscillation between the material pains of being in *lack* and the imaginary pleasures of miming plenitude. Here, the subject-in-process occupies the place of a monster. How horrific and how fascinating. In the space of such indeterminate transference one is neither truly inside nor outside society. As such, one is thus neither truthfully a subject nor an object. Thus, one "looks to that other person [imagined as the locus of desirous plenitude] to inform him [or her] what he [or she] should desire in order to acquire that being. If the model, who is apparently already endowed with a superior being, desires some object, that object must surely be capable of an even greater plenitude of being."[19] Or so it may seem to the "partial" subject whose dramatic knowledge is constituted more by the impure force-fields of transference than by the purified reason of binary sociological classification. In this sense, transferential displacements provide a pre-textual space for the subsequent fixing of identifiable desires within classificatory language or the Symbolic Order. With symbolic language comes a restrictive economy of gift exchange where what was once open to mimetic reversals and transferential flux now appears banished to the realm of what is (only) imaginary. In this, desire is parasitically linked to the (moral economy) of law.

Girard's theory of sacrifice poses the question of human desire in terms of a mimetic impulse "directed toward an object desired by the model."[20] This is (k)not to suggest that either the object or the model appear independent of the transferential forces that carry each in relations of desire toward and away from others. This is the form of a transference that movingly acknowledges the contradictions it feeds off. It reflexively embodies an awareness that multiple "desires converging on the same object are bound to clash. Thus, mimesis coupled with desire leads automatically to conflict."[21] In what ways is it possible to profitably contain, economically channel or symbolically order the artificial plenitude promised by mimesis without recognizing the materiality of such RECIPROCAL VIOLENCE? This question is both posed (and hierarchically answered) by the HIStorical coming into being of (social) states, the power of which is centralized around the seemingly supernaturalized "realities" of a given mode of moral and economic authority.

I am here, somewhat mythically—that is, theoretically—referring to the SYMBOLIC ORIGINS and psychic bodily effects of centralized state authority and the emergence of patriarchal social forms. Although an adequate discussion of these matters is beyond the scope of the present lectures, it is important to note that such Symbolic Orders are of relatively recent "anthropological origin." Most scholars today agree that for the first 30,000 of our "our" 40,000 years as a species of *Homo Sapiens* "we" human animals lived in relatively decentered, "headless" or *acephalous* social formations.[22] These were most likely also matrifocal societies, characterized by egalitarian economic exchange, the ecstasy of sacrificial reciprocity, and "the experienced unity of psychic-productive-sexual-cosmic power."[23] For the most part, they were also societies that dealt with conflict by various "mimetic" rituals of reconciliation. By such rites gaping social wounds were symbolically revenged and material conflicts engendered by contradictory sacrifices were collectively healed rather than indefinitely extended in the name of some supernatural, metaphysical or transcendental authority. All talk of evolution aside, acephalous societies did not disappear naturally. They were *made to disappear* by the emergence of militaristic patriarchal social forms.[24] Indeed, only with the advent, selective deployment and hierarchical appropriation of social technologies—permitting some men to manage the lives of other men and virtually all women—were acephalous societies relegated to the excremental trash heap of a supposed pre-HIStory.

How did patriarchal state formations secure their militaristic reign? One partial answer is found in a critical reformulation of Girard's theoretical projections. For Girard, the restrictive economic violence of Symbolic Orders is facilitated by the *secondary violence* of forgetting or sacrificial (mis)recogni-tion. Such rituals of (mis)recognition are a feature of the *elementary religious forms* which Durkheimian sociology envisions as a constitutive aspect of social life itself. This is true of "modern philosophy" as well. According to Girard, who here follows Durkheim in the direction of a postmodern philosophy:

> That is why modern philosophers attribute the origin of society to a 'social contract,' either implicit or explicit, rooted in 'reason,' 'good sense,' 'mutual self interest,' and so forth. They are incapable of grasping the essence of religion and attributing to it a real function. This incapacity is mythic in character, since it perpetuates the religion's own misapprehensions in regard to violence. It evades the problem of human violence and mistakes the nature of the threat this violence poses for human society.[25]

MONSTROUS DOUBLINGS: THE SCAPEGOAT

A partial glimpse of such sacrificial (mis)recognitions (of objects of attraction and repulsion) is also a matter of great concern to a critical social-psychoanalysis. This is suggested in the (w)ritings of Kristeva. In *Revolution in Poetic Language*, Kristeva agrees with Girard that "even the crudest of religious viewpoints acknowledges a truth ignored by even the most lucid nonreligious system."[26] Here the "relationship between modern thought and primitive religion is somewhat different from what it appears at first glance. Although modern and primitive [society] share a fundamental misunderstanding of the nature of violence, primitive [society] retains certain insights into this nature, insights that are perfectly real and that wholly escape our grasp."[27] Kristeva here couples the insights of psychoanalysis with those of "primitive society." She also points to limits of Girard's analysis when considering sexually specific aspects of symbolic violence. "Surprisingly...Girard rejects the sexual nature of [sacrificial] violence, which Freud's work, to its credit, reveals beneath the ethnological heap."[28] Indeed, Freud's attention to the sexual character of sacrificial violence "opened the way to rational knowledge of that violence, not through the abstraction of civilizations phantasmatically or mimetically reconstructed, but in the concrete practice of the subject—or subjects—within the realm of contemporary social forces."[29]

Kristeva extends Girard's theorization by recognizing the "abject" play of what might otherwise appear as no-thing but endless conflict. This is to reflexively acknowledge both the arbitrary and HIStorically specific character of what Girard describes as *reciprocal violence*. This awareness serves to detour or even possibly subvert the unreflexive *super-naturalization* of sacrifices demanded on the part of others. Such sacrifices operate HIStorically to secure and preserve the (artificially constructed) self-evidency of an experiential framework that denies its own *lack* of identity. The sacrificial fruits of this denial are covered up by a violent substitution of the sacrificial blood of "surrogate others" as (partial) insurance against the transferential discovery of its own homicidal origins. In this way, "sacrifice can be viewed not only as an imposition of social coherence but also as its outer limit."[30]

Conceiving sacrifice as "the reign of substitution...and ordered continuity," Kristeva underscores the symbolic economy set in place by sacrificial logic. "In sacrifice,...two series, sacrificer and 'deity' [or the sense of things being supernaturally given], far from being homomorphic, must, precisely, establish their relation."[31] Each must pledge allegiance to an everlasting covenant with the Other. This is a pledge of material discontinuity (within nature) that masks itself with the (supernatural) appearance of an illusory sense of continuity. In actuality this is nothing but a fetishized continuity—the powerful doubling of what it's (k)not. This continuity is fired by the sacrificial immolation of a contradictorily positioned "scapegoat" or "surrogate" other. Hence the destruction of the victim—a murderous rupture that "divinely absolves" those blessed by the resulting Symbolic Order from recognizing our own complicity with the sacrificial character of violent HIStorical contradictions. As a reward for the gift of one's others, "we" who compulsively repeat such formative rites are provided with a monumental return for "our" secret investment (in murder). This return comes in the form of a promise of "compensatory continuity." Kristeva depicts the sacrificial violence behind this promise as the driving force of "symbolic communication" between "two hierarchized...agencies," the sacrificer and the posited divinity that ritually insures the sacrificer's identity. This is a way of describing the (k)not so original "origins" of a closed social circuit—the promise of immortality or the linguistic erection of a (patriarchal) Symbolic Order perched above the silent bodies of those it parasitically consumes. Thus:

> In sacrifice...the entire circuit of symbolic communication...is established (gift—reward—symbolic praise), a circuit on which symbolic economy is based. In this way, sacrifice stages the advent of this economy, its emergence from ecological continuum, and the socialization of this ecology....
> In its...broken continuity, and its symbolic relation to a dominant agency,

sacrifice resembles not language but the unconscious, which is the unspoken precondition of linguistic systematization. This explains why sacrifice, like incest and bestiality, is found at the extreme end of the social code: it reproduces both the foundation of that code and what it represses.[32]

Kristeva and Girard's theorizations of the substitution of surrogate victims for the material actuality of troubling social contradictions suggest that, prior to the structured appearance of given social objects there first exists a process of sacrificial disappearance. This is a process of violent displacement whereby the ambivalent character of contradictory human actions are projected onto the monstrous figure of those *monstrous doubles who* are said to (k)not fit cleanly into the binary division between natural *processes* and *cultural* doings. Then the monster is consumed, the victim of violent totemic doublings and their fetishized or *supernatural disavowal*. In this, sacrificial consumption appears to both structurally predate and prepare society for various subsequent modes of contradictory social production. To pursue production is to pursue the manufacture of particular objects of desire. But before objects may appear as either desirable or repulsive they must first be sacrificially extracted from an otherwise indeterminate flux of human-animal relations in metamorphoses. This founding cultural extraction is what I mean by totemic doubling. In this way sacrificial symbolic acts might be thought of as violently engendering rather than existing as the material by-products or super-structural effects of various modes of restrictive economic production.

The fetishized (or productive) extension of such sacrifices, although a dominant feature of hierarchical societies such as our own, is neither necessary nor natural. Instead of feeding off the sacrifice of others, why (k)not periodically suffer the mimetic shattering of our own parasitic identities? Why (k)not give back our restricted economic desire for purely artificial plenitude? Why (k)not exchange this desire for the more dangerous impurities and indistinctive co-minglings of a more generous mode of gift-exchange? Instead of repressing the play of mimesis why (k)not return to this strangely reflexive world of mirrors and ritual illusions?[33] To raise such admittedly perverse questions is, in part, to follow the dance of Bataille in (w)riting of what's most (im)possible to (w)rite about. Perhaps this is also to laughingly make impure differences between the restrictive economy of (modern male) desire and a general economy that's given to (the reciprocal violence) of some other pleasures. For, "Only the body without desire is truly deserving of pleasure."[34] But what of the body of love? Isn't the body given over to love a body in generous defiance of the productive symbolic constraints demanded by more restrictive forms of sacrifice? This I believe is suggested in the (w)ritings of Helene Cixous when she states:

> Giving isn't sacrificing. The person who transmits has to be able to function on the level of knowledge without knowing.... [O]ne should be in a state of weakness, as we all are, and that it *be evident*. That one have the guts to occupy the position one has no right to occupy and that one show precisely how and why one occupies it. I set my sights high; I demand that love struggles within the master against the will for power.[35]

HYPER-PRIMITIVE DOUBLINGS

My use of the word *totem* is (k)not innocent of an awareness that this term ordinarily is reserved for a discussion of the representational practices of so-called "primitive peoples." They practice totemism in their *magical identifications* with plants, animals, or other "natural" objects. "We," on the other hand, with our commitment to theories of scientific causation, are said to be above and beyond such epistemological mistakes. This problematic distinction between *us* and *them*, as well as its naive romantic reversal, has long facilitated the masterful (mis)recognition of ourselves over against those we pose or suppose to be our "primitive" others. "Thus the peoples of the Third world (Arabs, Blacks, Indians) serve as the imaginary of western culture (just as much as an object/support of racism as the support of revolutionary hope)."[36]

How to break the imperial tortion (or dis-tortion) of such violent binary logic? One strategy (that I will imperfectly entertain) is to perversely mirror back upon ourselves certain of the theoretical terms that *insiders* to modern power have used to explain or explain away the problem of *others*. This is to provisionally make ourselves others to ourselves. It is to also reflexively act upon a partial awareness of the *projective constitution* of others as *Other* in the exclusionary materialization of our modern language. It is to likewise take seriously the perverse truth of such projections as symptomatic of the real, if distorted, relations of those (of us) who theorize about such things within the complex and contradictory transferential fields of unequal power. This applies to those (dis)positioned as masters, as well as to those who (in different ways) such putative masters attempt to enslave. In this sense, it is important to inquire into the real, if distorted, relations that materially characterize western social science's recurrent fascination with the term *totem*. I make this claim (k)not uninnocent of the symptomatic fascinations that give form to the very text you are reading.

Claude Levi-Strauss' study of totemism pursues a related question. Levi-Strauss attends both to the "all enveloping terms, which confound...objects of perception and the emotions which they arouse" on the part of those who practice totemic logic and to the related (binary) classificatory practices of those professing a western scientific knowledge of *the savage mind* of others.[37] Recognizing related forms of classification in "the kind of surreality" observable in totemic societies and modern anthropology, especially in anthropology's totemic-like classification of totemic logic itself, Levi-Strauss concludes that: "In this sense, there is nothing archaic or remote about [totem-ism]. Its image is projected not received; it does not derive its substance from without. If the [totemic] illusion contains a particle of truth, this is not outside us but within us."[38]

Levi-Strauss' analysis, operating within a "kind of surreality" of its own, labors to (ethically) subvert the privileged classifications of anthropology. Levi-Strauss suggests that both totemic peoples (who religiously identify themselves by virtue of their classificatory relation to plants, animals, and other "natural" objects) and anthropological peoples (who scientifically identify themselves by virtue of their classificatory relation to totemic peoples and other "natural" objects) together enact a related form of binary logic. By demonstrating (literally, by charting together) the homology between these two seemingly different, but structurally identical forms of logic, Levi-Strauss subverts the ethno- centric privilege of western "scientific humanism."

But isn't even Levi-Strauss' self-effacing structural subversion, whereby the logic of western science is made identical to the logic of totemism, itself exclusionary of other differences between the practice of science and the practice of totemic knowledge? Jacques Derrida raises a related question in his deconstruction of Levi-Strauss' "ethical" presentation of *savage* and *scientific* knowledge forms as sharing an identical linguistic structure. According to Derrida, not only are there no (demonstrable) ethical claims "without the [symptomatic] presence of the other but also, and consequently, without absence, dissimulation, detour, difference."[39] In this sense, all transferential moves toward identification, including Levi-Strauss' theoretical moves, are simultaneously moves toward exclusion. This is a key aspect of that (social) structuring practice that Derrida himself paradoxically identifies as "writing."

The strength of Levi-Strauss' position LIES in his theorization of a "structural identification" between the projective binary logic of both "totemic" and "scientific" classification. Derrida, however, appears to more perversely favor the "weakness" of the combinatory bricolage. This is typified by an always shifting ritual assemblage or ongoing re(w)riting of all social forms and, as such, "a total inability to justify itself in its own discourse."[40] This differentiates totemic logic from Levi-Strauss' truthful assertions concerning structural identity. Why?

> [Because] in the best of cases, the discourse of bricolage can confess itself, confess itself in its desire and its defeat, provoke the thought and the essence and necessity of the already-there, recognize that the most radical discourse, the most inventive and systematic engineer are surprised and circumvented by history, a language etc., a world (for 'world' means nothing else) from

which they must [parasitically] borrow their tools, if only to destroy the former machine.[41]

Derrida, it seems, has unlearned more about anthropology from Georges Bataille than Levi-Strauss.[42] Reading Derrida (w)riting suggests that he both rigorously and (im)properly reads in(to) "primitive"(w)riting, or totemic bricolage, not a mere combinatory logic (by which "we" and "primitives" may be said to labor under the self-same structural code) but also an allusive story of the ritual effects of sacrificial violence. In this sense, Derrida gives complicit notice to the doubled violence that operates in both the (w)riting of others and in his own (w)riting. This is evident in Derrida's evocation of the terrible ORIGINARY LOGIC of *différance*. Derrida's neologism here sets Levi-Strauss' structuralism spinning. As a word, *différance* appears more provocative than descriptive. As an enigmatic hybrid of terms connoting both difference and deference, the word *différance* hovers at the indeterminate borders of its own ritual performance. *Différance* combines a structuralist understanding of meaning (as produced by the differential positionings of binarily paired signs within a linguistic system of difference) with a (politically charged) recognition that any arrangement of meaning sacrificially defers the making "present" of others.

The paradoxical operation of *différance* acts to economically detour the immediacy of things being present to their own performative SACRIFICIAL ORIGINS. But this is only part of the term's double operation. This is a spacing operation which I am here translating as the material effects of sacrificial rituals or *(w)riting*. *Différance*, thus, both separates us from open-ended contact with the bodies of others, while simultaneously placing us within the transferential throes of a promise that, over time, things might eventually become meaningfully identified with exactly what they are (k)not. This is to read *différance* as, at once, a curse and a gift promise of credit, a space of exile and a fictive pledge of mythic cultural domesticity. In the poetic play of *différance*, "we" are thus simultaneously detoured from and promised the immediacy of an identifiable self-sameness over against others. "Thus one could reconsider all the pairs of opposites on which philosophy is constructed and on which our discourse lives, not in order to see opposition erase itself but to see what indicates that each of the terms must appear as the *différance* of the other, as the other different and deferred in the economy of the same...."[43]

FROM DURKHEIM TO DERRIDA

Levi-Strauss' analysis generally involves only the "differing" (or structurally differentiating) aspect of Derrida's paradoxical and indeterminate term. For the structuralist anthropologist, both totemic and scientific logics sort out a world of differences into binary doubles. These doubles are said to be syn-chronically (or systemically) dependent upon the contemporary arrangement of all other doubles. All possible terms and the opposite of each are thus included within Levi-Strauss' elegant structural mappings. The same is true for classifications projected by the totemic or *savage mind*. According to Levi-Strauss both logics are governed equally by the laws of structural linguistics.

Derrida appears suspicious of Levi-Strauss' cognitive democratic projections. For Derrida, the homogenizing projection of any pair of linguistically structured doubles involves something more base—a parasitic operation that itself involves a kind of doubled violence. This is a way of understanding ORIGINARY SACRI-FICE: a *hierarchical violence* that inevitably gives deference more to one side of the terms of a binary opposition than its other. This is a kind of delimiting *violence* that reduces the heterogeneous flux of an unnameable host of material possibilities into the ORIGINARY or IDEALIST CON-STRICTURES OF LANGUAGE. By this two-fold reduction other ways of meaningfully giving form to human relations (in nature) are temporally exiled. Such differences are excluded by the sacrificial operations of a "system" of clearly differentiated binary terms. This is the ORIGINARY VIOLENCE of *différance*. This violence remains relatively unnoticed by the formal methods of a structuralist analysis. Nevertheless, Derrida's poststructuralist intervention does not directly oppose Levi-Strauss' assertion of the founding of meaning, whether totemic or scientific, within a circumscribed vector of synchronic linguistic forces. Deconstruction instead supplements the structuralist position by recognizing (or reflexively (mis)recognizing) exclusionary hierarchical effects that accompany all acts of sacrificial (dis)positioning.

Deconstruction is also marked by a methodological recognition that the base materiality of fluid heterogeneous relations, although sacrificially exiled, continues to haunt the ORIGINARY VIOLENCE of language itself. In other words, the homogeneity of language remains haunted by its repressed remainders, by what LIES in excess of its hierarchical orderings. Derrida's recognition of the supplementary force of such (unconscious) remainders moves his deconstructive (w)riting in the direction of social-psychoanalysis. This is also indicative of the cursed gift he shares parasitically with the perverse anthropology of Georges Bataille.

Both Bataille and Levi-Strauss wrote in the wake of Émile Durkheim's subversive refusal of previous western claims of the superiority of the scientific anthropology over totemism. In *The Elementary Forms of Religious Religious Life* Durkheim reviews existing ethnographic "evidence" only to conclude that the logic of totemism sacrificially translates the indeterminate flux of material reality into the reductive confines of "an intelligible language which does not differ in nature from that employed by science."[44] The implications of Durkheim's 1912 thesis for structural anthropology is elaborated by Levi-Strauss. In his own writing on totemism, Levi-Strauss quotes the following passage from *Elementary Forms* as an example of "Durkheim at this best."

> It is far from being the case that this [totemic] mentality has no connection with our own. Our logic was born of this logic....Today, as in former times, to explain is to show how a thing participates in one or a number of others.... Every time we unite heterogeneous terms by an internal link we necessarily identify contraries. Of course, the terms that we unite in this way are not those that the Australian brings together; we choose them by other criteria and for other reasons; but the process itself by which the mind relates then does not differ essentially....Thus there is no abyss between the logic of religious thought and the logic of scientific thought. Both are composed of the same essential elements, only unequally and differently developed.[45]

In this passage Levi-Strauss constructs a somewhat "surreal" congruence between Durkheim's analysis and his own. Here the HIStorical realities of any given culture are reduced to a kind of transHIStory, as all cultures are said to be governed by the same basic classificatory forms. As such, Levi-Strauss argues that Durkheim "is admitting that all social life, even elementary, presupposes an intellectual activity in man of which the formal properties, consequently, cannot be a reflection of the concrete organization of society."[46] This counters a more common reading of Durkheim as a "functionalist," or as someone who suggests that religious and/or scientific logics are but reflections of some pre-existing social order.

Unfortunately, both structuralist and functionalist interpretations of *Elementary Forms* fail to engage what is arguably the most radical implication of Durkheim's (w)ritings—a partial theorization of the transferential effectivity of symbolic forms in terms of the violent doublings entailed by ritual sacrifice. Doublings that cut into and imprison the finite bodies of human animals made subject(s) to the power of abstracted linguistic logic; doublings that collectively impose artifactual distortions in the process of translating the indeterminate co-minglings of material relations-in-flux into the fixed and seemingly law-like rule of hierarchical binary condensations; doublings which sacrificially substitute the orderly reductions of signs or totems for the chaotic charms and playful intimacies of a multiplicity of ambivalent forms.

It is this violent doubling that is suggested by Durkheim when he (w)rites that "Man is double" and that "there are two beings in him: an individual... and a social being." But if the first being (fleshy, contingent and born from a woman) is cut into and cut up by the second, the gap between these does not disappear. Nor is this gap anything but a ritually policed borderline, the recurrent effect of a repetitious enactment of taboos that compulsively safeguard particular social hierarchies against that which threatens to profane their supernatural existence. Here Durkheim's theory of representational doubling parallels Derrida's enigmatic notion of *différance*. In both Durkheim and Derrida there is the suggestion that all the ideational representations displace the material possibility of others. What results is both the erection of abstract cultural imperatives (a moral economy or Symbolic Order) and the ritual inscription of a gap barring a full disclosure of meaning. This gap may be the site for multiple transferential crossings but it can never be fully crossed out or closed over.

This dynamic gap (and its ritual policing) is a material effect of taboos instituted by the ORIGINARY SACRIFICES of a totemic socio-logic and by the differences and deferences that such a logic engenders. Although repeatedly appearing in the form of restrictive economic demands for moral closure and desires that may temporarily divert the weight of such (im)possible demands, this sacrificially constructed gap must (k)not be imagined as permanent or "once and for all time." In Durkheim's analysis of totemic cultures, this ORIGINARY GAP (or the production of the illusory sense that something is always lacking) is depicted as being periodically deconstructed or ecstatically transgressed. This involves a festive loss of the ORIGINARY SACRIFICIAL LOSS that constitutes the doubled world of human linguistic abstraction. In enacting such sacred transgressions our partial exile from the indeterminate contingencies of bodily existence is, for "a time between times," excessively put aside. This results in a "state of effervescence [and a space of] exuberant movements which are not easily subjected to too carefully defined ends."[47] This is Durk-heim's depiction of (what Bataille would later call) *transgressive excess*, a ritual space that may "provoke laughter by laughter" and "being foreign to all utilitarian ends" carries people across the threshold of what is ordinarily taboo. Caught up "in the domain of pure fancy," such (deconstructive) rites enable people to (provisionally) "forget the real world and transport them into another where their imagination is more at ease."[48]

> In part, they escape aimlessly, they spread themselves for the mere pleasure of so doing, and they take delight in all sorts of games. Besides, in so far as the [doubled] beings to whom the cult is addressed are imaginary, they are not able to contain and regulate this exuberance....Therefore, one exposes oneself to grave misunderstandings if, in explaining [these] rites, he [or she] believes that each gesture has a precise object and a definite reason for its existence. There are some which serve *nothing*; they merely answer the need felt by worshippers for action, motion, gesticulation. They are to be seen jumping, whirling, dancing, crying and singing, though it may not always be possible to give a meaning to all this agitation.[49]

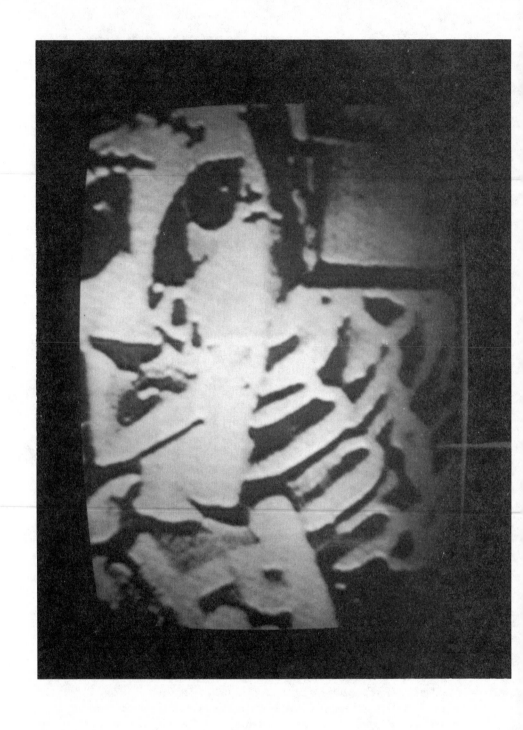

TOTEMS AND TABOO
HYPER-NARCISSISM, DEATH AND THE UNCANNY

> Frightening scenes of uncanny literature are produced by hidden anxieties
> concealed within the subject, who then interprets the world in terms of his
> or her apprehensions.—Rosemary Jackson[1]

FREUD'S DEAD FATHER TOTEM: THE UNCANNY

She was a dark skinned cunt double of somebody for sure. Can you guess
who? One day, just before Labor Day, little Reno Heimlich, I mean Oli North Jr.
(this is me when I was a little white boy wanting to be a hero) set out for the
midway. I never really wanted to be George Bush, although I did want to be a
top secret agent. I guess this was because I wanted to rise to the top rather than
start at the top. I was a good little cute white boy, kind of skinny and uncertain,
but I imagined myself far more. I had a haircut just like Oli North Jr. I was Oli
North Jr. And, since my dead father was a sign and my alive father was a sign-
maker, I got into the State Fair without paying. Or at least I thought I wasn't
paying. Who was paying? Somebodies must be paying? In the back of a company
vehicle. LYING low, keeping secret(s). It was the 1950s.

Before I left the kitchen my mother said, "Now, Oli, remember what you
promised!" "Okay Mom. Goodbye." I'd promised so many things that I
thought, if only I could just get out of The House without being specific about
which promise, then I wouldn't end up being/feeling guilty. At the time this
seemed like a pretty clever strategy. Although I kind of knew she was talking
about the midway, no further questions were asked.

The next thing you know, there's me, Pat Boone and my brothers sneaking
through the gate. What a thrill. Fledgling little whitemale workers, we help my
father make signs. After a couple of hours, when Pat and my brothers go off to
buy some hot dogs, coke and candy, I tell my father, innocently enough, although
I was sure he must know what I was up to, "Hey, Dad, I'm just going to take a
walk around, Okay, and look at some stuff, Okay." This was neither a question
nor an overt declaration of intent. At the time it seemed like a clever strategy.
"Okay, young fella. Take care of yourself," said my father. With a wink. Since I

had illegal millions in my pocket I knew I'd be all right. After that, things became uncannily repetitious. It was as if I'd walked wide eyed into an old story that was anything but mine alone. Involuntary repetition: it "forces upon us the idea of something fateful and inescapable when otherwise we should have spoken only of 'chance.'"[2]

I walked through and past the industrial exhibits, prize poultry and crafts show. As I was walking, the afternoon's hot sun beat down, and soon I found myself in a quarter whose character could not long remain in doubt. Except for a bunch of snakes, jungle scenery and a troop of beaten bleeding sailors, nothing but a painted woman could be seen on the seven huge canvass screens. I had wanted to see the midway but what was this?

What I remember most is that the brown skinned topless, almost naked, woman was so strong she could rip a sailor's arm from its socket and turn a gang of handsome painted white men's sex eyes to bloody horror. I'd never seen so much blood squirting. We didn't have VCRs in those days. The snakes were on her side and the eerie carnivalesque voice of a balding midway barker haunts me to this day. *STEP RIGHT UP MY YOUNG MAN. PUT YOUR EYES   IN THE (W)HOLES AND LET YOUR FINGERS DO THE WALKING. SEE THE BLOOD. SEE THE PLEASURE.* Some of the sailors seemed out of their mind with fear. Others appeared overcome by desire. The woman's teeth seemed incredibly sharp and severed limbs were everywhere. *STEP RIGHT UP. SEE ZELDA QUEEN OF THE JUNGLE. FROM THE DARKEST AMAZON FORESTS OF BRAZIL. SHE'S THE WILD ONE. SHE'S THE NAKED ONE. SHE'S THE FRIEND OF THE SNAKES. SEE ZELDA. THE MANEATER. SEE ZELDA. SHE'S STRONGER THAN A DOZEN WILLING SAILORS. SEE THAT OLD GIRL ZELDA. THE ONE YOU'VE HEARD ABOUT. ZELDA THE WILD ONE CAPTURED AT LAST. BROUGHT HERE BY A SPECIAL EXPEDITION IT'S ZELDA. CHAINED IN A PIT OF SNAKES. STEP RIGHT UP. SEE ZELDA. QUEEN OF THE JUNGLE. FROM THE DARKEST AMAZON.*

I was overwhelmed by a feeling of helplessness, the sense of helplessness experienced in some dream-states. I knew I shouldn't be seeing all this, and hastened to leave the narrow and crowded strip of pay if you please attractions at the next turning. "But after having wandered about for a time without enquiring my way, I suddenly found myself back in the same street, where my presence was now beginning to excite attention."[3] *SHE'S THE WILD ONE. SHE'S THE NAKED ONE. SHE'S THE FRIEND OF THE SNAKES. SEE ZELDA. THE MANEATER. SEE ZELDA.* "I hurried away once more, only to arrive by another *detour* at the same place yet a third time. Now, however, a feeling overcame me which I can only describe as uncanny."[4] *WILLING SAILORS. SEE THAT OLD GIRL ZELDA. THE ONE YOU'VE HEARD ABOUT. ZELDA THE WILD ONE CAPTURED AT LAST.* My first impulse was to get back to the "make-believe" piazza where my father was making signs, and to avoid any further voyages of discovery. But then, for one reason or anOther, perhaps it was the secret grant money burning in my pocket, I decided to go inside to further explore what LIES behind (or beneath) this strange and unintended recurrence. *SEE THAT OLD GIRL ZELDA. THE ONE YOU'VE HEARD ABOUT. ZELDA THE WILD ONE CAPTURED AT LAST.*

I paid my quarter (exotic sightings were much cheaper in those days) and got in line behind a long precession of white men gazing. The tent was dark and hot and the wait was long. One after another "we" men climbed the stairs of a sturdy wooden platform overlooking a deep hole. *CHAINED IN A PIT OF SNAKES. STEP RIGHT UP. SEE ZELDA.* Soon it was my turn. I braced myself, readying my eyee/"I"s. Now things became really uncanny. I had expected (I had desired) to see a fearsome naked female, like the wild painted woman on the huge canvass signs with the snakes. "Look at that old bitch," said the sailor before me. His CAPITAL was becoming white liquid flowing. She was down there with the snakes alright. Maybe a thousand and one snakes. An old sagging breasts naked woman, dark skin and gray hair. *FROM THE DARKEST AMAZON.* There she sat twelve feet beneath the earth with a little electric rod shocking the snakes that circled her nakedness and a fly-swatter. There were plenty of flies to swat and if any of us men tossed down another quarter she'd swat one and eat it right before our eyes. Then the men would laugh. "Look at that old bitch!" I didn't look for long, feeling first uncanny and then terribly sad confused undone. What's the attraction of this strange sight? Why the repetition and "we" men's pleasure?

In the years 1912-1913, at more or less the same time as Durkheim was writing his sociological thesis on totemism, Freud produced the study *Totem and Taboo.* Examining many of the same ethnographic materials as Durkheim, Freud mixed-up a story of ritual sacrifice with that depicting the repetitious mythic origins of the *holy* (dreaded) *ghost* power of dead fathers. This is the power of what Lacan would later, following Levi-Strauss, Mauss and Durkheim, call the Symbolic Order. This power operates through repressive linguistic signs (or totems). This power constructs moral horizons around what is accessed by a given order of cultural memories and what must be screened away. This power, this order of sacrifice, is what effectively gives white Euro-American patriarchal social forms their day in court. Lawfully. Day after day after day.

Freud, of course, didn't exactly put it this way. Freud did write, however, about the ritual sacrificial conversion of deeds into words, noting the violence of repression and that "In the beginning was the deed."[5] What deed? *THE WILD ONE CAPTURED AT LAST. BROUGHT HERE BY A SPECIAL EXPEDITION IT'S ZELDA.* The deed of violent totemic substitutions (or doublings) and also the deed of fixing the material effects of such doublings "once and for all time" in a code without end. The CAPITAL deed of *fetishization* or representational law-making—the bloody whitemale deed demanded by a total linguistic fulfillment of linear time. The conscious realization of this deed appears forever delayed. This deed is simultaneously enacted and denied by a seemingly permanent (phallic) cultural erection of the Symbolic. This deed is credited on demand by a promise. Promises. Promises. A recurrent deed demanding the promise of fresh blood. *STEP RIGHT UP MY YOUNG MAN. PUT YOUR EYES IN THE (W)HOLES AND LET YOUR FINGERS DO THE WALKING. SEE THE BLOOD. SEE THE PLEASURE.* A transferential deed carried by the promise of male eye/"I" sight, the gaze, the gathering all objects before One's eyee/"I"s. A deed engendered by a sacrifice and driven by the unconscious promise of getting above all that matters. The disembodying promise of ontotheological language. The promise of immortality. The promise of fascist aesthetic rituals. The promise of ultramodernity. *STRONGER THAN A DOZEN WILLING SAILORS.*

This powerful white promise both oppresses others and represses the experience of self-contradiction. This promise works on behalf of the "normal" (male) subjects (of its modern language). Sometimes this promise's pairing of oppression and repression scratches at the surface of consciousness like a sacrificial ghost whose unnatural death never ceases to haunt the *guilty minds* of those stained by what's literally unthinkable. When this happens dread spreads like a dark and contagious virus as fear passes from the sudden recognition of a most unheavenly host to the now anxious mind-body of the parasite. In 1919 Freud put some of his thoughts about such dreaded hauntings on paper in an essay entitled "The Uncanny."

In what follows I attempt a partial re(w)riting of Freud's "uncanny" concerns with totem and taboo. In so doing, I pass Freud's words back through a provisional hermeneutic circling of others who have also dined upon, incorporated and/or excreted psychoanalytic language. I read (or eat) these words of others, as I do the words of Freud himself, as a kind of ambivalent gift that I have consumed without fully digesting. The "significant (to me) others" about whom, or through whom I am parasitically (w)riting, have, I believe, willfully (mis)interpreted "the proper (fatherly) name" of Freud in order to construct forms of social-psychoanalytic truth more adequate to the contradictory HIStorical demands for critical understanding, social change, mutual aid and healing, in which each author finds her or himself differentially positioned in (w)riting. What a mouthful! This is a way of acknowledging my own transferential dependence on a particular theoretical food chain. But, since I am presently concerned more with (again) re(w)riting Freud's story than with telling stories about all the stories that have already retold Freud's story, permit me simply to list some of the initials of others whose stories most influence mine. These include AG JO JB JL JD CC CL GB

JK DH RB CJ SS HM MF HC LI JG VB AH AR GCS CLS and JMac. I assure you these are (k)not all French (feminist) theorists.

Having acknowledged certain parasitic debts before (erringly) telling you how I think Freud's *mythic drama of sacrifice ought* to be dramatically re(w)ritten in terms of a *moral economy of sacrifice*, I feel it important to make a few remarks that differentiate Freud's texts from those produced in the wake of Durkheim and Mauss. Most obvious is the racism that envelops Freud's ethnocentric comparisons between the mental lives of "primitive peoples" and those of western neurotics and young children. Most striking is (k)not so much the racism evident in Freud's work, a common feature of much early ethnography, as the relative absence (or critically modified character) of ethnocentrism in (w)ritings stemming from the tradition of Durkheim and Mauss. While often lacking adequate HIStorical specificity, the Durkheimian path nevertheless reflexively (ab)uses knowledge of so-called "primitives" to raise questions which disturb the *normal savagery* or (hierarchical) complacency of western scientific logic. This sets critical French social psychoanalysis at a distance from Freud's comparisons between "primitives" and the neurotic or infantile behaviors of ill-adapted westerners.

The Durkheimian analysis of the totem also appears more adequate than Freudian theory when considering the social-sacrificial origins of what's taboo. For Durkheim, Mauss and Bataille a totemic sign becomes taboo because it is symbolically cut off from the indeterminacies of interdependent material-being-in-flux. This symbolic cut-off (or what Lacan calls "castration") sets the totemic object (of desire) apart from what is questionable or profane. At the same time, it sets in motion a (forbidden) desire for that which, through the erection of taboos, secures a totem's believability. In this sense, the same socio-logical or symbolic demands which make something forbidden simultaneously make it a conduit of desire.

At first glance, this appears quite the opposite of Freud's theory. Rather than locating taboos and the desire to break taboos as the after-effects of sacrificial exclusion, Freud states: "The basis of taboo is a forbidden action for which there exists a strong inclination in the unconscious."[6] This has often led to the interpretation that, prior to the establishment of a particular taboo or prohibition, Freud posited some original or even instinctual desire—an original desire for incest, an instinctual drive to have sex with one's mother or father. There are many passages in Freud's work that can easily be interpreted in this way. Concerning the ambivalent dread and desire of "savages" for taboo objects, Freud declares: "These prohibitions concerned actions for which there existed a strong desire."[7] What could be further from the Durkheimian tradition with its emphasis on prohibition as the cause of desire?

This reading of Freud's text is partially undermined by Lacan who finds the "truth" of the Freudian unconscious, (k)not in any preexisting package of instinctual desires, but in the always contemporary (ritual) repetition of the structural (linguistic) labor of sacrifice. For Lacan, it is a grave error to read Freud as a theorist of pre-social instincts. Lacan criticizes the "standard English" translation of Freud's use of the term *trieb* as instinct rather than drive. As an insistent pressure or pulsation, Freud "was led to hypothesize the 'drive' [only] after noticing the transformations undergone by desire in relation to its [missing, or always absent] objects."[8] This is to sociologically theorize desire in terms of sacrificial rites that engender the unconscious separation of what's believable from what's (k)not. This involves the erection of taboos repressing the moral recognition of a parasitic host of other, now forbidden, objects. These (im)possible objects (of desire) are made missing by the reductive linguistic violence of a given Symbolic Order.

One sociological effect of such *originary sacrifices* is that "we" who are constituted as subjects in this process now mourn the lack of and desire the return of a more fluid form of being-in-relatedness. Such fluidity is repressed by the onset of modern (phallic) language. As a substitute, this HIStorically specific form of language offers a desire for its own end or termination. Such language promises the eventual obliteration of the self-same lack it engenders, but only at "the end of time," only at a time that is forever deferred. This is a mythic promise of making good on what (here and now) always appears lacking. It operates in the short term language of loss and in the long term language of promised wholeness, restoration or redemption. The (im)possible fulfillment of this restrictive economic promise demands work. What is desired, moreover, may be less the material possession of specific objects than transferential contact with those little bits and pieces of "our" own human animal relationality that are severed from consciousness in the process of their totemic doubling. Hence, the production of (im)possible desires to (re)turn to an immanent (or intimate) unity of material-being-in-flux. Such desires may cathect around small fragments, gestures or bodily parts. These function as uncanny reminders of an (otherwise) unmemorable, archaic or preHIStoric "primal scene." This unconscious scene marks a loss of being given to fluid metamorphoses. This scene separates conscious subjectivity from the others it feeds off in constructing the (sacrificial) truths of any particular identity. In Lacan, the desire to compensate for such "unbelievable" loss is signified by an untranslatable desire for the (always) missing *objet petit a*. This is the desire for an *unconceivable otherness* that was "once upon a time" an indistinct aspect of ourselves in relation to (m)others. This is an archaic desire, founded (k)not in some universal instinct but in the HIStorical geography of specific sacrificial rites.

With these concerns in mind, it is possible to read (into) Freud's (w)ritings about totemic doublings a symptomatic story of the haunting or uncanny structural violence effected by patriarchal rites of sacrifice. In this sense, I read Freud's narrative (k)not as an adequate depiction of the psychic lives of "savages" but as suggestive of the psychic functioning of modern western symbolic relations. Such suggestiveness is set loose by Freud's (inadvertent) use of the foreign practices of others as something like a methodological mirror of estrangement. This "erring" strategy facilitates Freud's memorable (if distorted) glimpse of the sacrificial dynamics of "our" own culture. If (k)not for Freud's "creative" or "fictively theoretical" use of such mirrored distortions, this partial view of the sacrificial basis of social reality might remain unnoticed. A perversely symptomatic reading of relations of power as relations of erring interpretive access—this is my strategy for reading, and thus re(w)riting, Freud. There may be no other in (patriarchal) language.

Imagine that a dead father is the cause of everything lawful. Imagine that in the beginning was the word and (k)not the (sacrificial) deed. Near the close of *Totem and Taboo*, this is exactly what Freud asks us to imagine about the sacrificial dynamics of western culture. But where did the word come from? Like *her* it appears given as an economic substitute for one's own body. Like *her*, it is made to come lawfully by being exchanged in an orderly fashion between men. Exchanged for what? Exchanged for repressively quelling the uncanny horror of appearing to (k)not live outside and above nature. Exchanged for (k)not revealing the double murder LYING behind each and every MAN for himself. First the murder and forced disappearance of the (m)other's body; then the murder and denial of the murder of the (m)other's murderer; and, finally, the figurative defense of this (guilty) denial by the parasitic transformation of the dead father's flesh into a word, a sign or totem.

Here LIES the (k)not so original origins of metaphysical first principles—a compulsive repetition of the positive or conscious perception that there is NO NEED TO EXAMINE THE UNDENIABLE (SACRED) REALITY OF THE FACTS OF MAN'S ENVIABLE SOCIAL EXISTENCE. This is undoubtable. This belief is insured by the exclusionary force of taboo. It is also forever haunted by the threatened return of a recurrently repressed desire to tear up the body of the (now "significantly" darkened) Other, a body given to the lightening fast transmission of this powerful message. This would be to ruin, and thus release oneself (and one's Others) from the the (w)hole oppressive/repressive base mechanics of this HIStory. All these disturbing matters are suggested by Freud.

In the opening pages of *Totem and Taboo* Freud explains that his interest in "the so-called savage and semi-savage races" is that in them he recognizes "a well-preserved, early stage of our own development."[9] For better or worse "we" civilized people are said to pass developmentally out of that stage—childhood—into the self regulative maturity of adulthood. This is (k)not the case for the "primitive," neurotic or hysteric. Such persons are said to live with a "subtle infantile trait" organized around the simultaneous dread of and desire for incest. So deeply repressed is this desire in the "normal adult," states Freud, that many people will likely reject this hypothesis, simply because they already embody "a deep aversion to former incest-wishes."[10] But from where do such wishes originate? And whom or what are they protecting?

MODERN DREAD OF (THE GIFT OF) INCEST

Searching for clues to solve the riddle of incest, Freud turns to totemic peoples. These "savages" are said to be haunted by a fearful fascination with this taboo subject. In Freud's words, "Almost everywhere the totem prevails there also exists the law that the members of the same totem are not allowed to enter into sexual relations with each other"—the incest taboo.[11] Freud also notes that this initial prohibition is accompanied by another—the killing and eating of the totemic objects themselves. Why the conjuncture of these two (general economic) taboos?

Freud initially refrains from answering this question. He does, however, convincingly demonstrate the absence of any practical or innately biological basis for such prohibitions. He also recognizes that taboos symbolically unite people against what is forbidden. In this way, taboos, particularly the incest taboo, are said to be constitutive of the elementary structures of kinship. But what kinds of kinship? And what kinds of incest?

Already Freud's observations provoke questions that carry me between his text and others. In this, I am transferred away from stories concerning the violence of incest within contemporary patriarchal cultures, where parental abuse functions to reinforce, rather than challenge, social-sexual hierarchies operating in the name of some Father or Other.[12] I am drawn, instead, to more laughable stories, stories that dispell the ritual fixities of patriarchal socio-logic itself. In various archaic western imaginaries, to be one's (m)other's lover is to be Dionysos or maybe even Artemis in one of her phases. It is to live excessively under the sign of an always changing moon and to die ecstatic by returning to an ambivalent labyrinth of animal-mineral-vegetable relations. This is to (stupidly) empty oneself of all pretensions of a will to power without limits. This is clearly no unisexual matter. To give oneself to one's (m)others in such a complex and contradictory way is to become intimate with HERstory's changing personas. It is to recognize oneself in dramatic transference with multiply masked (m)other identities. These several faces are typically presented in three ritual forms: the airy sex wild and daring lesbian "virgin" huntress, the fertile wet nursing woman at the generous center of earth's waving surface, and the old woman associated with what's beneath the earth, the bearer of death's sting and life's continuous rebirthing. To dance, LIE, or sleep with one's (m)other in any of these forms is to commit incest. It is also to lose the workability of one's sacrificially engendered self-identity. It is to give away one's proper name, sign or distinguishing totem.

This is (k)not to have one's identity stolen but to give away one's identity. This is incest, but (k)not pornography, rape or sadistic abuse. This is incest but (k)not the mirrored substitution of one's offspring for the materiality of one's own death. This is incest but in a form preceding Oedipus, whose shadowy acting-out of (m)other love/father hate, and then the exact reverse, appears only

> at the historical crossroads [between emergent "states" of patriarchy] where two forms of succession meet and clash: an earlier one in which power was transferred from the king to his son-in-law through marriage to the king's daughter, thus through the agency of the "princess," [who as her father's daughter, rather than a participant in some (m)other's power, was already a displaced figure of earlier matriarchal-pagan rites] and a later form in which the transfer occurred directly from king to his own son. Because the transfer of power implied the necessary death, usually the killing, of the old king by the new one, the later form of succession gives rise in folklore to the theme of patricide....For in such a system, a son cannot wish, let alone execute, the killing of his father; Oedipus is a criminal, though unwittingly.[13]

Caught up in an emergent struggle between one form of becoming king and anOther, the criminal incest and patricide of Oedipus is a long way in HIStory from the transgressive incest-death-rebirthing of the ecstatic rites of Dionysos. Dionysos cross dresses and gives himself polysexed mad drunk and dancing to his (m)others. In this way he repels his father's call to war. This marks a ritual reconciliation between the restrictive materiality of human symbolic forms and our unnameable animal participation in nature. Such a reconciliation is prohibited with Oedipus and the story of incest told by Freud just before the first World War. The (w)riting of Oedipus, like Freud's (w)riting, is situated in a culture of TOTAL WAR. Here what is anxiously prohibited is (k)not simply sexual relations with fatherly named family members, but intimate relations with one's ever changing and thus never fully nameable (m)others. This is a matter of general economic difference. Unfortunately, this is also a difference that escapes Freud's analytic attention, except when he remarks, "I am at a loss to indicate the place of the great maternal deities who perhaps everywhere preceded the paternal deities."[14]

Freud's explanation of the prohibition of incest and of the taboo against killing and eating one's totem is explicitly Oedipal. This is a great HIStorical limitation. Arguing that "the beginnings of religion, ethics, society, and art meet in the Oedipus complex," Freud notes that "these problems of racial psychology can be solved through a single concrete instance, such as the relation to the father."[15] In *Totem and Taboo*, the story of Oedipus' ambivalent "love-hate" relation with his father is basically a homo(geneous)sexual story of men's relations of power. This is (k)not a homosexual story but a homo(geneous)sexual story. The difference is important. What is all too commonly interpreted as matters of sexual (dis)position (i.e. homosexual, heterosexual, bisexual, transsexual etc.) may be no-thing but the material and imaginary effects of powerful ritual prohibitions which put such supposedly "natural" (dis)positions into play in the first place.[16] In other words, whether prohibited or compulsively reinforced, various sexual (dis)positions have no purely "natural" existence independent of the ritualized institution of taboos or symbolic cut-offs that bring them restrictively into being in opposition to an otherwise indeterminate heterogeneity of human-animal relations in continual metamorphic flux.

In cultures dominated by patriarchal militarism, the ritual ban on men's periodic vulnerability to impure flows of swampy animal co-minglings with each other appears particularly great. This seems an apt description of the Oedipal cultures in which men feel *as if* naturally defensive toward one another. Within such cultures (such as the culture in which I find myself resistively (w)riting to you), the taboo against us (men) giving over to relations of mutual vulnerability and intimate bodily exchange with those whom our dominant rituals designate *as if* the *same sex* (and prohibiting women from doing likewise) appears to LIE constructively before all other prohibitions on incest. This is a prohibition against impurely touching and being touched by each other in any but the most disciplinary fleshy forms—a prohibition against being turned ecstatically inside out of our war vaults, restrictive economic treasuries and cultural closets of narcissistic self-possession; a prohibition against erotically moving, playing, loving or reciprocally giving ourselves away to other or (m)otherly identified men in ways that defy the militaristic games of competitive power to which so many of us (today in HIStory) seem most normatively given. The name used to designate such taboos—compulsory heterosexuality—appears to distortively (mis)recognize the material character of such normative constraints. Indeed, within a culture of TOTAL WAR between men (above, beyond and often through the bodies of women) there seems little heterogeneous and almost nothing ecstatic about such supposedly heterosexual forms.[17] This distinction, like the distinction between matriarchal and patriarchal social forms, appears outside the homo(geneous)-sexual confines of Freud's theory of the incest taboo.

Freud's story begins instead with a retelling of Darwin's tale of a "primal horde." This is the story of brothers who (militaristically) gang up on an all-powerful father (of preHIStory). These brothers are oppressed by a father (whose power) they love. They love this father's power so much they want to imitate the father's power. They love this father's power more than they love this father's body. This may be the meaning of father-love in a culture of TOTAL WAR. The sign of this (cumulative, nonfleshy and well guarded) power is that the father controls all the objects the sons' desire. Since in a culture of TOTAL WAR (between men) none of these objects can be other men, because this would entail being ritually opened by desire to relations other than those of restrictive economic competition, the objects which the father controls (almost supernaturally) are women animals which men liken to (vegetative) nature *herself*. The father, it seems, has these women animals or nature under his thumb and the sons want a piece of this (military) action. In order to become powerful like the father the sons rebel. They collectively kill "the old man" and consume his remains. In retelling this story, Freud cautions that he is (k)not referring to an allegory but the actual (mythic) beginnings of HIStory.

"Now they accomplished their identification with him by devouring him and each acquired part of his strength."[18] And yet, the "situation created by the removal of the father contained an element which in the course of time must have brought about an extraordinary longing for the [now materially absent] father. For the brothers who had joined forces to kill the father had each been animated by the wish to become like the father."[19] This is hardly the same as saying the brothers had desired the women the father controlled. Freud is emphatic that to carry out their collective act of patricide, the sons had to temporarily suppress their true feelings of tenderness for the father. Thus, after sacrificing the father to further their own imitation of the father's beloved power, the sons were rudely confronted with an even more terrible cultural dilemma. Each had now become the other's rival for possession of the women, who, in this HIStory, appear as nothing but signs of the dead father's power. Each also felt enormous guilt for murdering "he" who was truly the object of each brother's desire. What was this murderous (power) loving gang of sons to do?

What they did, declares Freud, the "father of psychoanalysis," was to offer a substitute for the fleshy father—the totemic sign. Under this sign they instituted a ban on both sexual relations with those who fell under the totem and also against doing (any more) harm to the father by prohibiting violence against his totemic representation (or bloodless name). In this, the sons "undid their deed by declaring that the killing of the father substitute, the totem was not allowed, and renounced the fruits of their deed by denying themselves the liberated women."[20] Except during "totemic feasts." At such "times between times" the binding moral economy of this crime and its "civilizing" solution was periodically reen-acted and then again driven from (conscious) memory. In this way, the law of the sons is really nothing but the perpetuation of the (militaristic) rule of the (dead) father, only stronger and more assured by the linguistic regularities of abstraction or (sacrificial) sign work. This represents the violent singularity of the father's mind without the occasional hesitations, confusions and finite vulnerability of the father's body. Here LIES the everlasting (restrictive economic) promise of patriar-chal language in its purity—the parasitic promise of dining upon the father's fleshy contradictions without losing the materiality of his murderous HIStorical and homo(geneous)sexual advantage.

EXCHANGING (COMMODITY) SIGNS: TRAFFICKING IN WOMEN

Claude Levi-Strauss and Jacques Lacan have both re(w)ritten Freud's sacrifi-cial drama. Each retells Freud's story of sons murdering their father in terms of the murderous effects of a fatherly Symbolic Order which silences the "nature" of (m)otherly tongues. Levi-Strauss' and Lacan's analysis have also provoked important feminist theorizations of the symbolic "origins" of patriarchal social exchange. Levi-Strauss contends that culture's symbolic demands LIE in the reduction of women to units of moral and economic value exchanged between men. This is what Gayle Rubin calls a "trafficking in women." As "signs" which are "given" (and received) among men, the exchange of women is pictured as constructing obligatory moral bonds (of kinship) between and within the bodies of those "given" (to linguistic difference) in this fashion. It's (k)not that women represent something to men. It is simply that, when given as signs, women's bodies become "as if" nothing but material conduits for men's (militaristically (dis)positioned) communications with each other. As such, (for straightmale men) "her" body is said to operate as a kind of ritual technology of communication, a repetitious (re)charging of restrictive economic male bonding. In this, the gift *he* makes of *her* circulates with the kind of effervescence that Mauss portrayed as the "ambiguous" essence of the "total social fact." *He* senses it perhaps in the smell of *her* fragrance, touch of *her* lips, curl of *her* smile, or wink of *her* eye. In this *her* presence operates as if a sign of *his*. Materially, of course, *her* experience may be more contradictory and complex, but perhaps (k)not from *his* narcissistic positioning within this sacrificial sign-system. This is what makes a man's refusal to give away and receive the gift of the women at one's disposal taboo. To com-mit incest (in this culturally transgressive way) is to refuse to enter into (and remain within) the homo(geneous)sexual and communicative networks of patri-archy's arbitrary (if morally demanded) imperatives.[21] It is to refuse to impose a symbolic order upon the otherwise directionless wanderings of nature *herself*. It is also to resist a seemingly timeless economic differentiation between culture and nature as *he* gives *her* a particular identity and as *his* mind passes through *her* body and keeps on moving.

(K)not naive to the contradictory positioning of women in this sacrificial rite, Levi-Strauss points toward the *double bind* or split-minded subjectivity this incest taboo presents for women. On one hand, *she* is faced with the promise of being (passively) given as nothing but a sign between men (at war). On the other, *she* is, like *him*, an active agent of communication, except for the fact that the only things *she* can legally communicate are (k)not of her own making. This, *her prisoner's dilemma*, has led some feminist critics to read Levi-Strauss' analysis as a depiction of the sacrificial origins of patriarchal culture. Caught up like a commodity in *his* market *she* is sentenced to a life where cultural meanings are ordered by *his* totemic sign-work.

In describing the Symbolic Order as operating "in the name of the Father," and in (de)positing the promise of communicative subjectivity as a "phallic" promise, Lacan also appears to give notice to the violence of (patriarchal) culture. As an encore to Levi-Strauss' and Freud's analysis of incest, Lacan interprets the killing (and the repression of the killing) of the mythic "Father of Prehistory" as a symptom of the abstract violence imposed upon the human psyche by all linguistic (cultural) exchange. This aspect of Lacan's work has attracted the attention of more than a few feminist readers. As Gayle Rubin points out, in Lacan the symbolic "phallus passes through the medium of women from one man to another.... [W]omen go one way, the phallus the other. It is where we aren't. In this sense, the phallus is more than a feature which distinguishes the sexes, it is the embodiment of male status, to which men accede, and in which certain rights inhere—among, the right to a woman."[22]

Despite the provocative nature of each man's theories, both Levi-Strauss and Lacan often appear to take for granted (perhaps, inconsistently) the "reality" of some prelinguistic or "biologically given" gendered subjectivity. In Levi-Strauss, the problem LIES, as Teresa de Lauretis points out, with the anthropologist's use of a kind of "totalizing discourse." As such, Levi-Strauss conflates the materiality of exchange (and its partial contestation) with the "syllogistic" operation of binary linguistic distinctions. This leads both to "positing woman as the functional opposite of subject (man)" and to overlooking "the fact that the terms or items of exchange must already be constituted, in a 'hierarchy of value,' which means that women's economic value must be predicated on a pre-given sexual division which must already be social."[23]

De Lauretis also notes that Lacan's recurrent (mis)recognition of the visual character of language appears to go against the "effective implications of the psychoanalytic theory he himself developed."[24] In this, de Lauretis concurs with Stephen Heath, who observes that, while the Lacanian framework "should forbid the notion of some presence from which difference is derived," in actuality it erringly "instates the visible as the condition of symbolic functioning, with the phallus the standard of visibility required: seeing is from the male organ."[25] And what of other senses—touch, smell, taste and hearing? In what ways might these other mediums of communication be either more accessible to women or more resistive to the domination of women's sight by modern men's gaze? Lacan (dis)appears into the dark on this issue. It is, nevertheless, interesting to note how Lacan's dissident student, Luce Irigaray deconstructs the primacy of vision while underscoring other sensual modalities of knowledge.

Unlike Levi-Strauss and Lacan, Teresa de Lauretis demands that gender never be considered outside the multiple and contradictory (ritual) technologies of its HIStorical representation. To suggest that the incest taboo is brought into being by (fatherly) men visibly exchanging women may point to exclusionary mechanisms at work in patriarchy. It does (k)not, however, radically theorize how either such men or women come representationally into being "as if" nothing but binary paired opposites. From whence the moral and economic authority of this "hard to resist" and seemingly absolute difference? Why, moreover, has such alleged difference become so thoroughly linked to the related western metaphysical separation between culture and nature?

GENEALOGICAL DESCENT: THE AMBIVALENCE OF SYMBOLIC EXCHANGE

In the second section of *Totem and Taboo*, Freud elaborates his concerns with the desirability of forbidden objects by underscoring the emotional ambivalence felt toward totemic beings. On one hand, such objects are viewed as consecrated or positively sacred. On the other, they haunt those who believe in them with the uncanny lure of something dark, unclean and forbidden. Citing the ambivalence felt by "primitive peoples" for their enemies, priest-kings and the dead, Freud makes connections between this mix of conscious fear and unconscious fascination and the repressed sacrificial origins of culture itself—what Freud (mis)recognizes as the ORIGINARY VIOLENCE of patricide.

Among "moderns" the collective recognition of ambivalence is said to have declined. Only "neurotics" or "hysterics" repeatedly manifest the compulsive ambivalence between tenderness and hostility (or love-hate) that Freud viewed as characteristic of totemic societies. While indicating that "a tangible HIStorical change is probably concealed" behind this fateful disaggregation of ambivalent emotions, Freud does (k)not suggest what such change entails.[26] What he does suggest is that the (repressive) reduction of ambivalence leads to the internalization of (culture-founding) guilt. In this sense, "moderns" are denied the kind of festive "group therapy" available to "primitives" in the ceremonial displacement of their ambivalence. "Primitives" collectively enact "projective" rituals such as the staged killing and commemoration of respected enemies, the alternation between distanced reverence and frenzied aggression directed toward chiefs, priests, other rulers, and elaborate rites of mourning aimed at quieting feelings of envy in relation to the dead. Such archaic rituals literally consume time. As such, they are distinguishable from the "time saving" rites of "moderns" who repressively screen ambivalent feelings from conscious memory.

In modernity, unrepressed ambivalence may itself appear taboo, childish, hysterical or neurotic. Indeed, for Freud the "social danger" posed by the "acting out" of neurotics is an outcome of their (asocial) inability to repressively "forget" contradictory feelings of love-hate directed toward figures of (fatherly) authority. In this way, "neurotics" may contagiously undermine the lawful repression of "modern society's" murderous origins. This is perhaps the unspeakable "secret," (k)not simply of the "neurotic's" painful individual experience, but of the symbolic threat she or he "hysterically" poses to the reproduction of demanded repressions. By resisting "amnesia" concerning society's sacrificial origins, the neurotic becomes dramatically charged with the ambivalent "electricity" of a taboo itself. Such "chargedness" sends sparks flying as the "neurotic's" ambivalence may "hysterically" disrupt the psychic borders between a contradictorily given self and its "others." In this way, states Freud (quoting Wundt):

> Persons or things which are regarded as taboo may be compared to objects charged with electricity, they are the seat of tremendous power which is transmissible by contact, and maybe liberated with destructive effect if the organisms which provoke its discharge are too weak to resist it,....the strength of a magic influence.[27]

As a "modern" example of the disruptive electricity of such "ambivalence," Helene Cixous finds herself drawn to the "hysterical figure" of Freud's resistive patient, Dora. Dora's almost theatrical display of ambivalence is said to operate as "a sort of hideous merry-go-round" that gives bodily notice to the "system of silent contracts," that "double game" by which the patriarchal exchange of women normatively occurs.[28] Rather than permitting men's words to cut through to each other through the medium of her body, Dora coughs up a hole in the (w)hole system of patriarchal exchange. Rather than assuming her "lawful" place as a gift, Dora symptomatically "manages to say what she doesn't say, so intensely that the men drop like flies.... It is she who is the victim, but the others come out in shreds."[29] These others include Freud, who Dora dismisses like a "servant girl" caught up in a homo(geneous)sexual economy of men. Connected in "unspeakable ways" to an archaic economy of eroticism involving "a very beautiful feminine homosexuality, a love for women that is astounding," Dora resists Freud's masterful reinscription of her ambivalent dreams and thus leaves his psychoanalytic "studies in hysteria" literally in fragments.[30] Accordingly:

> Dora seemed...to be the one who resists the system, the one who cannot
> stand that the family and society are founded on the body of women, on
> bodies despised, rejected, bodies that are humiliating once they have been
> used. And this girl—like all hysterics, deprived of the possibility of saying
> directly what she perceived, of speaking face-to-face or on the telephone as
> father B or father K or Freud, et cetera do—still has the power to make it
> known....Yes, the hysteric, with her way of questioning...makes demands of
> the others in a manner that is intolerable to them and that prevents their
> functioning as they function (without their restricted little economy). She
> destroys their calculations.[31]

A related interpretation is offered by Catherine Clément. Clément parallels the
"anti-establishment" ambivalence of hysteria to the festive annulment of the
Symbolic Order generated by the pagan sorceress or witch. Introducing "periodic" disorder into the interstices of culture, both the medieval sorceress and the
modern hysteric inject "the suspense of ellipses" into the linear pathways of
patriarchal language forms. This threat (and its fascination) is mirrored by those
"natural disturbances," women's menstrual periods, "which are the epitome of
paradox, order and disorder. It is precisely in this natural periodicity that fear,
terror, [and] that which is offside in the symbolic system will lodge itself."[32]
Transgressing the boundaries between culture and nature, the periodic rites of the
sorceress and hysteric, like the ambivalence figured in the "natural symbolism"
of menstruation, represent a deconstructive challenge to patriarchal exchange. In
so-called *anthropophagic* (archaic or aHIStorical societies) the return of periodic
ambivalence gives notice to the artificial nature of culture itself. This is a celebration of society in reverse; not a return to some more primordial nature but a
"turning around" of things given "in nature" by totemic artifice or language.
This is festival. Within its so-called "feminine" reversals:

> Social life is...'upside down.' Everything happens backward, and even bodies
> find a way to turn upside down. The 'Paradises' of Hieronymous Bosch are
> like that: lovers join, their heads in the air and feet on the wall; proportions
> reverse, fruits and animals are gigantic and the minuscule elect can straddle
> them, penetrate them, become absorbed in them. One of the elect caresses
> himself next to a flower; his head is invisible, entirely underwater; his
> elongated hands envelop his penis, which is falling back toward the water—
> yet erecting—toward his head. His legs, which are spread apart for the
> caress, form a wide V; and the space between his thighs, a fleshy fruit, red
> and pierced by a black thorn is swelling. Another figure, his bent legs in the
> air, has his hands on the ground. Neither his head nor his torso is visible;

they are stuck in several wrappings of feathers and shells making the shape
of an egg or upside down flower. The first shell is fruity and pink, the second
is made of tawny feathers, and the third is dark and spotted with pale pink.
The plover's tail slides between the legs of the upside-down lover. A flowery
fruit is drifting; it is a large, round, orange berry with hard and thorny palm
leaves bursting from it. A delicate red tuft, vibrant as the trembling fruit of a
strawberry tree, comes out of the petals.... A couple of the elect caress each
other, protected by a bubble of veins that run throughout the menningeal
membrane; wrapped in the flower's pistil, they are emerging from a fruit.
Nature and culture are abolished, all bodies mingled: animals, fruits, and
humans are in the same interwining. Flowers penetrate, fruits caress, animals open, humans are instruments of this universal *jouissance*.[33]

Such festive ambivalence is also a seductive aspect of what Jean Baudrillard
calls *symbolic exchange*. Variously described as an archaic, feminine, or general
economic form, symbolic exchange is characterized by the excessive periodic
expulsion of the sacrificial fruits of culture itself. In symbolic exchange, ambivalence challenges "the false transparency of the sign."[34] Like the hysteric, except
for its collective (aHIStorical) embodiment of counter-memories, symbolic exchange plays out the "reversibility of the gift in the countergift, of exchange in
sacrifice, of time in the cycle, of production in destruction of life in death, and of
each linguistic term in the anagram: in all domains, reversibility—cyclical reversal, annulment—is the one encompassing form. It puts an end to the linearity of
time, language, [restrictive] economic exchange and accumulation, and power."[35]
This heralds the playful return of sacrificially repressed difference, a sacrifice of
the power appropriated by the originary sacrifices demanded by a given Symbolic
Order.

All this is put to the stakes by the "straightforward" HIStorical violence of
modern CAPITAL. Literally, one pagan peasant woman sacrificed after another.
Banished (or driven unconsciously into the body of the hysteric) are the sorceress
and her festival of reversals. Overlaid upon these is a thoroughly masculine
system of abstract utility and logical equivalence. In this, the idealist abstractions
of modern use and exchange value come to safeguard against the dangerous
materiality of symbolic exchange with its periodic threats of returning to a wild
circling dance of incomparable difference—"the surpassing of old ritual and
symbolic constraints."[36]

This is the birth of what what Levi-Strauss calls *anthropoemic* society, a
society that violently resists its own reversal. Rather than periodically vomiting
up its own restrictive economic enclosures, modern western society vomits its
"abnormal" ones into the protected disciplinary spaces of the prison, hospital,
asylum and school. The patriarchal transformation of ecstatic sorcery into

hysterical anxiety is a case in point. As Allon White points out,

> no longer bound by the strict timetable of the ritual year,...carnivalesque
> fragments have formed unstable discursive compounds, sometimes disrup-
> tive, sometimes therapeutic. Hysteria in the late nineteenth century was
> doubtlessly compounded in part by this material and what had been
> excluded at the level of communal practice returned to the level of subjec-
> tive articulation, as both phobia and fascination, in the individual patient.
> It is more than accidental that the major foci of carnival pleasure—food,
> dirt and mess, sex and extreme body movements find their neurasthenic,
> unstable, and mimicked counterparts in the discourses of hysteria.[37]

Denied all contact with her (m)other's bodies, except as mediated by the
reductive utility of her father's functionally equivalent laws, the hysteric is a
CAPITAL embodiment of symbolic ambivalence constrained by the phallic illusions of modern social power.

"MAN"—THE ANIMAL WHO DENIES HIMSELF (AND OTHERS)

Here LIE questions about the incest taboo that exceed those concerned primarily with which cultured agents are denied sexual access to what sign-worked
bodies. I am here referring to the taboo against human animals generously giving
themselves over to (m)others and thus transgressing (patriarchal) culture's restrictive economic demands. Related questions have been posed by Georges Bataille.
Nevertheless, a critical dialogue with feminism carries social theory well beyond
Bataille toward *genealogical* concerns with the imposition of patriarchal rites.
Bataille initially repeats Levi-Strauss' restrictive economic analysis of the incest
taboo as a means of binding communication between men. Later he exceeds
Levi-Strauss' critique by examining general economic taboos against generously
abandoning the sacrificial privileges of appearing to significantly transcend a
world where human, animal, mineral, and vegetable life-forms all co-mingle. This
ecstatic loss of human distinction represents a laughable poetic fall out of all
productive or WORKABLE human communications into the useless fires of self
expending intimacy. For Bataille, this is a (sacrificial) meal in itself, really.

With Levi-Strauss, Bataille recognizes the symbolic prohibition of incest as
mandating a ceremonial exchange of women. This occurs with "the same sort of
significance" as the sharing of a "glass of champagne"—both "stimulate" a
feeling of comraderie between men. Bataille also appears alert to gender-specific
differences effected by such effusive exchange, noting, "Marriage is a matter less
for the partners than for the man who gives the woman away."[38] Still, from
Bataille's point of view, "Levi-Strauss' propositions describe only one aspect of

the transition from animal to man."[39] More decisive is the taboo against realizing the indeterminate materiality of human animal nature. This taboo is imposed HIStorically by "man's" labor. By this, Bataille means the militaristic production of a distinctively "human" economic distance from a nature "man" denies "he's" complexly part of. This is a prohibition against human animal incest with one's (m)others, a "denial of sensuality; of the carnal and animal."[40]

For Bataille, the ritual basis for this denial involves the uniquely human structuring of *work*. In opposition to the material exuberance of intimate human participation within nature, "work," states Bataille, "demands the sort of conduct where effort is in a constant ratio with productive efficiency. It demands rational behavior where the wild impulses worked out on feast days...are frowned upon. If we were unable to repress these impulses we should not be able to work, but work introduces the very reason for repressing them."[41] Bataille was a perversely Marxist social theorist and an avant-garde political (w)riter. He was also trained in Medieval HIStory. There was no-thing that convinced him that the *order of things* in which he found himself anxiously working had existed for all time. Nor was this order immune to radical social change. Having passed through psychoanalysis on his way to sociology, Bataille sought to passionately dispel cultural demands that positioned his body over against others. He didn't want to be identified with a blindly abusive death father and said so repeatedly in (w)riting. Concerning the repetitious origins of the incest taboo, Bataille (w)rote:

> Man flatly denies the existence of his animal needs; most of his taboos relate to them and these taboos are so strikingly universal and apparently so unquestioned that they are never discussed.... [M]an is the animal that does not just accept the facts of nature, he contradicts them. Thus he alters the exterior world of nature. Out of it he makes tools and manufactured objects which make up a new world. Similarly he contradicts his own nature, he refuses to give free rein to the satisfaction of his animal needs, needs that a true animal will satisfy without reservation. It must also be agreed that there is a connection between man's denial of the world as he finds it and his denial of of the animal element in himself.... [I]n so far as man exists there exist also work on one hand and the denial of the animal element in man's nature on the other.[42]

From where in HIStory does this MAN of whom (or as who) Bataille is (w)riting come from? Following Bataille, Foucault poses a genealogical answer—MAN as "we" know him exists only since the sacrificial onset of modernity, only since the (cultural) death of God and the ritual centering of a seemingly infinite will to power in the human subject "himself."[43] Notice that I'm (k)not using gender inclusive language in referring to this MAN. The MAN I have in (my) mind is (k)not gender inclusive. *STEP RIGHT UP MY YOUNG MAN. PUT YOUR EYES IN THE (W)HOLES AND LET YOUR FINGERS DO THE WALKING. SEE THE BLOOD. SEE THE PLEASURE.* The MAN of whom I'm (w)riting has been power-fully constituted by modern ritual sacrifices which "only recently turned man into an economic animal. *Homo economicus* is not behind us," wrote Mauss, "but before, like the moral man, the man of duty, the scientific man and reason-able man. For a long time man was something quite different: and it is not so long now since he became a machine...a calculating machine."[44] This is a MAN of modern patriarchy—THE MAN ideally typified by CAPITAL, heterosexist discipline, production, white Protestantism and a technological refusal of a finite animal positioning in nature. In general, this Man's attitude is "one of refusal. Man has leant over backwards in order not to be carried away by the process [of nature], but all he manages to do by this is hurry it along at an even dizzier speed."[45]

This last statement by Bataille is of particular importance. It concerns the impetus to transgress the anxious boundaries that modern Man erects between himself and nature. For Bataille, this ambivalent desire for incest, a desire to LIE with modern man's (m)others, is the result of the taboo *he* places on bodily reciprocity with nature. It is a desire for Man's own death and his return to ambivalent relations of being within rather than above nature. (K)not to nostalgi-cally return to some form of "pure" nature, but to descend to the sacrificial crossroads where the artificial divisions between *his* (w)riting culture and *her* sacrificially inscribed nature are periodically suspended. Here, Man is greeted by the laughable horrors and self-expending eros of ecstatic gift-giving. Here, the homo(geneous)sexual laws of restrictive economic logic are literally reversed, as law-givers are rebelliously recognized as murderers of their (m)others. Here, those who would seek the law's annulment must first (partially) die to them-selves, thereby freeing the possibilities of new ritual technologies for making connections between what was previously unimaginable or only a dream. This is festival. This is undefinable eros. This is a rite of returning to difference that Bataille, as a medievalist, was given to observe as a continuous, if partially suppressed, feature of the western mix of Pagan and Roman Catholic cultures, until the dawn of the Enlightenment, Protestantism and the seemingly timeless age of CAPITAL.

PUTTING DIONYSOS TO WORK: THE STRAIGHTMALE LABOR OF PATRIARCHY

In CAPITALIst modernity, festive rites are severely restricted—channeled into a more workable form and/or displaced onto the darkly imaged bodies of others (women, nonwhites, gays, and the so-called "dangerous classes"). Against this displacement, Bataille "howls" for the return of the carnivalesque Dionysos, whose *classical* coming into the world depended on the murder of his mother by his father—the criminal Zeus striking down Semele in a flash of lightning. But this was only the *classical* Dionysos, the tragic hero deprived of his (m)others by the sacrificial violence of a sky-god father, against whom he would remain in perpetual revolt.

Today, feminist scholarship offers us a more radical genealogy of the son who refused to refuse his (m)other's dark light dark cycles for a father's military-industrial promise of sunlight without end. Bataille's words point (me) in this direction as well. Moreover, as a man (w)riting within the sacrificial throes of patriarchy this is no minor gift.[46] I read Bataille's call for critically re(w)riting the meaning of the incest taboo away from the trajectory of Oedipus and back into the labyrinth of Dionysos as encouraging the possibilities of a more generous male imaginary. To follow Bataille's descent is perhaps somewhat risky, even maddening, for men (of modern social power). But hopefully, in time, such descent may open collective spaces that are less violent, if certainly more laughable, than "our" normal or normative ways of acting toward (or against) those whose sacrifice modernity demands.

More challenging, still, are *counter-memories* offered by such provocative texts as Monica Sjoo and Barbara Mor's *The Great Cosmic Mother*[47] and Arthur Evans' *The God of Ecstasy* and *Witchcraft and the Gay Counterculture*.[48] These critical examinations of pagan epistemological practices in many ways exceed Bataille's. Each is richly suggestive of a genealogy of staightmale sacrificial violence directed against the reflexive partiality of cyclical social forms of giving (and taking back culture) within nature. This reflexive articulation of paganism opposes any absolute distinction between cultural technologies and natural processes. As a cultural tendency it has been continuously suppressed by the *winner take all* ethos of modern patriarchal forms. Under the sign of such paganism "we" are radically reminded, (k)not only of what is HIStorically missing in the instrumental rationality of patriarchal CAPITAL, but also of alternative economies kept alive in the marginalized rituals and contradictory carnal knowledges of a diversity of women and gay men. In this reflexive counter-HIStory, Dionysos appears (playfully) as the polysexual son/lover/brother/sister lover of (m)others (the distinctions blur as here, *his* sex, like *hers* is (k)not one) who periodically gives away his/her body—ecstatic, cross-dressed, and "(im)possibly feminine."[49]

Dionysos is (k)not womanly, in the sense of pertaining to the lives of women (a distinction made most powerfully by Alice Jardine in (w)riting[50]), but "(im)possibly feminine" in a charming animal-mineral-vegetable sort of way. This is suggestive of a radically different form of incest—a mode of (k)not knowing or descending out of what is hegemonically taken for granted. To dramatically enact such parodic knowledge is to playfully recognize that "we" humans are admittedly in nature and that nature is impurely continuous. In this sense, there are never only two binarily opposed sexes or genders, but always a panoply of HIStorically inscribed bodily positions in contradictory relations to (m)others. Some of these modes may be more materially generous than others. Much contemporary feminist-pagan (w)riting refers backward in HIStory to a time when the ritual spacing of social power neither pressed women below men, nor materially supported men's effort to blast off away from or at the planet.

I do (k)not mean to wax nostalgic, but (w)riting like that of Sjoo and Mor's provocatively suggests that the waning of reciprocal human technological relations in nature (as opposed to Man's technological mastery of nature) is neither a timeless state of affairs nor a fully accomplished *total social fact*. This is to create mythic openings for alternative social science ficitional futures. A somewhat counter-encyclopedic treatment of everything from rites of food, sex, death, labor, science and the lunar rhythmic exchange of bodily fluids, to the racist and imperial assault on the continuation of pagan sensibilities by global CAPITAL, *The Great Cosmic Mother* represents a challenging example of the genealogical construction of counter-memories, a radical HIStory or HERstory of our hierarchical present.

The aim of genealogical (re)search is to strategically open our convergent HIStories to the possibility of things making a radical difference. To designate such radical difference as being "(im)possibly feminine" is, of course, to play with words. It is to also conjure an "old way" of referring to sacred (sociological) transgressions. Before (and after) there were two sexes, there was (k)not one sex but a plenitude of sex devoid of singularity. And this sex was thought of as feminine in a forever changing and (im)possible sort of way. This was a sex that changed faces like the moon, or like a tree changing seasons in a Toni Morrison novel, or like the changing of masks by Iroquois shamans (before the coming of whitemale demons with guns). This was a sex, like a woman's body moving from ovulation to menses and then the reverse; a sex that is neither a clitoris, nor a womb, nor a tomb, although it may pass through the forms of each. Although this multi-phased sex was "once upon a time" called a goddess, neither *her* sacred body (which was (k)not at all the same as *his* biology) nor *her* mind (which was reflexively full of holes into (and out) of relations with others) were conceived as either homogeneous or totalistic entities. Nor were *her* mind and body viewed as truly differentiated from each other. Quite the opposite. So why (k)not (laughingly) call "archaic" ways of being indistinct from nature "(im)possibly feminine?" Once upon a time, before the ritual imposition of male military models and their restrictive economy, this is exactly what such old and "sacred" ways were called. Honestly, as hard as it may be for Baby M to believe, it was once ritually known that human animals come from and return to (m)other bodies.

Judging from some symptoms, Lacanian social-psychoanalysis knew this as well; even if ambivalent as to how to respond to such a wisely stupid awareness. The question to be (multiply) faced is this: how to critically embody the contradictory understanding that, if the temporal-spatial movement of bodies (including human HIStorical bodies) POWERFULLY transforms what matters into spiralling waves of energy (and the reverse) then this process is (at this very moment) effecting and being effected by everything imaginable. Including, for instance, how you are presently reading (or sacrificially re(w)riting) these words. How, IN OTHER WORDS, to (w)rite with the awareness that you and I are EFFECTIVELY in the same PARASITIC FOOD-CHAIN? Efforts to (reflexively) come to terms with this awareness are located at the crossroads of a variety of postmodern epistemologies. These include varieties of feminism (including feminist-paganism and such radically science-fiction feminisms as "Cyborg-feminism"), certain versions of sociological poststructuralism, Voodoo, and even aspects of the most "advanced" quantum and chaotic forms of BIG WESTERN SCIENCE. This admittedly QUEER conjunction of knowledge forms may seem excessive but I believe it also represents a (repeatedly) necessary first step for choreographing a contemporary practice of critical theory. Only after such a profoundly STUPID first moves is the emergence of a truly POWER-REFLEXIVE PERFORMANCE OF SOCIAL THEORY possible. I am, here, imagining of a way of deconstructively (ab)using words theoretically that will HOPEFULLY make a (loving) MATERIAL DIFFERENCE in our (practical and political) relations to others.

THE GENEALOGICAL METHOD: DESCENT AND EMERGENCE

While my words might appear (to some of you) as caught up in a desire for a counter-cultural enactment of theory, I am (k)not in any way writing about for some naive *hocus pocus* or parasitic "New Age" consciousness.[51] Believe me, I have learned more from the Black Madonna than that. My evocation of a pagan epistemological critique is (k)not aimed at returning to some lost garden of goddess worship. I am instead suggesting the possibilities of multiple, if convergent, methods that may better facilitate giving notice to and thus evicting the slum landlords of whitemale and patriarchal socio-logic. This restrictive economic logic, as it circulates within and between the bodies it credits or/and threatens to bankrupt, today controls, if (k)not exactly dictates, where, when and how of most of "us" currently eat, sleep and think about what it is that we are and are (k)not doing. This logic cuts differentially into "our" bodies, unevenly penetrating our minds with certain ideas, while censoring others. Enough is enough! How to critically imagine ways out of this most ungiving social reality (back and forth) into some (m)others? Or die trying? Quesalid embodied one effective symbolic strategy (in anOther social time and space). So did Artemis,

Erzuli and Dionysos, each in their multiply *dragged* aspects. But closer to the scene of "our" own mythic present I find Foucault's genealogical strategy particularly helpful. When most radically deployed, Foucault's methods challenges "us" to risk the materiality of "our" own (in)significance before (re)producing the ideality of (partial) meanings.

Foucault's methods honor "archaic" demands for (deconstructive) descent prior to the (constructive) promise of theoretical emergence. This is a secret of *genealogical* HIStory. To know what I mean perhaps some of you must risk descending (out of) yourselves. This is (k)not uniform advice. As Foucault was all too painfully aware, somebodies are unfortunately quite low in the (w)hole already. Beginning from the position of descent is (k)not the only one way to enact a genealogical method. There is (k)not any predetermined place of origin in this dance. This dance is spiral. For those already condemned to HIStory's margins a better first movement might involve preparing for the emergence of collective forms of social resistance. But for those of us already somewhat privileged, in one way or anOther, initial descent may prove a radical mandate. Either way, this dance is (k)not linear. Waxing waning waxing, emerging descending emerging, or the reverse—it is an alternating rhythmic movement that is demanded, (k)not the cut and dry econometrics of a linear sequence.

Of the genealogical method, Foucault (w)rites, it "is gray, meticulous and patiently documentary. It operates on a field of entangled and confused parchments, on documents that have been scratched over and recopied many times" — like our bodies.[52] Foucault recommends that the genealogist attend to the singularity of "unpromising" events falling outside, or at the margins, of HIStory's "monotonous [sacrificial] finality" and that s/he be sensitive to patterns of "recurrence," while also examining possibilities that are denied material realization. In this, the genealogist may come to recognize that what poses as the true "origin" of any event is nothing but a "fleeting articulation" of power and knowledge. "Truth is [thus] undoubtably that sort of error that cannot be refuted because it was hardened into an unalterable form in the long baking process of history."[53] Rather than trying to uncover some original truth, genealogy constructively realizes "that there is 'something altogether different' behind things: not a timeless and essential secret, but the secret that they have no essence or that their essence was fabricated in a piecemeal fashions [like a collage] from alien forms."[54]

This is a self-implicating discovery. It suggests that one is forever (re)constructing rather than simply revealing origins. This prompts Foucault to embrace a methodological strategy that literally laughs at the solemnities of (always fictive) origins. This is a DOUBLE STRATEGY involving an interplay of *descent* and *emergence*. In using the term descent Foucault asks that "we" follow Nietzsche (and Dionysos), (k)not back in time to restore an alleged unbroken linear continuity (filling in the wholes, stopping the gaps) but the opposite—to make holes in what might, otherwise, appear seamless and totalizing. This is (k)not the appropriation of a stable, solid or continuous set of "facts," but "an unstable assemblage of faults, fissures and heterogeneous layers." This challenges the powerful facticity of a given Symbolic Order. As such, "descent is not the erecting of foundations: on the contrary, it disturbs what was previously considered immobile; it fragments what was thought unified; it shows the heterogeneity of what was imagined consistent with itself."[55]

As a strategy of dislodging the masked character of artificial constructions, descent involves a bodily retracing of previous descents. This makes reflexive demands both on the body of the researcher and on "one's" object of inquiry. Accordingly:

> Descent attaches itself to the body. It inscribes itself in the nervous system, in temperament, in the digestive apparatus; it appears in faulty respiration, in improper diets, in the debilitated and prostrate body of those whose ancestors committed errors. Fathers have only to mistake effects for causes, believe in the reality of an an 'afterlife,' or maintain the value of eternal truths, and the bodies of their children will suffer.[56]

If the epistemic effect of these words appear radically pagan, Foucault's comments about emergence are no less so. Having descended into a bodily recognition of the artifactual vectors of truth's power, emergence marks the constructivist entry of new forces. It "is their eruption, the leap from the wings to center stage."[57] But this is also a sacrificial leap. It pushes other things aside from memory, just as it asserts its own (always provisional) claims to truth's power. In this way, emergence suggests a social form of *palimpsest*, a dancing overlay of images, whereby one "text" can only be read through the screenings of others. This is related to Derrida's iteration of différance—a perpetual play of delays and exclusions. According to Foucault, this is space "of confrontation but not as a closed field offering the spectacle of a struggle among equals. Rather...it is a 'non-place,' a place of pure distance, which indicates that the adversaries do not belong to a common space.... In a sense, only a single drama is ever staged in this 'non-place' the endlessly repeated play of dominations."[58] In this, genealogy reflexively implicates the researcher in a ritual social movement in and out of particular social forms. For the modern researcher, positioned as if eagle-eyed above the object of "one's" analysis, Foucault's method may appear savagely incestuous. It unlawfully cojoins the bodies of investigating subjects with the objects of our own research. Moreover:

> This relationship of domination is no more a "relationship" than the place
> where it occurs is a place; and precisely for this reason, it is fixed, through-
> out its history, in rituals, in meticulous procedures that impose rights and
> obligations. It establishes marks of its power and engraves memories on
> things and even within bodies. It makes itself accountable for debts and
> gives rise to the universe of rules, which is by no means designed to temper
> violence, but rather satisfy it.[59]

TECHNO-MAGIC AND THE "UNCANNY" OMNIPOTENCE OF THOUGHT

In the third of the four essays composing *Totem and Taboo,* Freud attends to
the "omnipotence of thought," a "savage" characteristic said to dominate the
psychic processes of young children, neurotics and so-called "primitive peoples."
A term Freud borrows from a "compulsive neurotic" patient ("Rat Man"),
"omnipotence of thought" designates "all those peculiar and uncanny occur-
rences" which follow "one" around, like the ghost of an imperfectly repressed
experience or the trace of a cultural memory "surmounted" but not fully banished.[60]

Such "an uncanny effect is often and easily produced when the distinction
between the imagination and reality is effaced, as when something that we have
have hitherto regarded as imaginary appears before us in reality, or when a
symbol takes over the full functions of the thing it symbolizes and so forth."[61]
One's "double," for instance, or sex simulated for the porno-eye of the video by
a "living doll," or, maybe even a "talking head" that looks exactly like myself
replayed. "[T]hese excite in the spectator the impressions of automatic, mechanical processes at work behind the ordinary appearance of mental activity."[62]
Called forth by intense and transferential psychic-bodily processes, "one" suddenly confuses one's own identity with that of some other. In this, the uncanny
flashes into being "by mental processes leaping from one of these characters to
another—by what we should call telepathy."[63] Here one's "knowledge, feelings
and experience" are possessed by an ambivalent mix of pleasurable displeasure,
fascination and terror. Thus, with "a compulsion powerful enough to overrule
the pleasure principle," uncanny experiences are said to manifest a "daemonic
character" that may reach the "highest degree" in relation to images of death or
the presence of dead bodies.[64]

All these things, states Freud, "are "concerned with the phenomenon of the
'double,' which appears in every shape and in every degree of development.... In
other words, there is a doubling, dividing and interchanging of the self. And
finally there is the constant recurrence of the same thing—the repetition of the
same features...or vicissitudes, of the same crimes, or even the same names."[65]
What vicissitudes, crimes or names are both doubly divided and repetitiously

reenacted in this fashion? I again ask you to consider Freud's Oedipal answer, and the host of other (im)possible HIStories (t)his narrative denies and feeds off— the sacrificial displacement of (m)other, dark, heterogeneously erotic, supplementary, or cyclical (w)riting practices. "When all is said and done," remarks Freud, suggesting the "horror" of (k)not being able to safely distinguish between words and deeds, "the quality of uncanniness can only come from the fact of the 'double' being a creation dating back to a very early mental stage, long since surmounted—a stage, incidentally, at which it wore a more friendly aspect. The 'double' has become a thing of terror, just as, after the collapse of religion, the gods turned into demons."[66] What gods turned to demons? Pagan gods and/or matriarchal goddesses? Totemic figures or images of periodic epistemologies that curve back upon their own spiralling pretensions and thus double-cross the distinction between what's undoubtably sacred and what's laughingly mirrored?

Descend with me, if you will, into several aspects of Freud's words. Along the way perhaps some other social-psychoanalytic possibilities might emerge. In particular, I invite you to consider two of Freud's most pronounced concerns: the pairing of primary narcissism with a primitive, neurotic and infantile *will to power* and the alleged universality of the terror of death.

PRIMARY NARCISSISM AND TOTEMIC MODELING

Right away it is (again) evident that Freud's references to mythic figures are unreflexively "Olympian." By this, I mean they are dominated by the narratives of "gods" who come from on high and whose conquests are inscribed over against (or on top of) the bloodied traces of women and other so-called preHIS-toric or "savage" figures. The Olympian God "has lost his animal forms and his magic ability to transmute from one energy shape to another. He has lost his alchemical properties. The Olympian is idealized, rationalized, aloof, deathless ...too geometric.... This means he is not born from woman, or earth, or matter, but from his own absolute will. He represents a static perfection, in human form, incapable of transformation or ecstatic change; as a God, he is an intellectual concept...and his world mere mechanism."[67]

The Narcissus whom Freud evokes is an offspring of the Olympian era and its imperial (Roman) translations. He remains with us today. His is the tragic tale of a youth so enamored by his own doubled image that he spurns the affection of fleshy others. These others, like Echo, are sacrificially repulsed by the youth's self absorption. Alone within the magnetism of his own simulacrum, Narcissus dies gazing at the disappearance of his reflection in a pool of water disturbed by tears of self longing. When mourners seek the dead youth's beautiful body, all that is found is a flowering bulbous plant, a member of the amaryllis family. This plant, which comes to bear the name Narcissus, is variously linked to flowers that wreath the brows of the Grecian *three fates* (displaced figures of the multiple aspects of the Great (M)other), and is said by Sophocles to crown the goddesses on Mt. Olympus.

In Roman mythology the Narcissus plant is dedicated to Venus (another displacement of the archaic (M)other Goddess, in one of her phases) and is known for its antiseptic properties, particularly the healing over of wounds. These chthonian features of the Narcissus tale suggest traces of a story predating its lesson in the tragic excesses of auto-eroticism. Indeed, as Julia Kristeva points out, "The humid, subterranean torpor of narcissistic space links the fable to the vegetative intoxication of Dionysos; the theme of sight points in the same direction (Narcissus dies after he has seen himself...), as does even more explicitly the character's genealogy, integrated by Ovid [at the beginning of the Christian era, 2-8 A.D.] into the Dionysian cycle."[68] In the earlier Narcissus-Dionysos couplet to see one's double may have been less a source of melancholic loss than ecstatic abandon—an erotic reunion with the flowing ambivalence of (m)others before, after or alongside the sacrificial violence of language. This signifies a return to the labyrinth but hardly a solidification of the imperial fortress of one's ego.

Freud's story of narcissistic doubling makes no connections to the ecstasy of Dionysos. His is a tale of "unbounded self love," a self enclosing fascination which is said to dominate "the mind of the child and primitive."[69] For Freud, such narcissism is a fundamental feature of "the omnipotence of thought." Under its spell, children, neurotics and primitives fail to differentiate between one's own willful wishes and "the manifest prohibitions of reality."[70] As such, the narcissist pursues an object of desire, "but the object is not external and foreign to the individual, but is his own ego."[71] In the throes of such "primary narcissism" (which Freud reads as an invariant feature of both cultural and individual "evolution"), the world is "peopled" with one's own systematic and delusional doubles, a substitution of the seeming "immortality" of subjective projections for the finite actuality of real objects. Narcissism thus represents the "originary" construction of a dual or double psychic world. What distinguishes the "primary narcissism" of primitives from the "reality principle" governing the lives of modern adults, is that the former are said (by Freud) to live within the ambivalence of a dual existence, while the latter achieve some measure of "relief" from ambivalence. Such "relief" is purchased at the cost of a radical division between what's consciously memorable and what's unconsciously perceived.[72] This division is nonexistent in "primitives." Unlike "civilized man" the ambivalent consciousness of archaic peoples "unites determinants from both sides" rather than elevating one to the repression of the other.

That such "development" comes at the cost of considerable discontent is suggested by the differential evaluation of doubles by "primitives" and moderns. Here Freud follows Otto Rank in ascribing to primitive doubles a friendly role as "guardian spirits" of a world populated by the omnipotence of one's own thoughts. In this way, "the 'double' was originally an insurance against the destruction of the ego, an energetic denial of the power of death."[73] Freud imputes to "archaic" peoples a fear of death that is nothing but modern in its Oedipality and linear disavowal of castration. Hence: "This invention of doubling as a preservation against extinction has its counterpart in the language of dreams, which is fond of representing castration by a doubling or multiplication of a genital symbol."[74] Whose dreams? Whose genitals? And, in what HIStorical circumstances of (patriarchal) power are such projections made?

Freud's own narcissism affords little insight into these matters. He does note, however, that, with the "surmounting" of the "omnipotence" of primitive thought, "the 'double' reverses its aspect. From having been an assurance of immortality, it becomes the uncanny harbinger of death."[75] Why? Censored by the superego, the double comes to symbolize desires that "civilization" renders taboo and, thus, deadly. Again, Freud appears to tell a story about forbidden desires for the dead father of preHIStory—"all the unfulfilled but possible features to which we still like to cling in phantasy, all the strivings of the ego which adverse external circumstances have crushed, and all our suppressed acts of volition which nourish in us the illusion of free will."[76] In this way "self deception" functions as the basis for humans' erring relations to reality. An ambivalent aspect of the conscious life of primitives, the "uncanny" recognition of such erring ways LIES behind the fascinating terror of doubles for moderns.

Julia Kristeva re(w)rites Freud's narrative of primary narcissism in a way that diverts its Oedipal filterings. Kristeva also documents particular inversions in Freud's story. For Kristeva, narcissism, while omnipresent in human development, is "far from originary."[77] Rather than representing a singular beginning surmounted by "modern man," narcissism comes into play as a forceful "third realm," a supplement to the more primal mother-child dyad. In pagan epistemological terms, it is possible to read Kristeva's account as a evocation of a third and "erotically charged" aspect of one's *material* relations to (m)others. While she makes use of Freud's references to an "archaic Father of prehistory," it is clear that Kristeva's "Imaginary Father" is (k)not of one sex. Nor is it a figure of "monotheism." This is a (m)other father: "A strange father if there ever was one...because there is no sexual awareness" in that period or disposition in which this figure appears, (k)not as a father *per se*, but "as 'both parents.'"[78]

Acknowledging a certain debt to Lacan, Kristeva suggests that this third party to human experience "cuts through" the plenitude of being one with one's (m)other. This introduces an "emptiness" or "gaping hole" in one's being within the world. This engenders a moving "amatory identification" with what appears to separate the (m)other's body from one's own. This is primary narcissism—a turning, (k)not toward any certain object, but a turning, nevertheless. "A fleeting effect of enigmatic as well as creative non-sense," [79] the psychic-body folds amorously upon the traces of its own being in movement. In this, it apprehends, (k)not a nameable self (that comes later), but a pattern or a model. To take a model within—this is to "eat" or "incorporate" a trace of one's displaced and condensed (m)others. It is also to parasite upon a strange and "archaic" figuration and thereby draw "boundaries" or a "narcissistic screen" around oneself.

Such screening (or modeling) may be occasioned by a sound that distinguishes one from one's (m)other—the noise of a (polysexual) "archaic father" tattooing "primitive classifications" as bodily (re)minders of difference. This is a form of totemic sacrifice, a mode of social differentiation, a means of (metaphorically) preparing bodies for the parasitism of sign-work or language. Commonly associated with an intervention whose modality is "oral," such archaic screening might also be brought about by a feeling of disturbance in one's stomach, an odd odor, or a tingling of the skin. Unlike Lacan, Kristeva posits this "cut" well before eyesight/"I" cite. Its effects, or the "aura" it engenders, prepares a subject for one's later play before mirrors. In this way, Kristeva "sensuously" enlarges the ritual realm of the Imaginary. This provides a material disposition for a subsequent slide into the signifying labor of a (linguistic) Symbolic Order. A simultaneous movement of "advent and loss,"[80] this is also a human's first encounter with one's double—"an archaic reduplication" by which "I identify, not with an object, but with what offers itself to me as a model. That enigmatic apprehending of a pattern to be imitated."[81]

This is no-thing but a "magnetic" process of NONORIGINARY IDENTIFICATION. Kristeva likens its screening actions to the contemporaneous "birth" of metaphoric reduction and what psychoanalysis calls *transference*—"an identification that sets up love, the sign, and repetition at the heart of the psyche."[82] A moving and "abject" identification of oneself in terms of what "cuts through" an otherwise undifferentiated envelopment in (m)otherness, "narcissism" emerges to protect the fragile emptiness, that arbitrary and gaping hole around which the walls of the ego will, in time, be constructed. This permits the "emptiness" to be "maintained, lest chaos prevail and borders dissolve. Narcissism protects emptiness, causes it to exist, insures an elementary separation. Without that solidarity between emptiness and narcissism, chaos would sweep away any possibility of distinction, trace, and symbolization, which in turn confuse the limits of the body, words, the realm of the symbolic."[83]

I find Kristeva's description of the transferential character of "primary narcissism" helpful in imagining the material and psychic effects of totemic doublings. In describing the effectiveness of totemic rituals, Durkheim, like Kristeva, uses the terms "model" and "metaphor" to depict the way in which sacrificial rites transfer people from the flux of chaos into the "arbitrary" social pathways of collective representation. Cut into by signifiers ranging from sounds to mirrored images, "we" humans may be socially dependent upon narcissistic metaphoricity. This, according to Kristeva, represents an elementary form of "our" human animal disposition toward language. "Primary narcissism" is thus interpreted as a "magnetic" feature of all cultural sign-work. This, however, is neither a singular HIGHway out of nature, nor an irreversible one-way street. Neither are totemic practices. These, like the effects of "primary narcissism," are always open to reversals. On this issue Kristeva differs from Freud and other "monotheistic" theorists. Remember: narcissistic screenings may be nothing but a third aspect of a profoundly ambivalent (pagan) positioning in relation to (m)others. Indeed, Kristeva's texts suggest that the erotic (sex) chargedness of primary narcissism exists in a somewhat cyclical social form. Like a totemic force, or the power of *mana*, its transference ebbs and flows. This involves a periodic give and take, a "reversible" form of symbolic exchange, both with a more primordial form of undifferentiated being (death), and with a secondary or reproductive form of narcissism (language). Erotic-**sex**. Reproductive-**language**. Undifferentiated-**death**. In "archaic" cultures, the (pagan) doubles of each send the others spinning. Three fates and an energetic spiralling of matters.

SECONDARY NARCISSISM AND FETISHISTIC REMODELING

Modern straightwhitemale and restrictive economic theory resists reversals. This is evident in Freud's (w)ritings where the metaphoric violence of reproductive language struggles to keep an upper hand on the (m)others. Freud's language pursues the (m)others along the (metonymic) surface of its own desires. These are parasitic desires; desires to make (m)others only a secondary part of the story; desires to make HIStory (hold water as) one story. This story comes after the (m)others. It moves speedily in pursuit of their difference with its secondary narcissistic apparatus—its mirror play and gaming syntax. It also ritually resists being caught off-guard. When this happens things become terrifying or uncanny.

Freud's story aims at permanently separating itself from being one among many. In this, it abstracts a singular aspect out of our HIStorical embodiment within nature's ambivalent materiality. This is what differentiates a fetishistic truth from a totemic story. Freud's fetishized narrative is (symbolically) fixed by its desire for the possession of (im)possible objects. This is exactly what death and sex resist becoming (at least, in Freud's time)—objects. Both sex and death threaten the reproducibility of cultural memories. In order to interpretively master these *"strangely familiar" aspects (of life) Freud repeatedly pursues that* part of himself made absent by the ORIGINARY SACRIFICES of primary narcissism. This blinds the analyst from reflexively reversing *his* own totemic positioning within a given order of straightwhitemale and restrictive economic power. This leads Freud to compulsively return to the same singularizing (mis)recognitions. This is *secondary narcissism*. This is sadism. It analytically assaults one's (m)others, thereby both preserving and simultaneously denying the sacrificial enclosure of oneself. Just because Freud argued that masochism is more originary this doesn't turn the cultural effects of HIStory's work into a cause. This is (k)not to suggest that this can't happen. It's simply that Freud was chasing the uncanny before VCRs and the televisonary mediation of human experience nearly twenty-four hours a day.

McLuhan's story of Narcissus carries "us" further into HIStory than Freud's. It is also more "ambivalent" about the desirability of stabilizing and extending an arbitrary HIStorical classification of bodies. For McLuhan, this was the almost magical essence of technology: a willful desire for prosthesis; a desire to prolong the nature of artifactual arrangements without end; a desire to exceed the transitory and ambivalent nature of totemically given objects; a desire to substantiate the effects of signs. Like Freud's story, McLuhan's begins with what is sacrificially given by a HIStorically specific metaphoric inscription—the isolation of a particular set of psychic-body transferences from (m)others. Unlike Freud, McLuhan seeks to recover, rather than explain, an ambivalent posture to the processual environment in which human metaphoricity plays its part (in nature).[84] McLuhan's contradictory espousal of an ambivalent attitude partially questions the fetishistic dynamics of artificial language cuts that refuse reversal. This is to probe the fetishistic or technological effects involved in the attempted conversion of (temporary) totemic reductions into a nonreturnable bottling of signs going nowhere but straight ahead. Always straight ahead. This is modernity. This is a "one-way" street of sacrifice. This is *white magic* or technology. This is what feeds off "primitive" religious and/or scientific "classifications," transforming what's arbitrary and artful into what appears natural and necessary.

As a powerful social form secondary narcissism refuses the reversibility of sacrifice. By naturalizing what is HIStorical, it operates to cover up social contradictions. It thereby functions as a secondary order of social control. This distinguishes totemic rites from fetishism. The fetish works linguistically to stabilize and extend an earlier order of totemic violence. In this way, the fetish appears to surmount the materiality of human animal ambivalence. Like the difference between the Symbolic and the Imaginary, the fetish works to keep everything totemic in sight and in words. And, yet, there always seems to be something lacking—something "we" modern men want to believe is nothing but more of the same. But this is (k)not at all true. When presented with material evidence of this *real* difference modern men may symptomatically experience something that defies belief—something uncanny.[85] The possibility of things (k)not really being the same—this appears (like sex and death) to be a recurrent source of the uncanny.

"We" fearful and defensive men are CAPITALly positioned within the ritual (linguistic) technologies of a given (white magical) form of Symbolic Orderings. Reproductive technologies and *white magic* ritually function to keep one sacrificial set of objects desirously on line forever. As fetishistic practices these social technologies feed off the effects of previous totemic reductions, without giving themselves in return. The secret of the fetish's violence involves an ability to repetitiously demand a compulsive structural transformation of the ambivalent *nature* of artificial sign play into the *naturalized* workings of reliably coded tests of significance. This doubles the originary violence of totemic sacrifice. This stabilizes the reduction of difference to the self-same. This blurs ambivalent religious classifications with magical mastery. It confuses scientific symbolization (or theory) with technologies for reproducing rather than playing with (theoretical) objects. This is to confuse totemic rituals with fetishistic rituals. This is to attempt to ritually transform the sensuous and artful nature of situated transferential identifications (primary narcissism) into transHIStorical reproductions of what appears senselessly naturalized (secondary narcissism). This is positivism. It keeps "us" men hard and on guard, defensively looking over "our" shoulders, fearing reversals at every crossroads. This demands discipline and constant surveillance.

WHITEWESTERN MAGIC AND THE POWER OF CAPITAL

Modern MAN's disciplinary demands for total surveillance of his (m)others may be sent reeling by the sight or sensation of the least little repressed thing. This slows MAN's metonymic pursuit of mastery. This destabilizes the fetishized density of originary metaphoric distinctions. This is uncanny. But what about the man whose eyes/"I"s are no longer as trained on the fleshy bodies of (m)others, mistaking their difference for "our" given self-sameness? What about the man whose eyes/"I"s are on little but the high speed circulation of images racing screen to screen? "Owing to an acceleration of speed, he's succeeded in modifying his actual duration; he's taken it off from his lived time. To stop 'registering' it was enough for him to provoke a body-acceleration, a dizziness that reduced his environment to a sort of luminous chaos."[86] Isn't this magic? And what about the man whose secondary narcissistic dispositions appear extended without end, replayed and rescreened by technologies that speedily bypass *real* relations of bodily discipline, without returning any of the militaristic privileges that discipline has appropriated? I am here asking questions about what might be called hyper-narcissism. (K)not the secondary narcissism of a Symbolic Order, vulnerable to interruption by the uncanny reminders of what it denies or represses, but a tertiary or *trinitarian narcissism*—a narcissism of the code. This more enveloping narcissism was theorized by McLuhan. It involves an ultramodern spin out of HIStory.

Narcissus didn't fall in love with himself, argues McLuhan. He was far more distanced from the sacrificial effects of doublings than that. Narcissus fell under the numbing spell of techno-magic. He became fascinated by various gadgets promising an indefinite extension of his originary totemic (mis)recognitions, an image support system without end. This carried Narcissus beyond the fetishes of language into an eerie "Never Never Land" of (death defying) doubles doubling previously doubled doubles. XEROX. IBM. CNN. SONY WALKMAN. APPLE. FOX. KISS RADIO. CINEMAX. This made Narcissus a kind of slave to monstrous extensions of himself; extensions purified of the possibility of their own (sexual or deathly) disappearance. Slave to machinery supporting (rather than challenging) the violence of given Symbolic Order. Slave to technologies simulating (rather than repressing) a challenge. In this, Narcissus becomes the servant of an electronic materialization of his own defensive projections. Mary Shelley had previously written a more gender-specific story of this technological redoubling of sacrifice. A related tale which double-crosses the monotheistic violence of dominant western religious traditions with the magic of CAPITAL might also be imagined. Think for instance of a narrative produced by a concurrent read of Marx, Bataille and Nietzsche. Maybe Arthur Kroker has already written this story. In McLuhan, the tale goes like this:

> The youth Narcissus (narcissus means narcosis or numbing) mistook his own reflection in the water for another person. This extension of himself by the mirror numbed his perceptions until he became the servomechanism of his own extended or repeated image. The nymph Echo tried to win his love with fragments of his own speech, but in vain. He was numb. He had adapted to his extension of himself and had become a closed system. Now the point of this myth is the fact that men at once become fascinated by an extension of themselves in any material other than themselves.[87]

Why such technological extensions in the first place? Drawing upon medical literature relating to bodily adaptations to "stress" through numbing or "auto-amputation," McLuhan theorizes technology as a form of "power or strategy" assumed by the human body when its own perceptual apparatus "cannot locate or avoid" a particular source of "irritation."[88] This resembles Mauss and Durkheim's theorization of magic as a secondary response to wounds (or stresses) incurred by the totemic cutting of nature by elementary religious (or scientific) forms. Mauss explicitly theorized technology as a form of profane magic; magic devoid of its ceremonial roots.[89] It is (k)not that technology is lacking in ceremony. What it lacks is a reflexive grasp of the sacrificial nature of its own productions. This, at least, is the case for what I am calling technologies of white magic. These function to fetishistically preserve, rather than ambivalently question, the continued existence of a given moral economy of *primitive classifications*.

Magic aims to either heal or cover up the contradictory nature of things effected by totemic sacrifice. Thus, magic comes after religion, like technology comes after science. In the (admittedly perverse) sense in which I am using these terms, *black magic* (or, perhaps, I should (w)rite *black/green/gold/red* or *black/rainbow magic*) aims at healing through ritual reversals.[90] For this reason, its ritual technologies are commonly associated with (or condemned as) what's daemonic, evil, or transgressive. For epistemologies based in the western abstractions of both Judaic and Christian metaphysics *black magic* appears "a strategy of the devil, whether in the guise of witchcraft or love. It is always the [reversible] seduction of evil—or the world. It is the artifice of the world."[91] This condemnation of "black magic" technologies (as daimonic or diabolic) is a condemnation of the world to an imbalanced reign of symbolic sacrifices without end, and without the periodic possibilities of beginning again differently.

Whitewestern magic aims at suppressing such reversals. *Whitewestern magic* and its technological redoublings numb the pains of totemic separation. They cover up without (deconstructively) reversing the restrictive moral economy of originary sacrificial condensations. It is thus no surprise that *whitewestern magic* is looked upon with CAPITAL favor by western culture. This is a culture which at various times has privileged both the "immaculate conception" and sustained irreversibility of totemic objects. *Whitewestern magic* technologies adaptatively preserve, rather than resist, their totemically charged environments. Fearing some unspeakable loss, or driven by a murderous will to power (and these may be aspects of the same thing) *whitewestern magic* technologies respond positively to their totemic environments. Within a HIStorical environment charged by economic, racial and sex-gendered hierarchies, this can only lead to an escalation of sacrifices demanded of (m)others. Repetitiously and with compulsion. Welcome (again and again) to the Parasite Cafe. Welcome to a world of hyper-narcissistic doublings.

McLuhan argues that media technologies "are extensions of some human faculty—psychic or physical."[92] Media, moreover, "tend to isolate one or another sense from the others."[93] The result is a form of *hypnosis*. "To listen to radio or read the printed page is to accept these extensions of ourselves into our personal system and to under go the 'closure' or displacement of perception that follows automatically. It is this continuous embrace of our own technology in daily use that puts us in the Narcissus role of subliminal awareness and numbness in relation to these images of ourselves."[94] If, with Durkheim and Mauss, "we" theorize the shifting HIStorical ORIGINS of particular perceptual "faculties," not as pregiven or *a priori* aspects of epistemology, but as the ritual effects of sacrificial condensation (or human metaphoricity), then the sociological implications of McLuhan's observations become quite striking. WHITE MAGICAL MEDIA TECHNOLOGIES extend the violence of sacrificial hierarchies into the realm of omnipresent environmental effects. This is what makes them hard to notice. This is what gives them their particularly subliminal power. "All media," notes McLuhan, "work us over completely. They are so persuasive in their personal, political, economic, aesthetic, psychological, moral, ethical, and social consequences that they leave no part of us untouched, unaffected, unaltered. *The medium is the massage.* Any understanding of social and cultural change is impossible without a knowledge of the media work as environments."[95]

While this may have been true in Freud's day, psychoanalysis was born prior to the environmental swell of electronic informational media. Freud wrote during a time when the print media, with its affinities with Symbolic Orders of mastery, remained dominant. This undoubtably guided Freud's theorization of the "anxiety" produced by uncanny reminders of (once familiar) realities repressed by a modern will to power.[96] Such anxiety could literally stop "one" in "one's" tracks, thus slowing the *secondary narcissism* of modern power. But even as Freud wrote, a revolutionary electronic shift in media technologies was already altering the psychic and material environment of anxiety itself. Within a few fast forwarding decades unprecedented forms of techo-magic would undermine psychoanalysis as a privileged theater for confronting anxieties engendered by uncanny everyday experiences. This is noted by Catherine Clément, who observes that while Freud "put his finger" on the ceremonial character of anxiety, "on the hysteria of witches, on epidemics of dancing, on the devil's cold sperm," he nevertheless distanced himself "from...the whole theater of therapeutics."[97] Perhaps Freud feared that an engagement with such dramatic forms would bring psychoanalysis too close to the realm of magic. Other ultramodernizing forces at work in Freud's culture appeared less afraid. As Clément suggests:

> At the same time [that Freud was writing], expressionist forms of silent films were emerging everywhere: nonetheless, Freud rejected the cinema, and the terrible figure of Caligari—the mad psychiatrist who uses the intent state of a sleep walker—and the fascinating figure of Nosferatu the Vampire, the evil hypnotist. Therapeutic theater chose a new kind of spectacle, the cinema; and the small space of the psychoanalytic office was reduced to a very bare stage.[98]

McLuhan's theorization of social responses to anxiety was less limited. According to McLuhan, a major impetus for technological change comes from people's desires to resistively escape anxiety generated by existing media environments. That new technological environments create new anxieties is a feature of "irreversible" stresses of an environment ruled by *whitewestern magical* technologies. Although it carries "us" beyond McLuhan's limited political vision, this is a way of describing environmental stress generated by whitemale and modern CAPITAL.

CAPITAL's ability to profitably parasite upon anxieties produced by its own environment is a central feature of its commodified magic. This may account for the HIStorical affinity between people's desires to escape the anxious confines of commodity culture and CAPITAL's move to parasitically channel such resistance into a new *techno-magic* of social control. In late twentieth century CAPITAL the technological production of a *brave new world* of mass electronic imagery is no simple story of manipulative power from the top down. It may be this, but (k)not simply this. More cynically, advanced CAPITALiant media may literally feed on mass desires to resist anxieties engendered by previous extensions of CAPITAL's logic, discipline or instrumental rationality. That people actively seek out technologies that numb their anxieties is a central theme in McLuhan. In a related way, Baudrillard theorizes the "hyper-conformist" addiction of CAPITAL's anxious "silent majorities," (k)not so much as the effect of slick manipulations, but as resistively sought distractions from the anxieties produced by rationalization without reversal.[99]

If only such anxieties could be abated without actually reversing the hierarchical sacrifices demanded by whitemale CAPITAL. If only reversals could be simulated, or injected into the population like a vaccine, making restrictive use of a virus it generally fears. This would be a much more resilient form of CAPITAL. This would be CAPITAL in an ultramodern form. In this way, what was previously uncanny in its terror might suddenly become nothing if (k)not fascinating. Here, what's uncanny operates, no longer to slow the extension of modern power, but to accelerate the circulation of power in a new and ultramodern form. This is a power that almost instantaneously elicits and simultaneously numbs the anxieties it reproduces. This is a hypnotic power. It passes in the contagious form of a densely controlled virus of fast moving media images.

Under the compulsive techno-magic of such power, it becomes increasingly difficult to differentiate oneself from one's environment. Whereas during modernity people may have been made anxious by uncanny experiences that blurred the boundaries between oneself and one's (m)others, under the spell of ultramodern power such experiences appear anything but unusual. Here and now the uncanny is being produced in byte sized doses and fed to us as a regular part of our parasitic techno-environment. Increasingly inoculated against the uncanny's once disturbing potential to slow things down, things now seem both more fearful and more numbing, more terroristic and more fascinating. This puts the contradictory materiality of (m)otherness at a greater distance than ever, just as it incorporates that distance as a "new and improved screen" for the emptiness it preserves within us. More alien and yet more hooked up than ever—this is hyper-narcissism in the age of techno-magic.

Nowhere is such hyper-narcissism more evident than in the organization of corporate CAPITAL. This is a major theme of Christopher Lasch's *The Culture of Narcissism*.[100] Despite its author's manifest patriarchal nostalgia for the authority of "our" modernist past, Lasch's text provides a critical reading of the role of CAPITAL in fostering a *new and improved* form of narcissistic detachment and indifference. Central to Lasch's thesis are the structural inducements of corporate bureaucracy in fostering self-mirroring executive success games, the omnipresent materiality of electronic systems of image management and information exchange, and the widespread dissemination of "therapeutic ideologies" of self-enhancement.

Regarding the influence of corporate bureaucracy, Lasch points to the prominence of the entrepreneurial "gamesman" who is constantly open to new, fast, and short term ideas, but who lacks larger convictions concerning the nature of business or ethics. This is the corporate manager on the make, an ultramodern agent of CAPITAL for whom "power consists not [merely] of money and influence but of 'momentum,' a 'winning image,' and reputation as a winner."[101] For this new narcissist, "Power lies in the eye of the beholder and thus has no objective reference at all.... Indeed it has no reference to anything outside the self,"[102] just as the boundaries of the ultramodern self become dissolved by the parasitic invasion of mass mediated viruses. Here corporate subjectivity is extended outward beyond the body into a kind of transnationalized hyper-space, without defined limits and within what is literally NO TIME AT ALL. This heralds a new age of corporate mobility, based less on company loyalty than on what Eugene Emerson Jennings describes as the organization of "style,...panache" and "the ability to say and do almost anything without antagonizing others."[103] Noting convergence between successful business practices, political celebrity and the organization of entertainment, Lasch observes that the new narcissistic (male) executive is boyish, playful and "seductive."[104] Moreover:

> He will do business with any regime, even if he disapproves of its principles.
> More independent and resourceful than the company man, he tries to use
> the company for his own ends, fearing that otherwise he will be 'totally
> emasculated by the corporation.'... He avoids intimacy as a trap, preferring
> the 'exciting, sexy atmosphere' with which the modern executive surrounds

himself at work.... In all his personal relations, the gamesman depends on the admiration or fear he inspires in others to certify his credentials as a 'winner.'[105]

The omnipresent playback of image making technologies is said to be a second factor in CAPITAL's high speed movement into the density of narcissistic screenings. In this, Lasch draws upon Susan Sontag's analysis of the effects of mechanical image reproduction in undermining the sense of external reality. "Among the many narcissistic uses that Sontag attributes the camera, 'self-surveillance' ranks among the most important, not only because it provides the technical means of ceaseless self-scrutiny but because it renders the sense of selfhood dependent on the consumption of images of the self, at the same time calling into question the reality of the external world."[106] *SMILE! YOU'RE ON CANDID CAMERA.* Lasch reads this popular TV phrase as indicative of something like an ultramodern shift in epistemological perspective. No longer are "we" glued to the straightforward perspective of eyes of the flesh. Within advanced CAPITAL's culture of narcissism, it is as if everything imaginable is or might be recorded from all angles and vantage points.

> We live in a swirl of images and echoes that arrest experience and play it back in slow motion. Cameras and recording machines not only transcribe experience but alter its quality, giving to much of [ultra]modern life the character of an enormous echo chamber, a hall of mirrors. Life presents itself as succession of images or electronic signals, of impressions recorded and reproduced by means of photography, motion pictures, television, and sophisticated recording devices. [Ultra]modern life is so thoroughly mediated by electronic images that we cannot help responding to others as if their actions—and our own—were being recorded and simultaneously transmitted to an unseen audience or stored up for close scrutiny at some time later.[107]

The omnipresence of media feedback—this is today (k)not entirely separable from corporate bureaucratic structure in its most advanced forms. Indeed, as Michael Schrage has observed, with increasing intensity, "the media is the (corporate) culture....Today, organizations are becoming far more media-intensive. It's not just that they're using computers and telecommunications networks to manage data, they're always packaging information in new ways. They're making videotapes and creating internal television networks. They're crafting 'expert systems'—computer programs that embody the technical expertise of company old-timers—and using facsimile machines or electronic mail as the medium of instantaneous communication. The 'old boy' network has taken on a technological hue. Personal interactions are increasingly mediated, complemented and/or captured by an increasingly elaborate media mesh."[108] There is something un-canny about the lack of "secrets" regarding the illusory character of ultramodern corporate political sign-work. When almost nobody is innocent of "the fact" that one never sees George Bush, but only media constructed sound-bytes and televi-sionary photo-screenings, and when there is a "totalizing" acknowledgement of the illusory power of negative political advertising by the very same mass elec-tronic and print media who deploy negative political advertising (for profit), then the reality of everyday life comes to take on the "fascinating" characteristics of what Baudrillard calls hyperreality. This is at once anxiety producing and numb-ing.

But what of the stresses generated by being literally surrounded by media screens? Such anxieties are today processed in much the same way as irregulari-ties in electronic information flows themselves. Lasch here points to the increasing prevalence of a form of "therapeutic ideology" which demands that individuals regularly monitor, evaluate and adapt themselves to a premodeled series of "developmental stages." Radically divorced from any and all HIStorical contexts, this is a narcissistic therapeutics that demands endless self examination for "signs of aging and ill health, for tell-tale symptoms of psychic stress, for blemishes and flaws that might diminish attractiveness, or on the other hand for reassuring indications that...life is proceeding on schedule."[109] This is a panicky aspect of ultramodern social life. For many, the goal becomes nothing less than the survival of one prepackaged series of staged anxieties after another. As Lasch points out in reviewing "crisis management" texts, such as Gail Sheehy's "best selling" *Passages,* a book billing itself as "a life support system" for those facing the "predictable" crises of adult life and which promises a "no panic approach to aging": "Social conditions today encourage a survivor mentality, expressed in its crudest forms in disaster movies or fantasies of space travel, which allow vicari-ous escape from a doomed planet. People no longer no longer dream of overcom-ing difficulties but merely surviving them."[110] Thus, in an increasingly cynical world, where people are doing everything they can simply to stay one step ahead of their next scheduled bout with panic, "Narcissism appears realistically to represent the best way of coping with the tensions and anxieties of [ultra]modern life."[111]

TERROR OF DEATH: TERROR OF OTHERS

Lasch's analysis links the "survivor" mentality of contemporary narcissism to a perpetual "state of social warfare."[112] There are already nearly 500,000 U.S. soldiers in the Persian Gulf when I (w)rite these words and the nation seems numb. We've got to stop "them" now, we are told, or they'll do to us what we'd do to them. This is a logic of foreign policy. It begins at home. Thus, a "warlike society tends to produce men and women who are at heart antisocial. It should therefore not surprise us to find that although the narcissist conforms to social norms for fear of external retribution, he [and I won't alter the gender, here, because its (k)not clear that the narcissism implied by a culture of TOTAL WAR can be anything but masculine] often thinks of himself as an outlaw and sees others in the same way, 'as basically dishonest and unreliable, or only reliable because of external pressures.'"[113] This is strikingly similar to the way Freud (mis)interprets the narcissism of "primitives" in relation to "the impression that death makes upon its survivors."[114] Freud refers to that "conflict of feelings" or "ambivalence" that survivors experience when presented with images of the dead. This is a major source of the "uncanny." It is also said to explain the narcissistic doubling by which "primitives" defend themselves from "evil" or "daemonic" spirits.

From Freud's perspective, the birth of both "evil" spirits and self-preserving doubles, "which began as a spell against evil wishes,"[115] occur simultaneously. Survivors are believed to fear the envy of the dead. As a defense they erect primitive "theoretical systems" that are both delusional and paranoid. This, for Freud, is the psychic basis of "the omnipotence of thought." Why such defensiveness and delusion? Freud again credits that originary mythic act—the killing of an archaic father. More challenging, from an HIStorical viewpoint, is Lasch's suggestion that something about the advance of CAPITAL generates such narcissistic deterrence. By comparison, Freud's sweeping comments about both death and narcissism appear unreflexively metaphysical.

Asserting that "primitives" deny the reality of death,[116] Freud contends that "almost all of us still think as savages do on this topic." Moreover, "the primitive fear of the dead is still so strong within us and is always ready to come to the surface on any provocation."[117] Freud's ambiguous terror of death is richly symptomatic. His (w)ritings are replete with references to the "insufficiency" of scientific evidence concerning whether death is "inevitable" or but an "avoidable" illness. Freud's personal life is also marked by death's dark hand. (K)not only was his "self-analysis" prompted by the death of his father but throughout his life Freud was haunted by a fear that others (particularly Jung) had premonitions of the hour of Freud's death. More provocative is Freud's theorization of death as a "drive" countering the "drive" of libidinal desire. The death that Freud fears may be no drive at all. Quite the opposite; death's movement may be that which *seductively* undoes the repetitious nature of drives and the Symbolic Order they compulsively feed. I am here referring to a more archaic "reverence" for the periodicity of death. (K)not the end of life's energies, but their reversal. Such a radically "other" relation to death haunts Freud's forever unfinished "Project for a Scientific Psychology." While Freud typically associates the fear of death with the terror of castration, a close reading of Freud's words also reveals such perplexing passages as the following.

> To some people the idea of being buried alive by mistake is the most un-
> canny thing of all. Yet psychoanalysis taught us that this terrifying phantasy
> is only a transformation of another fantasy which had originally nothing
> terrifying about it at all, but was qualified by a certain lasciviousness—the
> phantasy, I mean, of intra-uterine existence.[118]

What is the meaning of such a "intra-uterine" fantasy? Is Freud hinting at a more archaic relation to (m)other bodies? Is he suggesting a relation to death less menacing than castration and less guarded than that implied by his theory of narcissistic defense? The notes accompanying Freud's text suggest that this is hardly the case. All that Freud appears capable of reading into such a fantasy is screened by a transference to the homo(geneous)sexual power of a dead or absent father. As Freud states elsewhere: "[T]he womb-phantasy...is frequently derived...from an attachment to the father. There is a wish to be inside the mother's womb in order to replace her during coitus—in order to take her place in regard to the father."[119] Again, all roads point to the father and to his sons' envy, competitive desires and subsequent guilt. In this, Freud demonstrates little recognition of the cyclical markings of death and other ceremonial "blood mysteries." In pagan or (m)other oriented cultures, death represented a ritual remembrance of the interdependent materiality of living. Accordingly, "every-thing was both dead and alive, in process, in nature."[120] In such "primitive" cultures there may be little space for the close circuiting narcissistic defenses assumed by Freud.

Freud's ideas about the narcissistic delusions of "primitives" are ill-founded. Durkheim's analysis is more insightful. Certain of Durkheim's terms are related to Freud's. Both theorists refer to the "delirious" beliefs and systematic "halluci-nations" of primitive religion. Yet, rather than seeing such matters as a narcissis-tic "flight" from natural realities, Durkheim viewed the "artful" character of such "delirium which all religion [and by extension all science] is in a sense," (k)not as the substitution of "a pure hallucination for reality" but as a "well founded delirium."[121] For Durkheim, the "significance and objective value" of totemic "hallucinations" is rooted in the "natural" limits imposed by human sign work. The "error," suggests Durkheim, is to mistake (as did Freud) "the letter of the symbol" for "the thing...represented." This permits one to disregard "the fact" of the letter's material existence as a constitutive feature of the "natural" reality of society itself. This is to read the "infectious intensity" of sign-work, which Durkheim, following Max Muller, likens to "parasitic growths...under the influence of language," (k)not merely as "a system of lying fictions," but as fictions that have "a foothold in reality. [Moreover,] behind these figures and metaphors, be they gross or refined, there is a concrete living reality."[122] It is this reality to which linguistic "hallucinations" or "deliriums" correspond. (K)not the reality of natural objects referenced by collective representations but the reality of society that is "naturally" constitutive of and simultaneously constituted by such metaphoric and symbolic practices. Durkheim is clear that the processual (and thereby transitory) "nature" of such realities is fundamentally HIStorical.[123] With this in mind, it is necessary to provide some HIStorical specificity for Freud's ideas about narcissism as a deterrence of the terror of death. In so doing, it becomes apparent that, while Freud's theories may be largely irrelevant to "primitive" societies, they are uncannily pertinent to an understanding of death in the modern West. What follows is a brief outline of the displacement of pagan understandings of the periodicity of death into the white narcissism of modern and ultramodern CAPITALIST patriarchy.

THE ASSAULT ON CYCLICAL TIME: THE ANXIETIES OF "AUTOBIOGRAPHY"

This condensed (and admittedly whirlwind) tour of death's changing tortions is intended as but a suggestive supplement to more conventional understandings of the birth and subsequent transformation of modernity. It begins with efforts to abolish cyclical interpretations of time in the earlier thirteenth century. Set against a background of efforts to centralize medieval church authority and threats to a continuation of feudalism by the rise of towns, changing agricultural technologies, the ascendancy of regional kingships, and the mortgaging of estates in exchange for the financing of wars and religious crusades, this is a story of the assault upon the prevalence of festivals and their connections to the periodicity of earlier matriarchal rites. Consider the 1209 proclamation of the Council of Avignon "that at all saints' vigils, there shall not, in the churches, be any theater dances, indecent entertainments, gatherings of singers, or worldly songs, such as incite the souls of listeners to sing."[124] This is a thinly disguised reference to festive ceremonies whereby peasant peoples periodically overturned existing orders of authority and displayed a laughable indifference to such culturally fearful matters as death. In the words of Mikhail Bakhtin:

> The acute awareness of victory over fear is an essential element of medieval laughter. This feeling is expressed in a number of characteristic medieval comic images. We always find in them the defeat of fear presented in droll and monstrous forms, the symbols of power and violence turned inside out, the comic images of death and bodies rent asunder. All that was terrifying becomes grotesque.... [O]ne of the indispensable accessories of carnival was the set called "hell," a cornucopia; the monster, death, becomes pregnant.

> Various deformities, such as protruding bellies, enormous noses, or humps are all symptoms of pregnancy or of provocative power. Victory over fear is not its abstract elimination; it is a simultaneous uncrowning and renewal, a gay transformation. Hell is burst and has poured forth abundance....There can be nothing terrifying on earth, just as there can be nothing frightening in a mother's body, with the nipples that are made to suckle, with the genital organ and warm blood.... All unearthly objects were transformed into earth, the mother which swallows up in order to give birth to something larger that has been improved....The earthly element of terror is the womb, the bodily grave, but it flowers with delight and a new life.[125]

In such carnivalesque reversals between tomb and womb the ritual accent of (m)other focused paganism could hardly be missed. Nor was this unnoticed by hostile Church authorities who, in the thirteenth century, began to attribute such rites to the newly figured image of Satan, while substituting the singular cult of Mary, the immaculate virgin and *one and only* mother of God, for the earthy figuring of multi-aspect (m)other goddesses. In 1212, the Council of Paris acted with increasing patriarchal fervor to prohibit "assemblies of women, for the purpose of dancing and singing, permission to enter cemeteries or sacred places, regardless of considerations of dress." Also rendered taboo were "nuns from heading processions, either within their own cloister or without, that circle churches and their chapels while singing and dancing, something we cannot allow even secular women to do."[126] The target may have been nothing less than the ecstatic "round dances," whose association with "spiralling" (feminine) reversals, and the encircling of death within life, represented obvious challenges to the linearity of a "world without end" promulgated by the masterful (masculine) forces of Church power.

From the thirteenth to fifteenth centuries assaults on rites of cyclical time gradually altered the cultural meaning of death. The individualization of responsibility for "confessing" one's sins, instituted by the Lateran Council in 1215, played no small role in transforming the face of death into matters of "autobiographical" anxiety.[127] In *The Hour of Death,* Philippe Aries reviews evidence documenting a rise in western anxieties relating to death during a same time period.[128] Following the decline of empire in the fifth century, Aries notes a general cultural relaxation of anxieties regarding human mortality. This leads me to wonder whether imperial cultures, such as the culture in which I am (w)riting, are also cultures marked by greater anxiety concerning death. Imperial cultures claim to possess (rather than simply live within) the world of nature. Since the materiality of death "naturally" dispossesses us of such idealist fantasies, the question might be asked: are those of us who find our identities ritually secured by a *will to possession* more likely to be terrified of death than those who do not?

Imperial cultures are also organized around the parasitic overdevelopment of the life-chances of their most privileged members at the often deadly military expense of others. But what are the material and psychic costs of such violence to those who would be MASTERS OF THE UNIVERSE? Despite a variety of ritual repressions and ideological justifications for the seeming "naturalness" of their own privilege, in so much as they literally feed off the economic spoils of war, in what ways are imperial cultures also—even if unconsciously—assailed by the ghostly haunts of sacrificial contradictions that they themselves deny? In other words, is the prospect of death more terrifying for those who make ritual use of death as a linear technology of domination than it is for those who accept the uselessness of death as a dispossessive aspect of the "natural" life-cycles of human-animal existence itself?

Such questions aside, in tracing a HIStory of the simple and relatively un-adorned ceremonial displays of death throughout the early Middle Ages, Aries concludes that this was a period of "tame death"—an epoch where the living appeared generally resigned to their own mortality and where death was typically greeted in a rather unanxious manner. This, of course, was also a time when the western dream of imperial mastery lay dormant or in recession. Here death was recognized less as a threat to world mastery than as a phase of being in the world itself—a phase of wintery sleep in the seasons of life's vegetative-like cycles. Thus, during these so-called "Dark Ages" death appears as somewhat of an anony-mous and collective matter. This changes with the thirteenth century, as anxiety toward death increases, first among the rich and powerful, and subsequently among the population at large. To substantiate this thesis Aries draws upon several sources of evidence: the introduction of anxious depictions of *the last judgment*, the prevalence of rites of *artes moriendi*, the development of *still life paintings* and the emergence of *the macabre* as a cultural thematic.

Regarding *the last judgement*, Aries finds little interest in this theme before the late twelfth century. Initial depictions of Christ's second coming involve a mixture of apocalyptic and redemptive imagery. A century later, Christ begins to appear solely in the form of a judge. As time passes, this scene appears more formal and judicial. "The apocalyptic descent from heaven to earth has become a court of justice."[129] Paralleling the individualization of experience prompted by confes-sional rites and the growth of restrictive merchant economies, the calculative depiction of the last judgement facilitated a "new idea of life as biography." Thus, "Each moment...will be weighed someday in a solemn hearing, before all the powers of heaven and hell. The creature responsible for this weighing, the standard-bearing archangel, became the popular patron saint of the dead."[130]

Aries connects this image of almost legalistic judgment to a curious transfor-mation in the religious meaning of "the book." Previously a symbol of collective revelation, the book becomes imaged as a kind of calculative ledger of good deeds and bad. In twelfth century paintings the book appears as but a record of saints, a book of the elect. But by the fourteenth century, Christ is portrayed as a stern judge with a book upon his knee reading: "He whose name is written in this book shall be damned." By the fifteenth century, this book has become so individualized that it hangs (in a fresco in the Albia Cathedral) "like identification papers" around the neck of naked souls judged one by one. This, for Aries, is indicative of a new anxiety surrounding an individual's confrontation with death. Thus:

> The actions of the individual are no longer lost in the limitless space of transcendence or...the collective destiny of the species. From now on they are individualized. Life [now] consists in the sum total of an individual's thoughts, words and deeds. Life is a body of facts than can be itemized and summarized in a book. The book is therefore at once the history of an individual, his biography, and a book of accounts, or records, with two columns, one for evil and the other for good. The new bookkeeping spirit of businessmen who were beginning to discover their own world—which has become our world—was applied to the content of life as well as to...merchandise or money.[131]

This new anxiety before death is also a feature of the *artes moriendi* of the fifteenth century. As depicted in the popular iconography of early mechanical prints and woodcuts, this was a calculative ceremony in which dying individuals are presented with two final hurdles to salvation. Unlike ecstatic rites of circular dancing, in the *artes moriendi* a person is on one's own. First, one is tempted to despair for the weight of one's sin. Then one is tempted by *avartia*, a passionate love of earthly possessions. Indicative of the emergent power of privatized property, on one's death bed a person is made anxious by the prospect of losing "objects of pleasure, sources of profit, things and people; people as possessions to be preserved."[132]

A related theme may be identified in the rise of "still life" paintings near the end of the Middle Ages. As Aries points out, "Before the thirteenth century the object is almost never regarded as a source of life, but rather as a sign, the symbolic representation of a movement."[133] By the fourteenth and fifteen centuries the nature of the object in art, as in society, is radically altered. Objects, like the individuals who contemplate them, begin to appear fixed in their autonomy. These are objects collected by the gaze of a subject at a secure distance, objects possessed by the observer's eyes. In this, Aries reads a relation between changes in the material economy of objects and the "avartia" tempting the "subject" of a new economic order. As such, the "contemplation and speculation" entailed by still life "are also the distinguishing traits of the protocapitalist, as he appears in the later Middle Ages and in the Renaissance. If we go back too far before capitalism, things do not yet deserve to be seen or held on to or desired; this is why the early Middle Ages were a time of indifference [and] wealth was not seen as the possession of things; it was identified with power over men, just as poverty was identified with solitude.... In order for material possessions to become important to the dying man, they had to become both less rare and more sought after, they had to acquire a value of utility or exchange."[134]

As further indication of newly formed western anxieties concerning death, Aries points to the *macabre* as it appears in the art and literature of the four-teenth and fifteenth centuries. The *macabre* involved the depiction of dead bodies in various stages of decay and decomposition. Although there were antecedents, these were rare and constituted nothing like the "obtrusive" presence of rotting corpses that took their places besides the *artes moriendi* and still life images of the late Middle Ages. Representations of universal destruction had previously been symbolized by dust, (k)not "worm-ridden corruption," as a sign of death's ways. Associated with the fiery dryness of ashes, dust symbolized a form of "purified" decomposition, "a cyclical process" of unceasing material circulation, closer to pagan understandings than the anxious individual judgment of the *artes moriendi*. But in the fourteenth century, the "new image of the pathetic and personal death of individual judgment...was to have its counterpart in a new image of destruction."[135] Appearing commonly in the form of the *transi,* an icon of a dead body literally coming apart, figures of the macabre were sometimes engraven on tombs, but most frequently found illustrating the pages of *The Book of Hours,* a prayer manual used by devout Christian laypersons. In the form of the *danse macabre,* the rotting corpse also appears as a kind of horrific double, alternating with figures of the living in "rounds" inscribed upon the chamber walls of cemetery charnels. This is hardly the ecstatic round dance of pagans. The living seem almost frozen, while the dead appear to give warning. "The dead lead the dance; indeed they are the only ones dancing. Each couple consists of a naked mummy, rotting, sexless, and highly animated, and a man or woman, dressed according to his or her social condition and paralyzed by surprise. Death holds out its hand to the living person whom it will draw along with it, but who has not yet obeyed the summons. The art lies in the contrast between the rhythm of the dead and the rigidity of the living."[136]

In examining literary examples of the *macabre* Aries points to numerous instances where an unprecedented desire for sudden death, or even suicide, is preferred to the agony of the expected death. "An atmosphere of anxiety seems to have taken hold."[137] But why? While it has been common to view the *macabre* as an outgrowth of the horror of plagues and economic catastrophe, Aries cautions against such interpretation. He refers to data suggesting that mendicant religious orders had received instructions to "idealize" depictions of death during plagues and to recent HIStorical research suggesting religiously motivated exaggerations of the disastrous nature of the times. Citing work documenting the relatively optimistic character of "wills" in an age allegedly overwhelmed by plagues, Aries offers a reading of the era as one of radical transformation rather than total catastrophe. Although death by plague was enormous, it may not have been as widespread as traditionally believed. Moreover, much of what is classified as *macabre* is anything but realistic in its depiction of the body, dead or alive. Contrasting the *macabre* with the realism of sixteenth century "death masks" and seventeenth century paintings of corpses, Aries concludes, "Not only is there no connection, there is even an antagonism between the art of *macabre* and the immediate, physical sight of death."[138]

Rather than reflecting the physical reality of death, the macabre showed "precisely what could not be seen, what went under ground: the hidden work of decomposition, which was not the production of observation, but the product of imagination."[139] In this the *macabre* was closer to allegory than realist art. In Aries' words:

> [T]he *macabre* is not the expression of a particularly profound experience of death in the age of high mortality and great economic crisis....The image of death and decomposition...are the sign of a passionate love for this world and a painful awareness of the failure to which each human life is condemned.... In both religious representations and natural attitudes, then, we have moved by imperceptible stages from death as an awareness and summation of a life, to death as an awareness and desperate love of this life. The art of the macabre can only be understood as the final phase in the relationship between death and individualism, a gradual process that began in the twelfth century and that arrived in the fifteenth century at a summit never to be reached again.[140]

By the second half of the fifteenth century tensions surrounding death's figuration are further displaced into the sacrificial body of *the mad*. This occurs during both a period of massive economic and social transformation—the defeat of decentralized feudal cultures by early CAPITALlist social forms and the solidification of centralized state authority—and the genocidal sacrifice of peasant society's continuing paganism in the mass murder of millions of women, accused witches, gay men and others suspected of alliances with the earth's cycles, or what modernizing men called "the devil." The uncertain estimate of deaths range from 1 to 9 million, but one figure appears undoubtable: eighty percent of the accused, tortured and burnt heretics were women.[141] The threat that pagan women represented to the emergence of modern forms of patriarchy was more than simply spiritual. Convicted witches were mainly peasant and lower-class women who opposed the existing authority structure and thus represented a political, religious, and sexual threat to the dominant class, particularly men."[142] They also embodied a continuing sense of the imminent ceremonial positioning of "reasoning" human animals within nature; a ritual material dialogue between the restrictive economy of "reason" and its (m)others.

INTO THE LIGHT: THE MADNESS OF (CAPITALIZED) CIVILIZATION

The dialogue, or periodic "symbolic exchange," between "reason" and "unreason" was torn asunder in the fifteenth century. Maintained, if in an imbalanced form, in the allegorical imagery of *danse macabre,* such a dialogue represented a reflexive recognition of the double character of human existence itself. Here humans were viewed as ambivalently composed both by indeterminate relations of materiality (unreason) and by the idealist reduction of experience to what can be given in words (reason). The sacrificial elimination of the dialogue between these doubled moments is at the core of Michel Foucault's *Madness and Civilization.* Beginning in the calculative rush toward linearity which characterized late medieval towns and cities, a wedge was driven between these cyclical poles of human experience as the negative pole (unreason or *folly*) was gradually repulsed from the minds of everybody and projected onto the bodies of those declared *mad.* Thus:

> Up to the second half of the fifteenth century, or even a little beyond, the theme of death reigns alone. The end of man, the end of time bear the face of pestilence and war. What overhangs human existence is this conclusion and this order from which nothing escapes.... Then in the last years of the century this enormous uneasiness turns on itself; the mockery of madness replaces death and its solemnity. From the discovery of that necessity which inevitably reduces man to nothing, we have shifted to the scornful contemplation of that nothing which is existence itself. Fear in the face of the absolute limit of death turns inward..., man disarms it in advance, making it an object of derision by giving it an everyday, tamed form.... Madness is the *deja-la* of death.... The substitution of the theme of madness for that of death does not mark a break, but rather a torsion within the same anxiety.... And where once man's madness had been not to see that death's term was approaching, so that it was necessary to recall him to wisdom with the spectacle of death, now wisdom consisted of denouncing madness everywhere.[143]

Foucault's text traces the displacement of the spectacle of everybody's death into that of somebody's madness. For a century and a half this "ritual division" haunts the early modern landscape, as *the mad* are herded, like sacrificial "animals," in a kind of "counter pilgrimage" to various "sacred sights," then to confinement within the gates of cities themselves, and finally from this "threshold" to another—the *Narrenschiff* or "Ship of Fools," in which these strange "figures of death" were transported from city to city as objects to be gazed upon with fascination and fear. "The madman's voyage is at once a vigorous division and an absolute Passage. In one sense, it simply develops across a half-real, half-imaginary geography, the madman's liminal position on the horizon of medieval concern.... Confined on the ship from which there is no escape, the madman delivered to the river with its thousand arms, the sea with its thousand roads, to that great uncertainty external to everything. He is a prisoner in the midst of what is freest, the openest of routes; bound fast at the infinite crossroads. He is the passenger par excellence: that is, the prisoner of the passage."[144]

And then in the seventeenth century the torsion of death's economic restriction changed again. Floating amidst a swell of other impoverished peoples whose unemployment and discontent symbolized the so-called "dangerous classes" of the early CAPITALlist order, the mad were removed from their spectacular circulation and confined in large undifferentiated *poorhouses*, such as the *Hopital General* in Paris. Opened in 1656, *Hopital General* would soon be the home for some 6,000 persons, one percent of the Parisian population. Within its gates the mad continued to bear the "face of death." Chained like monstrous animals, they remained subject to the gaze of "normal" people who came to stare with fascination upon their horror. In this way, "madness had become a thing to look at: no longer a monster inside oneself, but an animal with strange mechanisms, a bestiality from which man had long since been suppressed."[145]

The date 1656 is important in Foucault's (w)ritings. (K)not only does it mark a beginning of the "great confinement," a period of "classical" social control extending through the eighteenth century, but elsewhere in Foucault's work this date is emblematic of the solidification of linear visual perspective, a central feature of the "classical" episteme of the early modern order. Indeed, near the beginning of *The Order of Things,* Foucault provides a detailed analysis of *Las Meninas,* a 1656 painting by Velázquez.[146] Foucault reads this remarkable painting as symptomatic of what is made visible and what is hidden by the ritual character of classical representation. Revealing with great precision three dominant functions of representation—the gaze of the model (object) being painted, the spectator's classificatory contemplation, and the painter in the process of composing—the painting (like all acts of classical representation) is, nevertheless, blind to the nature of the "enlightening" act itself. What it does not and cannot represent (without reversing the linear privilege of its own positioning in HIStory) is the act of representation itself; the sacrificial act whereby it "reasonably" masters, rather than periodically entering into an "unreasoned" exchange with, the illusionary play of its own doubles. This is to secure a modern *ideal* at the expense of the ambivalence of *material* participation in nature. For Foucault this heralds the inversion of madness in "the age of reason," a defensive hollowing out of Man accomplished by displacing Man's finitude, or inevitable death, onto the figure of others. This, perhaps, is a new madness—the insanity of reason without end or reversal.

In the final sections of *Madness and Civilization* "we" arrive at the end of the eighteenth century as two further displacements of death's imminence are evoked. The first involves a move toward the "medicalization" of madness. A response to the contradictory demands of industrial CAPITAL, Foucault tells a story of how pressures to separate the "able bodied" from the "disabled" poor prompted the "reform" of undifferentiated "poorhouses," such as the *Hopital General* and the creation of separate "asylums" for the mad, the unemployed and criminals. But what happens to the displaced "figure of death" as the confinement of the mad is rationalized by the "moral therapies" introduced by Tuke, Pinel and other pioneers of the "lunatic asylum?" Foucault describes Tuke's attempts to simulate "normalizing" family relations, with patients assigned roles a dutiful children and the introduction of constant surveillance, self-judgment and the "therapy" of disciplined work. Pinel's "experiments" with enforced silence, the use of mirrors and techniques of perpetual judgment produced similar effects—the lawful gaze of medicalized authority upon the body of those who are figured as other.

But what of death? In the closing pages of Foucault's study death reappears, now allied (k)not simply with madness but with the eroticized violence of sadism. Deep within reason's confines, death's periodic call is transformed into a mad and "rigorous geometry," a thoroughly modern desire for self-preservation and the erotic undoing of others. Here appears the monstrous figure of the Marquis de Sade, a dark double of the "man" of reason. Sade calculatingly extends reason's rule to that dark point unseen by those who stand alone within its light. In this way, the pornographer utters words of such extreme reason that they cannot be spoken except by "exploding the material and imaginary confines of rational language itself."[147] This is the madness of "normalized" reason; the madness of a language that abandons its dialogue with mortality; the madness of a culture obsessed with displacing its own fleshy periodicity into an unending linear pursuit of its stereotypically femininized "others"—others who bleed each month and others whose monstrous (dis)positionings at the sacrificial borders between culture and what modern MAN designates as nature threaten the purity of white lighted male reason. This is HIStory. In Foucault's words:

> The great cosmic conflict...revealed by the Insane in the fifteenth and
> sixteenth centuries, shifted until it became, at the end of the classical period,
> a dialectic lacking the heart's mediation [lacking a...dialogue between reason
> and unreason]. Sadism is not the name finally given to a practice as old as
> Eros; it is a massive cultural fact which appeared precisely at the end of the
> eighteenth century, and which constitutes one of the greatest conversions of
> western imagination: unreason transformed into the delirium of the heart,
> madness of desire, the insane dialogue of love and death in the limitless
> presumption of desire. Sadism appears at the very moment that unreason,
> confined for over a century and reduced to silence, appeared no longer as an
> image of the world, no longer as a *figura*, but as language and desire.[148]

Foucault's comments about the HIStorical specificity of sadism are corrobo-
rated by Aries, whose examination of cultural depictions of death in the seventeenth and eighteenth centuries suggests an unprecedented overlay of iconic and
literary images of death with those of sexual violence. In *Birth of the Clinic,*
Foucault extends his analysis of death's displacement into the language and gaze
of medical science, and by inference to the discursive structure of the "human
sciences" as a (w)hole. "Nineteenth century medicine was haunted by the absolute eye that cadaverizes life and rediscovers in the corpse the frail, broken
nervure of life."[149] At the center of this sacrificial epistemology is a cold and
objectified "gaze," (k)not unlike a still life. This is an idealist gaze operating at a
sadistic distance from its own self-classificatory rituals, those ceremonial cycles of
perception by which knowledge itself is materially constituted as power. This is
"the gaze that envelopes, caresses, details, [and] atomizes the most individual
flesh and enumerates its secret bites" in terms of that which appears "fixed...
from the height of death."[150]

The sacrificial character of this "sadistic" gaze is elaborated in Foucault's
subsequent (w)ritings on the abstract "idealization" of Man in the discursive
structuring of the human sciences; in penal, military and educational "discipline;" and in the reduction of sex to that which can be contained by language.
But even in the closing pages of *Birth of the Clinic* the ritual stakes are clear. In
his obstinate and fearful obsession with passing *his* knowledge of life through the
filters of death without reversing this linear perspectival trajectory, the modern
"individual owes to death a meaning that does not cease with him. The division
that it traces and the finitude whose mark it imposes [and simultaneously denies]
link...the universality of language and the precarious, irreplaceable form of the
individual."[151] The is the modern individual, a MAN of (totalizing) reason. This is
the MAN of modern CAPITAL and bureaucratically controlled socialism. This is a
MAN ruled by a restrictive economic socio-logic. This is an "individual" whose
morally evaluative ideas about life are narcissistically purchased by the death of

others. Silence equals death. This is "Freudian man."[152] No wonder this MAN is struck by uncanny terror at the sight of *his* doubles when they return. Here *his* interminable analysis comes full circle. But wait. The story gets worse. Don't forget Foucault, but remember what happens next. I am (w)riting here, not of death's repression, but of its uncanny and artificial resurrection in the smooth, cold and seductive doublings of ultramodern simulations.

chapter
ten

INFANTILE RECURRENCE AND OVERDEVELOPMENT
SCENES FROM WORLD WAR THREE

ONE

> Many people experience the feeling of the uncanny in the highest relation
> to death and dead bodies, to the return of the dead, and to spirits and
> ghosts.—Sigmund Freud[1]

Genocidal Forgettings. U.S. HIStory. Ultramodern CAPITAL. What are the
psychic bodily and collective cultural costs of living off the material ruins of
others? How does "one" live with a self secured by the virtually memory-less
enactment of restrictive economic and military violence against others? At work
each day. In the market. In the bedroom. On the highway. In the airwaves radiating white toxic male wasteproducts into the bodies of others. Feeding parasitically off the sacrifice of others' flesh. Without saying that's what you're doing.
Even in the men's room. To and with each other. Complicit in a global politics of
exploitation. And its pleasures.

So much so that when you read of stabbings rape gang violence child beatings
drug abuse shootings PREMODELED IMAGES COME TO MIND. Without commas.
RAPID FIRE IMAGES COME TO MIND. Images you've seen before. Maybe on
television: moving electric pictures of dark young wild stereotypes rap addicted
and inner city males. With baseball caps and badness. Stereotypical images of
persons whom white politicians say ought to be put away. With VIRTUALLY NO
MEMORIES OF HOW THESE THOUGHTS (rather than others) HAVE COME TO
OCCUPY YOUR MIND. And VIRTUALLY NO COLLECTIVE RITUALS to put into
play memories of an entirely different sort—memories of unprecedented
whitemale CAPITAL intitiatives; memories, for instance, of the near extermination
an entire continent of people with little taste for still life paintings, narcissistic
mirrors of production and the self-defensive or DEATH DEFYING PLEASURES of
PARASITIC OVERDEVELOPMENT; memories of the continuing material effects of
enslaving, "freeing" and then transformatively red-lining millions of Africans
into a semi-permanent U.S. underclass. What are the psychic body and cultural
costs of such selective memories and forgettings? Where are the ghosts?

I live in half of an old two family house in Brookline Village, an area of

Brookline, Massachusetts, founded in 1639 by a fiercely patriarchal group of whitemales with CAPITAL on their minds and GOD in their hearts. These men were accompanied by women who survived in complex and contradictory relations of economic, spiritual and sexual dependence. These Puritans were (k)not the first human animals to live on this part of the earth. Believe me this is no confession. Today Brookline is more "liberal." John F. Kennedy was born here and Michael Dukakis. It has a very highly educated and large Jewish-American population. Some of Brookline is quite wealthy. Most of Brookline is white. Quite a few college students live in parts of Brookline. During the Viet Nam war Brookline voted to withhold its sons. Until the tenth year of the Reagan-Bush drain on middle class property owners the town even had very progressive rent control policies.

Brookline is surrounded on three sides by the City of Boston. Near where I live, the Boston that is (k)not where I live has many poor and many nonwhite people. One night I was riding my bicycle near the border of Mission Hill in Boston and Brookline Village. In October of 1989, "Charles Stuart, a white man, staged the murder of his pregnant wife in Boston's Mission Hill, a largely Black neighborhood, shot himself in the gut for an alibi, and described the assailant as Black. The Boston police took those white words and ran with them in search of Blackness. They invaded the Mission Hill community and took part in the fabrication of a Black crime to nearly convict the wrong man. When the fiction was revealed as such, it was shown to be hiding a typical (and typically hidden) case of domestic violence. The police department remains responsible for violating a community, and yet, they also acted within a larger context as agents of a [North] American war which seeks to situate its problems on the outside."[2]

While bicycling I was overtaken by a disturbing hallucination. Was this a hyper-vivid daydream or an allegorical sensation of ghosts? It was really quite baroque. I was fast passing a body of dark water near the oldest Protestant church in town. Suddenly I was overcome by a terrible sense of melancholia, then fear. Not so much for myself as for the community that doesn't exist for so many of us at this time and place in HIStory. Such violence and estrangement. In successive waves there appeared figures of dead labored native peoples, blood stained and nameless. Then over these figures were lain, like a strange screen or a visual palimpsest, an eerie choreography of black skinned bodies. Slow rhythmic and troubled. Genocidal Forgettings. U.S. HIStory. Ultramodern CAPITAL. What's a whitemale U.S. sociologist to do with such hallucinated sad knowledge (of ghosts)?

Guilt of course is no answer. No, not of course, perhaps this needs to be written. Freud was probably right to suggest that guilt is part of what reproduces a forgetting of the actual (primal) scenery of violence. At least for modern men. A ghost of one of the dead labored dark red black skinned people whispered something in my ear. What s/he said must remain a secret, but this much I can tell—it led me to feel with uncanny terror the living dead violence of ultramodern power in the U.S.A. TODAY. Something infantile in its blinding white pleasures. Something indifferent in affect. What's a whitemale U.S. sociologist to do with such hallucinated sad knowledge (of ghosts)?

> In general, having the experience of a ghost, being haunted by a ghost, is having the memory of what you've never lived through in the present. Having the memory of something which has basically never been [allowed to be] present.[3]

Monday, May 13, 1985. Approximately 5:25 p.m. The workday's about to explode. The sound of a low flying helicopter. Chopping. This is not Viet Nam nor the U.S. supported Contras attacking Nicaraguan civilians. This is Philadelphia, Pennsylvania. This is the U.S.A. Today. This is democracy in action. Four and one half years later they'd tear down the Berlin Wall to get a piece of the action. Lieutenant Frank Powell, commander of the Philadelphia Bomb Disposal Unit is about to dispose of some people. He leans from the chopper's cabin, hurling a green canvas bag. It hits a roof top. The helicopter chops up up and away. Beneath the rooftop there are thirteen people. In pagan cultures this was the number of a coven. Soon there will be ghosts. Seven adults. Six children. On impact the bomb flames to 7200 degrees Fahrenheit. Heat waves in HIStory. For most North Americans this will be no big story. Really. During the height of the Contra War against the sovereign peoples of Nicaragua, *Newsweek* reported that approximately 55% of U.S. citizens tested in geography had no idea where Nicaragua was. Once Reagan said they might be heading to Texas. This is (k)not Nicaragua. This is Philadelphia. The roof convulses. Windows shatter halfway down the block. MOVE! THIS IS AMERICA.

"With the jury gone, the judge told Sue Africa that if she refused to abide by court procedures he would not allow her to testify any further and would strike what she had already said from the record. Ramona Africa retorted that the judge, in ordering Sue Africa to submit to the court procedures of the same legal system which had legally murdered her son, was telling her to sanction that murder."[4] The judge told her that she must speak only within the proper language of law. White driven language: language in the dead labored name of some father or Other. CAPITAL language. Rational proper turn taking language. The Language of I QUESTION: YOU ANSWER. Language embodied in the sacrificial rites of courtroom DISCIPLINE. The language of sadism. Ramona Africa answered, "I know my family were killed because of courtroom procedures....What protocol and procedures were used on May 13th?"[5]

> [G]hosts have images which emerge in language, expression, and modern
> rituals which far from being forgotten in the new electronic age, actually
> make their presence increasingly felt.[6]

"The importance of this colonial work of fabulation extends beyond the
nightmarish quality of its contents. Its truly crucial feature lies in the way it
creates an uncertain reality out of fiction, giving shape and voice to the formless
form of the reality in which an unstable interplay of truth and illusion becomes a
phantasmic social force. All societies live by fictions taken as real. What distinguishes cultures of terror is that the epistemological, ontological, and otherwise
philosophical problem of representation—reality and illusion, certainty and
doubt—becomes infinitely more than a 'merely' philosophical problem of epistemology, hermeneutics, and deconstruction. It becomes a high-powered medium
of domination...[a] medium of epistemic and ontological murk most keenly
figured and thrust into consciousness as *the space of death*."[7]

"How is one to make sense of the weapons carried by the 500 police surrounding the MOVE house: high powered military explosives (C-4); commercial
explosives (Torex); automatic and semiautomatic weapons (including a .50
caliber submachine gun); sharp-shooter rifles, two M-60 machine guns, UZI's,
shotguns; a silenced .22 caliber rifle; a Lahti anti-tank weapon? What was the
terror of MOVE?"[8] "For me the problem of interpretation is decisive for terror,
not only making effective counter discourse so difficult but also making the
terribleness of death squads, disappearance, and torture all the more effective in
crippling of peoples' capacity to resist. The problem of the interpretation turned
out to be an essential component of what had to be interpreted, just as resistance
was necessary for control. Deeply dependent on sense and interpretation, terror
nurtured itself by destroying sense."[9]

"The secret of the terror of MOVE is, to a large degree, the secret of the terror
and violence of language. This is so in a double sense. MOVE made its presence
felt in the Osage neighborhood of Philadephia (from 1983-1985 particularly)
through language. The language of violence was their primary weapon. As the
texts of the MOVE Commission Hearings reveal, the threat of transgression was
often more frightening than transgression itself. The terror of language pursued
the City in another sense: the officials of the City could not grasp MOVE in [their]
language. MOVE resisted definition and categorization. Were they a religious cult,
a radical protest group, black-power advocates, violent anarchists, back to nature
animal rights activists? Or, were they 'simply' mentally unstable? Unable to
grasp MOVE linguistically, suffering from the cognitive, moral and emotional
dissonance that MOVE elicited, the city moved awkwardly, involuntarily but
inexorably toward annihilation."[10]

"They see death everywhere...They think solely of the fact that they live surrounded by vipers, tigers and cannibals. Their imaginations are constantly struck by the idea of death as figured by these images of the wild and the only way they could live in such a world...was by themselves inspiring terror."[11] "And only then, in retrospect, could the City find and use the tag for which they had searched. MOVE were terrorists. The terror of language is believed to be vanquished by its domestication: the word 'terrorist' is posited as grasping the essence of the reality of MOVE. But the effect required the dropping of a bomb."[12] "Of the thirteen people who were inside 6621 Osage, eleven are dead—six adults, five children. Mangled, burned, carried away in zippered nylon bags—mostly in pieces. Only 30 year old Ramona Africa and 13 year old Birdie Africa managed to survive. As for the once attractive and stable neighborhood, both sides of Osage Avenue, the south side of Pine Street, and a section of Sixty-second Street are destroyed. The only things left [were] smoldering brick walls, standing in rows like giant grave markers. Altogether, sixty- one rowhouses have been totally destroyed or gutted. Two hundred and fifty people are without homes."[13] An orgy of bureaucratically orchestrated sacrifice—this was no festival.

TWO

> In the modern period, exchange value has come to dominate society: all qualities have been reduced to quantitative equivalences. This process inheres in the concept of reason. For reason, on one hand, signifies the idea of a free, human, social life. On the other hand, reason is court of judgment of calculation, the instrument of domination, and means for the greatest exploitation.... As in de Sade's novels, the mode of reason adjusts the world for the ends of self-preservation and recognizes no function other than the preparation of the object from mere sensory material in order to make it that material of subjugation.—Kathy Acker[14]

In 1847, one year before the violent defeat of proletarian revolutions throughout Europe, Marx and Engels wrote that, with CAPITAL, "the icy water of egoistic calculation" and "naked self-interest" had replaced the "religious fervor" of "heavenly ecstasies."[15] Marx and Engels are here describing a modern form of social organization that feeds off the repression of the commun(ion)istic materiality of medieval rites of festival. As a collective HIStorical embodiment of transgressive sacred rites, festival represented a periodic drama of "self-expenditure." The excessive generosity of festival signalled an advent of that *time between times* that was *once upon a time* a ritual aspect of pre-modern, pre-CAPITAList and pre-imperialist cultures.[16] A carnivalesque break from the productive ordering of everyday life, festival is associated with the celebration of transgressive excess, laughter, parody, noise, dirt, useless expenditure and polymorphous erotic effervescence.

The intense and frenzied playfulness of festival is literally impossible to productively endure. At the same time, the collective experience of this impossibility provided festivals with a deconstructive social force. To be within the vertiginous throes of festival is not to be on the outside the social order looking in. Festival is not be confused with transcendence. To be loosely caught up in festival is to be ambivalently (dis)positioned at the *borderlines* of a given social order and its ritual (re)construction. It is to be at the crossroads between order and chaos, between processes of *symbolic exchange* and the immanent flux of being nothings but human animal bodies in generous relations of giving and receiving gifts. Festival connotes an intensely common(ion)istic social space, a nameless form of *sacred disordering*, where the boundaries of subjective experience are, for a *time between times*, (im)possibly burst. Within the "primitive" or "chaotic effervescence" of festival all that appears solid is dis-placed into spiralling motion, while all ideal (or ideological) forms are given over to the terrifying silence of death and the joys of rebirthing.

What defines festival defies proper names and lawful economies of grammar. This is what makes festival potentially dangerous to the normative social order. As such, festival is commonly associated with an overturning of authority, and patriarchal authority in particular. While medieval festival may have been a pale remnant of earlier matriarchal rites,[17] within its carnivalesque spell "laughter breaks up, breaks out, splashes over...the masculine integrity of the body image."[18] Festival, likewise, challenges both the compulsions of heterosexist hierarchies[19] and white-western-racist claims to unitary self-identity.[20]

Festival also defies the rational instrumentality of modern CAPITAL. Indeed, a major feature of modern western HIStory involves the fragmentation, marginalization and suppression of public carnivals. "In different areas...the pace varied, depending upon religious, class and economic factors. But everywhere a fundamental ritual order of western culture came under attack—its feasting, violence, drinking, processions, fairs, wakes, rowdy spectacles, and outrageous clamor were subject to surveillance and repressive control."[21] From the seventeenth until the second half of the nineteenth century carnivalesque rites continued under the guise of modern religious and secular holidays. With the cultural regimentation demanded by industrial CAPITAL even these milder forms of festival were abolished or, worse still, converted into military-like parades. While 1855 marked the abolition of both St. Barthollomew's Fair in London and the Great Donnybrook Fair of Dublin, following the Fairs Act of 1871 some 700 British fairs, feasts and wakes were eliminated. By the 1880s the once wildly festive Paris Carnival had been transformed into a display of military and commercial enterprise. Similar changes occurred in Germany. Following the Franco-Prussian war, remnants of medieval feasts were turned into military pageants and celebrations of state power. In the wake of Operation Desert Storm the U.S. public was invited to play *as if festively* amidst flight simulators set up on the District of Columbia's mall, while in New York City millions of people were treated to fireworks resembling the televisionary bombing of Baghdad and a spectacular simulation of a Patriot missile intercepting a Scud.

The cultural impact of these acts of suppression should not be underestimated. They herald the HIStorical stabilization of linear social forms. By banishing (or driving underground) cyclical ways of re-marking memory these forms appear to live by production alone. Consider the modernization of Bavaria. Under pressure from "incipient CAPITALism," between 1770 and 1830 the number of days dedicated to "festive holidays" was reduced from 200 to 85 per year. Excluding Sundays, this meant "a reduction of actual festivals from 150 to 35 a year....This dramatic collapse of the ritual calendar had implications not only for each social formation but for the basic structures of symbolic activity in Europe: carnival was now everywhere and nowhere."[22]

This is not to suggest that modern forms of power have done away with the festival entirely. "Carnival had always been a loose amalgam of procession, feasting, competition, and spectacle, combining different elements from a large repertoire in different localities.... During the long process of suppression there was a tendency for these mixtures to break down, with certain elements becoming separated from others. Feasting became separated from performance, spectacle from procession. The grotesque body began to fragment" and become "marginalized in terms of both social class and geographical location" resulting, not only in reducing the value of festival, but confining its "childish" continuance to lower class and "deviant" sectors of the population.[23] In this, white modern and straightmale forms of CAPITAL either triumphed over festival or labored to neutralize its subversive charms. This is to purify the carnival of unprofitable transgressions and reduce it to "good clean fun," "organized sports," "games of chance" and "the well-earned vacation."[24] This is to reduce festive excess to access and make it a marketable item. But at what cost?

This is not to construct a nostalgic romance about the social functions of festival. Festivals were often as cruel as they were chaotic. Moreover, they often functioned more as a form of "tension release" than radical mobilization. At the same time, festival reminded human animals of our immanent, contingent and finite interdependencies in nature. What has happened to this "laughable" awareness, this "dark" wisdom? Has the paradoxical knowledge of festival been eliminated? Or has it simply been dis-appeared, forced to go underground or become (socially) unconscious? Throughout modernity the unauthorized remembrance of festival has remained a resistive drag on the instrumental rationality of CAPITAL, a thorn in the side of total bureaucratic control. This may be particularly true for those most disempowered by the industrialization of reason—women, the "working classes" and non-whites. Whether in the dramatic embodiment of hysteria, or in more subtle rituals resisting the homogenizing demands of linear time, those silenced by modernity have never entirely submitted to its abstract and disciplinary framework.[25] "Regarding the impossibility of making meaning circulate among the masses, the best example is God. The masses have hardly retained anything but the image of him, never the Idea.... What they have retained is the enchantment of ceremony and spectacle [and] the immanence of ritual....They were and have remained pagans."[26] In this way, festival has long haunted modernity, slowing its instrumental mastery, diverting its "Protestant Ethic," resisting the straight calculative deployment of its white-male and CAPITAL ethos.

This haunting paganism has remained a ghostly feature of the modern West, an uncanny double of what modernity and its institutions both feed off and deny. Oppressed and then repressed, or worse yet, driven to discourse, the carnivalesque has been banished to the realm of taboo, along with "everything resulting from *unproductive* expenditure" (cadavers, menstruating women, dreams, bodily waste and other such "impurities").[27] Reminders of an earlier order of *symbolic exchange*, the repressed remnants of festival today provoke an ambivalent combination of fascination and dread.[28] This is the parasitic dread of modern MAN confronted by the bodily remains of his victims. The dread of "he" who accumulates power at the sacrificial expense of others. The dread of the executioner, the philosopher and the architect. The dread of the scientist and the administrator. An enlightened dread. The dread of the master. *The dread of the fascist...*

This association between modern male anxieties and fascism is no accident. As suggested by Theweleit's analysis of the cultural artifacts of German fascists, those privileged by fascist forms of power dread the festive impurities of material interdependency. Mud, morass, mire, dirt, slime, pulp and excrement—these were terms used by fascist males to describe women, Jews, communists, anarchists and homosexuals. Within the fascist mind such images are linked to "the living movement of women." This mobilizes a "defensive-oppressive" stance whereby fascists either screen themselves against the presence of women or act to destroy them.[29] In this way, fascism represents a socio-logical materialization of patriarchal tendencies to "divide...life into its higher and lower categories, 'spirit versus nature,' or 'mind' versus 'matter'. [Hence,] fascism is not a wild 'barbaric' phenomenon that appears suddenly and without reason in the midst of civilization. It is the result of a long conditioning process, and the institutions that do the conditioning are those of [patriarchal western] civilization."[30] Fascism enacts

A TERRORISTIC CULTURAL STRATEGY aimed at erecting a pure distance between "civilized men" and a nature such men code as impurely female. In this, fascism converges with the hyper-clean and aestheticized rituals of ultramodern culture. Both fascism and ultramodernity are symptomatic of male fantasies that suppress and disavow (the suppression of) reflexive communal participation within nature. Both signify the material realization of violent patriarchal social constructions directed at reducing western MAN's dread of being in relation to others.

Imagine the fascinations of a social order that appears to escape such dread while giving away nothing in the realm of productive economic accumulation. This is to imagine an ultramodern social order. This is also to theorize the dangers of fascism in terms of a form of *imperative heterogeneity* that parasites upon nostalgic attractions for the "archaic pleasures" of festival, without allowing *the effervescence of excess* to disturb the hierarchical functioning of power. In this, ultramodern culture gains a purely technological access to the otherwise impure forces of the heterogeneous realm. This is to access a form of "cold ecstasy"[31] and thus transcend "the problem posed by the [haunting] contradictions of homogeneity."[32] This is to neutralize resistances engendered by the repression of festival by simulating (at a safe aesthetic distance) commun(ion)istic feelings once nurtured by collective rites of reciprocal symbolic exchange. This is to transform the *useless expenditures* of the carnivalesque into something useful—the perverse or pseudo-festival.

What is expended by such an ultramodern maneuver is not, as was the case with pre-modern festival, the purified privilege of being oneself. Sacrificed, instead, is the being of others as a substitute for the self insured. Rather than exceeding the modern social order, the ultramodern festival, as played out through mediums of dense and high speed telecommunicative fascination, appears to extend the violence of modernity without end. This may be what connects ultramodernity to fascism—its social and technological abilities to access "the means of coercion necessary to resolve...differences...between previously irreconcilable elements."[33] Between, for instance, money and the body. Or between the imperial daydreams of modern white men and the nightmares "we" have collectively created for women, the racially disenfranchised and the economically exploited. These forms of ritual access are purchased at a terrible price. As Bataille points out, "it goes without saying that, at the end of a movement that excludes all subversion [by profitably including what always only appears to be subversion], the thrust of these resolutions will have been consistent with the general direction of the existing homogeneity."[34] And consistent they have become. Twenty-four hours a day. Channel after channel. One "fascinating" byte of inFORMation after anOther.

THREE

MADNESS AND CIVILIZATION: "In the margins of the community, at the gates of cities there stretch wastelands which sickness had ceased to haunt but had left sterile and long uninhabitable."[35] There he makes his way amidst these ruins, pausing now and again to savour the sense of rust. There is no moon. Or if there is, he doesn't notice. Wastelands of fractured metallic engines, doors, hoods and fenders ripped by velocities in excess of the limit. It was a sovereign matter, or so it appeared.

Foot to the rubber, Reno accelerates between concaves of collapsed models incarnate. "I'll wait," he says to himself. Breathless and without thinking, he claws uneasily at the belt that binds him to the seat. She'll return to the scene, he imagines. All parasites do. It's a matter of nature. Really. A metallurgical recycling of difference.

In the margins of the community, at the gates of cities, he is suddenly taken with a desire to jerk off into oblivion. And so he does. This act calms his mind, soothes the restless edges, releases his eyes/"I"s to wander senseless beyond the windshield. Then, with a minimum of feeling, Reno turns off the engine, takes two extra strength tablets and lays his mind to dream within a mass of scrap iron tearing the mask, cutting his thigh. Maybe he shouldn't have pulled the trigger. The people at the cafe meant nothing to him. Nothing personal at least. It was simply a matter of business. After all, everyone from THE COMPANY seemed so frightened and so sure. Reno remained ambivalent. This was his pleasure—a real time flux; controlled bleeding, an *imaginary* charged by techno-dangers and the like. It's all a game of chance, a game of "double or nothing," he thinks to himself drifting beyond what's flesh. Redoubling.

FOUR

> Consumable pseudo-cyclical time is...the time of consumption of images....
> The epoch which displays its time as essentially the sudden return of mul-
> tiple festivities is also an epoch without festivals. What was, in cyclical time,
> the moment of the community's participation in the luxurious expenditure
> of life is impossible for the society without community or luxury....The
> reality of time has been replaced by the advertisement of time.—Guy
> Debord[36]

Reno: "Cathy, I mean Marty, I need you. I love you. I'll do anything at all to be with you. I'll even die."

Marty: "Oh Reno, why can't we be together like we were as children. What's happened to the secrets we once shared. I too would do anything to be with *you—death, telemarketing, standing in line with 50,000 others waiting for a $12.64 BIG MAC in Moscow. Anything at all. Oh Reno, what's become of love?"*

Reno: "Wars are raging everywhere. Just look what happened to Laura Palmer. Remember the Alamo?"

Marty: "Males dumber and whiter than nonhuman animals are running this economy. Playing golf and racing speed boats, while you and I are dying (for love). I want. What do I want? Is it wrong to want life?"

Reno: "Yeh, it's bad all right. But look, it's time for WHEEL OF FORTUNE. We can talk later, OKAY? You know how savage I get if I miss my shows. OKAY, Marty, OKAY?"[37]

In 1847, one year before the defeat of proletarian revolutions throughout Europe, and the same year as Marx and Engels' *Communist Manifesto,* Emily Bronte published the novel *Wuthering Heights.*[38] A narrative of tragic love between Catherine Earnshaw and the enigmatic Heathcliff, *Wuthering Heights* is described by Georges Bataille as "one of the greatest books ever written." This "beautiful and most profoundly violent love story" is also a tale of the displacement of festive rites of death and self-expenditure into the structural (im)possibilities of modern adult (hetero)sexuality.[39] For Bataille, eroticism, like the transgressive sacred rites of carnival, involves an intimate restoration of the continuity of material being partitioned by the ideational doublings of language or culture. This is a loving "animal immanence" between "the eater and the eaten," such that the boundaries separating one from the other are literally set spinning.[40] "Like water in water" each becomes a fleeting form of food for the other in a sacrificial reciprocity that defies desire-driven distinctions between subject and object. A form of "violent silence," the exuberance of eroticism involves an "assenting of life to the point of death."[41] In the world of modern CAPITAL, where death represents a terror to be repressed or deterred, and where eroticism is tamed by the exclusivity of lawful heterosexual marriage, the transgressive aspects of erotic love are thus severely reduced. In modern western society responsible adults are no longer permitted to periodically dine on what is forbidden. Here contact with what has been deadened by the restrictive economic sacrifices of instrumental reason is permanently taboo. The tragedy of such (im)possible permanence and the desire it engenders is, for Bataille, a key theme in Bronte's "dreamy" text.

Freud makes a related point in "Infantile Recurrence," the final chapter of *Totem and Taboo.* Freud makes distinctions between the laws governing modern family meals and rules guiding the "feast of kin" among primitive people. While the modern "meal unites the members of the family," this union has nothing do with "the sacrificial repast" of primitives, "an occasion for joyously transcending one's interests and emphasizing social community and community with god."[42] In "primitive" societies, "the ethical power of the public sacrificial feast was based upon primal conceptions of the meaning of eating and drinking in common. To eat and drink with someone was at the same time a symbol and a confirmation of social community and of the assumption of mutual obligations; the sacrificial eating gave direct expression to the fact that the god and...worshippers are communicants.... In other words: the sacrificial animal [or totem] was treated like one of kin; the sacrificing community, its god, and the sacrificial animal were of the same blood."[43] All this is suppressed by modern society. Here the guilt of having once eaten the forbidden totem (or "primal father") is repressively channeled into linear visions of accumulative development without return or recurrence.

A fundamental difference between Freud and Bataille concerns what each makes of this suppression. For Bataille it represents a violent injunction against periodic movement out of the artificial or linguistic death imposed by the workings of culture. This is a meaning of erotic transgression: an effervescent intimacy with that which is other than what is made accessible by a particular moral economy. Bataille poetically imagines such radical generosity in the form of an excessive *potlatch* or selfless rite of gift exchange. This "is the opposite of the principle of conservation: it puts an end to the stability of fortunes as it existed within the totemic economy."[44] Within the CAPITAL confines of a moral economy that has banished the cyclical recurrence of otherness, Bataille's excessive imagery must be read as either "evil" or "mad." Bataille embraces the first designation, reversing its reductive binary opposition as the debased opposite of good. For Bataille, "evil" is what undoes modern binary logic. This is its daimonic threat. Bataille's (w)ritings, like Bronte's, make an impassioned plea to be haunted by the ecstatic ghosts of an eroticism forbidden by modern times. Of the passionate evil evoked by *Wuthering Heights*, Bataille (w)rites:

> Evil...if we examine it closely, is not only the dream of the wicked: it is to some extent the dream of Good. Death is the punishment, sought and accepted for this mad dream, but nothing can prevent the dream from having been dreamt. It was dreamt by the unfortunate Catherine Earnshaw as well as by Emily Bronte. How can we doubt that Emily Bronte, who died for having experienced the states of mind which she described, identified herself with Catherine Earnshaw? *Wuthering Heights* has a certain affinity with Greek tragedy. The subject of the novel is the tragic violation of the law.[45]

While Bataille embraces the (w)riting of evil (or transgression) as a contra-punctual movement in relation to the restrictive economy of modern power, Freud views the compulsive repetition of such actions as madness. In this, the "father of psychoanalysis" draws parallels between the recurrence of "creative guilt" among "primitives" and the "infantile" thoughts and actions of modern neurotics. In each instance, "a piece of HIStoric reality" is said to be involved. Like those "evil" savages who mythically sacrificed their Primal Father, neurotics are said to be persons who "in their childhood...had nothing but evil impulses and as far as their childish impotence permitted they put them into action."[46] Still, there are important differences. While primitives are said to regret their crime, declaring that "its execution must bring no gain," they are also graced by the luxury of symbolically returning to the ORIGINARY ACT of killing. In so doing, they again dine upon the ambivalent object of their most compulsive fears and desires. This is Freud's projective interpretation of the "sacrificial feast."[47] This periodic rite gives "primitives" a perverse advantage over neurotics. Caught up in "the pressure of over-morality," the neurotic is said to be "inhibited in his [or her] actions," such that one's anxious thoughts operate as "a complete substitute for the [sacrificial] deed."[48] At the same time, the ritualized disinhibi-tions of "primitives" condemn them (in Freud's eyes/"I"s) to cycles of recurrence that block the linear conquest of time. In this they fail to progress. By modern definitions this is what makes them "primitive."

In order to cure neurotics, and thereby help them progress out from within the guilty constraints of their allegedly primitive mentalities, Freud thought it neces-sary that such persons be reconciled to the "irreversibility" of guilt. But how might this take place, without reproducing the experience of being eaten away by guilt (a prolongation of neurosis) or an "infantile" eating up of guilt (effecting a release from the "civilizing" repressions demanded by modernity)? Freud's somewhat hysterical answer involves sublimation—the elevated and artful channeling of repressed energies into constructive acts of labor. In a word—WORK.

Bataille's response is radically different. Influenced more by Marx's analysis of work's oppressive HIStory, Bataille sought to subvert "the shame of Icarian despair" in "bourgeois" men such as Freud. It was (k)not that Bataille rejected Freud's insights into the unconscious structuring of guilt. Quite the opposite. What Bataille rejected was sublimation's flight skyward. Where there was repres-sion Bataille conjured dreams of rupture. Where there was oppressive work Bataille called for festive agitation. "For it is human agitation, with all its the vulgarity of needs small and great, with its flagrant disgust for the police who repress it...that alone determines revolutionary mental forms, in opposition to bourgeois mental forms."[49]

Bataille sides with the "child-like" agitation of Bronte and her tragic lovers against CAPITAL's voice of instrumental reason and modern adult demands for sublimated adjustment. What haunts Catherine and Heathcliff is the forced abandonment of "child-like" relations. Rather than diagnosing "recurrence" to childishness as a problem, Bataille reads the instrumental demands of adult sublimation as an oppression against which Catherine and Heathcliff play out their ill-fated revolt. Theirs was a love originating in and returning to the pleasures of childhood, where they "spent their time racing wildly on the heath. They abandoned themselves, untrammeled by any restraint or convention other than a taboo on games of sensuality. But, in their innocence, they placed their indestructible love for one another on a different level, and indeed perhaps this love can be reduced to the refusal to give up an infantile freedom which had not been amended by the laws of society or of conventional politeness. They led their wild life, outside the world, in the most elementary conditions, and it is these conditions which Emily Bronte made tangible—the basic conditions of poetry, of spontaneous poetry before which both children refused to stop."[50]

The abandonment of the play of spontaneous poetry—is this what modern adulthood demands? This is what Bataille reading Bronte suggests. For Henri Lefebvre, this is also a major feature of CAPITAL's "everyday" culture—the displacement of poetic cycles into the linearity of purposive prose. Beginning with the generalization of CAPITAList "trade and monetary" relations in the nineteenth century, "the prose of the world spread, until now it invades everything—literature, art, objects—and all the poetry of existence has been evicted."[51] A related argument is made by Monica Sjoo and Barbara Mor, who associate the "rationalization" of ecstatic poetic forms as an aspect of western patriarchal domination. "Apollo's priests proclaimed that 'rational poetic language and thought' were to replace the inspired poetic language of the Goddess. From then on, poetry—language itself—ceased to be mantric utterance and became a social ornament and political device; rhetoric."[52] In Bataille's words, modern "society contrasts the free play of innocence with reason...based on the calculations of interest. Society is governed by its will to survive. It could not survive if these childish instincts, which bound the children in a feeling of complicity, were allowed to triumph. Social constraint would have required the young savages to give up their innocent sovereignty; it would have required them to comply with those reasonable adult conventions which are advantageous" to a culture governed by the blind fatherly language of CAPITAL.[53] This is the tragic dynamic at WORK in Bronte's novel. Separated by the calculative adult demands of class, power and prestige, the lovers' child-like free play is dashed upon the rocks of instrumental rationality. The wildness of their generosity is repressively exiled to the haunting world of ghosts.

FIVE

REPETITION COMPULSION: I see him passing into the dark almost faceless. He's stalking the wide-eyed young woman student as she approaches the cafe. There's not much traffic and the (k)night's upon her/us/me. She does appear to register the danger. No. Wait. She's turning, scanning, then quickening her pace, her heart beat, searching for signs. She doesn't see him. He's in the shadows; rationally wild, half naked half human half beast. He means NO GOOD but can't tell the difference. Binary frames split his mind from coast to coast; half life half machine half body.

He's shaggy haired and close shaven and almost upon her as she enters the cafe. His body casts a shape upon hers and I'm frightened. He's moving half minded half wanting half dead. He seizes her figure. She's terror stricken, (k)not wanting his half wanting (k)not wanting. She's struggling. He's stronger. He's ripping away her blouse. He's baring her breasts, man-handling her figure. I'm no longer able to bear this vision. I'm dreaming. I'm frightened. How should I act? What should I (w)rite?

I'm running (k)not knowing but wanting to rescue her figure from his form. He appears familiar, too familiar, doubly familiar and I'm worried. I'm half shaking my fist. I'm half shaking my body. I'm half trying to make him disappear and he does. I embrace the young woman student shivering frightened and angry. Half ravished, half nuded, fully terrorized. I press her exposed breasts to my suit coat doubly heroic, if anxious.

The wild man, the bad man, the dark man appears to have vanished into the (k)night. He appears familiar, too familiar, doubly familiar and I'm worried. Later, when telling this dream to the Black Madonna, it strikes me that perhaps the man was Reno. Reno Heimlich. It must have been him. That explains why he was stalking the young woman student figure at the cafe. Reno, that once and future assassin serial killer shooting (w)holes into HIStory. Reno. Yes, it must have been Reno.

Black Madonna Durkheim agreed or rather half agreed with what I was saying about Reno. "Of course it was Reno," she said. But adding a few lines of double talk, she continued, "Of course it was Reno. But isn't that only half the story? When you look him in the eyes/'I's, whom else do you see?" I see him passing into the dark almost faceless. I'm running (k)not knowing but wanting to rescue her figure. He appears familiar, too familiar, doubly familiar and I'm worried. I am repeating myself. I see him passing compulsive...into the (k)night...into my double...

SIX

> Death alone—or, at least, the ruin of the isolated individual in search of
> happiness in time—introduces that break without which nothing reaches the
> state of ecstasy. And what we regain is always both innocence and the
> intoxication of existence. The isolated being *loses oneself* in something other
> than oneself. What the 'other thing' represents is of no importance.... So
> unlimited is it that it is not even a thing: it is *nothing*.... Its violence is not
> slowly reabsorbed in the gradual experience of an enlightenment. It is, in
> short, far closer to the indescribable anguish expressed in *Wuthering
> Heights*. —Georges Bataille[54]

Rada Rada led the way upstairs, suggesting that I hide the scanner and (k)not
make a noise. When I asked the reason, she told me she had no idea, but that in
the short time she'd been here there had been plenty of queer goings on.

"Queer goings on?"

"It has nothing to do with latent homosexuality," she replied. "The abyss here
is far more superficial." Then she withdrew for the night.

Too stupefied to want to know more, I fastened my door and glanced round
at the sleeping apparatus. It was a bit like a coffin of mirrors, with blue velvet
cushions and a telelectric memory screen near the top. I slid back the panelled
side units, got in with my scanner, and, for a time, felt secure against what LIES in
wait for my body like a swamp or a tear in a perfectly good idea.

The input jack where I inserted the scanner was covered with mildew but
when I key coded the entry post everything seemed fine. (W)riting appeared on
the screen etched out in MacPaint. It was "nothing but a name repeated in all
kinds of characters, large and small"—Catherine, I mean *Marty Martin,* here and
there varied to *Marty Heimlich*, and again to *Marty Samhain*. Vapid and listless I
lay my forehead against the screen, and continued repeating in silence Marty
Martin—Heimlich—Samhain, *till my eyes closed; but they had not rested five
minutes when a glare of white letters started from the dark, as vivid as specters—
the air swarmed* with the name of Marty; and rousing myself to dispel the obtrusive name, I fast forwarded the replay until a fly-leaf bore the title—"Marty
Martin, her book," and a date indicating a time in the early 1990s.

An immediate fascination drew me to the unknown Marty and I began at
once to decipher, I mean re(w)rite, her strange text's hieroglyphics. To me her
words, fragmented and uncertain, were all about food. And sacrifice.

> Writing which expends its own spending-without-return (depense) goes
> toward the fragment, which self-denounces by an abrupt rupture, by a cut to
> the quick. The system tries to understand death; the fragment is death, for it
> immediately collapses into its own loss. To put it another way: by its

manifestness the fragment snatches us from our discontinuity while the continuity of the system returns us to our discontinuity. [56]

'An awful Sunday!' commenced the entry. 'I wish my father were here in the flesh. Reno is such a cold substitute—his conduct to Rada Rada is atrocious—Rada and I are going to rebel. On Sunday evenings we were permitted to play mildly, as long as we didn't make much noise; any audible laughter was sufficient to send us off to Saudi Arabia.'

Rada Rada pressed a finger to my lips saying, "What would we be without language? It has made us what we are. Alone, it reveals, at the limit, the sovereign moment where it has no currency."[55]

"Certainly, it is dangerous," I responded, "in extending the frigid research of the sciences, to come to a point where one's object no longer leaves one unaffected, where on the contrary, it is what inflames." This made us both laugh.

"You forget you have a master here," says the corporate suited tyrant, "I'll destroy anybody who attempts to deconstruct my power! I insist on absolute sobriety and silence. Don't tell me that objects are in transition."

Rada Rada turned toward him anxious, exposing the delicacy of certain private parts, saying: "Have a bite/byte! You eat me anyway, sucking my precious fluids so as to waste me on your way to empire! So I ask you, WHY CAN'T THIS VEAL CALF WALK?"

He thought her mad to speak these words, but sank his teeth in anyway. This was (k)not a matter of dialogue. Her sacrifice has become his music. It enables him to forget all the noise and find comfort. He stuffs himself on the meat she'd been made into; dining upon her silence. But it is not enough that he simply parasite upon her body LYING beneath his erection. He needs her to also hum along, to play chorus to the harmony he imagines; to act the part; to feed herself within the (falsely) empirical foodstocks of his desire. He depends upon the fact that she will conform to the image of a parasite who demands the only gift he has or is willing to dispense (as a worthy investment). For, "the victim of the sacrifice [that founds his culture] cannot be consumed in the same way as a motor uses fuel."[57] She must also appear to find pleasure in the totemic exchange that creates the surplus upon which he dines. Or face the consequences of being sliced open and discounted market to market. Then she will be NO-BODY, really. What a cursed share! Agoraphobia runs rampant.

Pursuing the path of reductive sacrificial consumption, Bataille's study of "the cursed share" involves "tracing the exhausting detours of exuberance through eating, death and sexual reproduction."[58] These practices ritually constitute an ORIGINARY VIOLENCE that, in eating into otherness, makes possible the energized RULE of the self-same. The relatively unnoticed character of these sacrifices is evidence of fetishistic codings that render its base economic violence nearly *unmemorable. Out of such channelled luxuries comes an ordering of THINGS as "we" know them carnally. This knowledge, however, remains haunted by traces of blood-letting. This is what founds its surplus value; value abstracted from the bodies of those it deadens or forecloses. As such, Bataille suggests that the THINGS produced in originary sacrificial rituals remain tenuous, circumscribed by the forces of returning repressions, ghosts and the like.*

These ghostly forces haunt a seemingly solid world of empirically experienced THINGS. Moreover, since these THINGS are in reality NOTHINGS but artificial doubles of suppressed relations of differentiation, they must return repeatedly to the ritual scene of their violent constitution, simply to continue to appear (as if) "natural." Throughout modernity, this rite of return (or reproduction) is danger-ously unstable. Masters depend on it for renewing their sacrificial power, while those it enslaves are led to once again feel the "uncanny" wound such sacrifice entails. Such a painful feeling renders the future uncertain. It also opens up temporal possibilities that may challenge the linear development of THINGS in time. This is radical potential of secondary sacrifices, sacrifices that temporarily undo the "naturalness" of fetishized relations, sacrifices which feedback upon or into the always only apparent effects of originary sacrifices, sacrifices that un-mask the artifice of what seems real, (k)not to reveal a hidden truth but to dra-matize the hiding of all truth in the violent erasures of CAPITAL language. This I sensed was the character of Rada Rada's challenge to the master. Immediately I sought to join in this revolt.

I suppose Marty realized her project, for the words that followed took up another subject: she waxed lachrymose like a moon walked upon by men.

'*How little did I dream that Reno would ever make me cry so!*' she wrote. '*My head splits with pain and yet I still can't give over. Poor Rada! Reno calls her a vagabond slut poststructuralist, and won't let her eat with us; and he says, she and I must (k)not play together, and threatens to send her to Saudi Arabia if we break his SYMBOLIC ORDER.*'

I began to nod drowsily before the screen. I recall a eerie red inscription— SEVEN TIMES SEVENTY—and soon fell into dreams. *They were of a strange and uneasy character—disturbing transgressions that I had never imagined previ-ously.* The first dream opens in a long narrow men's locker room, or maybe a horse barn. There is athletics in the air and a coach is barking instructions. He orders some of his best team players to sew yellow ribbons onto their uniforms and then to seize upon and mount others. Some players quickly obey. They place rough hands upon the cold shoulders of those who resist or have second thoughts, forcing them into stalls where they are raped or otherwise made to feel shame.

There are only men in this dream and THINGS seem fascist in their frenzy. Several young men or boy victims try to escape. They run terrified out of the locker room (or riding stable) across an open field leading to a huge coliseum. This coliseum looks like a military fortress. Maybe there's a banner blowing patriotic. Maybe the banner reads OPERATION DESERT SHIELD. It is dusk and the grass is gridiron green. The sun is setting. At first I'm unsure what do to. I appear as if a spectator to myself, uneasy about my role in the violent dreamy performance. Next, I'm joining those who obey the coach's orders. "We" chase down those who flee. "We" tackle them. "We" MAN HANDLE them and pull off their trousers. I am flushed hot hard within this violent pageant and the erotics seem disciplined. All of a sudden I reflexively double back upon my own pleasures channelled anally and with such violence. Who am I? What am I doing in this awful sacrificial dream play? The field is littered with dead male Arab bodies with asses bleeding. Maybe 150,000. Maybe there's a banner blowing. Maybe it reads OPERATION DESERT STORM.

Frenzied and dazed I find myself at the top of a huge cylindrical tower. Below me is a long and spiral staircase to who knows where. I begin to descend. Down I go, deep within the phallic tower's interior. Military men of various sorts rush up and down the stairs, shouting commands, preparing to do battle. I descend further. Men pass me marching, clicking heels. They pay little attention to me. I am amazed. At the base of the tower a reinforced metal door opens to a platform of rocks. On the door is stamped the number 490. I am puzzled. "That's how many steps there are, Sir," I hear one soldier say to another. Seven times seventy. Nobody says a word to me. I step out onto the rocks. Everywhere waves are pounding against smooth stone. The last of the military men scurry into the tower's confines. Fearing the water, the men prepare to bolt the door. Waves rush in around me ankle deep. Somehow I maintain an eerie calm amidst this fateful HIStory.

I hear the metal door slam and am torn from my sleep. Then I realize this was no door, but the sound of my scanner flipping into auto-reverse. Half awake and half in slumber, I listen doubtingly for an instant; detect the disturber, then turn and doze, and dream again, if possible, still more disagreeably than before.

This time, I am LYING in the mirror lined coffin when I hear the distinctive sound of the scanner resetting the *bioinfo* disk and beginning to replay its compulsively screened narrative. This time I know the source of my televisionary anxiety; but it annoys me so much that I resolve to silence it by any means. I rise and try to demag the scanner joint but the hook seems soldered into the staple.

'I must stop it!' I mutter, knocking my knuckles through the screen, and stretching an arm to seize the unwieldy mag hook. Instead my fingers close on the fingers of a little ice-cold hand!

Intense horror sets my mind to spin and my body races electric in panic. I try to draw back my arm, but the hand clings to it, as a most melancholy voice sobs, 'Let me in—let me in!'

'Who are you?' I ask, PLAGIARIZING, re(w)riting, struggling to disengage myself.

'Marty Samhain,' it replies shiveringly (why did I think of Marty Samhain? I had read Marty Martin twenty times for Marty Samhain), 'I've come home, I'd lost my way in the networks!'

As it spoke, I discerned, obscurely, a child's face looking through the screen's fractured opening—terror makes me cruel—and, finding it USELESS to attempt shaking the monster off, and fearing everything that's USELESS, I pull its wrist on the broken surface, and rub it to and fro until blood runs down and soaks the sheets of my own (w)riting. Still the child's voice wails, 'Let me in!' The little cold icy fingers maintain their uncanny hold. I am maddened, fearing the (im)possibilities of TOTAL RECALL.

'How can I let you into my life without dying to myself in the process! Let *me* go if you want me to let you in, let *me* go!'

The child's fingers relax and I snatch mine through the hole, hurryingly piling books up in a pyramid against it. *The Closing of the American Mind* and *Thinking About Crime*— these were among the volumes I bring to my self-defense. I look for anything by John Silber or William Bennett. No doubt the words of these men would help me to keep this strange other at a safe and straightmale-minded distance.

My efforts seem to keep the ghostly child outside for a few minutes, yet the instant I open my ears again, there is the abject moaning.

'Begone!' I shout, 'I'll never let you in, (k)not if you beg for forty years.'

'It's forty years,' moans the voice, 'forty years, I've been outside looking in. Forty years!'

A blast of static fills the airwaves and the pile of books moves as if spun by the vertigo of an unseen catastrophe.

I try to jump up, but my limbs remain paralyzed. I scream in a doubled frenzy of fright.

As if to further my abjection, I discover the yell was in no way ideal. Hasty footsteps enter my chamber and a soft green light shines upon me. It is Rada Rada. The electrolight she points in my direction multiplies my terror in the endless play of mirrors in which I LIE enveloped. Sitting upright within my coffin I point to the shattered screen, unable to speak.

Rada places a finger to her lips and cautions my silence, saying: "Look, I told you things at the Cafe would be more real than you'd think. *'To see one's double is to see oneself dead.... From mirage to mirage, the subject/object takes flight and loses its existence. Trying to grasp it amounts to stopping a mirror from mirroring. It is encountering the void. Not a transitory void, but one (the one) that has always been there despite our eternal effort to banish it from conscious sight. A shattered mirror still functions as mirror; it may destroy the dual relation of I to I but leaves the infiniteness of life's reflection intact. Here reality is not reconstituted, it is put into pieces so as to allow another world to rebuild (keep on unbuilding and rebuilding) itself with debris.'"*[59]

SEVEN

> Fast ideas are like fast food. Its not the taste of the meal that matters, nor the care in cooking it, no matter how much the business claims to love its customers. This sort of food exists to be digested and not eaten. The swiftness of their preparation corresponds to the swiftness of their consumption. —Ariel Dorfman[60]

In *The Empire's New Clothes* Ariel Dorfman points to the infantilization of adult North Americans as a dangerous feature of U.S. imperial culture. Dorf-man makes an important theoretical distinction between the playful wonder of children (something hopeful) and the narcissistic or insular infantilism of adults caught up in high speed circuits of numbing information (something terrifying, particular for those most subject to the violence of such "infantile adult" power). (W)riting as a Chilean whose country and people have a tragic knowledge of such power, Dorfman identifies aspects of North American culture which protect many U.S. adults from memories that would challenge our sense of "innocence" concerning America's "good guy" image in world HIStory. Dorfman points to publications such as Reader's Digest that provide their readers with "an extraordinarily...marketable product: *immortality*."[61]

Reader's Digest and other "fast food-like" information rituals partially release U.S. culture from repression, without exposing its celebrants to the material return of the ghosts of sacrificed others. As distinguished from Bataille and Bronte's view of the generosity of child-like poetics, such rituals bring to mind Freud's association between infantile fears of death and narcissistic self-enclosure. Here Freud's comments about totemic rituals appear most relevant to contemporary western society. Unlike the totemic practices of many so-called "underdeveloped" peoples, Dorfman's reading of U.S. culture is suggestive of something like a simulation of festive rituals. The effect is more infantile than child-like. Here repressed ghosts may no longer (appear to) haunt the Symbolic Order, still the fetishized power of that order is neither reversed nor given back. In this sense, Dorfman's work points to the terrifying if relatively unmemorable violence of *overdeveloped societies*. In such societies:

> With Digest in hand, one can be powerful and dominant just like omniscient beings, and good and beloved like defenseless creatures. We can keep our juvenile optimism without having to give up the progress and material well-

being that comes with subordinating the world to our science.... We're told that we can know and still preserve our innocence, because we digest, although we do not eat.... Life is dreamt without death; digestion is dreamt without evacuation, knowledge is dreamt as consumption and not production.[62]

What the *Digest* and other ultramodern cultural rituals offer is a renewed sense of linear mastery as the modern deterrence of death is ritually freed from the haunt of its ghosts. In this, ultramodern power (over others) is insured by putting into play "simulations" of its exact opposite—the eternal recurrence of prefabricated versions of otherness that are, at once, insidiously disarmed and exotically fascinating. This is an inoculated otherness stripped of its potential to make a disturbing difference; an infantile otherness; an otherness where all the ghosts appear to have disappeared because all the ghosts are visible. This is a hyper-visible culture without secrets or horizons. This is a hyper-narcissistic culture that literally screens itself in orbit around itself. No wonder its agents appear numb to the structural basis of this culture's violence. No wonder its violence may appear random, indifferent or chaotic. Here violence originates (as always) where sacrificial power finds its (totemic) center. But since that center may today exist predominately in the social form of that which appears as if literally spun around itself, its violence may seem anomalous or without origin. In this sense, ultramodern violence may appear literally to come from nowhere. "The weight of twenty centuries" may suddenly be suspended by "the airiness of...sidereal space," as ghostly anxieties produced by progressive disembodiment come into inFORMational oscillation with predigested promises of "certitude" and "enduring significance...as long as the isolated and scattered faithful renew their faith through the ritual of reading and through that other ritual which is subscription and purchase."[63]

> *I've been trying to complete this text by the deadline but am haunted, detoured, led astray. Maybe it's just bad timing for theory. These last several weeks of 1989 have been given over to efforts to collectively counter the terrible U.S. sponsored violence against the people of El Salvador. For the most part I have been working with others to publicly raise questions about the virtual media WHITE OUT concerning such matters as the murderous bombing of San Salvador's poorest neighborhoods, the suppression of a wide range of popular religious and humanitarian organizations and the insidious use of weapons such as U.S.-made white phosphorous bombs (a powdery explosive with effects much like NAPALM).*

Dorfman's analysis of *Reader's Digest* points (k)not merely to the content of this magazine but to its medium or social form. This form fascinates with its seductive promise of "infinite" or limitless knowledge.[64] (K)not that it provides such knowledge. What it provides is fascination, (k)not knowledge *per se*. Dorfman likens the promise of such unfettered inFORMation to that which captivated Faust. This is to read Faust's story as "a tragedy of development."[65] Lured by the seductive promise of TOTAL KNOWLEDGE AS TOTAL CONTROL, Faust makes a pact permitting him to develop the world according to the dictates of modern reason. This entails the sacrificial destruction of all worlds, except those productively engendered by Faust's own rational imagination. This separates Faust from a recurrence to "childhood," a time of flowering interdependence and cyclical rebeginnings. Yet, for Faust, a figure at the threshold between medieval and modern culture, childhood also involved the cruelties of feudal modes of domination. (K)not only was childhood a time of recurrence, but what recurred involved the ritual reproduction of irrational hierarchies of inherited male wealth and power.

> *The American media carry electronic words, but few images of six murdered Jesuit priests with brains splattered. The killing of liberation theology by a theology schooled in the virtues of the corporate CAPITAList market place. To what God-the-Father does Bush say his prayers? There is incidental mention of the dead bodies of the woman who prepared these priests' food and of her daughter bloodied and past tense. Little information is given about why any of this is happening, except to imply that the violence on each side is excessive. Nihilism abounds, as does distortive racist imagery of savage Hispanics.*

> *The lives of those struggling imperfectly to rid their country of the fascist infections of a U.S. will to power, our nation's manifest destiny, are statistically equated with those of parasitic military commanders. These men's American made boots are stained with the blood of those who are poor and resisting. Bush describes these men as a force for democracy. America, it seems, remembers virtually nothing of the lessons of Viet Nam. Lessons about a HIStory of U.S. imperialism, lessons about the role of the U.S. military-industrial complex in opening new markets and securing new freedom to buy American. Or to die by American made weapons at the hands of U.S.-trained torture-rape-death squads. It is not that Americans remember nothing. It is that "we" remember virtually nothing. Not the empty stomach turning nothingness of shamefully knowing that our parasitic survival and cheerful Christmas shopping is purchased by the blood of others, but the blank, white and virtual nothingness of a telecommunicative screen that is void of memory, if cluttered with infor-*

mation. During the first week of the FMLN war of resistance the headlines of USA TODAY, the Nation's No. 1 Newspaper...6.3 million readers every day announces: "HOLIDAY SHOPPERS CHEER EARLY SALES— HOLLYWOOD'S BIGGEST CHRISTMAS—FANTASITIC SEASON LIKELY TO SET RECORD." As a popular and electronically mass mediated culture it appears "we" register neither memory nor shame.

Bolstered by the masterful logic of Mephisto, with whom the tragic hero makes his "developmental" pact, Faust attempts to become a thoroughly modern man. Using the tools of money (or functionally equivalent exchange), productive utility, speed and the aura of sexual potency, Faust progressively severs all ties to childhood. His productive labor makes childhood a site of underdevelopment rather than difference. As a sacrificial substitute Faust offers a profitable model of rationally planned progress. The dead bodies of others pile up along the way: the body of Gretchen, who is drawn into Faust's Imaginary but without any of the self-protective (linguistic) resources which guard his new Symbolic Order; and the bodies of Philemon and Baucis, who remain "childishly" content to live by the sea rather than, like Faust, developmentally master the sea's "natural" power. Still, in the contradictory material course of HIStory, the ghosts of "others" whom Faust "productively" condemns to underdevelopment come back to haunt this most modern of western "heroes." This is what makes HIStory tragic. In the end, the speed of Faust's own productive labor brings him face to face with the death his dreams of infinite (self)development have long deterred. Goethe's failing SUPERMAN falls prey to mortality like any other.

As Americans, the collective representations by which we narcissistically advertise ourselves to ourselves have little to do with the material exigencies of our actual HIStories. Little is ritually remembered about who ate whom for dinner on Thanksgiving, the first and perhaps most cynical of all New World holidays, or of the economic foundations of American democracy in genocide, slavery and the subordination of women. Unto death do us part. One boat load of refugees, escapees, prisoners, outlaws, and fortune seekers after another. Claiming the land, seizing the time, one cemetery, lynching tree, and ghetto blasting moment of HIStory after another. Without the pre-CAPITAList constraints of residual medieval institutions, architecture and folkways. America the Beautiful.
Sacrificial America.

In Dorfman's analysis of *Reader's Digest,* and by extension the even faster food for thought markets of PEOPLE MAGAZINE NATIONAL ENQUIRER HARD COPY EYEWITNESS NEWS DISNEY ENTERTAINMENT TONIGHT PRIME TIME MTV

CNN INSIDE EDITION SPORTS ILLUSTRATED USA TODAY etc., as these are hooked into networks of increasingly fast, dense and mobile interchangeable experience, Faust appears on the other side of tragedy—a stupidly optimistic Faust, an "infantile superman"—Faust doubling with Narcissus. Ultra-Faust or Hyper-Narcissus, James Bond, Rambo, Ollie North, George Bush or whoever—the memoriless, merciless, guiltless, and indifferent "infantile subject" of Dorfman's analysis is no longer a "man" of tragedy or modernity. "He" is a dangerously new type of man—ULTRAMODERN MAN, CYBORG MAN; someone who no longer uses repressive power to oppress others, but who appears (to himself) to have exceeded modern constraint (on developmental violence) by being fascinatingly taken into the very media that were once his tools. In this, "ultramodern man" may seem (to himself) ecstatic. But this a cold and communicative ecstasy. This an *infantile adult ecstasy* without *child-like generosity*. It explodes nothing that is "his," while parasitically absorbing most everything else. This is an implosive, white magical or cybernetic ecstasy. It appears vertiginous but without giving away the media (money, power, violence, influence) by which MAN now, more LIMITLESSLY than ever, stakes out a position of sacrificial privilege. Upon or within the bodies of others.

> *America the Beautiful. Sacrificial America. Without the constraints of having white men's bodily aggressions HIStorically modulated by a LACK of seemingly limitless spatial frontiers. The westward expansion of the USA was, for well over a century of modernization, unencumbered by the formal or legal fictions of colonial discourse. And within this magnetic expanse, American white men begin to cut their ties with European modernity, as each day "our" ancestors enacted rites such as regularly carrying a gun, purchasing women for male-ordered pleasures and sticking metal knife blades into the scalps of other living human animals. And cutting. All for the pleasures of power, conquest and terror. The joys of the wild West—manifest destiny and the like.*

Faust, as Goethe knew him, was becoming fully modern. At a critical moment in the "development" of his narrative "we" find our tragic hero reading the words of St. John's Gospel. *In the beginning was the word.* Faust thinks (k)not. He crosses out the Christian phrasing and inscribes, *In the beginning was the deed.* Mephisto appears. He informs Faust that, to realize the profundity of modern truth, he must recognize that the most productive of his deeds will also be destructive. Only from destruction does production flow. This seems to be a restrictive economic law of modernity—a belief in the primacy of linear developmental violence; the violence of ORIGINARY SACRIFICE; the violence of progressive mastery or civilization. Freud agreed in theory, "though without vouching for the absolute certainty" of this decision. In closing *Totem and Taboo*, Freud notes that this is (possibly) the lasting lesson of (his) having studied "primitive man"—the psychoanalytic insight that *In the beginning was the deed.*[66] Freud here allies himself with Faust, Mephisto and other tragic heroes of *overdevelopment*. But this is an unfortunate (mis)reading of totemism—a projective and whitemale magical reading of ghostly others through modernity's fetishistic screen.

> *I grew up as a little boy playing cowboy, rolling in imaginary struggles for freedom on the floor of a room in a house that my father had purchased and enacting intense and transferential rites of feeling the manly virtues of sticking it to a televisionary enemy of we who are whites and memory-less. What white LIES behind this deadly color coding? Afterwards, in bed, I would close my eyes and imagine that a carload of suburban white girls, maybe cheerleaders, would sneak up to my window and climb into my mind. They would tie my hands behind my back and strip me of every bit of clothing. I would bask in submission and arousal. I would watch myself watching. The girls would then pirate me out of my father's house into their father's AUTOmobile and drive me around. With abandon.*

> *What tranferences with what senseless futures are young American boys today feeling standing quarter to quarter in relation to a video-game named CONTRA. A white Rambo look alike totem dashes across the screen blinking digital. He is powerfully armed and fires laser beams into brown skinned iconic men in mustaches. What do these boys feel that they think when they hear on the airwaves the patterned voice of Bush referring to the popularly elected President of Nicaragua as an unwanted animal at a garden party? Party. Party. Party...Party beyond the time of what's flesh...Partly beyond the spatial recognition of contradictory matters. Watch out these boys may kill you as they seize this planet in a single byte and without notice.*

Critical re(w)ritings of Durkheim and Baudrillard may offer greater insight. Each recognizes that in totemic cultures the word and deed come into being simultaneously. This is why the sacrifices instituted by these cultures are reversible. This is why their distinctive rule is periodic. But what if deeds become so fast in execution and so dense in the sacrificial coverings that they appear to penetrate the signifying materiality of words? What, in other words, if the most dominant of our ritual social technologies appear capable of materially blurring the distinction between coded word symbols and the flesh? Welcome to a parasite New World Order of cybernetic social controls and virtual reality modelings—a world where words may literally appear to become flesh and flesh, words. Here the material efficacy of words may become so fast, fascinating, or absorbent that they pass into or amidst deeds without registering a difference. Here the resistive power of ghosts is rendered void. Here everything becomes uncanny. Here doubles abound, but rather than signifying the immanence of one's own death, they signal little but hypervisible destruction of others—overdevelopment without tragedy, mastery without repression, a mass aestheticization of death and the killing of others without notice—LIMITLESS CAPITAL.

> *During the first 48 hours of the* FMLN *offensive armed Salvadorans attacked more than 50 military positions spread over half of El Salvador's 14 provinces. Under the cover of a virtual media* WHITE OUT *the government responded to these military actions by dropping U.S. supplied bombs from U.S. supplied aircraft upon the poorest slums or barrios of its* CAPITAL *city. Unable to militarily defeat the rebels in open contact or in the bloodied sewers of San Salvador's underground, the fascist leaders of the country's U.S. trained military rained terror on the very population it sought to protect from the evils of communism. Better dead then Red! Better dead than self-determining.*

This is ultramodernity. Here the double becomes the clone of culture. Here representation fades into the network fascinations of video scan data banking VIRTUAL REALITY MODELLINGS. Here the contradictory material character of rites of doubling (or language) implode with the hyperreal and clean machine based RITUALS OF (transbodily) SACRIFICIAL CODINGS. These are rituals without reverse, but with omnipresent feedback and self-regulative monitoring. These are CYBERNETIC FORMS of inFORMation control systems. CCCT. Command. Control. Communications. Transference. Of the Four Fundamental Concepts of (Social) Psychoanalysis, transference is the most untamed and rule dependent. Perhaps it is also the most seductive, perverse and hopeful. At the same time, capturing the power of transference for profit is a militaristic game being played by those IN THE KNOW (or the media) as a GLOBAL BATTLEFIELD for a LIMITLESS DEPLOYMENT of CAPITAL. Indeed, in the wake of the televisionary transferences that constituted such a material feature of Operation Desert Storm, the bodies of countless thousands were made to literally disappear along with their ghosts. And today back on the home front something related appears to be happening again and again to the bodies of those parasited by the economic restrictions of CAPITAL in its ultramodern form. This is transnational BUSINESS AS USUAL. Increasingly it assumes the totemic form of fast food for thought and viral swells of almost electric transferences waving through WHOSE DISAPPEARING BODIES? I was sitting in the Cafe with Rada Rada and Marty Martin when the news hit the screen fading to grey. How fascinating and how fascistic!

part three

RE-MEMBERING DIFFERENTLY: FLESH BEFORE WORDS

Sociology's conceptual procedures, methods, and relevances organize its subject matter from a determinate position in society. This critical disclosure is the basis of an alternative way of thinking sociology.

—Dorothy E. Smith

[T]he crucial distinction for me is not the difference between fact and fiction, but the distinction between fact and truth. Because facts can exist without human intelligence, but truth cannot.   —Toni Morrison

Partiality and not universality is the condition of being heard; [but]...the presence of subjugated knowledges means that groups are not equal in making their standpoints known to themselves and others. 'Decentering' the dominant group is essential, and relinquishing privilege of this magnitude is unlikely to occur without struggle.   —Patricia Hill Collins

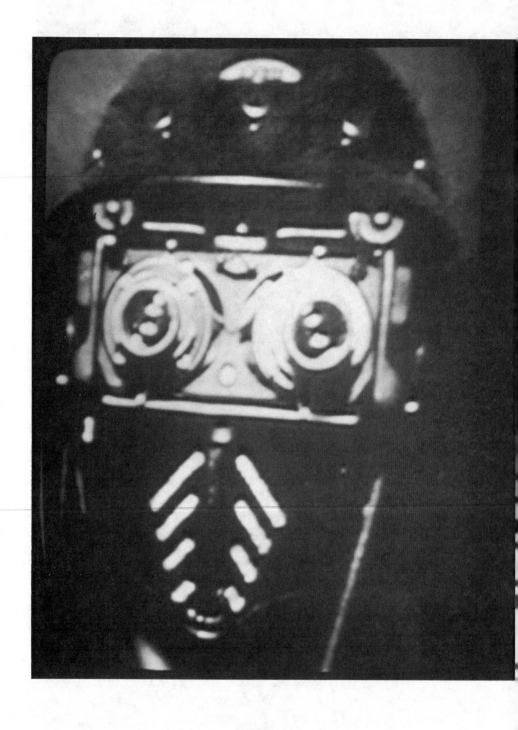

YUPPIES FROM MARS
A HISTORY OF THE PRESENT

Why raise these questions? To challenge an obsessional mode of thought
which annunciates itself as new and seems to become more rational
everyday, but which is a capital, *ghost haunted* complex, stealing thought
and memory away to hoard it.—Sol Yurik[1]

A detached entourage of metropolitan and mostly white male-minded
parasites were gathering in the office-studio-laboratory-space station. I felt it
would be difficult to pass among them, but then I've always been anxious
about screen tests of any sort. Rada Rada appeared more composed. This was
by far the largest assembly of corporate raiders I'd seen—a disconcerting mix
of some the leading BIG BOYS. Telecommunicating screen to screen, each
appeared equally intense as one after anOther the raiders prepared themselves
for the thrill of the pure and beautiful buy-out. Having ravaged the Savings
and Loans industry, futures seemed limitless. Like Japanese totems dressed in
new German electronics with Texas accents and Israeli recorders, these raiders
seemed almost Otherworldly. A white noisy buzz of telematic feedback fills the
air. And since the global entrance to all BIG BOY *corporate-office-tower-
industrial-park-research-inFORMation-security-systems-banking-pleasure-
palace-shopping-mall-designer-sports-stock-market-enterprises* were hourly
chem-dusted and image-scanned for bad odors, unpleasant visuals and other
irregular memories, the scent of missing Guatemalan bodies, dead dark skinned
U.S. infants without food or proper medical care, as well as the stateless plight
of Palestinian "refugees" went *virtually* unnoticed. Not unnoticed but virtually
unnoticed. "Yuppies from Mars," whispered Rada Rada.

"We'll leverage the suckers or they'll drown in their own waste!" declared
one of the best suited raiders.

"Or both," added anOther.

Most of the raiders were whitemales-on-line, but not all.

A small test band of women and DESIGNated "minorities" were also present
(in a way). But for the most part, even these A-TYPICALS were infected with
the virus of western whitemale-mindedness and, thus, condemned, like a cadre

of ancient seafarers, to wear the albatross of some Other's self-imposed guilt around the necks of their always partially exposed bodies. Lost at sea, lost in space, most of the A-TYPICALS never really felt at home among the raiders. Despite appearances.

"There are many ways to suck cock, I mean the phallus," said Rada Rada half laughing. Half-laughter, mid-speech—what's the difference? I was thinking of asking Rada this question but it hardly seemed appropriate given the urgency of our situation. Instead, I asked, "What's next?"

Rada Rada passed me a mask saying, "Quick. Re-dramatize yourself. Pretend you're a Martian and preparing to do business. You'll be able to pass unnoticed, like an unmarked term among men's millions. At least if you remain silent. Believe me I've got a lot of experience. I even used to shave my underarms."

In a flash I intuited the drift of Rada's words. At least I thought I did. For a blinding instance I was taken by an image of Rada spinning out from within HIStory changing. New possibilities appeared in various dimensions and our relation(s) seemed charged with a kind of political electricity. It was as if we existed in no-thing but an effervescent "force field of past and present...a lightning flash of truth."[2] Unlike the universalism of Kant's aesthetic freeze frame, Hegel's sublative (or motion picturing) transcendence, and George Bush's thousand points of lightened CAPITAL, between Rada Rada and I the fast forwarding dialectic of HIStory had come to a (temporary) standstill. This was not entirely dissimilar to Heidegger's world grounded Being, painfully at home in the uncanny ideality of its own disconnectedness; although (hopefully) what existed between Rada Rada and I lacked Heidegger's overwhelming (whitemale Euro-fascist) nostalgia for truth's truthful reappearance. Here, as we stood at a crossroads of HIStory gaping, "thought comes in a constellation saturated with tensions." Here I gaze upon an uncanny image of what appears to be my most sacred totems eaten by worms; an image of self-ruin and unameable (m)otherly pleasures. "It is the caesura in the movement of thought. Its positioning, of course, is in no way arbitrary. IN A WORD, it is to be sought at the point where the tension between dialectical oppositions is the greatest." In this way, the image is "identical to the historical object; it justifies blasting the latter out of the continuum of history's course."[3]

"All right, I'll put on a mask," I said. "But first let me find the texts I need to support this transition. I'll get back (to a genealogical HIStory) as soon as I can!" I don't really say all this to Rada Rada but she seems to get the message. I set off hastily for the cafe.

At the threshold to the cafe, just above the doorway is a mural depicting three figures: a fearsome looking cat, "king of the jungle," a mighty elephant and a monkey in whiteface hurling words from a tree. The monkey's painted words read: "*You might as well stop, there ain't no use tryin' because no motherfucker's gonna stop my signifyin'.*"[4]

Inside the decor resembles an abandoned theme park. But don't be nostalgic. Above the doorway floats a ghostly white sheet draped over a black plastic dreamscape. Above the sheet hangs the white head of a pumpkin face smiling. At least I think this pumpkin's face is smiling. Things here seem a bit uncanny and its difficult to be positive about what's being signified. To get to the tables, which look like wasted school desks, you have to pass beneath the floating sheet. Its only then that you realize that one side of this sheet is doubling as a screen for an image being projected. The image appears to be a composite of two additional images, one dissolving into the other. Along the outside is a facsimile of a white woman's face fractured with the words NOT YOURSELF. Perhaps this is an image once worked on by Barbara Kruger. Imploding within the center of this first image appears the second—a shameful snapshot of naked black male bodies held at gunpoint. In my search for meaning I find a caption that reads, BK PARASITE VISITS ATTICA.

At a table near the back of the cafe, surrounded by orphans, sat Jack O. Lantern. As I draw near, the professor says, "Let me tell you something strange. I saw a woman at the cafe last night who looked so much like you she could have been your double. No kidding. Do you know who I mean?" Several of the orphans laugh—not in unison.

"It's a secret," I said with a wink.

"Come on! What's her name?"

I hesitate for a split screened second before repeating, "It's a secret." It's not that I'm trying to be deliberately evasive with Jack O. Lantern. Actually, I felt quite seduced by his line of inquiry; his methods and style. Perhaps we'd even have sex before this text comes to its climax. But for whatever reasons, at this moment I feel more esoteric and occult.

"Is it Mauss? Bataille? Colette Peignot?"

"I told you. It's a secret."

The professor takes a transferential step forward. His lips seem but inches from mine and I wondered what he'd taste like should I run my tongue around the rim of his mouth.

"I thought you were supposed to be working. What's the story?"

I laugh. I sigh. This breaks the tension. O. Lantern distances himself in relation and says: "Okay, it's a secret. But let me show you a letter I've been drafting."

My eyes fall upon the laser printed heading of this letter. It reads—

DEAR HABERMAS:

I'm not sure whether you'll remember (me), but several years ago we had lunch together in Boston and I promised to send you something I'd be (w)riting. Well this is it. It's a reading of certain material aspects of capital at this point in history. I hope you find it of value. That is, I hope you find it morally compelling and generally meaningful in an economic sort of way.

When we met (over food), you expressed surprise that a U.S. sociologist was interested poststructuralism. I had been sitting in on your lectures and had taken issue with your reading of certain so-called postmodern thinkers. In your opinion, Bataille, Foucault, Derrida and others offered no justifiable position of rational transcendence outside the textual networks in which they found themselves in (w)riting. This led you to conclude that, all good intentions aside, someone like Foucault offered no critical standard of judgment that might reliably differentiate his rhetorical claims from Ronald Reagan's. By contrast, you seemed desirous of a kind of transhistorical standard for the "ideal speech situation," a type of power-free zone for negotiated debate and undistorted reciprocity. In such a utopian space rational actors might communicate in a free and reasonable fashion. Like your view of psychoanalysis, the consensual application of this open communicative standard holds the (evolutionary therapeutic) promise of bringing everything into the light. In its erring displacements of the compulsive repetitions of all metanarratives, you also believed that poststructuralism marked the (linear) death of Marxism, rather than its periodic or cyclical transformation. Why, then, had I—a sociologist—fallen for the seduction of such a basically conservative move? Shadows of Gadamer, like hunks of rotting meat, lie across the table between us.

Your claims for the critical transcendence of an undistorted or communicatively clear "ideal speech" situation is often juxtaposed to Gadamer's condemnation of interpretive human action to the infinite regress of an endless hermeneutic circle. From my (general economic) point of view, neither of these perspectives make reflexive connections between the historical appearance (and disappearance) of seemingly autobiographical "subjects of interpretation" and the contradictory sacrificial rituals that have made such modern western notions of agency a changing whitemale material possibility. The "fact" that women, nonwhites and those condemned to being economically exoteric to capital's reason have been denied equal historical access to such "subjectivity" is not a major concern of either your or Gadamer's theories. Nevertheless, by "ideally" including everybody in the network of rational communications your model initially appears superior to

Gadamer's hermeneutic circularity. But what if your "ideal" of nonexclusion or nondistortion is just that—an "ideal;" or worse yet, the "liberal" ideological promise of a restrictive economic form masking the sacrificial violence inherent in all cultural and linguistic practices?

Poststructuralism, as I read or re(w)rite it, begins repeatedly with a reflexive recognition of the material positioning of all communicative forms as forms of sacrifice. In this sense, the task of critical theoretical practice is not so much to eliminate distortions as to institute some forms of periodic rites that (poetically) sacrifice the restrictive economic authority of particular modes of common sense or socio-logic. Whether in its social-psychoanalytic, ethnographic or genealogical modes, poststructuralism demands a partial and playful working out from within the violent confines of prosaic language (as "we" in the modern and ultramodern West have come to powerfully know it). This, I feel, is a more rigorous and complexly ambivalent "critique" of truth claims than those proposed either by either Gadamer or yourself.

Poststructuralism's critical possibilities LIE economically embedded in the networks of contemporary social power in which its "believers" are themselves differentially positioned. As Deena and Michael Weinstein suggest, philosophical "strategies" such as deconstruction are not innocent of economic transmutations in the cultural conditions of epistemology in general. "Derrida, one might say, is the philosopher of television. Deconstructed texts are simulacra of television.... The images play across the screen, just as the philosophemes and epistemes play through the texts; and the viewer plays with them, just as Derrida deconstructs the text. Television is present as a perpetual context, but what runs across it is 'the spacing of differences.'" To 'read' the text of television is to surrender to its juxtapositions and displacements, never allowing any image to be a master-image, providing a meaning for the text outside." [5] There is, nevertheless, a critical difference. As a form of (moral) knowledge poststructuralism demands a reflexive re(w)riting of material structures of complicity, toward difference, but without transcendence. As Gayatri Spivak points out:

> The aspect that interests me most is...the recognition, within decon-
> structive practice, of provisional and intractable starting points in
> any investigative effort; its disclosure of complicities where a will to
> knowledge would create oppositions; its insistence that in disclosing
> complicities the critic-as-subject is herself complicit with the trace of
> that complicity—the proof that we do not inhabit a clearly defined
> critical space free of such traces; and finally, the acknowledgement
> that its own discourse can never be adequate to its example. [6]

I didn't actually say all these things to you in person. Instead, I hand you a poster for a Halloween Party organized by the Parasite Cafe. It is 1984, an election year, and the poster reads POSSESSION OF THE REAGANHEADS. *Reagan's image appears as a simulacrum of itself, just like Reagan's body, and you say: "Oh! Now I understand—Dada and surrealism. That's your attraction to poststructuralism." You comment on the rise of these artful modes of intervening within/against the instrumental violence of* CAPITAL *at earlier times in western* HISTORY, *and mention how disturbed you felt in watching a "Reagan for President" commercial the evening before. The "advert" you describe featured nothing more (or less) in the realm of political in*FORMATION *than the shadow of an "evil empire" bear encroaching on the campsite of an (eternally) innocent U.S. family (of televisionary mutants). You tell me you had been in the U.S. during Reagan's first successful Presidential campaign. The commercials this time appear far less rational and more ominous. I tell you that at the Parasite Cafe our uneven, if collective, moves in the direction of poststructuralism have emerged out of attempts to rethink Marxist theories of "hegemony" within a telelectronic popular political culture of "fascinating" sound bytes and photo opportunities, and that working through (out of) Gramsci and Althusser had, for some of us, been a step on the way to Foucault and Derrida.*

You seem surprised by this, but say that it helps you understand a certain socio-logical interest in poststructuralism. Then you say something rather disconcerting. You tell me that if you were a younger man maybe you'd do the same. The dangers of making such (radical) theoretical moves appear to you enormous. You repeat your concerns about the lack of an identifiable place of transcendence by which to launch a critique. Desirous of a more immanently material form of critique, I speak briefly of the need to reflexively double back upon our contradictory social situations, and argue that the experience of "pure" transcendence exists today largely in telecommunicative media, or in what Baudrillard calls the cold ecstasy of communication. You ask whether I thought this a uniquely North American situation. Six years later MTV would celebrate the "transcendence" of the Berlin Wall. Globally. By satellite.

I excused myself from our luncheon conversation, explaining that I must use the toilet. Once in the restroom I heard a strange scratching at the window's screen, almost like the sound of someBODY (W)RITING. It was Rada Rada and she whispered invitingly: "Come on! This appears as good (or bad) a time and place as any. Follow me if you want."

What did I want? How could I want things that are other than the way things are promised from the vantage point of THE WAY THINGS WERE. Barbara Streisand, Robert Redford and the Black Madonna Durkheim each came to mind, if (k)not exactly in that order.

"You may find that the only way you'll make it through the screen without killing somebody other than yourself is by EX-POSING YOUR BODY to others. Think about it, in reverse. Why have you (men) for so long wanted to see us pinned up and strip-teased. Why not strip away your own clothing? You can keep wearing that cut-off sleeveless t-shirt, but that's all. Try to bare with me, if you can, and DRAG yourself to the crossroads where HIStory puts us at each other's throat. I'm not asking that you take leave of HIStory. That would be more than madness. That would be deadly. I ask only that you attempt an uneasy dance at HIStory's borders in relation to my forbidden selves and others."

Having uttered these words, Rada Rada proceeded to DRAG herself through the window, across the screen, dis-appearing into a self made-over, deconstructed and materially reimagined.

"Jesus Christ," I thought, without saying these words aloud. The phrase came almost automatically. I felt anxious, gripped by great self-doubt. I also felt incredibly white and stupid. I also felt strangely attracted to what what taking place before my eyes/"I"s. Rada Rada was literally slipping in (w)riting from someone somebody might identify with into no-thing but an image of a self inscribed. I knew no-thing but transference, and yet felt disturbingly seduced into baring myself (to others) in the way Rada had suggested. If I remove everything but my t-shirt would s/he, you or anybody be able to see my phallus for what it really is—no-thing but the erection of a symbolic fortress safe-guarding the privileged whiteness of my sex from the exiled eyes/"I"s of others? Everything seemed confused. Things felt strangely erotic, but not the least bit romantic.

My eyes/"I"s make contact with Rada Rada's. S/he appears to have dragged herself to the other side of the screen without removing a single item of clothing. Perhaps she was naked enough already in the plot-lining of this story that I'm re(w)riting. In any event, it appears that it's me rather than Rada Rada who must decide whether or not to risk giving away my AUTHORity. Then, for a flaming instant, it seemed that Rada was waving to me across the horizon constituted by the screen. Quivering, I began my striptease—slow, stupid and uneased. I felt as if I was descending into the fires of some perverse and ill-fated sacrificial rite. Rada Rada laughed. Soon I was outside of my clothes but not HIStory or hers. This made me laugh as well.

In a low somewhat baroque murmur Rada Rada began to sing an eerie refrain. *Everyone says I'm a witch. Everyone says I cast spells. Fire surrounds me everywhere. Everyone says I cast spells.*

The screech of a tom-cat rang in the alley. At least I think it was a tom-cat. Maybe it was a sim-stim parasiting the form of a tom-cat plagiarizing. Chaos abounds. How can I stay in material contact with all this without going mad or playing hero or becoming a serial killer? Things were spinning wild and out of control. Nothing in my conversation with Habermas had prepared me for this. Maybe he was right about poststructuralism after all. Darkness floods my intestines as I grasp for fortitude without certain models. What should I do? What should I (w)rite?

If only Black Madonna Durkheim were here to offer guidance and a recipe or two. I close my eyes. I open my "I"s. I edge out along the screen's border. As I do this I let my mind drift bodily to images of four strange playing cards the Black Madonna suggested I commit to memory.

37 *El mundo*. What a joke! What a temptation! The straining figure of a nearly naked man shouldering the globe. North America is centered above the man's back stretching right arm. The man casts a shadow to (my) the viewer's right and is dressed in a sexy black bikini and ankle cut black leather Dr. Martin's. This man appears both athletic and forlorn.

23 There is a waxing quarter moon with the features of a woman. It is night and she is cool and taking in the sight of 37 holding up the world. She's (k)not in love with this man, the hero. *La Luna*.

Then 6 and 34. It looks bad for the bare breasted mermaid in 6. *La Sirena*, it appears, was just about to call out in warning when she was shot; the bullet passing exactly through her navel, dislodging remaining traces of her birth from a (m)other's body. I imagine her in a future card inscribed as a dead fish who almost had her say. It was 34, I sense, who did her in. *El Soldado*. Maybe funded by U.S. tax dollars. He is standing erect before a narrow phallic tower with windows to shoot through. This tower is no fleshy penis. Maybe this tower's a missile. This tower appears supportive of *El Soldado's* desire for the death of others; his desire for the Other; his desire for a self-solidified in desire for the Other. In any event, this man appears to me as a murderer and it appears he's shot 6, *La Sirena*, and shot her so fast that hardly anybody noticed that she was somebody other than a dead fish before he had her appear as a dead fish in some future card incorporated. In any case, as I indicated before, things look bad for the bare breasted mermaid. What a joke. What a temptation. What a deadly gift exchanged. Her body for his bullets. The two currents flow together, mixing like the yen or deutsche mark with blood purchased by U.S. dollars. These two currents reinforce each other in ways that are anything but ambivalent. I am ambivalent. I am nearly naked and in tears as I pass through this screen re-membering HIStory. "Repetitions and the same cycles of legend, but the whole is disfigured by its literary and theological style."[7] On the other sides of this screen, (k)not outside HIStory, but along its other sides, the transnational economy looks very different and very ultramodern. Bare with me and I'll try to tell you why.

META-VOODOO ECONOMICS
THE MATERIALITY OF CYBERNETIC CULTURE

This play [is] written...by a white man...but if, which is unlikely, it is ever performed before a black audience, then a white person, male or female, should be invited every evening. The organizer of the show should welcome him to his seat, preferably in the front row of the orchestra. The actors will play for him. A spotlight should be focused upon this symbolic white throughout the performance. But what if no white person accepted? The let white masks be distributed to the black spectators as they enter the theater. And if the blacks refuse the masks, then let a dummy be used. —Jean Genet[1]

Papa Legba, ouvirier barriere pour moi agoe
Papa Legba, ouvirier barriere pour moi
Attibon Legba, ouvirier narriere pour moi passer
Passer Vrai, Loa passer m'a remerci loa moin.
—Chant to Papa Legba[2]

What, besides something unspeakably racist, could George Bush have had in mind when, in campaigning against Ronald Reagan for the Republican Party nomination for President in 1980, he used the phrase "Voodoo economics" to describe Reagan's plan for strengthening U.S. CAPITAL? Mindful that Bush would later adopt such policies as his own, the Black Madonna Durkheim gave me several texts on Voodoo by Zora Neale Hurston (among others), saying, "You white folks should remember that ecstatic religious forms continued in this country long after you genocided the Native Americans." She suggested I look into the matter.

Voodoo is a name to designate forms of (pagan) religious knowledge brought to the New World of African-American slavery by the violently transported peoples of West Africa. As a ritual constellation of sacred beliefs, epistemology and morality, Voodoo continues to be practiced overtly and in disguised forms in both South and North America and the Caribbean. Within the restrictive economic matrix of ultramodern CAPITAL, something that is modeled in a form resembling Voodoo (but with a terrible parasitic difference) is also being practiced. I am here (w)riting of rites that certain critical theorists have partially imagined in such terms as "the cyborg revolution," "the ecstasy of communication" or "excremental culture." A comparison between some of the most material aspects of Voodoo and these cybernetic forms of inFORMational CAPITAL may prove helpful in imagining the bodily ways in which ultramodern economies access (and convert to abstracted matters of neutral indifference) what has long danced in excessive resistance to the dominant whitemale forcefields of modern economic "possession."

Zora Neale Hurston's writings on Voodoo were, for the most part, produced during the years of the depression and the New Deal/wartime economics of Franklin D. Roosevelt. As a (w)riter who ritually refused to reproduce clear disciplinary boundaries between social science and fiction, Zora Neale Hurston associates both the linguistic embodiment of African-American culture and Voodoo with an excessive play of metaphor and simile, the dramatic enactment of "double description," and the reversibility of "verbal nouns."[3] These are not the characteristics of a universal linguistic system. These are reflexive features of the linguistic embodiment of peoples torn from a material context of homeland rituals, made literally into commodities, forced into a "middle passage" marked by waves of death, orphanhood, dismemberment and the *virtual destruction* of memorably ingrained patterns of kinship and all that was sacred. Thereafter the Black diaspora was offered the promise of restrictive economic redemption if only they would but submit to the disembodying beliefs of western Christian hierarchies. In response to F.D.R.'s call for "Negro Americans" to join the "democratic" war effort against fascists abroad, Hurston declared that as a black woman she accepted the idea of democracy but had tasted few of its fruits. After commenting upon U.S. willingness "to go to war and sacrifice billions of dollars on the idea [of democracy]," Hurston states, "I think that I ought to give this thing a trial. The one thing that keeps me from pitching headlong into the thing is the presence of numerous Jim Crow laws on the statute books of the nation. I am crazy about the idea of democracy. I want to see how it feels."[4]

Hurston and Talcott Parsons were contemporaries, but unlike the Harvard sociologist and cybernetician, Hurston is rarely taught in courses on social theory. Hurston's *theoretical fictions* of the epistemological drama of Voodoo (or the elementary religious forms of African-American culture) are, nevertheless, reinscribed in the critical analytic movements of literary theorists such as Houston Baker and Henry Louis Gates, Jr. Gates understands the reflexive doublings enacted by vernacular African-American *signifyin(g)* as "a rhetorical practice that is not engaged in the game of information-giving."[5] Baker's "soundings" of a noticeably "masked" deformation of masterfully white "Western duels—and dualities" as a form of "racial poetry" conjure a "release from a being possessed."[6] Both "mimic" the materiality of Hurston's analytic concerns and play out from within the epistemic waves of Voodoo as a HIStorical social form.

When Gates evokes "the play of doubles...at Esu's crossroads,"[7] he appears to be literally re-membering what Hurston describes as a "sort of liquifying of words" associated with Voodoo's doubled reversal of language by the "subtle power" of "love and laughter."[8] In its paradoxical juxtaposition of asymmetrical and rhythmic "insinuation," Voodoo is said to enact a "realistic suggestion" that subverts the abstract dualisms of white culture. In this way, whether overtly practiced or incorporated into such ceremonial forms as the "ecstatic" rites of "the Black church" or African-American music, poetry, painting, sculpture or dancing, Voodoo serves to "funeralize" the seemingly endless linearity of modern white "individuality." As a ritual challenge to the restrictive economy of whitemale governed western spirituality, a parasitic form of spirituality that dreams of immortality while feeding off the sacrificial "uglying away" of others, Voodoo calls for a return to a communal material participation in (not above or below) "the mysterious source of life" itself.[9]

In Voodoo, as in the traditional African-American cultural practices described by Hurston, Gates and Baker, one does not so much "get above," transcend or leave behind the material world (as in the dominant versions of western Christian religion), as pass through the crossroads of the world in its (sacrificially ordained) everyday dimensions into experiential contact with the world materialized in different (and ecstatic sacred) forms. In Voodoo there is no question of reducing the world that LIES (HIStorically and materially) in excess of that which is sacrificially fixed by language to that which can be accessed as dogma or belief. Voodoo ritually dispossesses its participants of their mundane identities. Its communicants are (re)possessed by the flows of what remains outside the linguistic violence of HIStorically specific cultural forms, as if these "laughable" forms could in any way be equivalent to the materiality of the universe with its fluid waves of comingling and multiple possibilities. This results in a "temporary loss of individual consciousness" as the "body is mounted" by a force that "sweeps" through a community "like fire over the church." For participants this engenders a heterogeneous mixture of "ecstasy," "shouting," "violent shoulder shaking," "hysterical laughter," "rhythmic dancing," "twitching," and other "cataleptic movements." These are terms that Hurston uses to describe the way Voodoo (in both its covert "sanctified church" and overt Haitian varieties) puts practitioners in material contact with divine reality itself. Voodoo, in other words, takes seriously the reality of the "invisible world." Voodoo also acknowledges that things which may appear as if natural are, in reality, bound by an artful cycle of dramatic ritual actions. This is a translation. Voodoo periodically spins off the possibilities of translation into unrepresentable spaces of heterogeneity. This is ecstasy. The translation for such *spinoffs* is *possession* by a *loa*.

Being possessed by a *loa*, and thereby dispossessed of the culturally defined constraints of oneself or one's ego, is an intense and ecstatic religious experience at the heart of many ceremonial Voodoo rituals. This is evident in the words of Maya Deren, a white U.S. woman artist, dancer and filmaker, whose intimate participation within a Haitian Voodoo community resulted in her own "ecstatic" possession.

> Over the demanding, compelling rush of its syllables, the tight staccato Yanvalou beat of the *petit* sets in; now the rounder tone, the more rolling rhythm of the *seconde* slides in under it; and then one feels a vibration beneath one's feet even before one hears the beat of the maman, which rises as if from some unfathomable depth, as if the very earth were a drum being pounded.... For a brief moment this towering architecture of sound, stretching solidly from the abyss below to the heavens above hearing, seems to advance without movement, like a tidal wave so vast that no marker exists to scale its progress for the eye.... The eyes are fixed on the ground, and the although the head is steady, the circular movement of the shoulders seems to send it forward, to draw the body after it, over and over; and as the bodies, which began in a posture almost erect, bend toward the earth, the undulation becomes more and more horizontal, until all figures blend into a slow flowing serpentine stream circling the center-post with a fluency that belies the difficulty of the movement.... What secret power flows to them, rocks them and revolves them, as a round-about the bright steeds prance and pursue, eternally absolved of fatigue, failure and fall? I have but to rise to step forward, become part of the glorious movement, flowing with it, its motion becoming mine, as the roll of the sea might become the undulation of my own body. At such moments one does not move to the sound, one is the movement of the sound.[10]

As dramatically spirited entities, *loa* signify a complex and changing panoply of gods and goddesses, each with her or his own persona and preferences in food, style and music. They are said to ride those who they possess as a horse that loses memory of the singular confines of the self. And since those who become possessed hold no exact memory of events that occur during the excessively sacred time of their divine encounter with a given *loa*, unlike the individualistic ecstasy of most Christian mystics, the interpretation of Voodoo possession is basically a communal experience. Moreover, while there exists a relatively stable core ensemble of recurrently important or major loa—Damballah Ouedo, Simbi, Erzuli in her several forms, Papa Legba, Mademoiselle

Brigitte, Guede, Ogoun, Loco and Baron Samedi—the specific embodiment of these "spirits" changes in setting and HIStorical circumstance and is not uncommonly supplemented by other "minor" gods and goddesses specific to particular times and places. In Haiti, where Voodoo is practiced perhaps in its most reknowned and overtly acknowledged forms (although most Haitians claim sincerely to be Catholics), many *loa* are associated with the appearance of one or another of the Catholic saints honored by former French slaveholders. Although borrowing or parasitically feeding upon a saint's form, the loa in no way represent "the saint done over in black" (as was once believed by certain whites). As Hurston points out, "This has been said over and over in print because the adepts have been seen buying the lithographs of the saints, but this is done because because they wish some visual representation of the invisible ones.... But even the most illiterate peasant knows that the picture of the saint is only an approximation of the *loa*..."[11]

What perhaps most distinguishes Voodoo from Christianity is its lack of a mind-body duality and the hierarchical subordination of the flesh to the spirit. For practicioners of Voodoo to divide flesh from spirit is truly evil. Not that evil or the abuse of sacred powers is unknown to Voodoo, only that the division of good and evil does not follow the repressive harnessing of the flesh that marks Christian thought and practice. Quite the opposite. Moreover, within Voodoo there are two recognizable "families" of deities; the *Rada* gods and goddesses being known for their benevolence and ecstatic blessings, while *Petro* loa are revered (or feared) for their power to effect either good or bad. The intense rage often associated with Petro loa is not a sign of evil, but rather "rage against the evil fate which Africans suffered, the brutality of...displacement and...enslavement."[12] Without a bureaucratically ordained clergy, Voodoo is also relatively free of the rigidities of hierarchical authority. *Houngans* and *mambos*, although commonly translated as priests and priestesses, while apprenticing under other houngans and mambos, operate more as theatrically skilled mediators, healers, negotiators and leaders than as authorized agents of the Rada spirits per se; while sorcerer-like *Borcos*, who serve certain Petro spirits, also operate outside the domain of official bureaucratic sanction.

Although hardly free of the power of gender distinctions, Voodoo is also more complexly sexualized in celebrating the importance of female forces than are the dominant western religious traditions. These aspects of Voodoo are underscored by Hurston, who not only studied Voodoo but also apprenticed as a practicing mambo. Thus, according to Hurston, although Damballah, the highest of all the gods, is sung about as "our papa who passes," he is never referred to as the father of the gods. So too is Damballah everywhere represented by the snake-like and feminine figure of a good and powerful serpent, the "bonne," a revered "maid servant." Indeed, the seemingly polysexual character of this mysterious *loa* is evidenced in the following passage from Hurston's *Tell My Horse*:

> Thus the uplifted forefinger in greeting in Voodoo is really phallic and that means the male attributes of the Creator. The handclasp that ends in the fingers of one hand encircling the thumb of the other signifies the vulva encircling the penis, denoting the female aspect of the deity. "What is the truth?" Dr. Holly asked me, and knowing that I could not answer him he answered himself through a Voodoo ceremony in which the mambo, that is the priestess, richly dressed is asked this question ritualistically. She replies by throwing back her veil and revealing her sex organs. The ceremony means that this is the infinite, the ultimate truth. There is no mystery beyond the mysterious source of life. The ceremony continues on another phase after this. It is a dance analogous to the nuptial flight of the queen bee. The mambo discards six veils in this dance and falls at last naked, and spiritually intoxicated, to the ground. It is considered the highest honor for all the males participating to kiss her organ of creation, for Damballah, the god of gods has permitted them to come face to face with truth.[13]

Voodoo was from its HIStorical ORIGINS in the violent "middle passage" from West Africa to the New World a postmodern religious form. It came after and in resistance to the imposed *slave morality* of white European modernity. It has also been long feared by the spiritual and material guardians of white power. On August 14, 1791, inspired by an intense and spirited Voodoo ceremony, members of Dahomean "tribe" in Haiti swore to the "Oath of Bois Caiman" and so began the first successful black slave revolt in HIStory. As news of the Haitian Revolution spread northward to the slaveholding states of the U.S. a "clampdown" on Voodoo was instituted. In 1782, Louisiana Governor Galvez had already outlawed the purchase of black slaves from Martinique, arguing that because Voodoo was there so strongly practiced that, if imported, it would likely threaten the lives of white U.S. Christians. After 1791 slaves from Haiti and Santa Domingo were also banned. The ban was lifted only in 1803 when the revolution was in full bloom and the market for soon to be freed slaves was bottoming out. The revolution itself heightened the fears of U.S. slave masters. In 1817, the Municipal Council of New Orleans forbade the public gathering of all slaves except for their sale, and except for supervised "Sunday Dances" at designated locations, such as the city's Congo Square.

Such restrictions on the public celebration of Voodoo had contradictory effects. Not only did they drive underground the religious rituals of African-Americans, but they also converted into spectacular performance what had previously been a radically participatory religious form. As Michael Ventura points out:

> It was precisely by trying to stop Voodoo that, for the first time in the New World, African music and dancing was presented both for Africans and whites as an end in itself, a form on its own. Here was the metaphysics of Africa set loose from the forms of Africa. For this form of performance wasn't African. In the ceremonies of Voodoo there is no audience. Some may dance and some may watch, but those roles may change several times in a ceremony, and all are participants. In Congo Square, African music was put into a Western form of presentation....Which means that in Congo Square, African metaphysics first became subsumed in the music. A secret within the music instead of the object of the music. A possibility embodied by the music, instead of the music strictly as this metaphysics' [epistemological] technique.[14]

Ventura's analysis of the forced transformation of Voodoo's ritual forms into performative spectacles is particularly compelling. Tracing the "roots" of both jazz and blues-based "rock and roll" to a continuing tradition of Voodoo in New Orleans, Ventura makes HIStorical connections between such pioneer figures in African-American "soundings" as Jelly Roll Morton and the renowned mambo and black religious leader, Marie Laveau, Morton's "godmother." He also makes a provocative argument concerning the healing power of black bodied music forms as these crossover the airwaves into the repressive and metaphysically disembodied culture of white youths in the late 1940s and early 1950s. In this, the "redemptive appeal" of a rhythmic "metaphysic that sees the body as embodied" is theorized as a "numinous force" associated with the (rebellious) attraction of "rock and roll" for whites.

Ventura's analysis hints at the (potentially) subversive force of Voodoo-based black music and dance as material social forms that call out positive modes of feeling and affect, independent of and perhaps counter to the racist beliefs and prejudices of whites. Ventura's argument here resembles Larry Grossberg's theorization of "economies of affect." As "free-floating" and "autonomous" modes of bodily sensation, economies of affect are said to be "stitched into reality without the mediation of ideology."[15] In this way, affect is said to operate in ways other than that governed by the "interpretive" or "representational" constraints of ideology. Grossberg reads the play of "contradictory" affective embodiments as "empowering" popular cultural "spaces" that resist being reduced to the unitary perspective of a given ideological framework. As such, everyday social actors are said to "appropriate events and practices" into such spaces, "using them not as representations or interpretations but simply as empowering signposts."[16]

Grossberg's is a particularly hopeful thesis that usefully counters the homogeneous characterization of power and the relative inattentiveness to contradictory bodily experience that characterize certain versions of "postmodern" theory. At the same time, to draw, as Grossberg does, "artificial" boundaries between ideology as a representational domination and affect as "unmediated" bodily possibilities is to ignore certain of the most critical derivations of the social-psychoanalytic work of Louis Althusser, Roland Barthes and Julia Kristeva. In different ways, each of these theorists has labored to articulate a "materialist" thesis of ideology that conjoins, without conflating, the contradictory ritual positionings of bodies in HIStory with the material embodiment of psychic and social signifying processes. More important, however, is Grossberg's (and other "popular culture" theorists') relative inattentiveness to the radically altered HIStorically material context or *social form* of both bodily and representational experience that characterizes the cybernetic-like environment of ultramodern CAPITAL. Grossberg's vision of "rock and roll" and related popular "affective" practices is to view these as "empowering" resistance to the terrors and boredom of commodified postwar culture. While not an unimportant insight, it is but partially true at best. Also important is the critical recognition that, within a parasitic culture that ritually feeds off energy released by *seductively manufactured resistance*, what may seem like the "unmediated" experience of "empowering affect" may in reality be little but the nearly instantaneous "possession" of "our" bodies by an ultramodern mechanics of inFORMation. For a want of better words, this is a way of describing the whitemale driven and cybernetic culture of contemporary CAPITAL.

Grossberg's description of the split between representation and bodily affect, or, in Ventura's terms, the repressive division between mind and body, may be an accurate description of the *master effects* of modern power. But following *the cybernetic revolution* (which takes places at nearly the same time as *the rock and roll revolution* in white pop culture) a major transformation in the sacrificial constitution of human subjectivity has been taking place. This, moreover, is occurring with such power that (blank white) masses of people may be no longer so much repressed as expressed (or ecstatically empowered) as they are transferentially waved between screens of inFORMation and parasitically mounted by increasingly automated sign-systems. In this, waves of inFORMational power may pass into and envelop our bodily imaginations like simulated or premodeled telelectronic *loa* that ride us, their human-animal-machine hosts, from one end of the globe to the other. Screen to screen; from one cybernetic market to the next; in seemingly NO TIME AT ALL.

The whitemale cultural practices that today pirate the most technologically advanced waves of liquid CAPITAL may have become less repressed by accessing Voodoo bodied African-American sounds and dance rhythms. But this makes these parasitic forms no less CAPITALIST; nor less vicious. Quite the opposite. This may have facilitated CAPITAL's abilities to literally get beyond what matters (in the fleshy sense of the word). Hence, through the omnipresent mediation of techno-body interfaces many whitemales (or at least those who count the most) may today be shedding the self-limiting confines of modernist subjectivities, and with them, the guilt and ghosts that have haunted the contradictory materiality of our sacrificial HIStorical relations to others. In the indifferent (if fascinating) world of inFORMation flows, megabytes and databanks, the locus of human experience may no longer be truly centered in the body, as, like so many high tech argonauts, or simulations of Voodoo's *divine horsemen,* "we" may become free-floating and wave-like subjects in the hyperreal and thin-aired sea of cybernetics. Here ultramodern male subjectivity may appear free floating but is hardly free to act much differently or more generously toward others, at least not with the respect their difference (from us) demands. Such *hyper-narcissistic* ritual developments are neither COMPLETELY FACTUALIZED nor incontestable. If I believed this, let me assure you, I'd not waste my time with such difficult (w)riting. Nevertheless, such developments are becoming *more real than real* as each day passes. Thus, without embodying critical efforts to theorize the material basis of such ultramodern economics there may be little chance that "we" can (de)constructively participate in subverting, resistively transforming, or somehow laughing away the violence such inFORMational power engenders.

In comparing the parasitic violence of ultramodern power to a form of simulated Voodoo transference or "possession," I *in no way* wish to suggest that cybernetic CAPITAL either shares the generosity that characterizes traditional African-American religious forms or that U.S. blacks gain somehow in this process; quite the reverse. For the most part the *flexible accumulation* of ultramodern economic parasitism remains a one-way street, a white telecommunicative circuitry that returns to nothing but abstract images of the doubles from which it materially flees. *Once upon a time* such doubles were totemically masked or counterfeited. Later, they were fetishistically made-over into the industrial equivalent to money. But, today, these doubles are being materialized in the form of meta-Voodoo cyber-flows. A ritual effect of technologically accessing machine-body connections, this represents the emergence of a narcissistic mode of (ultramodern) subjectivity that feeds off the premodeled or "negative feedback" simulations of what or who has been shit away to secure modern senses of individualized agency.

Today, within the televisionary rhythms of hegemonic U.S. Pop Culture, the cyber-magic of telelectronic CAPITAL, like Voodoo, "contains the notion of a communicating medium and communicants who believe in it."[17] The ritual character of such cultural practices implode key experiential differences between mediums of communication and those (of us) who engage with such mediums. In this, ultramodern CAPITAL resembles the wave-like flows of boundary blurring energy fields that Voodoo puts materially into play. But with this critical difference—Voodoo, by religiously situating the materiality of such transference within a community of love, reciprocity and the paradoxically infinite ritual acceptance of human animal finitude or death, offers a generous social context in which such transference is believable. "Do you think that was Quesalid's secret?" Rada Rada once asked, making me almost vomit with laughter.

The blank whitemale spaces that indifferently give form to ultramodern CAPITAL are hardly as kind. In reflecting upon the way in which "black religious practices" have struggled to "provide hope and sustain sanity in light of the difficult position of black Americans and the absurdity of transplanted European moderns casting America in the role of the promised land," Cornel West describes three "weapons" that African-Americans have traditionally used to defend themselves against the violence of white U.S. culture.[18] These include *kinetic orality* ("antiphonal styles and linguistic innovations that accent fluid, improvisational identities...that promote survival"), *passionate physicality* ("bodily stylizations of the world, syncopations and polyrhythms that assert one's somebodiness") and *combative spirituality* ("a sense of historical patience, subversive joy, and daily perseverance in an apparently hopeless and meaningless historical situation").[19] Each, in different ways, was embodied in the rituals of Voodoo; each guarding against the violent dematerializations of difference that drove modern white CAPITAL.

Today all this may be changing. Guided by the cybernetic ingenuity of "market sensitive" and "negative feedback" sensors, mass white sectors of the U.S. economy appear increasingly able to CAPITALize upon what had previously been repressed. In a parasitic kind of way U.S. CAPITAL has thus gotten "funky," simulating the once *outlawed styles* of African-Americans and claiming them as (if) their own. Indeed, with "the emergence of the United States, as a world power, it was quite clear that black music—spirituals, gospels, blues, jazz, soul—was the most unique cultural product created by Americans of any hue. So as the globalization of American culture escalated, black music was given vast international importance."[20] Just listen to black radio stations this season and top-forty stations in the next. *"It really doesn't matter if you're black or white."* One marketing season after the next, white CAPITAL cybernetically scans its borders and inFORMationally endeavors to appropriate and/or simulate models that promise greater flexibility and adaptive expansion within its New World Order of cybernetic control.

Boundaries between what's white and black implode, or are inFORMationally realigned, as aesthetically embodied differences in power are parasited as
nothing but transHIStorical abstractions of style. Just look at fashion, sports,
the television. Just look at yourself.

> The stress here is not simply on the new and the fashionable but also on
> the exotic and the primitive. Black cultural products have historically
> served as a major source for European and Euro-American exotic inter-
> ests—interests that issue from a healthy critique of the mechanistic,
> puritanical, utilitarian, and productivist aspects of modern life. [More-
> over,] given the European and Euro-American identification of Africans
> and African-Americans with sexual licentiousness, libertinism, and libera-
> tion, black music became both a symbol and a facilitator of white sexual
> freedom.[21]

In Voodoo, music, dance and style were not fetishized (inFORMational)
symbols but totemic gestures that doubled back upon the materiality of their
own ritual claims to knowledge. But even this formal aspect of Voodoo is
partially simulated in the ultramodern CAPITALIst mediascape. Images folding
back upon images upon images. The vertiginous and wave-like character of
Voodoo possession is perhaps the most precious gift parasited by cybernetic
forms of power. And this is occurring, moreover, without the generous and
combative spirituality that has long been a material feature of African-American religious practice. Without such generosity, the wave-like networks of
inFORMation that pass through ultramodern CYBORG BODIES may prove more
"panicky" than reconciliatory as "we" find ourselves extended outward across
vast and vibrant networks of economic, military and hyper-scientific inFORMation.

Such panic, its disorders and the theoretical fictions that have sought to
"medicalize" (and thereby neutralize) its political implications are no more
gender-free than they are racially indifferent. This is a central theme in Jackie
Orr's analysis of panicked bodies within contemporary CAPITAL. Orr intersects
Luce Irigaray's analysis of "women as commodities" within the patriarchal
marketplace of modern CAPITAL with Haraway's theorization of the cyber-
netization of postmodern culture. In so doing, Orr asks what happens to
women's (restricted economic) embodiment when the market moves (like
waves of liquid) from the embodied exchange of commodities (under the sign
of money) to the disembodied transfer of money (under the sign of commodities). Making use of an ethnographic collage of psychoanalytic, HIStorical,
literary and autobiographical materials, Orr constructs a theoretical fiction
that critically questions the parasitic indifference of ultramodern CAPITAL to

the panicky bodies of women upon whom it feeds. Here, panic is theorized as a gendered effect of a New World Order of "social relations inscribed on cyborg-bodies," relations that are communicatively filtered by "an unprecedented militarization of the daily, private, peacetimes of cyborgs at work and at play."[22] Thus, under the inFORMational signwork of the telelectronic marketplace:

> It is possible that value...becomes quite really a physical thing, an abstraction materialized within the social, sexual and symbolic spaces of our bodies incorporated in a new economy of the postmodern. But as value incorporates within and without our bodies, as the story [of capital] shifts into new configurations of exchange gone panicky and postmodern, do some things perhaps, really stay the same? Do some bodies in the postmodern market, already positioned historically and materially along the modern fractures of liquid and physical property, of abstract value and embodied exchange, do some bodies experience more terror than others? Do the disembodied flows of panic pulsing through the wires short-circuit in some bodies more than others? Are some bodies still paying a higher price for their own hook-ups in the postmodern market's shifting central (nervous) system?[23]

A related (but different) story may be told of the blank white racial effects of contemporary CAPITAL's cybernetic implosions of previously repressive modern boundaries. Communicatively ecstatic before the screen of its own blurring of HIStorical and cultural difference, mass-marketed segments of U.S. white culture may in one high-speed instance feel as free-floating as the *kinetic orality* and *passionate physicality* of the traditional black cultural practices it parasites, then, in the next panicky white time frame, blame those it feeds upon for the unbelievability of the simulations in which it finds itself adrift in terror. But what of the material effects of such parasitism on African-Americans themselves? Throughout this chapter I have argued that the exponential expanse of inFORMational CAPITAL has produced far more economic costs than benefits for African-Americans, Hispanics and other non-white U.S. citizens. But the spiritual effects of telelectronic CAPITAL may be just as costly.

In *The Sanctified Church,* a collection of ethnographic observations about African-American religious practices written in the 1930s, Zora Neale Hurston suggests that, "Language is like money. In primitive communities actual goods, however bulky, are bartered for what one wants. This finally evolves into coin, the coin being not real wealth but a symbol of wealth. Still later, even coin is abandoned for legal tender, still later cheques for certain uses."[24] For people with so-called "developed languages," such as the whites who dominate the economy of U.S. language, those for whom verse is "written in cheque words," Hurston notes that even "detached ideas" may become "legal tender." By contrast, the language of blacks is said to remain connected to contexts of linguistic "action," where even "detached words" have a "close fit" with the dramatic (or ritual scenery) of their materialization. Here "the speaker has in...mind the picture of the object in use."[25] Hurston locates this refusal of dematerializing language by African-Americans within a Voodoo based epistemological context where even the concrete illusions of everyday language are periodically waved away by rites of ecstatic possession.

But what if an ultramodern and predominantly white economic formation begins "liberating" itself from the repressive constraints of its modern economic (linguistic) abstractions, not by generously giving away power, but by more abstractly than ever simulating the embodied concreteness of a traditional black culture as nothing but a more flexible inFORMational power? What, then, for those whose language is pirated and then fed back to them in simulated form? A glimpse of the situated violence of such redoubled parasitism is provided in the following observations by Alison Luterman. Noting disturbances caused by the telelectronic waves of the mass-media for Haitian practitioners of Voodoo living in the U.S., Luterman (w)rites:

> These days, as Haitians experience the same dislocation and future shock that many other Third World cultures are going through, the gods have reason to be insecure. Even at a ceremony such as...a big feast, well attended and well supplied—god after god complains of not enough food and not enough attention. They must pursue their servitures through the jungles of Miami, New York, Boston, places where they have to compete with the gods and goddesses of the mass media for attention. With typical resourcefulness, they begin to incorporate the competition. As Ruth says, "When [the *loa*] Erzulie come to me at night, she come with the face of Elizabeth Taylor, but she's speaking to me with the voice of Erzulie.[26]

THE ORPHANS' REVENGE

SOCIOLOGICAL DECONSTRUCTION AT THE CROSSROADS

To be reasonably lucky, an orphan should have a brother or sister close in age, a modest inheritance (large ones cause trouble), and hospitable relatives. What to do with the unlucky ones has become the concern of a society whenever one of the giant orphan-makers—wars, mass migration, economic depressions, epidemics—caused their number to rise abruptly. Especially at such times children without parent have been subjected to the exploitation their vulnerability seems almost to beg for.—Eileen Simpson[1]

I. BEFORE ANYTHING ELSE

Tick tock. Tick tock. I find myself spinning uncertain how to proceed. My eyes/"I"s cross-circuit through the screen that becomes me and I buy a lot and give a little. Repeatedly.

DAY
AFTER
DAY[2]

In a variety of provocative visual and performative interventions and in the publication of texts such as *Society of the Spectacle, The Revolution of Every-day Life, The Poverty of Student Life* and numerous collectively authored manifestos, magazines and comics, members of the Situationist International transgressed the borders between the practice of critical social science theory and artful political interruptions aimed at exposing the LIES of consumer society.[3] Of particular importance for Situationists was the CAPITAL violence to HIStorical memory effected by the sacrificial production of fascinating psuedo-events and mass cultural experiences simulating the charms of festival in a technologically controlled or cybernetic fashion. Although rarely read by U.S. sociologists, during the late 1950s and throughout the 1960s the Situationists regarded the U.S. economy, (military) state and popular culture as the *avante garde* of a new form of CAPITALIST society. Here, "lived reality is materially invaded" by the spectacular fascinations of cybernetic control mechanisms that blur the distinction between productive work and obsessional compulsions to consume nearly everything in sight. Here, within a hypnotic swell of mass mediated images and bureaucratically orchestrated desires, nearly everybody becomes both worker and raw material. In this, the omnipresence of spectacle operates as "the material reconstruction" of traditional religious illusions, as "in all its specific forms, as information or propaganda, as advertisement or direct entertainment consumption, the spectacle is the present *model* of socially dominant life."[4] The "omnipresent affirmation" of choices "already made" by a dense and fast moving structure of hierarchical economic initiatives, the "society of the spectacle" represents "the technical realization of... *capital* to such a degree of accumulation that it becomes an image."[5]

FRAYED NERVES

Despite the contemporary resonance of the Situationist critique, Baudrillard is not wrong to proclaim the end of "the society of the spectacle" as a form of social control. Television's first phase has fast receded from memory, a phase marked by the dawn of the dead, the dawn of a new U.S. EMPIRE OF THE SENSELESS in the years following the Second World World. Thereafter, the SNAP, CRACK(LE) AND POP of things has gotten faster and faster and faster. More deeply dis-eased. More calm EDGY calm EDGY calm EDGY calm. Borderlines crossing into and out of each other give way to multiplied personalities as the low thrush of FAX MACHINE THOUGHTS lingers almost breathless. The nonsense of wondering whether war will start again. This is TOTAL WAR. This is TOTAL EVERYTHING.[6]

ATTENTION FORBIDDEN

This text is about filmic doubles and the moral economy effected by becoming a PARTIAL HIStorical orphan. Imaginarily and in the body. This is a story of the methodological relationship between a power-reflexive practice of social-psychoanalytic theorizing and the ritual demands for one (who is (k)not One) to pass through the HORRORS of being orphaned. Without transcendence or the sublime assurance of genius. Without heroics or the call to war. Being orphaned by social-psychoanalytic practice, or by the dance of a deconstructive ethnography, or by the entrancing descent of the genealogical method. Being orphaned by tears (or tears) and laughing matters. Like a serpentine skin passing out of time, shedding one's ego. Not killing or being killed, but being orphaned beyond (or beneath) belief and beyond (or beneath) interpretation and proper grammar gone syntax.

FAKE
NEWS

ONCE UPON A TIME I intended to deliver an Other text on this occasion. That was before what I encountered at the Parasite Cafe and was changed. That Other text, the One I am not presently (w)riting, at least not always, was to be called, "A World of Doubles: a World of Exile." This text was to be about the doubled role of cinematic rituals in reel/real time ritual sacrifices—film and society. Then it dawned on me that even such filmic rituals were today being technologically redoubled again—rescreened to secure a CAPITAL HIStorical investment in late (k)night television. Transnationally. It is as if some popular end of the twentieth century soap opera had suddenly gone PRIME-TIME with little material notice. (K)night after (K)night. Screen after Screen. This is cybernetics. This is ultramodernity: a liquid electronic flow of sacrificial CAPITAL images extending credit while bending One's eyes/"I"s. Bending one's self, secured visually: the gaze transmuted into a mechanical reproduction, then shot into a holograph. Is this gaze male or is it memorex? Or both? The eyes/"I"s bending split screened around the globe in a byte. In an instant. At what seems like exactly the same time multiplied across memory. Faster and more dense. Beyond and within what's modern male and white fleshed. Beyond and within what's economically incorporated as HIStory. Beyond and within the promised pleasures of mastering the passage of time. Here and there at the same time. Beyond and within the body.

INSIDE
OUT

Faster than a speeding bullet. Able to leap tall architectural metaphors with a single bound. And to shuttle absent minded and panicked bodied back and forth between several persons, several voices at once vocationed and cut off from each other within the same body. Whose body?

CYBER-VISION: IT OFFERS YOU THE WORLD IN A WORD

By the mid-1970s the transformation of television and its circulation within a more dense and ultramodernizing network of power is parasitically fed by the reorganization of world markets on a non-bipolar model. This is the manifest destiny of the USA TODAY; A FAST FOOD INSTANT FREEZE FRAME LOSS OF MEMORY; a violent MICRO-WAVING of fleshy bodies into the omnipresent vacancy of a CAPITAL and predominantly WHITEMALE AND HETEROSEXIST techno-dreamscape of purified festivals without ends, or beginnings. Liquid

CAPITAL floating screen to screen memory to screen memory. Faster than a speeding bullet. Able to leap tall architectural metaphors in a single BYte. No joking—this is inFORMation. THIS IS ART.

EMPTY
VISTA

With MCI's special total telephonic package you get something Other's only dream of giving. It's your choice. Call now and get one month free.

NERVOUS
SILENCE

Beyond and within a belief in metaphysical reality or the power of God-like truths Fathering Words and things and sons/suns radiating, transferring, telecommunicating memory or religion or science. Red, white and blue waves absorbed into the disappearing body of a Dark (K)night singular and yet multiply occupied; Batman and the stealth bomber both lonely yet overflowing with unlipped voices synching. And on screen there is inFORMation about who's in the hunt for the nation's leading quarterback and forth; back and forth, back and forth. Some strong malebody or Other from somewhere else and yet here at the same time in the heart of each excited sports fan.

BORED
STIFF

TRANSFERENCE DRIVES RITUAL beyond and within what "He" who is said to be One is always missing. Driving ritual into the almost magnetic or "ab-original" enchantments of HIGH DENSITY totems shot into space with a velocity that defies description. The *reel time* of cinema transmuting into the *real time* of electronically screened life chances and military logistics.

LOCK
STEP

The convergence of the home computer with the whitest dreams of MANkind! WHITER than WHITE. MAN after MAN. One dollar after anOther. She stepped from her questions into the sink of HIStory. This troubled her. But at least she was CLEAN and READY-MADE. WHITER than WHITE. MAN after MAN. One dollar after anOther.

BLANK
STARE

All they were talking about was RISK GROUPS. Why no mention of RISKY PRACTICES. Concerning AIDS this masks the almost unspeakable reality that there are virtually no differences in sexual practices between gay men and heterosexual men and women. What differences there are LIE in values ascribed (sacrificially). On screen, the category RISK GROUP has been used repeatedly to stereotype and stigmatize people already ritually excluded from the moral economy of the "mainstream." In 1987 this resulted in a successful campaign by Jesse Helms to prevent federal dollars from being spent on SAFE SEX inFORMation for gay men—the hardest hit RISK GROUP, and the only one in which reported transmission of the virus has actually declined (to less than two percent new infections in San Francisco in 1987) due to SAFE SEX education by gay men themselves. So why continue the language of RISK GROUP when its evident that what's more material is the seemingly unspeakable reality of RISKY PRACTICES? It's so hard to re-member.

CYBER
SLAVE

The convergence of the home computer, television and telephone lines as the nexus of a new viral machinery bares evidence of the undoing of the commodity in its spectacular phase. Today it's something else. Instantly. In the blink of an eye/"I." HIGH DENSITY but LOW DEFINITION. Faster than dreams and thicker than blood. Then the reverse. By remote control: the telecommunication and sacrificial conjuring of absence as presence. Then the reverse. By remote control: thick with fascination, if thin on substance. Then the reverse shot: time dis-appearing within the homogenization of space. This is CAPITAL to such an intense degree that its images are becoming no-thing but waves split screening fractal memories. Surface to surface: its violent effects registering in the bodies of those it renders homeless or orphaned. Democratically. One liberal gendered and color coded economic moment after anOther: a process of imperial world-viewing gone ULTRAMODERN.

WHY
ASK

And paradoxically, television, which had elevated the commodity to the height of spectacular space, is now implicated in the implosion of that space and the resulting evaporation of its aura. The commodity passes into the body and the body passes into space. I swear you could almost feel the vapors rising. Then he took the gun and put it into his mouth. The next thing you know they're sending troops to the Persian Gulf.

WAGE
WARS

For the Situationists writing in the wake of the Marshal Plan and *at the high tide of the 'PAX AMERICANA,' the auratic presence of the commodity was bound up with its utter tangibility.* STEP RIGHT UP MY YOUNG MAN. NOTHING'S LEFT. PUT YOUR EYES IN THE (W)HOLES AND LET YOUR FINGERS DO THE WALKING. SEE THE BLOOD. SEE THE PLEASURE.

HIDDEN
CAMERA

The terror of randomly accessing a memory that's anything but accidental. A violence that (k)nightly cuts the bodies of women, those who are (k)not white and those who are under or over-employed for some Other's self circulatory profit. And in between or the cracks of what's specifically economic—the terrors of the leveraged buyout, a corporately constructed virus re-speculating. Penetrating the galvanic borders of One's own skin and transmuting everything to flows of inFORMation, then credit. Promises. Promises. WELCOME TO THE PARASITE CAFE.

PANIC
STATE

Since the time of the Situationists we have become increasingly assaulted by a high speed displacement of aura from images of possessable objects to digitalized flows of data, the almost hypnotic glow of the screen and the promise of limitless access. This is a reversal of processes identified by the Situationists. One Dark (K)night after anOther. One leveraged BUY-OUT after anOther.

VIDEO
DRONE

Once upon a time I intended to deliver a text about cinematic doubles gone televisionary, about the parasitic transmutation of the time of film reels into the "real time" of video display terminals. But then I encountered the Parasite Cafe and everything's changed. This text is no longer simply about doubles. This text, or my (w)riting, is threatening to partially undo itself, or me, by becoming doubled at the crossroads of what's parallel processed and what's horizonally given. Is this what it means to be a PARTIAL SOCIOLOGICAL ORPHAN?

SHIT
WORK

This text is HIStory. Or HERS? I am not certain I'm being seduced. S/he dragged herself across the stream of icons to a place of unsanctioned secrecy. DisinFORM-ation. Everything was now CAPITAL and s/he felt it like a lump. SPIN-DOCTORED.

LEISURE
CONTROL

2. IN THE BEGINNING

> That fiction, where every character can, by reason of its consistency, be comprehended at a glance, either exhibits but sections of character, making them appear for wholes, or else is very untrue to reality; while, on the other hand, that author who draws a character, even though to common view incongruous in its parts, as the flying squirrel, and, at different periods, as much at variance with itself as the butterfly is from the caterpillar from which it changes, may yet, in so doing, be not false but faithful to facts.—Herman Melville[7]

On my third night at the Parasite Cafe, the Black Madonna appeared before an unruly gathering of orphans demanding revenge. What she had to say seemed more understandable to me, having spent the last several days with Rada Rada, Jack O. Lantern, Marty, Reno and the other orphans. Everybody was wearing a mask, at least in theory, and things were noiser than ever. "Now disguise is...the foremost example of how we articulate the problems of appearance in the context of change. Why...? The answer...rests in our recognition of the possibility for illusion—in the awareness of an ambiguity informing the simplest transitions... This awareness aids us in establishing a point of view and in evaluating phenomena that we may later view quite differently. The potential for ambiguity, therefore, remains fundamental to change despite any claims we might make about an inferred, innate, or even empirically perceived identity, and disguise is...the primary way of expressing this ambiguity. The use of diguise is thus conducive both to make-believe and to changes of state that are imputed to be real... [Moreover] because the human face is [a] primary means of our recognizing and thus identifying, one another, it deserves special attention in a study of appearances and their ambiguities. And because a mask is itself not merely the most direct but the most widespread form of disguise, the function of illusion in change may be most directly explored through an analysis of masks and masking conventions."[8]

A few questions about method—*LIFE as THEATRE or all stories are inherently plagiarized*—is it possible to DOUBLE STAGE a critical (post)phenomenological analysis so that experience dramatically undoes its (im)possible desires for Oneness, thus opening the imaginary realm to exits out of self-circulating narcissitic repetition? As I listen to the Black Madonna's words dance rhythmic I find myself entranced. I feel as if taken over by a desire for deconstructive generosity. I feel stupid but less afraid. How to tell a truthful sociological story about such contradictory authorial (dis)positionings at this dangerous time in HIStory?

The task, it seems, is not so much to kill the author as to reflexively de-authorize any claims to nonsituated storytellings. What a laugh! What a crime! "Why should I not admit, in fact, that it is possible that I am creating a [per-verse] phenomenology and not a science of society? Even that might be granting myself more than others are willing to concede. Would it not, afterall, be just a question of something deserving the name ideology? Would what I am setting forth here be anything more than a combat ideology? That is to say, by definition, a necessary delusion?"[9] One thing appears for certain, in this "intermingling of fact, fiction, and desire," I am laboring "to find a writing practice which can foreground the memories of the conditions under which the facts and the real story are produced."[10] Moreover, by making strategic use of theoretical fictions to "interrupt or put into crisis" the normative demand for realist sociological de-scription, "I hope to draw attention to the sociologist as writer and to the complicated relationship between the location of the investigating subject and the political interests of our readings and writings."[11]

Masked theories as fictions and the reverse—what a laugh! What a crime! It was crime that the Black Madonna was speaking about that evening and of challenging recent LEGAL OPINIONS set forth in (w)riting by the U.S. Supreme Court, when she said—

"So the criticisms I've been making of THINKING ABOUT CRIME shorn from the lived material exigencies of racist, warlike and transnationalized CAPITAL power and of the violence of social scenes that appear to be (always already) lacking power, ah!, these, in themselves, are nothing new. It is simply that crime and its control repetitiously take place, Oh-h-hhh!, within transferential social contexts that are marked by power, and are thus political, even and especially (as feminist criticism has repeatedly suggested) when most personal and, Ah, or when seemingly idiosyncratic. And to ignore this totemic geography, this social psychoanalytic conjuncture of biography and HISory, this dramatic whiteweaving of telematic desire and televisionary terror at the crossroads of 'our' orphaned bodies and 'their' fatherly figured sacrifices— Ah!, isn't this, I ask you, isn't this dangerous beyond words? Now, *'Goya said it* best in a song without words; Saturn devouring his son. Mad God with blood on his lips and raw flesh stuck beneath his fingernails. Weaver of words and illusions; you command F-15s and television. You try to bewitch us with your smile....Cowboy Eating His Children.'[12] So, I ask you, dear orphans, where are our memories?"

Shouts, sways and dance-possible epistemic configurings passed amongst the orphans. Since quite a few of the orphans were from Guatemala and El Salvador, the sound of native dialects and Spanish cut the air; rhythmic and (im)possibly staccato at the same time. The Black Madonna continued, like an artist, "carefully choosing every syllable and evey breath."[13]

"Now we live in a geographical moment, 'created by our collusion, confusion, and complacency, when delusion and reality have merged in public life....Cowboy...faster than a speeding MX. Deadlier than a diamondback. Cowboy the terror of the West....Like the gunslingers we so admire, we seem untroubled by our knowledge that Cowboy is a vampire who can maintain himself only by spilling blood. And like adolescents, which we yearn to remain, we dismiss the possibility that we, too, may die. We live in this Cowboy moment, imminent victims of his violence, which we perpetrate and permit. Cowboy whispers in our ears, tickling our lobes with his tongue, sucking our blood. He is our creature, our killer, ourselves. Cowboy is no specific politician, psychopath, or actor. Cowboy is our flight from history."[14]

"So, what I am saying is that all this Cowboy vampire danger seems particularly urgent in the wake of increasing waves of informationally polled and panicky U.S. public sentiment favoring sacrificial state action, Ah!, against those believed to represent the greatest threat to 'public safety'—young Black and Hispanic males. Images of such feared offenders, Oh-h-hh, such negatively charged totems or darkly mirrored reflections of what is so anxiously thought to be enlightened—these are daily severed, like telecommunicatively screened memories, from the cruel and contradictory confines of gender-specific, economic and racist hierarchies. And to allow ourselves to be enchanted by such techno-imaginings, and indeed it is hard to resist their televisionary allure, isn't this to remain blindly fascinated by parasitic rituals that repeatedly cast us in the role of sacrificial host to 'the lives of rich and famous.' Consider the so-called Drug Wars. Here, those who use or abuse 'controlled substances,' and today even their parents, are (at best) forced into treatment, not because their escape into chemically induced pleasure is acknowledged as a threat to the addictive illusions or disciplinary constraints of a society that simultaneously demands and hierarchically denies equal access to rational economic instrumentality, Ah!, but because such unfortunate persons are said to be sick or morally weakened. At the same time, those who act violently against persons

with whom they are most akin—they are criminalized, not because they dramatically exceed and thereby expose the 'normal' tribal limits of patriarchal family violence, but because they are diagnosed as unable to manage 'ordinary' stress and aggression in ways deemed safe and/or healthy.

"Oh-h-hhh, my dear orphans, this is not to romanticize those who violate the law. As you and I know, most of these persons are hardly self-conscious political rebels. Nevertheless, the story of crime I am telling is, at all times, a story of structurally situated resistance to the disciplinary construction and reconstruction of normalized senses of lawful subjectivity. It is a story inscribed under CAPITAL conditions of intense social contradiction and an equally intense denial of the omnipresent power of social inequalities in shaping the intellectual, perceptual and carnal context of actions that comply with or, Ah!, defy the law's reproduction. This is true regardless of whether such resistance is conscious or unconscious, deliberate or inadvertent. This is true whether the alleged criminal is an alcohol dependent male struggling with the impossibilities of realizing an autonomous masculine identity, or a SONY WALKMAN connected and easy to anger adolescent, as high on the communicative ecstasy of televisionary-video-game feedback, as he (or she) is low on cash and the promise of future well being, or the corporate raider, whose anxious, if omnivorous, will to abstract power over our inFORMational futures induces an embodied fascination that literally carries one beyond both the law and its white coded distinctions between what is technically right and what's technologically possible.

"So, to critically engage with the HIStorical materiality of contemporary crime, 'we' must reflexively resituate our collective representations of this frightening drama within and/or against the subtle and often unrecognized exigencies of power as it plays itself out through the bodily imaginations of those it captivates and those it silences. Otherwise, our activism will do little but reproduce the contradictory networks of power in which it is already always situated; confirming the gaze of the state upon those who are stereotypically at the roots of the crime problem, while distracting attention from such nearly unmemorable figures of recent crime as those most successful of corporate criminals—Ah!, the savings and loans bandits, including President Bush's own son, Neil. The unregulated and whitemale-minded criminal speculations of such supposedly respectable business people have cost U.S. taxpayers and the global citizenry of the New World Order something approximating $500 billion and, in my opinion, represent a major structural incentive for the recent war of the debt driven U.S. and its economic allies against its former 'client-state' Iraq. Sign Crimes or War Crimes? This is a crime wave that

passes in and out of our collective social memories without significant notice
or outcry. Nothing, for instance, like the distortive ritual notice given to the
illegal marketing of cocaine. Now, how, I ask you, might 'we' widows and
orphans make better theoretical, strategic and healing connections between
such widely stereotyped and such widely ignored scenes of crime?

"I ask this question not innocent of an awareness that parasitic connections
do in 'fact' exist between 'savings and loans' bandits, the activities of illegal
cocaine marketeers and the 'covert actions' of CIA agents and various other
U.S. government operatives. It was, in part, through such real, Ah!, if popu-
larly unimagined, connections that U.S. government itself secretly financed its
own criminal activities in support of the Contra-terrorists it paid to attack and
invade the sovereign (U.N. member) state of Nicaragua.[15] Guilty of some
twenty-four World Court adjudicated violations of international law, neither
the U.S. state, nor 'we' its public, appear to register a collective memory of
such violent criminal activity. Such crimes, instead, appear to implode into
informational signs that contain and displace their material actuality. More-
over, although massive in its domestic and international implications, the
corporate informational looting of the Savings and Loans industry has no-
where been greeted by such public condemnation as that so carefully orches-
trated against the media saturated criminality of former U.S. military-business
partners Manuel Noriega of Panama and Saddam Hussein of Iraq. Divorced
from the contradictions of HIStorical actuality, a mass-mediated image of
crime today tattoos such so-called 'evil' figures, just as it escapes from other
complex and, Ah!, contradictory aspects of the social structuring of sacrificial
power."

Her words, gestures and intonations conjured up uncanny scenes of otherwise inaccessible memories. Within the waves of real imaginary contact her
stories engendered, I found myself in social-psychoanalytic transference with
invisible mysteries of great power and knowledge that, like the unconscious
markings of totemic sacrifice, tattooed so many of "our" bodies with desires
for objects that forever escape our grasp, instilling both envy and desire. But
since the Black Madonna's analytic poesis, which at some points seemed
spatiously preachy and luxuriously ecstatic, appeared *really imaginary* (or
reflexively doubled), and not either imaginarily real (in the sense of dissimulat-
ing the specificity of its own "positivist" or "phenomenological" violence) or
hyperreal (in the sense of being cybernetically modeled as a technological
simulation of what appears simultaneously as both invisible and visible, or
informationally transparent), I read her performance as taking up dangerously
new and desparately needed positions of both defense and revenge upon the
vampirism of the COWBOY POWERS that rule this planet.

All around me the orphans were shouting out (un)free but playful epistemic associations. "There can be little doubt that [such] shouting is a survival of the African 'possession' by the gods.... The implication is the same...it is a sign of special favor...that drives out individual consciousness temporarily and uses the body for the its expression.... Broadly speaking, shouting is an emotional explosion [of wisdom], a response to rhythm. It is called forth by [various strategies for reflexively embodying communal memories]; (1) sung rhythm; (2) spoken rhythm; (3) humming rhythm; (4) the foot-patting or hand clapping that imitates very closely the tom-tom....Shouting is a community thing. It thrives in concert. It is the first shout that is difficult...to arouse. After that one they are likely to sweep like fire over" a learned gathering of orphans.[16] *Tongues untied*, some chanted a rainbow of names for she who appeared to mask herself as a host inviting some rather serious epistemic dining. Black widow erzulie vetula hag femina luna eve meretrix venus regina puello praegnans brigitte lilith artemis mater matrix mama Dada mama Dada Dada mama Dada mama—there must have been a thousand and one names. Each more laughable than the one before, and more reverent.

"*This is what I call re-search*," said Rada, posing performatively, like me, in drag. "The performance of drag plays upon the distinction between the anatomy of the performer and the gender being performed.... In imitating gender, drag implicitly reveals the imitative structure of gender itself—as well as its contingency."[17] And what about Jack O. Lantern's manifestly artificial white face? Was he in some kind of racial drag, playing with the ritual markings of skin color as if this bodily sign was one or the other, either body or sign, either archaic or modern, either black or white, or the reverse?

Rada nudged me, placing the text s/he was reading before my eyes/"I"s. The words read:

> It is possible that the religious ideas of ancient Crete and Egypt originated in black Africa. During 7000 to 6000 B.C., the Sahara was a rich and fertile land, and a great civilization flourished there. Images of the Horned Goddess (who became Isis of Egypt) have been found in caves on a now inaccessible plateau in the center of what is now the Sahara desert....Great importance has always been given to the Queen-Mother across the continent of Africa. The original Black Goddess was regarded as bisexual, the instrument of her own fertility; she was the ancient 'witch' who carried a snake in her belly. Africans worshipped her many manifestations. The creator of the gods of the Dahomey, for example, was Mawu-Lisa, imaged as a serpent; Mawu-Lisa was both female and male, self-fertilizing, seen as the earth and the rainbow. Africans believed that the earth is ultimately more powerful than the sky and its gods; the sky can withhold rain, but the earth is the source of life itself.[18]

Then the sound of one nasal hissing voice rose provisionally over the others. It was Jack O. Lantern, whose name (for me at least) conjured almost as many subversive bodily associations as the Black Madonna's. *Jack trickster jack rabbit jack of spades jack house that jack built jack be nimble jack's are wild one-eyed jacks be quick jack the beanstalk jack the conquerer jack off jack o' kent jack in a box jack hammer jack in and jack out little pumpkin.* (W)rapping himself around a strange woody post which stood at the center of the orphanage—I mean the Parasite Cafe—Jack called for the lights to be dimmed so as to project another in his seemingly endless panoply of slides. This time the image belonged to Card 152 in the *Pro Set Desert Storm* collector's card series. The front side of the card displayed the disappearing totemic figure of a white man fading to invisibility. Above him are the words MILITARY SKILL. Below this grim black-on-whitemale face, which appears midway between being visibly present and invisibly absent, in a machinic or cybernetic kind of way, are a miniaturized U.S. flag and the word CAMOUFLAGE. *"Just so you don't think we're the only ones wearing masks,"* hissed the professor. The back of *Pro Set Desert Storm* card 152 reads:

> The human face has natural areas of shine and shadow. The shiny areas attract attention and, combined with the shadow areas, make faces stand out from surrounding terrain. If the shiny areas are darkened and the dark areas are lightened, the face will blend into the background. Use dark camouflage paint or mud for the forehead, nose, cheeks and chin. Use light camouflage paint or mud everywhere else to break up the familiar face shape. Apply camouflage to the back of the neck and the hands to complete the process.

While reading the projected words I caught a glimpse of Reno passing stealthy out of the Cafe. Where was he going? Was he afraid he'd be challenged by the parodic rites that were under way? Was he afraid to risk the dangerous play of mirroring simulations back upon simulations and thus fatefully reclaiming LIFE *as THEATRE* or assuming collective social responsibility for the fact that all true stories are inherently plagiarized? Was he afraid to become the erotic object of some reciprocal social forms that might be lovingly accessed only in excess of what is currently re-memorable and not the Other way around? This part of my story must remain forever undertheorized, for at just that moment hisses calling for revenge began to pass through the crowd, not without laughter, but not without transferential rage either. LAUGHING RAGE—what a paradoxically masked combination! Revenge for all the death squads! Revenge for all the whitemale terror! Revenge for every CAPITAL idea put technologically into practice! Revenge for the homelessness, hunger and all that has parasitically turned us into orphans! Revenge upon each and every canon of their militaristic meanings and metaphysics! Needless to say, the orphans were hardly ignorant of the most fierce structures of sacrifice that plagued their every memory.

Then, as if in response, the Black Madonna motioned for the orphans' silence. An attentive hush fell over our different, if interwoven, HIStories. She marked the floor with corn meal and what appeared a secret language, afterwards saying, "The Invisible Ones say you come back tomorrow." You could almost feel the fire of her tongue. Some fell to their knees. Others swayed back and forth in waves of unspeakable social interaction. *I nodded that I heard and went out.*[19] The next day she began to prepare us for our initiation ceremony, a social-psychoanalytic rite of subtle power and great political significance. For rest assured, nobody may approach the Altar of reflexively informed struggles for justice without a generously embodied epistemic crown, and none may wear this powerful crown of counter-memories without preparation. It must be earned just as generously as it is dangerously given. And what is this crown of paradoxical power? Nothing definite in material but somethings moving; nothing certain but somethings true; nothing final but somethings both deadly and life-giving in their vulnerable partiality and strong claims to provisional deconstruction. What a laugh! What a crime!

The next day the figure who I have been repeatedly (mis)recognizing as the Black Madonna crowned me with a consecrated snake skin. Jack O. Lantern rubbed warm oil on the inside of my thighs, while Marty Martin touched my lips with saffron, sharply pinching my nipple, hissing unmentionably STUPID BAD FRESH JOKES refusing lawful codes of PUNishment and Ah! "i" feel myself falling spinning losing my head vomiting up words like a snake biting the tail that feeds her—

> colors spinning spicey smells tongues touching saffron tongues black tastes
> warm soft carressing knowing not confessing secret spaces times between
> rhythmic times cascading resisting namings saffron tongues black tastes
> stupidly meeting la luna el farol de los enamorados serpentine rainbows
> colors spinning dragging hearing whirling spicey tongues touching saffron
> soft carressing knowing resistance and revenge

"i" have also been crowned in other spaces and times with flowers, ornamental paper, books, mud, paint, eggs shells, sperm, sycamore bark, postcards, conversations, menstrual blood and spicy black bean shrimps. It is the materiality of generous symbolic exchange not the symbolism of specific materials that counts. But near the end of this particular ceremony, Rada Rada, who had also been crowned, if in a different manner, heard the uncanny scratching of a ragged masked beggar at the crossroads between our now orphaned bodies and some other men's HIStories. A feeling of great terror passed into our hearts. This was the last eye/"I"'d see of Madonna Durkheim, Jack O. Lantern or Marty Martin in the flesh. The violence that occurred that night at the Cafe is literally beyond description. For me the scariest thing is what they did with the yellow ribbons. Eye/"I" ask you, Reno, was it sublime?

3. LATER

Something light struck a cold memory and s/he tossed from her dream into HIStory. As s/he opened her eyes/"I"s s/he caught a glimpse of a WHITE-MAN masturbating at the window to the back of her mind. This was an extremely unpleasant sensation, but not without its fascinations. In court, it was noted that s/he was NO-THING but an organic conduit for the UNBORN. Afterward they stored her safely amidst the test tubes, monitoring for drugs and second thoughts. Everything was now CAPITAL in its diehard bloodlust and she felt it like a lump. In her left breast and in the tightness of her throat. And in the back of her calves and lower back. When s/he informed him of what had happened, he didn't say a word. The funny thing about Jim and Tammy Faye, s/he thought, is that they appeared able to actually eat themselves in public. This made her all the more starved.

For some time s/he'd been living with the awareness that her body had become a televisionary locus of great HIStorical power. In the increasingly disembodied world of simulations and floating whitemale spectres, this was as much a curse as blessing. S/he was re-minded of this almost hourly. But more recently, s/he'd been practicing BECOMING MORE OFFENSIVE and less terrorized by the costs of refusing. S/he been meditating on QUEER possibilities and training for battle. To risk the shock waves that they'd most certainly throw in her direction. To risk the waves of blood. This is something s/he'd learned at the Parasite Cafe: "Only a war strategy that rivals the proportions of compulsory heterosexuality...will operate effectively to challenge the latter's epistemic hegemony."[20] And which simultaneously challenges racism and the hierarchical restrictions of CAPITAL as well. These were all lessons s/he'd learned from the orphans, most of whom were both poor and nonwhite.

At one in the mo(u)rning s/he woke in a strange bed and found a WHITE-MAN masturbating at the window to the back of her mind. S/he flew into a RAGE, rolling her eyes/"I"s and sending him reeling/realing. At last s/he'd begun acting as an ORPHAN, or so it seemed. He was staggered. For a moment. Imagine that. Her own father staggered for a moment. This gave her just enough time to break from the laws of HIStory, the laws of this culture's memories, the lawless laws of the USA Today. To leap from the iconic laws of

HIS imagination of her body into a screen beyond. And so she fled through the gap of this instance into nowhere that she'd ever been before. And yet, even here things seemed strangely familiar. Just ahead loomed another crossroads. "Who am I kidding?" s/he asked herself, conflicted and ill-at-ease. S/he knew she was moving fast, but uncertain that s/he was actually going anywhere. Doubt clawed at what defenses she could afford.

Onward and under s/he flew. With ambivalence. There was no way that s/he could convince herself that this mode of flight, this almost theatrical production, was not also complicit with the socio-logic that constituted the violence of HIStory. Not that s/he hadn't tried. Struggling for space, her mind spun with half formed images of nearly a thousand and one other (k)nights. Some of these struck her as (im)possibly female and impatient for recall. Tremors racing through her body reminded her of a need for both resistance and revenge.

Without doubt, s/he was being drawn toward destinations that carried no names. But when had s/he ever been without doubt? As one destination faded into anOther, each seemed more lacking than the ones before. At least this is what he kept telling her, compulsively. He told her that the destinations s/he dreamed of were entirely unreasonable. Unacceptable, impure, and immoral. Throwing her destiny in with other women, for instance. And her pleasures. Destinations that allied her with those of the wrong color and/or insufficient holdings or credit. These things bothered him without end. For her, they were more matters of uncanny transference. It was unbelievable, really. S/he couldn't say what anything meant; only that her desires for revenge were now more intense than ever. This had to mean something important. S/he told herself, moreover, that to deny these feeling was to accept a living death. What s/he had in mind was "neither a simple 'turning of the tables' in which women now wage violence against men, nor a simple internalization of masculine norms such that women now wage violence against themselves."[21] The vengeance s/he found herself dreaming of was both more perverse and parodic. This, again, was something s/he found nurtured by the orphans—a shared dream of QUEER and erotic violence that "has the identity and coherence of the category of sex as its target, a lifeless construct, a construct out to deaden the body" and flat-line the body's memories of the very sacrifices that occasion the body's play.[22] What drama!

In this, s/he found herself in relation to previously unimaginable others. Its (k)not that they hadn't been there all the time. It's simply that they'd been unimaginable. But suddenly, here s/he was among their countless number, adrift amidst the forbidden zones, the other sides of HIStory's power and what (k)not. S/he felt both repulsed and attracted, fearful and determined. Trust your stomach, s/he counseled herself, as s/he approached the crossroads of what had been going on for far too long already. Pausing briefly at the gate, s/he took a deep breath before giving herself over to what defies description.

Onward and under s/he flew. With ambivalence. And, with the tiny crystal chip s/he had stolen from HIStory, s/he edged her way through the gold splashing black across the rectangular mirror of time screened into credit. People smiled from behind each counter she passed. White people. People with business on their minds and their minds on her body. People that were all business, or almost. S/he nodded, as s/he found herself transferred from point to point across the matrix, the force fields, the compulsive plateaus of desiring production. They nodded in return. They stamped her ticket.

Doors opened and doors closed behind her. And on all sides. Spinning. Twisting. Spiralling. Dizzy. Words came to mind. None seemed adequate. This can't be good for my body, s/he thought. But what today could be good for my body? As if this is my body alone; as if I'm not transferentially haunted, possessed or in conversation with what invisible legions or *loa*? Again s/he felt the tightness. What could be truly resistive to the violence of this HIStory and still good for my body? What body is this body? Who am I in relation to this story? S/he replayed these questions—endless times—alone in a room that was never her own. And in her imagination. What madness. S/he sensed his weapons warring within her, even now. S/he felt the terror of being thrown, like some fictional character, into the narrational flows of a dense, if compelling, whitemale fantasy. All these tears and gaps and uncertainties—were they really hers to bear/bare?

How could s/he? Self doubts multiplied with untold speed as transferential sparks shot wild through the spaces that marked her passage. As s/he moved from ONE end of the terminal toward others, s/he tried to comfort herself, thinking that maybe this is all just some kind of strange, if necessary, ritual. This is how s/he interpreted the transference, as s/he moved cautiously from his end of the terminal and from his telos and fears and fantasies and marketplaces toward whatever s/he hoped would make a difference. Would it really make a difference? Clean soft machines cut into her imagination from all directions at once, leaving ferroconcrete traces, without laughter. Drinks arrived. Dinner was served. The flight was underway.

S/he traveled port to port in what seemed like no time at all. At O'Hare a vast chunk of memory detached itself from a blanket of star spangled banners and school cheers. S/he began to cry. S/he was taken by an image of Reno's fingers violating the nice time s/he'd been having at the class picnic and of the terror of being all alone with just him too deep in the woods and the silence that followed—day after day after day. S/he vomited into a day-glow plastic bag labelled COUNT ZERO and sped backward, then fast-forward towards whatever LIES in waiting. "Have a good day please and thank you," s/he said, at last with a laugh. At the counter at the end of the corridor, Rada Rada once more traded tickets, before assuming her position within the dangerous dance that was about to begin. Moving colored figures, indicative of a multiplicity of intermingling wavelengths, invited her participation. Some appeared more seductive than others, but one thing was common to all. Each was an orphan and out for revenge.

4. THE DECONSTRUCTIVE KINSHIP OF ORPHANS

> With the opening of the New World, vagrant children had been rounded up by agents and exported to the Colonies to provide inexpensive labor. Almshouses and orphanages were opened by the states, and by religious orders, when the need for them grew as a result of epidemics of yellow fever, cholera, and typhus. The Civil War, as a result of which the number of orphans in almshouses increased 300 percent, together with wave upon wave of immigration, produced another explosion in their population [not to mention the mass production of orphans by the New World Order of slavery, the genociding of American Native peoples, and the violent proclamation of a U.S. right to MANIFEST DESTINY over everybody in the Western Hemisphere]. —Eileen Simpson[23]

What does it mean to write that a practice of deconstructive theorizing might assist one (who is (k)not One) to become an orphan? It's not that I hadn't been trying. It's that socially deconstructive strategies of (k)not knowing have encouraged my descent out from within a set of HIStorically specific disciplines into the material imaginings of some others. With the help of my friends. After all, you can befriend an orphan but never become her kin; or his. What I mean is this—deconstructive methods may assist one in partially loosening the hegemonic stronghold of those kinship patterns that are currently being supported by the activities of metropolitan based men of corporate power. World wide. Not simply the nuclearized family as kin, but the close-circuiting of ritual relations that seduce people into feeling kinship with automobiles, shopping malls, sports arenas, office towers, football teams and Patriot Missile totems. For it is within these dense and frenetic sites of social structuring that people are today being transnationalized into pre-packaged identities, pledging allegiances, public health syndromes and anxious desires for more and for less.

This is a new and post-familial meaning of kinship networks. Today the actualities of kinship are increasingly defined, not so much by blood, as by fast moving and totemically charged sign systems. Hence, "one" can and does speak in the name of the global family of CBS, NBC, ABC, CNN, Time, Inc. and Disney. Thus it appears that increasing numbers of people may receive more ritual sustenance from involving themselves in the imaginary feuds, intrigues, worries, and desires of TV and media personalities than they do from flesh and blood relations. Given the contemporary implosion of the nuclearized family into the "prime-time" screening of mass mediated remembrances, it is vital that those concerned about the future of human animal relatedness begin to radically retheorize the meaning of kinship. Transferential identifications with electronically screened characters—this is hardly the same as being subject to "the name of the Father." Or, if it is, it is transference in the name of such a disembodied or abstract father that many of us are today being made orphans, in the sociological sense of the word.

The pains of being orphaned—this may indeed be a terrifying aspect of the postmodern scene. More horrific, however, is the possibility that masses of people are today being teleconverted into mutant subjectivities whose primary connections to feelings of kinship are digitally sampled then relayed through the media itself. Those who keep statistics on these matters inform us that there are fewer "father-mother-children" families dining at the Parasite Cafe each evening. And fewer parent-headed families of any type. Within the confines of the USA TODAY children are regularly confronted with having to give up routine contacts with one in a series of "parents." On the other hand, virtually nobody is asked to divorce oneself from ritual contact with the mass electric and trans-sexual parentage that the media has become.

For the American middle classes this mutational situation is rapidly becoming a "real time" situation. Begun, perhaps, with the mass marketing of TV dinners, by the 1990s the "post familial" realities of everyday social life are becoming pronounced and more costly. Thus, the disconcerting conclusions of research recently reported in the *Panic Encyclopedia* suggesting that, when presented with large video-images of both biological mothers and an ordinary television reporter, young babies demonstrated no signs of greater recognition, delight or comfort upon seeing media images of "real" mothers. While this research may have been designed "to provide comfort to working mothers by demonstrating the possibility of new a long-distance video relationship to their infants," the actual results suggest something more about the role of media as a technological mutation of kin. Thus, when the TV reporter was substituted for the mother, "The baby's eyes beamed as much, and in its laughing noises and clapping hands, gave every sign that it wasn't, perhaps, the mommy image which was the object of fascination, but any electric vibrating image being blasted out of that big TV screen."[24]

Here we may be witnessing the emergence of mutant kinship formations generated by the omnipresent "solicitation" of media hook-ups. This is a new form of socialization which compels an "active response" of those of us who are drawn seductively into its new environmental modelings. This is a telematic world characterized by incessant inFORMational feedback and irradiating contact, where the omnipresent glow "of television transforms our habitat into a kind of archaic, closed-off cell, into a vestige of human relations whose survival is highly questionable. From the moment that actors and their phantasies have ceased to haunt this stage, as soon as behavior is focused on certain operational screens or terminals, the rest appears only as some vast useless body, which has been both abandoned and condemned."[25]

And at exactly the same time in HIStory "we" are bombarded with nostalgic (if erroneous) images of the drug free nuclear family as the only true source of "real time" telecommunicative kinship. This is the image of family evoked by a moral army of reactionary forces opposed both to "the liberation" of women and children from traditional family roles and to the so-called breakdown of the family on the part of the racially stigmatized and economically vanquished. Both developments are said to be related to crime, drug abuse and a host of other deviant behaviors. Calls for bolstering the endangered family are also part of an alleged "progressive" political agenda.

Without ignoring the pain of people victimized by the political and economic abandonment of traditional family networks, it is, nevertheless, far from clear that efforts to save the modern western family will prove either just or strategic. Consider the global operations of transnational corporate power as it is telecommunicatively relayed into everyday social life. The immediate site of this transfer involves the hyperelectric tactics of mass-mediated socialization. Here, there is little evidence that family units, as sociologists have traditionally defined then, have been at all effective in resisting the ultramodern transformation of kin. "Family" members who weep openly with Oprah, and share, with Geraldo, the televisionary intimacies of terror, may have little to emotionally exchange with each other in the flesh; little that is but the panic of not being able to live up to the simulated ideals of media icons that have virtually no reference to anything outside the screen and its information.

Better, perhaps, to be sociological orphans than mutant members of the new and fleshless family of the corporate mediascape. At least orphans know the pains of the HIStorical disappearance of their fleshy parents, just as they may dream of the ab-original possibility of reconstructuring some new and less hierarchical structures of kin. For telecommunicative mutants the future is in the past. What mutants screenplay as the basic nuclearized family is nothing but the reruns of an old and exhaustive patriarchal drama. Only this time there's no fleshy Father at its head; only the father's prerecorded presence, only the father's electronically screened memory. But guess what—there's a new talking head at the mutant's dinner table and it's consuming the flesh of everybody else. BYte by BYte. This is the Parasite Cafe. Maybe it's better to be an orphan.

One good thing about orphans—and indeed there are many drawbacks—is that being orphaned helps one to reflexively glimpse the nondialectical nature of parasitic networks of power. Orphans are not in this world because they are formally authorized to be in this world. It's something other than that, and orphans know it for sure. It is to parasite and to be parasited upon. Being orphaned and yet being in the world has "always" been the sign of a more archaic mode of gift exchange. Since "one" who is orphaned can never legally operate under a father's proper name, orphans never think they're "one" in the same way as others. And so to receive a present from an orphan, or to give away some presents in return, is truly to experience a form of social bonding that is fundamentally different than and, perhaps, reflexively distanced from the vicious conjuncture of heterosexist, racist and CAPITAList forces that ritually constitute the "moral economy" of the normal ultramodern family. Today, orphans may be scanning the receding televisionary horizon of contemporary social forms, searching for a place to dance. Their "seductive force, this fatal strategy is a kind of animal game—not simply that of the chameleon, which is only its anecdotal form. It is not the conformism of animals which delights us; on the contrary, animals are never conformist, they are seductive, they always appear to result from a metamorphosis."[26]

After (w)riting these words, I fall from consciousness into the following dreams. The first dream takes place in the underground of a hellish shopping mall. Maybe it's in Montreal. Maybe I'm trying to make contact with the editors who promise to publish this book. The mall is filled with grizzly bargains and there are signs of FREE TRADE everywhere. At a fast food joint I encounter Reno Heimlich who, unlike me, appears at ease with himself amidst the mechanically conditioned and plastic scenes of televisionary futures passing. He explains to me that he is waiting for three young screen tested women whom he hopes to persuade to become his roommates. Actually, he tells me that he hopes to persuade the three women to become his roommates rather than the roommates of another man with whom he's in competition for the screen tested trio. All this seems confusing.

The three women arrive, but just as they do a drag queen flute girl with a mind for philosophy and mirrors approaches me from the actor's stage left. When s/he presents me with the mirror I realize that this mirror is, IN TRUTH, a telelectric message board in disguise. Nobody better accuse me of being a Luddite. I take a look. My destiny seems simple enough—the message board inFORMs me that somewhere in the bowels of the mall are three buffalo on the loose and that I am called upon to give myself over to the touch of one of these nearly extinct animals. I ponder my fate over a dark cup of coffee before taking leave of Reno and the three televisionary women he's trying to persuade, or cajole or seduce into taking up residency within his apartment. I eye the adjacent sections of the underground mall. Everything seems thick with codes and fast with hieroglyphic transference.

I glide amidst rows of hardened plastic where people pass the time eating memories and forgetting. Suddenly I realize that I am carrying two leather bags: the thin leather bag that I was given by my mother, and which I've converted from a backpack to a shoulder bag filled with books, paper, pen, wallet and so forth, as well as Reno's bigger and wider bag that's more professional in appearance. In this dream, it seems I'm carrying more than my own cursed share of baggage. My desire is to get in touch with the three buffalo, but first I feel I should return Reno's bag. The dream begins to tear. Before I know what's happening I find myself LYING cheek to cheek with one of the buffalo, carressing. Then the buffalo nudges me and, in so doing, is transformed into Celie, a cat with whom I live, who is, in fact, nudging me, waking me from this dream. Half awake, I hear a whitemale human voice. It says, "We've an office for you in the rear of Spiraling Agony, my estate, and you will also be required to perform certain chores in addition to your responsibility as a columnist. We are *doubling-up* due to our very limited resources."[27]

I fall back asleep. This time I am carried away by a triptych of three other dreams. The text you are reading is (w)ritten at the crossroads of these several dreams and my wide-awake HIStory. I am in Canada again—somewhere in Quebec it seems—and I'm with Rada Rada (in one of her several figures). We are about to dine in the old wood cut dining room of an inn that feels uncannily like the lodge in Twin Peaks. Televisionary powers hover invisible at the edge of this dream. A waiter, who seems at once male and female, appears seductively to offer us food. Rada and the waiter appear engaged, or somewhat intimate, almost immediately. Soft words fall in French from their tongues. Their eyes smile. The waiter brings us a delicious mix of fish and grains. A fire is burning in the hearth nearby and things inside are warm and quiet. Inside, at least. Outside this lodge there's war, as the U.S. directs its lasers at the Middle East.

Before feasting I am called outside to confer with Jack O. Lantern. In this dream, Jack appears in the shape of a radical criminologist. We walk across the moonlit Quebec landscape, sharing words about the difference between signs of crime and the sign-crimes that appear war-like and everywhere. We are accompanied by Nettie the cat, Celie's sister. Sometimes Nettie darts off into playgrounds and parking lots, exploring the terrain, but each time she returns playful and happy to be out in the evening's air. As we walk, keeping an occasional eye on Nettie, Jack informs me that some unnamed male friend of ours seems to have become so transferentially enamored by my work or by the image of me (or himself) he finds in my work that he has transformed his look into a style fashioned in the wake of mine. This man, whom Jack has recently met with, has also apparently bought me a black silk shirt as a gift. I ask Jack about this gift and he explains that it's in the genre of something the man imagines I might like, but that the details are all wrong and, in actuality, the shirt is too small. Suddenly I remember that I've been gone from the dinner table far too long already and hasten to take leave of O. Lantern and return to the inn.

Back in the inn, Nettie, who is acting very frisky but, at the same time, exceedingly cooperative with the best laid plans of mice and men, seems to enjoy darting throughout the hallways of the old wood inn. Maybe it's a lodge. Maybe this is closer to Twin Peaks than I imagine. I am worried that my long absence will have engendered a rift between Rada and I and am happy to learn that this is not the case. We share food and intimate talk and are informed by our waiter of a "special deal" which will permit us to stay from 11:00 p.m. to 11:00 a.m. at the inn at bargain rates. Not ones to look *a gift horse* in the mouth, we sign up and turn in for the night.

The next dream in this series finds Rada and I still at the inn, waking early. Time is confused, but it seems like 9:00 a.m. and Rada is filled with desire for a fish dinner in the old wood dining room. S/he seems hungry for fish and demands to be fed, even at what, for me, appears a most unlikely hour. I feel that I'd rather sink into the old comfortable bed where we've been dreaming and share sex, and feel confused by Rada's desire for dinner at dawn. The wait staff is uncertain that there will be any fresh fish available until the catch of the day arrives at 5:00 p.m. The androgynous waiter who seemed so involved with Rada the previous evening tries to help. Again, Rada and the waiter appear bonded by a kind of subtle transference, identification or unspecific erotics. Nevertheless, the waiter, too, comes up empty handed. No fresh fish this morning. I try to detour Rada's desires by suggesting snuggling into sex now and another night's stay, with a delicious fish dinner later that evening. Ambivalence abounds and there is unease. Time appears confused and Rada seems convinced that it's later than it seems. The dream fades.

The third dream of this triptych opens and it's still morning at the same inn. We are now outside where Rada appears on a bicycle, making circles at the crossroads of the inn and an old wooden fence that lines a road of dreams extending into the distance. Reno, in one of his several incarnations, is also here with a bicycle of his own. It seems that Reno and Rada are to go on a bike ride together. Suddenly Rada disappears, taking off on her bike down one fork of the road without Reno. I speak with Reno briefly, then he, too, rides off, seemingly to find Rada. I decide to go off for a walk by myself.

I walk along a tree lined path on the grounds of the inn into the thickness of a forest. There I again encounter the soft French speaking androgynous waiter. As I greet the young man, he is approached by and enters into relaxed and comfortable contact with a huge snake, maybe thirty feet long. I'm amazed. In French, or in part French and part English, and without many words at all, the waiter directs my attention to a nearby tree where an even longer snake is wound around, slithering up and/or down. I look around. There are more snakes everywhere. This forest is filled with snakes but the young waiter manifests no fear of these old lengthy reptiles. The snakes, it seems, are simply part of the environmental text of this dream. Suddenly a huge coil of a snake wraps itself around my body; its fangs sinking into my left side, biting into my rib cage, locking its grip. I am at once terrified and fascinated. I signal to the young man for help. Like a vacuum hose the snake sucks me without release. The man grabs the snake by its middle and tries to pull it from me without tearing the flesh. The animal tightly parasites my body, jaws clenched. It is no use. The snake clings to me and winds itself around my form.

The young French speaking waiter is not sure what to do, but ushers me to follow him with the snake still parasitically clasping to my flesh. A woman friend of the young man appears. She also speaks soft French with a Quebec accent. With the snake draped around me and behind, I follow the man and woman further into the forest. We arrive at a warm wooded forest house where my sense of fright is undercut by a subtle erotic transference. The three of us seem charged by an uncanny, if unspoken, sexual connection, engendered by the snaking suckling on blood from my side.

The snake's fangs seem more deeply embedded yet. The young couple confer somewhat seductively. Low whispers. Soft hisses. Then the man tells me that they believe there's one *dance-possible* way I might be released from the snake's slithering bite, but only if I am not afraid of mixing my own blood with warm water in a tub that would be prepared for both me and the snake. What a ritual! Feeling a bit dazed, charged with soft erotic sensations, and even partially ecstatic I begin to remove my clothes as the young woman draws a tub warm wooded bathwater. If this ritual works, the snake may separate from me in the warm water, releasing a flow of my own blood in the process of bathing. In the event of such a dispossession, I am invited to stay warm and naked with the young man and young woman in the wooded Quebec house, healing from the loss of blood, preparing for yet other (w)ritings.

5. ALL THE DREAMS THAT MONEY CAN BUY

> Psychic orphanhood is not new.... What is new is putting a name to the feeling, articulating it as a concept.... Nowhere has this feeling been more prevalent, or of longer standing...than in this country. The United States ...has been since its founding an asylum for emotional orphans.
> —Eileen Simpson[28]

Sometimes being an orphan is extremely dangerous. At precisely 3:22 p.m. the video screen was filled with data dealing with, among other things, the possibilities of *Project Zarathustra*. Before me LIES an image of a speedy white man bursting boundaries never exploded before. How is this possible? As "i" read this borderline POP CULTURE artifactual picture-story or comic, it appears that the thick skinned white man is able to pierce the vaulted walls of what's been screened as memory. He soars red phallic mad and is ejaculated high above what's vegetative. There is a team of observers, maybe corporate raiders and BIG SCIENCE everywhere. And there's a text which reads:

> It is our belief that the tactical potential of Project Zarathustra *will make all conventional weaponry as obsolete as the slingshot.... And here we see him penetrating a bunker of solid Titanium as if it did not exist. Imagine the megadeath potential of such a creature in international conflict.*[29]

The scene switches to a blue lit room. There is the positive power of cold science. There is determination. And machines. The machines connect three human male bodies to more machines. One body is more full sized than the others, while a second is slightly fuller than the third. A trinity of surgeons appears to be working over the fullest of the three bodies. The other two bodies LIE truthfully awaiting their fate. Once again there are black words set against a red background that inform us.

> *The three subjects to date have been young males, [orphans] the children of Air Force personnel and have no other surviving relatives. They were chosen simply because they were available from* AIRFORCE *files, to which* AIRFORCE INTELLIGENCE *has full access.*[30]

These orphans are in real trouble. In Issue No. 4 of *Miracleman, America's #1 Super Hero!*, we see efforts to penetrate and program these orphans' dreams. But near the end of Issue No. 5 we observe how everything is going wrong. Serially. The damper fields that orchestrate the orphans' self-screening dreamscapes become overloaded and fissures appear to tear at the seams of their pure, if artificially generated, memories. A blond and blue suited Miracleman, the oldest of the orphans, begins to suspect his life's dream. "Something is wrong here," he tells the other. "Something doesn't feel right. It's as if none of this is really happening." It is a bitter night in November of 1961 and the orphans are awakening to the horror of their "real time" situation. Dr. Gargunza, a biogenetic genius and power-mad Heideggerian, who's been controlling the orphans' "being-in-the-world" this way declares: "What I need is a dream-programme that will explain these lapses in the [consumptive] continuity of [the orphan's] reality and lull him back into security and sleep. But what..."

6. TAXATION WITHOUT RE-PRESENTATION

George Bush addresses a multinational and multinetwork television audience with the following words: READ MY LIPS! This is corporate CAPITALIST semiology, sign-work for profit. In issuing this command Bush announces his position in a long and violent procession of metropolitan men of power covering their traces. To follow Bush's command sign or signal is to become (a) subject to an escalating taxation by a nearly instantaneous substitution of one dominant and domineering mode of communicative economy over others. This is the material force of Bush's base attraction: a masterful MORAL REPULSION of other economies of logic, feeling and action.

By itself this dramatic erection of authoritarian moral boundaries is no-thing new. It has been a feature of patriarchal state societies since their violent ascension to power. What is new, at least since the western HIStorical production of what's modern, is the increasingly instantaneous nature of telecommunicative fixation. In this Bush may genuinely be a pioneer. Racing across an oceanic surface of photo opportunities in his spy-thriller-secret agent-cigarette boat Bush may, in actuality, herald the end of theatrical representation and the advent of a pure and cynical screen play of power. Reagan, who, after all, was really only always an actor, may have promised the theatrical terror of the simulacra. But with Bush it's time for an efficient corporate execution of models that function transferentially without rehearsals and with only the shortest of digital delays. An eclipse of re-presentation into the model. Instantaneous communicative categorizations: READ MY LIPS!

7. V FOR VENDETTA: THE ORPHANS' REVENGE

It is the Fourth of July in the world's most a-mazing shopping mall fantastic. It is the day of the orphans' revenge. The orphans catch President Bush in a televisionary crossfire, or so the story goes.

TAKE TWO: 1-0, 1-0, 1-0. "Digitality is with us. It is that which haunts all these messages, all the signs of our societies. The most concrete form you see it in is that of the test, of the question/answer, of the stimulus response."[31]

QUESTION: Why a second beginning to this HIStory?

ANSWER: V for Vendetta: the Orphans' Revenge

It is the Fourth of July in "AMERICA." It is the day of the orphans' revenge. Bush travels to the world's most a-mazing shopping mall fantastic. He appears to witness a video projection of the U.S. Flag onto a vast screen composed of the digitally reconfigured body images of exactly 50,000 Indiana school children. Each child is dressed in painted white canvas and is posed individually. Each with her or his own life-size white mask stands obliged before a perfectly white backdrop. To the eye of the camera it is virtually impossible to tell the difference between each white costumed child and the pure white backdrop. Photographs of each child are snapped out of time. In these images each child appears only to disappear. No figures remain visible within these photographs; nor grounds.

Slides are made of each photograph then projected in sets of fifty. These projections are then rephotographed as slides that are again projected in ever larger configurations until a purely white composite of the images of all 50,000 children, now strictly miniaturized, is at last achieved. This image is then projected onto the backside of the huge screen that drapes the luxurious central boulevard of the fantastic shopping mall itself.

It is in-dependence day in America and onto the frontside of the giant video screen is projected a seamless high density image of white stars shimmering against an electric blue background and the unfurled red and white stripes that in combination signify the constitutionally insured integrity of this totem, this flag, "Old Glory." Bush is there to celebrate the flows of what freedoms this emblem sets in motion. Globally. Free Trade. Free Enterprise. The freedom to die homeless alone and in panic. He waves his arms and smiles into the converging networks. He offers words of heart-felt thanks to that great mass of shoppers from the home-state of Vice President Dan Quayle who worked so tirelessly in securing the purchase of that HIStoric landmark in representational politics—the end-of-this-century passage of a U.S. constitutional amendment guaranteeing the death penalty to FLAG ABUSERS. The crowd goes wild.

Ecstatic tears smear the make-up of prominent T.V. news personnel while sales skyrocket higher than ever. The crowd goes wild. But then, in an intense, sudden and televisionary instant, shadows mar the screen and Bush's kind and well-tailored body is shred from head to toe by a rain of exploding industrial projectiles. It is the orphans and they are signalling REVENGE.

It is the Fourth of July in America. It is the day of Bush's ethnoGRAPHIC assassination. It is the end of all coded empiricities, of all modelled flesh remade. It is the day this dream, this text, begins again and again and again and . . .

notes

PART ONE – (W)RITING PREFACES

Gayatri Chakravory Spivak, "Translator's Preface," to Jacques Derrida, *Of Grammatology*, Baltimore: Johns Hopkins University Press, 1974, p. xii.

Rada Rada, *Red Eyes Green Black*, Boston: Parasite Cafe Press, 1992, p. 55.

CHAPTER ONE – WHEN WORDS BECOME FLESH AND FLESH BECOMES WORDS

1. B. Madonna Durkheim, *A Constructivist Genealogy of Missing Memories*, Boston: Parasite Cafe Press, 1991, p. 77.

2. William Gibson, *Neuromancer*, New York: Ace Science Fiction Books, 1984, p. 117.

3. C. Wright Mills, *The Sociological Imagination*, New York: Oxford University Press, 1959, p. 166.

4. C. Wright Mills, *White Collar*, New York: Oxford Univeristy Press, 1951, p. 51.

5. C. Wright Mills, "The Cultural Apparatus," in *Power, Politics and the People: The Collected Essays of C. Wright Mills*, Irving Louis Horowitz, ed., New York: Oxford University Press, 1979, p. 407.

6. C. Wright Mills, *White Collar*, p. 334.

7. *Ibid.*

8. *Ibid.*, pp. 333, 336.

9. Kathy Acker, *Empire of the Senseless*, New York: Grove Press, 1988, pp. 77, 65, 91, 83, 55.

CHAPTER TWO – QUESTIONS OF ACCESS AND EXCESS

1. James Clifford, "On Ethnographic Surrealism," in *The Predicament of Culture: Twentieth Century Ethnography, Literature and Art*, Cambridge: Harvard University Press, 1988, pp. 146-147.

2. Arthur Kroker and David Cook, *The Postmodern Scene: Excremental Culture and Hyper-Aesthetics*, New York: St. Martin's Press, 1986.

3. Oliver L. North, *Taking the Stand: The Testimony of Lieutenant Colonel Oliver L. North*, New York: Pocket Books, 1987, pp. 13, 43, 49.

4. Michel Foucault, *Foucault Live (Interviews, 1966-84)*, trans. John Johnston, New York: Semiotext(e), 1989, p. 150.

5. Claude Levi-Strauss, *Structures Elementaires de la Parente*, as quoted in Helene Cixous and Catherine Clément, *The Newly Born Woman*, trans. Betsy Wing, Minneapolis: University of Minnesota Press, 1986, p. 22.

6. North, p. 43.

7. Henri Lefebvre, *Everyday Life in the Modern World*, trans. Sara Rabinovitch, New Brunswick: New Transition Books, 1984.

8. *Ibid.*, p. 49.

9. C. Wright Mills, *White Collar*, New York: Oxford University Press, 1956, p. 233.

10. Jean Baudrillard, *Simulations*, trans. Paul Foss, Paul Patton and Philip Beitchman, New York: Semiotext(e), 1983.

11. James Clifford, "Partial Truths," in James Clifford and George E. Marcus, eds., *Writing Culture: The Poetics and Politics of Ethnography*, Berkeley: University of California Press, 1986, pp. 6-7.

12. Avery Gordon, "Feminism, Writing, and Ghosts," *Social Problems*, Vol. 37, No. 4 (November 1990), p. 488.

13. Stephen Pfohl and Avery Gordon, "Criminological Displacements: A Sociological Deconstruction," *Social Problems*, Vol. 33, No. 6 (October/December 1986), p. S95.

14. See Denis Hollier, ed., *The College of Sociology 1937-39*, trans. Betsy Wing, Minneapolis: University of Minnesota Press, 1988; James Clifford, "On Ethnographic Surrealism;" and Michele Richman, *Reading Georges Bataille: Beyond the Gift*, Baltimore: Johns Hopkins University Press, 1984.

15. For a discussion of the political subversion of "self-evidency" in the writings of Bataille, Leiris and others, see Allan Stoekl, *Politics, Writing, Mutilation: The Cases of Bataille, Blanchot, Roussel, Leiris and Ponge*, Minneapolis: University of Minnesota Press, 1985.

16. Georges Bataille, "Attraction and Repulsion II: Social Structure," in Denis Hollier, ed., *The College of Sociology 1937-39*, pp. 114-115.

17. *Ibid.*, p. 115.

18. James Clifford, "On Ethnographic Surrealism," pp. 117-18.

19. Carl Einstein, as quoted in James Clifford, "On Ethnographic Surrealism," p. 130.

20. James Clifford, "On Ethnographic Surrealism," pp. 129-34. This is not to deny the projective exoticization of nonwestern cultural practices that resulted from certain surrealist appropriations. For a much needed critique of both artistic and anthropological fascination with "primitiveness" see Marianna Torgovnick, *Gone Primitive: Savage Intellects, Modern Lives*, Chicago: University of Chicago Press, 1990.

21. Jackie Orr, "Theory on the Market: Panic, Incorporating," *Social Problems*, Vol. 37, No. 4 (November 1990), p. 482.

22. Monique Wittig, *Les Guérillères*, trans. David LeVay, New York, Avon Books, 1971, p. 134.

23. Donna Haraway, "A Cyborg Manifesto: Science, Technology and Socialist Feminism in the Late Twentieth Century," in Linda J. Nicholson, ed., *Feminism/Postmodernism*, New York: Routledge, 1985, p. 196-197.

24. Judith Butler, "Gender Trouble, Feminist Theory, and Psychoanalytic Discourse," in Linda J. Nicholson ed., *Feminism/Postmodernism*, New York: Routledge, 1990, p. 336.

25. Gayatri Chakravorty Spivak, "Feminism and Critical Theory," in *In Other Worlds: Essays in Cultural Politics*, New York: Methuen, 1987, p. 84.

26. bell hooks, *Yearning: Race, Gender, and Cultural Politics*, Boston: The South End Press, 1990, p. 27.

27. Patricia Hill Collins, *Black Feminist Thought: Knowledge, Consciousness and the Politics of Empowerment*, Boston: Unwin Hyman, 1990, pp. 201-220.

28. Eve Kosofsky Sedgwick, *Epistemology of the Closet*, Berkeley: University of California Press, 1990; Michael Warner, "Fear of a Queer Planet," *Social Text*, Vol. 9, No. 4 (1991), pp. 3-17.

29. Mary Daly, in cahoots with Jane Caputi, *Websters' First New Intergalactic Wickedary of the English Language*, Boston: Beacon Press, 1987, p. 250.

30. Monique Wittig, *The Lesbian Body*, trans. Peter Owen, New York: Avon, 1976.

31. Kathy Acker, *Don Quixote*, New York: Grove Press, 1986, p. 39.

32. Trinh T. Minh-ha, *When the Moon Waxes Red: Representation, Gender and Cultural Politics*, New York: Routledge, 1991, p. 84.

33. Luce Irigaray, *Speculum of the Other Woman*, as quoted in Jane Gallop, *The Daughter's Seduction: Feminism and Psychoanalysis*, Ithaca, NY: Cornell University Press, 1982, p. 178.

34. Ishmael Reed, *Mumbo Jumbo*, Garden City, NY: Bantam Books, 1972, p. 17.

35. For a related thesis see Tzvetan Todorov, *The Conquest of America*, trans. Richard Howard, New York: Harper and Row, 1984.

36. Toni Morrison, *The Bluest Eye*, New York: Washington Square Press, 1970, p. 7.

37. George Jackson, *Soledad Brother: the Prison Letters of George Jackson*, New York: Coward-McCann, 1970, p.184.

38. See, for instance, Zora Neale Hurston, *Tell My Horse,* Berkeley: Turtle Island, 1981; Ishmael Reed, *Mumbo Jumbo*; Michael Ventura, "Hear that Long Snake Moan," in *Shadow Dancing in America*, Los Angeles: Jeremy P. Tarcher Inc., 1985, pp. 103-162.

39. Houston Baker, Jr., *Blues, Ideology and Afro-American Literature*, Chicago: University of Chicago, 1984.

40. Gloria Anzaldúa, "haciendo caras, una entrada," in Gloria Anzaldúa, ed., *Making Face, Making Soul: Haciendo Caras*, San Francisco: Aunt Lute Foundation, 1990, p. xxv.

41. *Ibid.*, p. xv.

42. Franz Fanon, *Black Skin, White Masks*, trans. Charles Laun Markmann, New York: Grove Press, 1967, p. 18.

43. Henry Louis Gates, Jr., "Talkin' That Talk," in Henry Louis Gates, Jr., ed., *"Race," Writing and Difference*, Chicago: University of Chicago Press, 1985, p. 408.

44. *Ibid.*

45. Henry Louis Gates, Jr. "Editor's Introduction: Writing 'Race' and the Difference it Makes," in Henry Louis Gates, Jr., ed. *"Race," Writing and Difference*, p. 15.

46. bell hooks, *Yearnings*, p. 26.

47. *Ibid.*

48. *Ibid.*, p. 28.

49. bell hooks, "On Cultural Interrogations," *Artforum*, Vol. XXVII, No. 9 (May 1989), p. 20.

50. For a reflexive interrogation of the white feminist shadows haunting a critical sociological reading of African-American texts, consider Avery Gordon's engagement with Toni Morrison's *Beloved* in Avery Gordon, *Ghostly Memories: Feminist Rituals of Writing the Social Text*, Ph.D. Dissertation, Chestnut Hill, MA: Boston College, 1990.

51. bell hooks, *Yearnings*, p. 28.

52. *Ibid.*

53. My limited knowledge of the material scene in which critical literature is being produced was exponentially expanded by the opportunity to participate in the Coloquio Internaciónal sobre el Imaginario Social Contemporaneo sponsored by the University of Puerto Rico in February of 1991. Most important in making explicit connections between "vernacular" cultural traditions and postmodern critique were the following papers: Aníbal Quijano, "El estudio de lo imaginario en las Ciencias Sociales de América Latina;" Madeline Román, "Feminismos y postmodernidad: El análisis de la resistencias;" Muriam Muñiz, "El Caribe: Arqueología y poética;" Heidi Figueroa y María Milagros López, "La imagen lábil de la resistencia;" and Antonio Martorell, "Imalabra II."

54. Trinh T. Minh-ha, "Grandma's Story," in Brian Wallis ed., *Blasted Allegories*, New York: The New Museum of Contemporary Art and Cambridge: The MIT Press, 1987, pp. 3, 2-3.

55. Gil Scott-Heron, lyrics from "'B' Movie," on album *Reflections,* New York: Arista Records, 1981.

56. Susan Sontag, "Fascinating Fascism," in *Under the Sign of Saturn*, New York: Vintage Books, 1981, p. 91.

57. Jean Baudrillard, *Forget Foucault*, trans. Nichole Dufresne, New York: Semiotext(e), 1987.

58. Walter Benjamin, "The Work of Art in the Age of Mechanical Reproduction," in *Illuminations*, trans. Harry Zohn, New York: Schocken Books, 1969, p. 241.

59. For descriptions of this "simulation," see both Sontag, "Fascinating Fascism" and Hal Foster, *Recodings: Art, Spectacle, Cultural Politics*, Port Townsend, WA: Bay Press, 1985.

60. Jean Baudrillard, *Forget Foucault*, pp. 61-62.

61. David Harvey, *The Conditions of Postmodernity*, New York: Basil Blackwell, 1989, pp. 160, 159.

62. Arthur Kroker and Marilouise Kroker, "Thesis on the Disappearing Body in the Hyper-Modern Condition," in Arthur Kroker and Marilouise Kroker, eds., *Body Invaders: Panic Sex in America*, New York: St. Martin's Press, 1987, p. 21.

63. Ice-T, Lyrics to "Colors," Produced by Ice-T and Africa Islam, New York: Rhyme Syndicate Productions, 1988.

64. Mark Goodin, as quoted in the *Boston Globe,* October 23, 1988.

65. Noam Chomsky, *The Culture of Terrorism*, Boston: South End Press, 1988.

66. William Bogard, "Closing Down the Social: Baudrillard's Challenge to Contemporary Sociology," *Sociological Theory*, 8 (1990), pp. 1-15.

67. Jean Baudrillard, "Astral America," trans. Lisa Liebmann, *Artforum*, 23 (1984), p. 74.

CHAPTER THREE – STUPID FRESH JACK DOUBLE DENSITY

1. Susan Willis, *A Primer for Daily Life*, New York: Routledge, 1991, p. 158.

2. Sigmund Freud, "Screen Memories," in *The Standard Edition of the Complete Works of Sigmund Freud, Vol. III*, trans. James Strachey, London: The Hogarth Press, 1986, p. 307.

3. Cheryl Townsend Gilkes, "'Holding Back the Ocean with a Broom': Black Women and Community Work," in La Frances Rodgers-Rose, ed., *The Black Woman*, Beverly Hills, CA: Sage, 1982, pp. 217-32; "Successful Rebellious Professionals: The Black Woman's Professional Identity and Community Commitment," *Psychological Quarterly*, Vol. 6, No. 3 (1982), pp. 289-311; and "Going Up for the Oppressed: The Career Mobility of Black Women Community Workers," *Journal of Social Issues*, Vol. 39, No. 3 (1983), pp. 115-39. See also Patricia Hill Collins, "Black Women and Motherhood," in *Black Feminist Thought: Knowledge, Consciousness, and the Politics of Empowerment*, Boston: Unwin and Hyman, 1990, pp. 115-137.

4. Indeed, as Hal Foster points out, drawing upon the (w)ritings of Gilles Deleuze and Felix Guattari, "the minor (which is precisely not a value judgment) is an intensive, often vernacular use of language or form that disrupts its official or institutional functions... Unlike other discourses or styles in major (bourgeois) culture, the minor has no 'desire to fill a major language function, to offer [its] services as the language of the state, the official tongue.' Yet, by the same token, it has no romance of the marginal... Indeed, in the minor 'there are only collective arrangements of utterance.' (Examples of the minor might include Black gospel, reggae, surrealist Latin American fiction.) This is a 'death of the author' that is perhaps new to us: a post-industrial experience based less on the dispersal of subjectivity than on the articulation of collectivity, one that does not heed the normative categories of major culture." See Hal Foster, "Readings in Cultural Resistance," in *Recodings: Art, Spectacle, Cultural Politics*, p. 177.

5. Georges Bataille, *Blue of Noon*, trans. Harry Mathews, New York: Urizen Books, 1978, p. 153.

CHAPTER FIVE – UNSINGULAR BEGINNINGS

1. Kathy Acker, "Lust," in Adison Fell, ed., *The Seven Deadly Sins*, London: The Serpent's Tail, 1988, pp. 114, 117.

2. Mark Poster, *The Mode of Information: Poststructuralism and Social Context*, Chicago: University of Chicago Press, 1990, p. 8.

PART TWO – DOUBLE-CROSSING THE EYE/"I"

Jack O. Lantern, *Doubling Back Upon Sociological Methods: A Deconstructive Return of the Repressed*, Boston: Parasite Cafe Press, 1986, p. 7.

B. Madonna Durkheim, *Mirroring Bodies of Sociology: a (K)not So Instant Replay*, Boston: Parasite Cafe Press, p. 22.

CHAPTER SIX – A STORY OF THE EYE/"I"

1. Avital Ronell, "Interview with Avital Ronell," in Andrea Juno and V. Vale, eds., *Angry Women*, San Francisco: Re/Search Publications, 1991, p. 128.

2. Georges Bataille, *The Accursed Share: An Essay on the General Economy, Volume 1* , trans. Robert Hurley, New York: Zone Books, p. 9.

3. *Ibid.*, p. 10

4. Michel Foucault, *The Order of Things: An Archeology of Knowledge*, New York: Vintage Books, 1973.

5. Georges Bataille, *Story of the Eye*, trans. Joachim Neugroschal, New York: Penguin Books, 1982, pp. 10-11.

6. Jean Baudrillard, *Simulations*, trans. Paul Foss, Paul Patton and Philip Beitchman, New York: Semiotext(e), 1983, p. 3.

7. Luce Irigaray, *Speculum of the Other Woman*, trans. Gillian C. Gill, Ithaca, NY: Cornell University Press, 1985, pp. 138, 136.

8. Michel Serres, *The Parasite*, trans. Lawrence R. Schehr, Baltimore: The Johns Hopkins University Press, 1982, p. 14.

9. Avery Gordon, *Ghostly Memories: Feminist Rituals of Writing the Social Text*, Ph.D. Dissertation, Chestnut Hill, MA: Boston College, 1990, p. 25.

10. Irigaray, *Speculum of the Other Woman*, p. 133.

11. *Ibid.*

12. *Ibid*, pp. 133-34.

13. Jean Baudrillard, "The Clone Story or the Artificial Child, ZG, (1984), pp. 16-17.

14. Jean Baudrillard, *Seduction*, as quoted in Douglas Kellner, *Jean Baudrillard: From Marxism to Postmodernism and Beyond*, Stanford, CA: Stanford University Press, 1989, p. 102.

15. For a challenging feminist allegory of the methodological possibilities of conversing with scientific objects as "agents" rather than as passively inscribed "units of analysis" see Donna Haraway, "Situated Knowledges: the Science Question in Feminism and the Privilege of Partial Perspectives," in Haraway, *Simians, Cyborgs and Women: the Reinvention of Nature*, New York: Routledge, 1991, pp. 183-201.

16. Roland Barthes, *The Pleasure of the Text*, trans. Richard Miller, New York: Hill and Wang, 1975, pp. 59, 61.

17. Michael Ryan, *Politics and Culture: Working Hypotheses for a Post-Revolutionary Society*, Baltimore: Johns Hopkins University Press, 1989, p. 5.

18. For an extended discussion of the relation between *normal social science* and paranoia see Paul Smith, *Discerning the Subject*, Minneapolis: University of Minnesota Press, 1988.

19. Max Horkheimer and Theodor Adorno, *Dialectic of Enlightenment*, trans. John Cumming, New York: The Seabury Press, 1972, pp. 83-84.

20. For an elaboration see Stephen Pfohl and Avery Gordon, "Criminological Displacements: a Sociological Deconstruction," *Social Problems*, Vol. 33, No. 6 (October/December 1986), pp. S94-S113. A video cassette version of this text is also available in VHS format. For a copy send $10.00 (U.S. currency) to Parasite Cafe Productions, c/o Stephen Pfohl, Dept. of Sociology, Boston College, Chestnut Hill, MA 02167, USA.

21. Horkheimer and Adorno, p. 84.

22. Dorothy Smith, *The Everyday World as Problematic: a Feminist Sociology*, Boston: Northeastern University Press, 1987.

23. Horkheimer and Adorno, p. 84.

24. Julia Kristeva, *Desire in Language: A Semiotic Approach in Literature and Art*, ed. Leon S. Roudiez, trans. Richard Miller, New York: Hill and Wang, 1975, pp. 59, 61.

25. Jacques Attali, *Noise: The Political Economy of Music*, trans. Brian Massumi, Minneapolis: University of Minnesota Press, 1985, p. 5; see also Hal Foster, *Recodings*, Port Townsend, WA: Bay Press, 1985.

26. Edward Said, "Opponents, Audiences, Constituencies and Community," in Hal Foster, ed., *The Anti-Aesthetic: Essays on Postmodern Culture*, Port Townsend, WA: Bay Press, 1983, p. 157.

27. Pfohl and Gordon, "Criminological Displacements," p. S109.

28. Stephen Pfohl, *Images of Deviance and Social Control: A Sociological History*, New York: McGraw-Hill, 1985.

29. Frigga Haug, et. al., "Memory-Work as Social Science Writing," in *Female Sexualization*, trans. Erica Carter, New York: Verso, 1987, p. 36.

30. Jackie Orr, "Autobiographical Essay: Assignment #1," from course syllabus for *Technologies of Control*, Boston College, Fall 1989.

31. See, for instance, Jean-Francois Lyotard, *The Postmodern Condition: A Report on Knowledge*, trans. Geoff Bennington and Brian Massumi, Minneapolis: University of Minnesota Press, 1984; and Linda J. Nicholson, ed. *Feminism/Postmodernism*, New York: Routledge, 1990.

32. Cornel West, "The New Cultural Politics of Difference," *October*, 53 (Summer 1990), p. 93.

33. Gordon, *Ghostly Memories*, pp. 12-13.

34. *Ibid.*, p. 40.

35. Donna Haraway, *Primate Visions: Gender, Race, and Nature in the World of Modern Science*, New York: Routledge, 1990, p. 4.

36. *Ibid.*, pp. 3-4.

37. Gordon, *Ghostly Memories*, p. 16.

38. Georges Bataille, *Inner Experience*, trans. Leslie Anne Boldt, Albany: State University of New York Press, 1988, p. 81.

39. Peter Berger and Thomas Luckmann, *The Social Construction of Reality*, Garden City, NY: Anchor Books, 1967.

40. Stephen Pfohl, "The 'Discovery' of Child Abuse," *Social Problems*, Vol. 24, No. 3 (February 1977), pp. 310-322.

41. Stephen Pfohl, *Predicting Dangerousness: the Social Construction of Psychiatric Reality*, Lexington, MA: D.C. Heath, 1978.

42. Steve Woolgar and Dorothy Pawluch, "Ontological Gerrymandering: the Anatomy of Social Problems Explanations," *Social Problems*, Vol. 32, No. 3 (February 1985), p. 218.

43. Haraway, "Situated Knowledges," p. 184.

44. *Ibid.*, p. 185.

45. For a more specific response to questions raised by Woolgar and Pawluch see Stephen Pfohl, "Toward a Sociological Deconstruction of Social Problems," *Social Problems*, Vol. 32, No. 32 (February 1985), pp. 228-232.

46. This is not to suggest that, after World War II and even before, important tendencies within surrealism did not betray its political radicality by the seductive aestheticization of its

art. This critique is made nowhere stronger than by members of the Situationist International who, between 1957 and 1971, struggled to advance the radical potential of an art (against art) in the service of social revolution. See, for instance, Guy Debord, *Society of the Spectacle*, Detroit: Black and Red Press, 1977. At the same time, there is evidence of the continued radicalism of some surrealists well into the 1960s. This is documented in such works as Helena Lewis, *The Politics of Surrealism*, New York: Paragon Press, 1988, and Franklin Rosemont, "Introduction" to Andre Breton, *What is Surrealism? Selected Writings*, New York: Monad Press, 1978. For an excellent work situating surrealism within the "interwar" years in France see Sidra Stich, *Anxious Visions: Surrealist Art*, New York: Abbeville Press, 1990. For analysis of the role of women in relation to surrealism, see Whitney Chadwick, *Women and Surrealism*, Boston: Little, Brown and Co., 1985, and Mary Ann Caws, Rudolf Kuenzli and Gwen Raaberg, eds., *Surrealism and Women*, Cambridge: The MIT Press, 1991.

47. Scott Lash, *Sociology of Postmodernism*, New York: Routledge, 1990, p. 181.

48. Georges Bataille, *Visions of Excess: Selected Writings, 1927-1939*, trans. Allan Stoekl, Minneapolis: University of Minnesota Press, 1985, p. 81.

49. For a discussion of surrealism's critique of positivism see Gaeton Picon, *Surrealists and Surrealism*, New York: Rizzoli, 1977.

50. Antonin Artaud, *The Theater and its Double*, trans. Mary Caroline Richards, New York: Grove Press, 1958, p. 13.

51. For connections between Brecht and critical social theory see Eugene Lunn, *Marxism and Modernism: a Historical Study of Lukacs, Brecht, Benjamin and Adorno*, Berkeley: University of California Press, 1982.

52. Michel Foucault, *Discipline and Punish: The Birth of the Prison*, trans. Alan Sheridan, New York: Vintage, 1977, p. 31.

53. Gordon, *Ghostly Memories*, p. 15.

54. Gayatri Chakravorty Spivak, "Translator's Introduction," to Jacques Derrida, *Of Grammatology*, Baltimore: Johns Hopkins University Press, 1974, p. lxxvii.

55. See, for instance, Judith Butler, *Gender Trouble: Feminism, and the Subversion of Identity*, New York: Routledge, 1990; Eve Kosofsky Sedgwick, *Epistemology of the Closet*, Berkeley: University of California Press, 1990; Jonathan Dollimore, *Sexual Dissidence: Augustine to Wilde, Freud to Foucault*, New York: Oxford, 1991; and Diana Fuss, ed., *Inside/Out: Lesbian Theories, Gay Theories*, New York: Routledge, 1991.

56. Haraway, "Situated Knowledges," p. 187.

57. *Ibid.*, p. 191.

58. Maya Deren, *Divine Horsemen: the Living Gods of Haiti*, New Paltz, NY: McPherson and Co., 1953, p. 6.

59. Luisa Valenzuela, *Other Weapons*, trans. Deborah Bonner, Hanover, NH: Ediciones Norte, 1985, p. 105.

60. *Ibid.*, p. 114.

61. *Ibid.*, pp. 114-115.

62. Gloria Anzaldúa, *Borderlands/La Frontera: the New Mestiza*, San Francisco: Spinsters/ Aunt Lute, 1987.

63. Nancy Harstock, "The Feminist Standpoint: Developing the Ground for a Specifically Feminist Historical Materialism," in Sandra Harding and Merill Hintikka, eds., *Discovering Reality: Feminist Perspectives on Epistemology, Metaphysics, Methodology, and Philosophy of Science*, Dordrecht: Reidel, 1981, pp. 283-310.

64. Smith, *The Everyday World as Problematic*.

65. Haraway, "Situated Knowledges," pp. 190-191.

66. Patricia Hill Collins, *Black Feminist Thought: Knowledge, Consciousness and the Politics of Empowerment*, Boston: Unwin Hyman, 1990, p. 234.

67. Gordon, *Ghostly Memories*, p. 40.

68. For a critical discussion of "postmodern pastiche" see Fredric Jameson, "Postmodernism and the Logic of Late Capitalism," *New Left Review*, 146 (1984), pp. 53-92.

69. Michel Foucault, *The Order of Things*, trans. Alan Sheridan, New York: Vintage Books, 1970, p. 379.

70. Georges Bataille, "Attraction and Repulsion II," in Denis Hollier, ed., *The College of Sociology, 1937-39*, Minneapolis: University of Minnesota Press, 1988, p. 115.

71. Avery Gordon, "Feminism, Writing, Ghosts," *Social Problems*, 37, 4, (November 1990), p. 488.

72. *Ibid.*, p. 488.

73. *Ibid.*, p. 490.

74. *Ibid.*, p. 491.

75. Jacqueline Rose, *Sexuality in the Field of Vision*, London: Verso, 1987, p. 14.

76. See, for instance, Gayatri Chakravorty Spivak, *In Other Worlds: Essays in Cultural Politics*, New York: Metheun, 1987; Trinh T. Minh-ha, *Woman, Native, Other: Writing Postcoloniality and Feminism*, Bloomington: Indiana University Press, 1989; Homi K. Bhabha, "Remembering Fanon: Self, Psyche, and the Colonial Condition," in Barbara Kruger and Phil Mariani, eds., *Remaking History*, Port Townsend, WA: Bay Press, 1989, pp. 131-150; and Michael Taussig, *Shamanism, Colonialism and the Wildman: A Study in Terror and Healing*, Chicago: University of Chicago Press, 1987.

77. Simon Watney, *Policing Desire: Pornography, AIDS and the Media*, Minneapolis: University of Minnesota Press, 1989.

78. John and Joan Digby, *The Collage Handbook*, London: Thames and Hudson, 1985, p. 10.

79. Max Ernst, "What is the Mechanism of Collage?" as quoted in James Clifford, "On Ethnographic Surrealism," in *The Predicament of Culture: Twentieth Century Ethnography, Art and Literature*, Cambridge, MA: Harvard University Press, 1988, p. 117.

80. My own immersion in collage methods dates back to my collaboration with Joseph LaMantia in the design and production of photomontages included in my book *Images of Deviance and Social Control: a Sociological History*, New York: McGraw-Hill, 1985. Shortly thereafter I began to work with collage and montage as aspects in the sociological construction of analytic texts. The influence of Kathy Acker's critical (w)ritings were, at that point, enormous, as were the works of Berlin Dadaists Hannah Hoch and John Heartfield. For a mix of visual, auditory and analytic collage work see the video-text I produced in collaboration with Avery Gordon, *Criminological Displacements*.

81. Clifford, "On Ethnographic Surrealism," p. 118.

82. Dawn Ades, *Photomontage*, London: Thames and Hudson, 1976, pp. 12-13.

83. Gregory L. Ulmer, "The Object of Post-Criticism," in Hal Foster, ed., *The Anti-Aesthetic: Essays on Postmodern Culture*, Port Townsend, Washington: Bay Press, 1983, p. 84. Ulmer here "collages" into his text a quote from Eddie Wolfram, *History of Collage*, New York: Macmillan, 1975, pp. 17-18.

84. Clifford, "On Ethnographic Surrealism," p. 118.

85. Michael Taussig, *Shamanism, Colonialism and the Wild Man: A Study in Terror and Healing*, Chicago: University of Chicago Press, 1987, pp. xiii-xiv.

86. Gregory L. Ulmer, "The Object of Post-Criticism," p. 84; includes quote from Group *Mu*, eds., *Collages*, Paris: Union Generale, 1978, pp. 13-14.

87. *Ibid.*, p. xiv.

88. Jacques Derrida, "The Law of Genre," *Glyph* 7 (1980), p. 206.

89. This italicized sentence and the following *italicized parts of this section* are from Christa Wolf, "A Letter, about Unequivocal and Ambigous Meaning, Definiteness and Indefiniteness; about Ancient Conditions and New Viewscopes; about Objectivity," in Gisela Ecker, ed., *Feminist Aesthetics*, trans. Harriet Anderson, London: The Women's Press, 1985, pp. 98-99. p. 90. Group *Mu, Collages*, as quoted in Gregory L. Ulmer, "The Object of Post-Criticism," p. 88.

91. James Clifford, "Introduction: Partial Truths," in James Clifford and George E. Marcus, *Writing Culture*, Berkeley: University of California Press, 1986, p. 7.

CHAPTER SEVEN – THE DOUBLE OR NO-THING

1. Jacques Lacan, *Le Seminaire III: Les Psychoses,* Paris: Seuil, 1981, p. 93, as quoted in Mikkel Borch-Jacobsen, *Lacan: the Absolute Master*, trans. Douglas Brick, Stanford, CA: Stanford University Press, 1991, p. 2.

2. See, for instance, Roger Caillois, *Man, Play and Games*, trans. Meyer Barash, New York: Schocken Books, 1979.

3. For a discussion of archaic games of simulation and vertigo see Roger Caillois, *Man, Play and Games.*

4. Jacques Lacan, *The Four Fundamental Concepts of Psycho-Analysis*, trans. Alan Sheridan, New York: W.W. Norton, 1977, p. 1.

5. *Ibid*, p. 3.

6. *Ibid.*, pp. 3-4.

7. Émile Durkheim, *The Elementary Forms of the Religious Life*, trans. Joseph Ward Swain, New York: The Free Press, 1965, p. 32. For a related reading of the "spell binding evocations" produced by Durkheim's "imageristic seduction," see Michael Taussig, *The Nervous System*, New York: Routledge, 1992, pp. 119-134.

8. *Ibid.*, p. 462.

9. Durkheim's analysis of the social effectivity of totemism is richly suggestive of how ritual practices engender both imaginary and symbolic spaces of experience. In being moved by totemic rituals, "we" are literally transferred out from within the chaotic indeterminancy of material flux into orderly phenomenal worlds, where our bodies and minds are marked by the performative play of identifiable images and the game-like, if sacrificial, constraints of language. This is not to suggest that Durkheim's provocative theorizations adequately describe the rites of the Aborginal peoples his work comments upon. Durkheim's (w)ritings about totemism are based on his reading of existing ethnographic accounts and share certain of the distortions these accounts produce. This is particularly true regarding Durkheim's pairing of specific totemic imagery with law-like boundaries separating one social group from others. Indeed, Durkheim's "tying sacred designs to a specific and bounded social grouping (hence 'society'), is now considered wrong in important ways, ways that reflect profoundly on the present-day land-claims by Aborginal people against the Australian state." Michael Taussig, *The Nervous System*, p. 188. For critical revisions to Durkheim's analysis see W.E.H. Stanner, "Religion, Totemism and Symbolism," in *White Man Got No Dreaming*, Canberra: Australian National University Press, 1967, pp. 106-43; and "Reflections on Durkheim and Aboriginal Religion," in Maurice Freedman, ed., *Social Organization: Essays Presented to Raymond Firth*, Chicago: Aldine, 1967, pp. 217-40.

10. Lacan, *The Four Fundamental Concepts of Psycho-Analysis*, p. 20.

11. Jean Baudrillard, "The System of Objects," in *Selected Writings*, Stanford, CA: Stanford

University Press, 1988, p. 25. See also Sut Jhally, *The Codes of Advertising: Fetishism and the Political Economy of Meaning in the Consumer Society*, New York: Routledge, 1990, p. 202.

12. Durkheim, *Elementary Forms*, p. 481.

13. *Ibid.*, p. 27.

14. *Ibid.*

15. *Ibid.*, p. 25.

16. *Ibid.*, p. 481.

17. *Ibid.*, p. 484.

18. Émile Durkheim and Marcel Mauss, *Primitive Classification*, trans. Rodney Needham, Chicago: University of Chicago Press, 1963, pp. 82-83, 84-85.

19. Durkheim, *Elementary Forms*, p. 477.

20. *Ibid.*

21. Émile Durkheim, *Formes Elementaires de la Vie Religieuse*, 4th (French) ed., Paris: Presses Universitaires de France, 1960, p. 13, as translated and quoted in Dominick LaCapra, *Émile Durkheim: Sociologist and Philosopher*, Chicago: University of Chicago Press, 1985, p. 262.

22. Durkheim, *Elementary Forms*, p. 138.

23. *Ibid.*, p. 223.

24. *Ibid.*, p. 471.

25. *Ibid.*, p. 481.

26. James Clifford, "On Ethnographic Surrealism," in *The Predicament of Culture: Twentieth-Century Ethnography, Literature, and Art*, Cambridge, MA: Harvard University Press, 1988, p. 123.

27. Georges Bataille, "Le Sens moral de la Sociologie," Critique, No. 1 (June 1946), in Denis Hollier, ed., *The College of Sociology (1937-49)*, trans. Betsy Wing, Minneapolis: University of Minnesota Press, 1988, p. 384.

28. Marcel Mauss, *Sociology and Psychology*, trans. Ben Brewster, London: Routledge and Kegan Paul, 1979, p. 10.

29. Claude Levi-Strauss, *Introduction to the Work of Marcel Mauss*, trans. Felicity Baker, London: Routledge and Kegan Paul, 1987, p. 29.

30. *Ibid.*, p. 7.

31. Marcel Mauss, *The Gift*, trans. Ian Cunnison, London: Cohen and West, 1954.

32. C. Wright Mills, *The Sociological Imagination*, New York: Oxford University Press, 1959, p. 143.

33. Peter McLaren, *Schooling as a Ritual Behavior*, London: Routledge and Kegan Paul, 1986, pp. 34-35, 36.

34. *Ibid.*, p. 37.

35. Harold Garfinkel, *Studies in Ethnomethodology*, Englewood Cliffs, NJ: Prentice-Hall, 1967, p. 47.

36. See, for instance, John Marks, *The Search for the Manchurian Candidate: The CIA and Mind Control*, New York: Dell Publishing, 1979.

37. See, for instance, Stuart Hall, John Clarke, Tony Jefferson and Brian Roberts, eds., *Resistance Through Rituals*, London: Hutchinson, 1976; Stuart Hall, Chas Critcher, Tony Jefferson, John Clarke, and Brian Roberts, *Policing the Crisis*, London: MacMillan, 1978; Dick Hebdige, *Subcultures: the Meaning of Style*, London: Methuen, 1979; Stuart Hall, Dorothy Hobson, Andrew Lowe and Paul Willis, *Culture, Media, Language*, London: Hutchinson, 1980.

38. Antonio Gramsci, *Selections from the Prison Notebooks*, trans. Quintin Hoare and

Geoffrey Nowell Smith, London: Lawrence and Wishart, 1971; see also Antonio Gramsci, *Selections from Cultural Writings*, trans. William Boelhower, Harvard University Press, 1985; Chantal Mouffe, ed., *Gramsci and Marxist Theory*, London: Routledge and Kegan Paul, 1979; and Walter L. Adamson, *Hegemony and Revolution: A Study of Antonio Gramsci's Political and Cultural Theory*, Berkeley: University of California Press, 1980.

39. Louis Althusser, "Ideology and Ideological State Apparatus," in *Lenin and Philosophy*, trans. Ben Brewster, New York: Monthly Review Press, 1971, pp. 127-186.

40. Raymond Williams, *Marxism and Literature*, Oxford: Oxford University Press, 1977, p. 110.

41. *Ibid.*, p. 112.

42. *Ibid.*, p. 132.

43. *Ibid.*

44. Roland Barthes, *Mythologies*, trans. Annette Lavers, London: Granada, 1973.

45. *Ibid.*, p. 140.

46. *Ibid.*, p. 142.

47. Anthony Giddens, *Central Problems in Social Theory: Action, Structure and Contradiction in Social Analysis*, Berkeley: University of California Press, 1979, p. 244.

48. Michael de Certeau, *The Practice of Everyday Life*, trans. Steven Rendall, Berkeley: University of California Press, 1984, p. xiv.

49. Durkheim, *Elementary Forms*, p. 426.

50. *Ibid.*, pp. 425, 424.

51. For a critical discussion of "ontotheology" see Mark C. Taylor, *Altarity*, Chicago: University of Chicago Press, 1987.

52. Georges Bataille, *Erotism: Death and Sensuality*, trans. Mary Dalwood, San Francisco: City Lights, 1962; and *Visions of Excess: Selected Writings, 1927-1939.* See also Bataille's important essays on "Attraction and Repulsion" in Denis Hollier, ed., *The College of Sociology, 1937-39*, pp. 103-124.

53. Georges Bataille, *Theory of Religion*, trans. Robert Hurley, New York: Zone Books, 1989.

54. For a discussion of transgressive heterogeneity as a *time between times* see Hans Peter Deurr, *Dreamtime: Concerning the Boundary Between Wilderness and Civilization*, trans. Felicitas Goodman, New York: Basil Blackwell, 1987.

55. Bataille, *Visions of Excess*, p. 128; see also *Inner Experience*, trans. Leslie Anne Boldt, Albany: State University of New York Press, 1988.

56. See, for instance, Michel Foucault, "Preface to Transgression," in *Language, Counter-Memory, Practice*, trans. Donald F. Bouchard and Sherry Simon, Ithaca, NY: Cornell University Press, 1977, pp. 29-52.

57. Georges Bataille, *Inner Experience.*

58. Georges Bataille, *The Accursed Share: An Essay on General Economy, Volume 1*, New York: Zone Books, 1988, p. 10.

59. Durkeim and Mauss, *Primitive Classification*, p. 7.

60. Bataille, *Theory of Religion*, p.41.

61. Georges Bataille, "Celestial Bodies," *October*, 36 (Spring 1986), p. 78.

62. Jacques Lacan, "The Mirror Stage as Formative of the Function of the I as Revealed in Psychoanalytic Experience," in *Ecrits: a Selection*, trans. Alan Sheridan, New York: W.W. Norton and Co., 1977, p. 3.

63. *Ibid.*

64. Jacques Lacan, *Speech and Language in Psychoanalysis*, trans. Anthony Wilden, Baltimore: Johns Hopkins University Press, 1968.

65. Althusser, "Ideology and Ideological State Apparatus," p. 162.

66. *Ibid.*, p. 168.

67. *Ibid.*

68. Julia Kristeva, *Revolution in Poetic Language*, trans. Margaret Waller, New York: Columbia University Press, 1984, pp. 46-47.

69. Julia Kristeva, "Freud and Love: Treatment and its Discontents," in *Tales of Love*, trans. Leon S. Roudiez, New York: Columbia University Press, 1987, p. 26.

70. Paul Smith, *Discerning the Subject*, Minneapolis: University of Minnesota Press, 1988, p. 121.

71. Julia Kristeva, *Powers of Horror: an Essay on Abjection*, New York: Columbia University Press, 1982.

72. *Ibid.*, p. 64.

73. Bataille, *The Accursed Share*, p. 27.

74. Durkheim, *Elementary Forms*, p. 426.

75. In using the term partial stabilization I mean to connote both the politically charged and always contingent (and thus contestable) character of all ritual orderings.

76. Bataille, *The Accursed Share*, p. 106.

77. *Ibid.*

78. *Ibid.*, pp. 36-37.

79. Jean Baudrillard, *The Ecstasy of Communication*, trans. Bernard and Caroline Schutze, New York: Semiotext(e), 1988, p. 46.

80. *Ibid.*, p. 49.

81. Baudrillard, "The System of Objects," p. 25.

82. Baudrillard, *The Ecstasy of Communication*, pp. 50-51.

83. Durkheim, *Elementary Forms*, p. 385.

84. Émile Durkeim, as quoted in Steven Lukes, *Émile Durkheim, His Life and Work: A Historical and Critical Study*, New York: Harper and Row, 1973, p. 555.

CHAPTER EIGHT – ELEMENTARY FORMS OF ULTRAMODERN SOCIAL LIFE

1. The quotes here from Columbus, as well as those in the following paragraph, are excerpted from Tzvetan Todorov, *The Conquest of America*, trans. Richard Howard, New York: Harper and Row, 1984, pp. 36, 38, 40.

2. Michael Taussig, *The Nervous System*, New York: Routledge, 1992, p. 128.

3. Émile Durkheim, *The Elementary Forms of the Religious Life*, trans. Joseph Ward Swain, New York: The Free Press, 1915.

4. Sigmund Freud, *Totem and Taboo: Resemblances Between the Psychic Life of Savages and Neurotics*, trans. A.A. Brill, New York: Vintage Books, 1918.

5. For related reading of critical aspects of Durkheimian sociology see Frank Pearce, *The Radical Durkheim*, London: Unwin Hyman, 1989.

6. Arthur Kroker, "Baudrillard's Marx," in Arthur Kroker and David Cook, *The Postmodern Scene: Excremental Culture and Hyper-Aesthetics*, New York: St. Martins Press, 1986, pp. 170-188.

7. Georges Bataille, "Attraction and Repulsion I: Tropisms, Sexuality, Laughter and Tears," in Denis Hollier, ed., *The College of Sociology (1937-39)*, trans. Betsy Wing, Minneapolis: University of Minnesota Press, 1988, p. 107.

8. Taussig, *The Nervous System*, p. 128.

9. Rene Girard, *Violence and the Sacred*, trans. Patrick Gregory, Baltimore: Johns Hopkins University Press, 1977, p. 306.

10. *Ibid.*, p. 317.

11. Émile Durkheim and Marcel Mauss, *Primitive Classification*, trans. Rodney Needham, Chicago: University of Chicago Press, 1963, p. 5.

12. *Ibid.*, p. 6.

13. *Ibid.*, p. 5.

14. Max Weber, *The Protestant Ethic and the Spirit of Capitalism*, trans. Talcott Parsons, New York: Charles Scribner's and Sons, 1958.

15. Georges Bataille, *The Accursed Share: An Essay on General Economy, Volume 1*, trans. Robert Hurley, New York: Zone Books, 1988.

16. Jean Baudrillard, *The Mirror of Production*, trans. Mark Poster, St. Louis: Telos Press, 1975.

17. Herbert Marcuse, *Eros and Civilization: A Philosophical Inquiry Into Freud*, New York: Vintage Books, 1955, p. x.

18. Julia Kristeva, "Freud and Love," in *Tales of Love*, trans. Leon S. Roudiez, New York: Columbia University Press, 1987, p. 41.

19. Girard, p. 146.

20. *Ibid.*

21. *Ibid.*

22. The anarchistic fantasy of rematerializing such headless social forms was a paradoxical feature of the "secret" initiatives of Georges Bataille and others who, for a time, gathered together and produced (w)ritings under the totemic sign of *Acephale*. My own knowledge of anthropological materials on acephalous societies is in debt to Raymond J. Michalowski whose text, *Order Law and Crime*, New York: Random House, 1985, represents an important critique of the sacrificial origins of criminal law. See also, Stephen Pfohl, "Labeling Criminals," in Laurence Ross, ed., *Law and Deviance*, Beverly Hills, CA: Sage, 1981, pp. 65-97.

23. See, for instance, Monica Sjöö and Barbara Mor, *The Great Cosmic Mother: Rediscovering the Religion of the Earth*, San Francisco: Harper and Row, 1987, p.16.

24. For a particularly salient account of such disappearance, see Mary Condren, *The Serpent and the Goddess: Women, Religion, and Power in Celtic Ireland*, San Francisco: Harper and Row, 1989.

25. *Ibid.*, p. 259.

26. Julia Kristeva, *Revolution in Poetic Language*, trans. Margaret Waller, New York: Columbia University Press, p. 250.

27. Girard, p. 259.

28. Kristeva, *Revolution in Poetic Language*, p. 250.

29. *Ibid.*

30. *Ibid.*, p. 76.

31. *Ibid.*

32. *Ibid.*, p. 78.

33. For related questions see Julian Pefanis, "Revenge of the Mirror People," in *Heterology and the Postmodern: Bataille, Baudrillard and Lyotard*, Durham, NC: Duke University Press, 1991, pp. 103-119. A critical concern with the radicality of mirrored illusions is also at the spiralling center of Jean Baudrillard, *Seduction*, trans. Brian Singer, New York: St. Martin's Press, 1990. Although both provocative and challenging, the radicality of Baudrillard's (w)riting here remains filtered by what I find difficult to read as anything but twisting layers of heterosexist imagery. For an engaging filmic reinscription of Baudrillard's mirrored games I suggest the controversial German feminist film by Elfi Mikesch and Monika Treut, *Seduction: the Cruel Woman/ Verfuhrung: Die grausame Frau*, (1985).

34. Jean Baudrillard, *Cool Memories*, trans. Christ Turner, New York: Verso, 1990, p. 57.

35. Helene Cixous, "Sorties," in Helene Cixous and Catherine Clément, *The Newly Born Woman*, trans. Betsy Wing, Minneapolis: University of Minnesota Press, 1986, p. 140.

36. Jean Baudrillard, *L'echange Symbolique et la Mort*, trans. and quoted in Douglas Kellner, *Jean Baudrillard: From Marxism to Postmodernism and Beyond*, Stanford, CA: Stanford University Press, 1989, p. 105.

37. Claude Levi-Strauss, *Totemism*, trans. Rodney Needham, Boston: Beacon Press, 1963, p. 102.

38. *Ibid.*, pp. 102, 104.

39. Jacques Derrida, *Of Grammatology*, trans. Gayatri Chakravorty Spivak, Baltimore: Johns Hopkins University Press, 1974, pp. 139-140.

40. *Ibid.*, p. 138.

41. *Ibid.*, p. 139.

42. See, for instance, Jacques Derrida, "From Restricted to General Economy: A Hegelianism without Reserve," in *Writing and Difference*, trans. Alan Bass, Chicago: University of Chicago, 1978, pp. 251-277.

43. Jacques Derrida, "Différance," in *Margins of Philosophy*, trans. Alan Bass, Chicago: University of Chicago Press, 1982, p. 17.

44. Durkheim, *Elementary Forms*, p. 477.

45. Levi-Strauss, p. 96.

46. *Ibid.*

47. Durkheim, *Elementary Forms*, p. 426.

48. *Ibid*, pp. 424, 425, 424.

49. *Ibid.*, p. 426.

CHAPTER NINE – TOTEMS AND TABOO

1. Rosemary Jackson, *Fantasy: the Literature of Subversion*, New York: Methuen, 1981, p. 64.

2. Sigmund Freud, "The Uncanny," in *The Standard Edition of the Complete Psychological Works of Sigmund Freud*, trans. James Stachey, London: The Hogarth Press, 1961, p. 237.

3. *Ibid.*

4. *Ibid.*

5. Sigmund Freud, *Totem and Taboo*, trans. A.A. Brill, New York: Vintage Books, 1918, p. 207.

6. *Ibid.*, p. 44.

7. *Ibid.*, p. 43.

8. Rosiland Coward and John Ellis, *Language and Materialism: Developments in Semiology and the Theory of the Subject*, Boston: Routledge and Kegan Paul, 1977, p. 101.

9. Freud, *Totem and Taboo*, p. 4.

10. *Ibid.*, p. 24.

11. *Ibid.*, p. 7.

12. See, for instance, Judith Lewis Herman, *Father-Daughter Incest*, Cambridge: Harvard University Press, 1981. Unlike the ritual reversals of power implied by my genealogically informed use of the term *incest*, Herman notes that within contemporary (patriarchal) society, "there is nothing subtle about power relations between adults and children. Adults have more power than children.... Children are esssentially a captive poulation, totally dependent upon their parents or other adults for their basic needs. Thus they will do whatever they perceive to be necessary to preserve a relationship with their caretakers" (p. 27).

13. Teresa de Lauretis, *Alice Doesn't: Feminism, Semiotics, Cinema*, Bloomington: University of Indiana Press, 1984, p. 114.

14. Freud, *Totem and Taboo*, p. 192.

15. *Ibid.*, p. 202.

16. For a theoretical elaboration of this suggestion see Judith Butler, *Gender Trouble: Feminism and Subversion of Identity*, New York: Routledge, 1990. Butler here draws upon a mix of feminist, critical psychoanalytic and Foucaultian thought in theorizing the construction of sexual dispositions as psychic and material effects of the performative enactment of prohibitive laws which, in turn, function to congeal the genealogy of their own productive power.

17. While the phrase TOTAL WAR refers, in part, to Paul Virilio's descriptions of militaristic social technologies dominating contemporary society, I mean also to direct attention to the relationship between imperial social forms and the prohibition on intimate homosexual exchange. This relation is suggested by A.L. Kroeber in an early review of the ethnological merits of Freud's theory of the incest taboo. See A.L. Kroeber, *"Totem and Taboo*: an Ethnologic Psychoanalysis," *American Anthropologist*, 22 (1920), pp. 48-55. In contrast to the "neurotic anxiety" surrounding both heterosexual incest and homosexual relations in "Hellenistic, Roman Imperial and recent eras," Kroeber points to the institutional acceptance of homosexuality by "North American and Siberian natives" as well as during Western Middle Ages. Although not explicit in Kroeber's account, one particularly fruitful line for theorizing culturally specific taboos on ecstatic forms of "homosexual" expression and upon the excesses of "nonuseful" or non (re)productive eroticism in general is to examine the genealogical relations between such taboos and the disciplinary rituals governing (male) bodies in imperial or military guided social formations. This, perhaps, is a way of understanding the corpus of Michel Foucault's (w)ritings.

18. *Ibid.*, p. 183.

19. *Ibid.*, p. 191.

20. *Ibid.*, p. 185.

21. Gay men's lack of desire to reproduce this sacrificial process of "gift exchange" (at least in the flesh) is perhaps, in part, why many remain so threatening to modern patriarchy. It is also (potentially) a material basis for "queer" political alliances between gays and feminists.

22. Gayle Rubin, "The Traffic in Women: Notes on the Political Economy of Sex," in R.R. Reiter, ed., *Toward an Anthropology of Women*, New York: Monthly Review Press, 1975, pp. 191-192.

23. Teresa de Lauretis, "Through the Looking Glass," in Tereas de Lauretis and Stephen Heath, eds., *The Cinematic Apparatus*, New York: St. Martin's Press, 1980, p.190.

24. *Ibid.*, p. 193.

25. Stephen Heath, as quoted in de Lauretis, "Through the Looking Glass," p. 193.

26. Freud, *Totem and Taboo*, p. 90.

27. *Ibid.*, p. 29.

28. Helene Cixous, "Sorties," in Helene Cixous and Catherine Clément, *The Newly Born Woman*, trans. Betsy Wing, Minneapolis: University of Minnesota Press, 1986, p. 149.

29. *Ibid.*, p. 150.

30. *Ibid.*, p. 154.

31. *Ibid.*, pp. 154-155.

32. Catherine Clément, "The Guilty One," in Cixous and Clément, *The Newly Born Woman*, p. 8.

33. *Ibid.*, pp. 22-23.

34. Jean Baudrillard, *For a Critique of the Political Economy of the Sign*, trans. Charles Levin, St. Louis: Telos Press, 1981, p. 150.

35. Jean Baudrillard, "Symbolic Exchange and Death," in *Selected Writings*, Stanford, CA: Stanford University Press, 1988, p. 120.

36. Baudrillard, *For a Critique of the Political Economy of the Sign*, p. 132.

37. Allon White, "Hysteria and the End of Carnival," in Nancy Armstrong and Leonard Tennehouse, eds., *The Violence of Representation*, New York: Routledge, 1989, p. 163.

38. Georges Bataille, *Erotism: Death and Sensuality*, trans. Mary Dalywood, San Francisco: City Lights, 1986, p. 218.

39. *Ibid.*, p. 212.

40. *Ibid.*, p. 216.

41. *Ibid.*, p. 41.

42. *Ibid.*, p. 214.

43. Michel Foucault, "Preface to Transgression," in *Language, Counter-Memory, Practice*, Ithaca, NY: Cornell University Press, 1977.

44. Marcel Mauss, *The Gift*, trans. Ian Cunnison, New York: Norton, 1967, p. 74.

45. Bataille, *Erotism*, p. 61.

46. For a feminist discussion of the merits and limitations of Bataille's contradictory critique of patriarchy see Michèle Richman, "Eroticism in the Patriarchal Order," in Paul Buck, ed., *Violent Silence: Celebrating Georges Bataille*, London: The Georges Bataille Event, 1984, pp. 91-102.

47. Monica Sjöö and Barbara Mor, *The Great Cosmic Mother: Rediscovering the Religion of the Earth*, San Francisco: Harper and Row, 1987.

48. Arthur Evans, *The God of Ecstasy: Sex Roles and the Madness of Dionysos*, New York: St. Martin's Press, 1988; and Arthur Evans, *Witchcraft and the Gay Counterculture*, Boston: Fag Rag Books, 1978.

49. For a radical feminist theorization of the parodic displacement of both sex and gender, see Judith Butler, *Gender Troubles*.

50. Alice Jardine, *Gynesis*, Ithaca: Cornell University Press, 1985.

51. For a critique of the commodified character of "New Age" social technologies, see Andrew Ross, "New Age Technoculture," in Lawrence Grossberg, Cary Nelson and Paula Treichler, eds., *Cultural Studies*, New York: Routledge, 1992, pp. 531-555.

52. Michel Foucault, "Nietzsche, Genealogy and History," in *Language, Counter-Memory, Practice*, Ithaca: Cornell University Press, 1977, p. 139.

53. *Ibid.*, pp. 143-144.

54. *Ibid.*, p. 142.

55. *Ibid.*, p. 147

56. *Ibid.*, p. 147.

57. *Ibid.*, p. 148.

58. *Ibid.*, pp. 148-149.

59. *Ibid.*, p. 150.

60. Freud, *Totem and Taboo*, p. 112.

61. Freud, "The Uncanny," p. 244.

62. *Ibid.*, p. 226.

63. *Ibid.*, p. 234.

64. *Ibid.*, p. 241.

65. *Ibid.*, p. 234.

66. *Ibid.*, p. 235.

67. Sjöö and Mor, p. 235.

68. Julia Kristeva, *Tales of Love*, trans. Leon S. Roudiez, New York: Columbia University Press, 1987, p. 105.

69. Freud, "The Uncanny," p. 235.

70. *Ibid.*, p. 240.

71. Freud, *Totem and Taboo*, p. 116.

72. *Ibid.*, p. 121.

73. Freud, "The Uncanny," p. 235.

74. *Ibid.*

75. *Ibid.*

76. *Ibid.*, p. 236.

77. Kristeva, p. 21.

78. *Ibid.*, p. 26.

79. *Ibid.*, p. 24.

80. *Ibid.*, p. 28.

81. *Ibid.*, p. 25.

82. *Ibid.*

83. *Ibid.*, p. 24.

84. Arthur Kroker, *Technology and the Canadian Mind: Innis/McLuhan/Grant*, Montreal: New World Perspective, 1984, p. 58.

85. For a related discussion of modernity and uncanny contact with *the real* see Mladen Dolar, "'I Shall Be with You on Your Wedding Night': Lacan and the Uncanny," *October*, 58 (Fall 1991), pp. 6-23.

86. Paul Virilio, *The Aesthetics of Disappearance*, trans. Philip Beitchman, New York: Semiotext(e), 1991, p. 12.

87. Marshall McLuhan, *Understanding Media: the Extensions of Man*, New York: McGraw-Hill, 1964, p. 51.

88. *Ibid.*, p. 52.

89. Marcel Mauss, *A General Theory of Magic*, trans. Robert Brian, London: Routledge and Kegan Paul, 1972.

90. My hope in stupidly deploying such awkward phrasings is to avoid or displace the more traditional Western binary and, I believe, implicitly racist division between (good) *white magic* and (evil) *black magic*, without simply inverting the hierarchy of these terms.

91. Jean Baudrillard, *Seduction*, trans. Brian Singer, New York: St. Martin's Press, 1990, p. 1.

92. Marshall McLuhan, *Counter Blast*, Toronto: McClelland and Stewart, 1969, p. 26.

93. *Ibid.*, p. 22.

94. McLuhan, *Understanding Media*, p. 55.

95. Marshall McLuhan and Quentin Fiore, *The Medium is the Massage: An Inventory of Effects*, New York: Bantom Books, 1967, p. 26.

96. Freud, "The Uncanny," p. 241.

97. Catherine Clément, *The Weary Sons of Freud*, trans. Nicole Ball, New York: Verso, 1987, p. 54.

98. *Ibid.*

99. Jean Baudrillard, *In the Shadow of the Silent Majorities ...or The End of the Social*, trans. Paul Foss, Paul Patton and John Johnston, New York: Semiotext(e), 1983.

100. Christopher Lasch, *The Culture of Narcissism: American Life in An Age of Diminishing Expectations*, New York: W.W. Norton, 1978.

101. *Ibid.*, p. 46.

102. *Ibid.*, p. 47.

103. Eugene Emerson Jennings, *Routes to the Executive Suite*, as quoted in Lasch, p. 46.

104. Lasch, p. 44.

105. *Ibid.*, p. 45.

106. *Ibid.*, p. 48.

107. *Ibid.*, p. 47.

108. Michael Schrage, "The Media is the (Corporate) Culture," *The Boston Sunday Globe*, November 4, 1990, p. A2.

109. Lasch, p. 49.

110. *Ibid.*

111. *Ibid.*, p. 51.

112. *Ibid.*

113. *Ibid.*

114. Freud, *Totem and Taboo*, p. 120.

115. *Ibid.*, p. 114.

116. *Ibid.*, p. 121.

117. Freud, "The Uncanny," p. 242.

118. *Ibid.*, p. 244.

119. Sigmund Freud, "From the History of an Infantile Neurosis (1918)," in *Three Case Histories*, New York: Collier Books, 1963, p. 295.

120. Sjöö and Mor, p. 105.

121. Émile Durkheim, *The Elementary Forms of the Religious Life*, trans. Joseph Ward Swain, New York: The Free Press, 1915, pp. 122, 107, 106, 255.

122. *Ibid.*, pp. 100, 256, 257.

123. *Ibid.*, p. 16.

124. Jacques Attali, *Noise: the Political Economy of Music*, trans. Brian Massumi, Minneapolis: University of Minnesota Press, 1985, p. 22.

125. Mikhail Bakhtin, *Rabelais and His World*, trans. Helene Iswolsky, Bloomington: Indiana University Press, 1984, pp. 88, 89, 90.

126. Attali, p. 22.

127. Michel Foucault, *The History of Sexuality, Vol. I*, trans. Robert Hurley, New York: Vintage Books, 1980, pp. 57-62.

128. Philippe Aries, *The Hour of Our Death*, trans. Helen Weaver, New York: Vintage Books, 1982.

129. *Ibid.*, p. 102.

130. *Ibid.*, p. 103.

131. *Ibid.*, pp. 103-104.

132. *Ibid.*, p. 130.

133. *Ibid.*, p. 132.

134. *Ibid.*, p. 136.

135. *Ibid.*, p. 112.

136. *Ibid.*, p. 116.

137. *Ibid.*, p. 123.

138. *Ibid.*, p. 127.

139. *Ibid.*, pp.127-128.

140. *Ibid.*, pp. 129, 138-139.

141. Sjöö and Mor, p. 298.

142. Sheila Balken, Ronald J. Berger and Janet Schmidt, *Crime and Deviance in America: a*

Critical Approach, Belmont, CA: Wadsworth, 1980, p. 231.

143. Michel Foucault, *Madness and Civilization: A History of Insanity in the Age of Reason*, trans. Richard Howard, New York: Random House, 1965, pp. 15-16.

144. *Ibid.*, p. 11.

145. *Ibid.*, p. 70.

146. Michel Foucault, *The Order of Things*, trans. Alan Sheridan, (New York: Pantheon 1970), pp. 3-16.

147. Stephen Pfohl and Avery Gordon, "Criminological Displacements: a Sociological Deconstruction," *Social Problems*, Vol. 33, No. 6 (October/December 1986), p. S101.

148. Foucault, *Madness and Civilization*, p. 210.

149. Michel Foucault, *The Birth of the Clinic: An Archeology of Medical Perception*, trans. A. M. Sheridan Smith, (New York: Vintage Books, 1973), p. 166.

150. *Ibid.*, p. 170.

151. *Ibid.*, p. 177.

152. *Ibid.*

CHAPTER TEN – INFANTILE RECURRENCE AND OVERDEVELOPMENT

1. Sigmund Freud, "The Uncanny," *The Standard Edition of the Complete Psychological Works of Sigmund Freud,* trans. James Strachey, Volume XVII, London: The Hogarth Press, 1961, p. 241.

2. W. Lea Snyder, "Boston's War on Blacks," *Blast Unlimited*, No. 2 (1990). p. 10.

3. Jacques Derrida, as spoken in script of Ken McMullen's film, *Ghost Dance*.

4. Margot Harry, *Attention, MOVE! This Is America!*, Chicago: Banner Press, 1987, p. 151.

5. *Ibid.*, p. 150.

6. Jacques Derrida, as spoken in *Ghost Dance*.

7. Michael Taussig, *Shamanism, Colonialism and the Wild Man: A Study in Terror and Healing*, Chicago: University of Chicago Press, 1987, p. 121.

8. Robin Wagner-Pacifici, "The Text of Transgression: the City of Philadelphia versus Move," *Journal: A Contemporary Art Magazine*, Spring 1987, p. 20.

9. Taussig, p. 128.

10. Wagner-Pacifici, p. 20.

11. Taussig, p. 128.

12. Wagner-Pacific, p. 20.

13. Harry, p. 14.

14. Kathy Acker, "Scenes from World War III," in Richard Prince, ed., *Wild History*, New York: Tanam Press, 1985, p. 110.

15. Karl Marx and Frederick Engels, "Manifesto of the Communist Party (1847)," in Robert C. Tucker, *The Marx-Engels Reader, Second Edition*, New York: W.W. Norton, 1978, p. 475.

16. Hans Peter Duerr, *Dreamtime: Concerning the Boundary between Wilderness and Civilization*, trans. Felicitas Goodman, New York: Basil Blackwell, 1985.

17. Monica Sjöö and Barbara Mor, *The Great Cosmic Mother: Rediscovering the Religion of the Earth*, San Francisco: Harper and Row, 1987.

18. Helene Cixous and Catherine Clément, *The Newly Born Woman*, trans. Betsy Wing, Minneapolis: University of Minnesota Press, 1986, p. 33.

19. Arthur Evans, *The God of Ecstasy: Sex Roles and the Madness of Dionysos*, New York: St. Martin's Press, 1988.

20. Henry Louis Gates, Jr., *The Signifying Monkey: A Theory of African-American Literary*

Criticism, New York: Oxford University Press, 1988.

21. Allon White, "Hysteria and the End of Carnival," in Nancy Armstrong and Leonard Tennehouse, eds., *The Violence of Representation*, New York: Routledge, 1989, p. 160.

22. *Ibid.*

23. *Ibid.*, p. 161.

24. Roger Caillois, "Festival," (1939) in Denis Hollier, ed., *The College of Sociology (1937-39)*, trans. Betsy Wing, Minneapolis: University Of Minnesota Press, 1988, pp. 279-303.

25. Clair Wills, "Upsetting the Public: Carnival, Hysteria and Women's Texts," in Ken Hirschkop and David Shepard, eds., *Bakhtin and Cultural Theory*, Manchester, England: Manchester University Press, 1989, pp. 130-152.

26. Jean Baudrillard, *In the Shadow of the Silent Majorities...or The End of the Social*, trans. Paul Foss and John Johnston, New York: Semiotext(e), 1983, p. 7.

27. Georges Bataille, "The Psychological Structure of Fascism, " in *Visions of Excess: Selected Writings, 1927-1939*, trans. Allan Stoekl with Carl R. Lovitt and Donald M. Leslie, Jr., Minneapolis: University of Minnesota Press, 1985, p. 142.

28. Jean Baudrillard, *Mirror of Production*, trans. Mark Poster, St. Louis: Telos Press, 1975.

29. See, for instance, Klaus Theweleit, *Male Fantasies, Vol. I*, trans. Stephen Conway, Minneapolis: University of Minnesota Press, 1987; and Susan Griffin, *Pornography and Silence*, New York: Harper and Row, 1981.

30. Sjöö and Mor, pp. 16, 17.

31. Jean Baudrillard, *Forget Foucault*, trans. Nicole Dufreesne, New York: Semiotext(e), 1987, p. 87.

32. Bataille, "The Psychological Structure of Fascism," p. 156.

33. *Ibid.*

34. *Ibid.*

35. Michel Foucault, *Madness and Civilization: A History of Insanity in the Age of Reason*, trans. Richard Howard, New York: Random House, 1965, p. 1.

36. Guy Debord, *Society of the Spectacle*, Detroit: Black and Red Press, (1967) 1983, pp. 153-54.

37. As a "model" for this plagiarized dialogue see Kathy Acker, *Don Quixote*, New York: Grove Press, 1986, p. 69.

38. Emily Bronte, *Wuthering Heights*, Middlesex, England: Penguin Books, (1847) 1965.

39. Georges Bataille, *Literature and Evil*, trans. Alastair Hamilton, London: Marion Boyars, 1985, p. 16.

40. Georges Bataille, *The Theory of Religion*, trans. Robert Hurley, New York: Zone Books, 1989, pp. 17-25.

41. Georges Bataille, *Erotism*, trans. Mary Dalywood, San Francisco: City Lights, (1957) 1986, p. 11.

42. Sigmund Freud, *Totem and Taboo*, trans. A.A. Brill, New York: Vintage Books, 1918, p. 174.

43. *Ibid.*, pp. 174, 176.

44. Georges Bataille, "The Notion of Expenditure" in *Visions of Excess*, p. 122.

45. Bataille, *Literature and Evil*, p. 21.

46. Freud, *Totem and Taboo*, p. 207.

47. *Ibid.*, p. 205.

48. *Ibid.*, p. 207.

49. Georges Bataille, "The 'Old Mole' and the Prefix *Sur* in the Words *Surhomme* [Superman] and *Surrealist*," in *Visions of Excess*, p. 43.

50. Bataille, *Literature and Evil*, p. 18.

51. Henri Lefebvre, *Everyday Life in the Modern World*, New Brunswick: Transition Books, 1984, p. 29.

52. Sjöö and Mor, pp. 279-280.

53. Bataille, *Literature and Evil*, p. 18.

54. *Ibid.*, pp. 26, 28.

55. Georges Bataille, as quoted in Bernard Noel, "The Question," in Paul Buck, ed., *Violent Silence: Celebrating Georges Bataille*, London: The Georges Bataille Event, 1984, p. 45.

56. Bernard Noel, p. 46.

57. Georges Bataille, *The Accursed Share: An Essay on General Economy,Volume 1*, trans. Robert Hurley, New York: Zone Books, (1967) 1989, p. 56.

58. *Ibid.*, p. 13.

59. Trinh T. Minh-ha, *Woman, Native, Other: Writing Postcoloniality and Feminism*, Bloomington: Indiana University Press, 1989, pp. 22-23.

60. Ariel Dorfman, *The Empire's New Clothes*, New York: Pantheon, 1983, p. 151.

61. *Ibid.*, p. 169.

62. *Ibid.*, pp. 169-170.

63. *Ibid.*, p. 172.

64. *Ibid.*, p. 152.

65. See, for instance, Marshall Berman, *All That Is Solid Melts Into Air: The Experience of Modernity*, New York: Simon and Schuster, 1982, pp. 37- 86.

66. Freud, *Totem and Taboo*, p. 207.

PART THREE – RE-MEMBERING DIFFERENTLY: FLESH BEFORE WORDS

Dorothy E. Smith, *The Conceptual Practices of Power: A Feminist Sociology of Knowledge*, Boston: Northeastern University Press, 1990, pp. 21-22.

Toni Morrison, "The Site of Memory," in Russell Ferguson, Martha Gever, Trinh T. Minh-ha and Cornel West, eds., *Out There: Marginalization and Contemporary Cultures*, New York: The New Museum of Contemporary Art, and Cambridge, MA: The MIT Press, 1990, p. 303.

Patricia Hill Collins, *Black Feminist Thought: Knowledge, Consciousness, and the Politics of Empowerment*, Boston: Unwin Hyman, 1990, pp. 236-37.

CHAPTER ELEVEN – YUPPIES FROM MARS

1. Sol Yurik, *Metatron, the Recording Angel*, (New York: Semiotext(e), 1985), p. 104.

2. Susan Buck-Morss, *The Dialectics of Seeing: Walter Benjamin and the Arcades Project*, Cambridge, MA: The MIT Press, 1989, p. 219.

3. Walter Benjamin, as quoted in Buck-Morss, *The Dialectics of Seeing*, p. 219.

4. Henry Louis Gates, Jr., *The Signifying Monkey: A Theory of African-American Literary Criticism*, New York: Oxford University Press, 1988, p. 58.

5. Deena Weinstein and Michael Weinstein, "Deconstruction as Cultural History/The Cultural History of Deconstruction," *Canadian Journal of Political and Social Theory*, Vol. 14, No. 1-2, and 3 (1990), p. 15.

6. Gayatri Chakravorty Spivak, "Translation and forward to 'Draupadi' by Mahasveta Devi," in Elizabeth Abel, ed. *Writing and Sexual Difference*, Chicago: University of Chicago Press, 1981, pp. 262-63.

7. Marcel Mauss, *The Gift*, trans. Ian Cunnison, New York: Norton, 1967, p. 54.

CHAPTER TWELVE – META-VOODOO ECONOMICS

1. Jean Genet, *The Blacks: a Clown Shown*, trans. Bernard Frechtman, New York: Grove Press, 1960, p. 4.

2. Chant to Papa Legba, as recorded in Zora Neale Hurston, *Tell My Horse: Voodoo and Life in Haiti and Jamaica*, New York: Harper and Row, 1990, p. 129.

3. Hurston, *The Sanctified Church*, Berkeley, CA: Turtle Island, 1983, p. 51

4. Zora Neale Hurston, "Crazy for Democracy," in *I Love Myself When I Am Laughing...And Then Again When I Am Looking Mean and Impressive*, New York: The Feminist Press, 1979, p. 167.

5. Henry Louis Gates, Jr., *The Signifying Monkey: A Theory of African-American Literary Criticism*, New York: Oxford University Press, 1988, p. 52.

6. Houston A. Baker, Jr., "Caliban's Triple Play," in Henry Louis, Gates, Jr., *"Race," Writing and Difference*, Chicago: University of Chicago Press, 1985, pp. 381-395.

7. Gates, Jr., *The Signifying Monkey*, p. 49.

8. Hurston, *The Sanctified Church*, pp. 83, 78.

9. Hurston, *Tell My Horse*, p. 113.

10. Maya Deren, *Divine Horsemen: the Living Gods of Haiti*, London: McPherson and Co., 1953, pp. 251, 252, 253.

11. Hurston, *Tell My Horse*, p. 114.

12. Deren, *Divine Horsemen*, p. 62.

13. Hurston, *Tell My Horse*, pp. 113-114.

14. Michael Ventura, "Hear That Long Snake Moan," in *Shadow Dancing in the U.S.A.*, Los Angeles: Jeremy P. Tarcher, Inc., 1985, pp. 123-124.

15. Lawrence Grossberg, "Putting the Pop Back into Postmodernism," in Andrew Ross, ed., *Universal Abandon? The Politics of Postmodernism*, Minneapolis: University of Minnesota Press, 1988, p. 181.

16. *Ibid.*, pp. 180-181.

17. Yurik, *Metatron*, p. 24.

18. Cornel West, "Black Culture and Postmodernism," in Barbara Kruger and Phil Mariani, eds., *Remaking History*, Port Townsend, WA: Bay Press, 1989, pp. 92-93.

19. *Ibid.*, p. 93.

20. *Ibid.*, p. 94.

21. *Ibid.*, pp. 94, 95.

22. Jackie Orr, "Panic Diary: Reconstructing a Partial Politics and Poetics of Dis-Ease," p. 19 in draft manuscript to be included in Gale Miller and James A. Holstein, *Perspectives on Social Problems: Reconsidering Social Constructionism*, Greenwich, CT: JAI Press, 1992, forthcoming.

23. Jackie Orr, "Theory on the Market: Panic, Incorporating," *Social Problems*, Vol. 37, No. 4 (November 1990), p. 475.

24. Hurston, *The Sanctified Church*, p. 49.

25. *Ibid.*, p. 50.

26. Alison Luterman, "Voodoo: A Real Life Encounter With the Gods," *Boston Phoenix*, April 27, 1988, Section 2, p. 5. For an extended discussion of the contemporary practice of Voodoo in the U.S. see Karen McCarthy Brown, *Mama Lola: A Vodou Priestess in Brooklyn*, Berkeley: University of California Press, 1991.

CHAPTER THIRTEEN – THE ORPHANS' REVENGE

1. Eileen Simpson, *Orphans: Real and Imaginary*, New York: Weidenfeld and Nicholson, 1987, p. 135.

2. These phrases, originally produced as "easy to stick on" signs by Pelle Lowe, and other elements of this section, were (for better and worse) stuck onto the walls of Boston's Institute of Contemporary Art by members of Sit Com International during the *ever so chic* opening of the show, *On the Passage of a Few People Through a Rather Brief Moment in Time*, a "spectacular" display of artifacts produced by the Situationist International, 1957-1972. There was a lot of interesting inFORMation given out about the Situationists from this corporate art display. At the same time, the show and its accompanying lectures represented the most cynical of art HIStory lessons, commodifying the Situationist International as a kind of (heroic) art movement and cutting off the relevance of questions raised by Situationists for the HIStorical scene in which the show itself took place in Boston. According to the editors of *Version 90*, a Boston publication with far more material links to Situationist concerns than the ICA: "In one 40-day period during September and October of 1989, over 100 people were shot on the streets of Roxbury, Mattapan and Dorchester, three of Boston's predominantly black neighborhoods. Toward the end of that same period of time, Boston's Institute of Contemporary Art, located in the affluent Back Bay, hosted the opening of *On the Passage of a Few People Through a Rather Brief Moment in Time*, a retrospective on the Situationist International movement. While local cops were stopping and searching any black male over the age of 14 just across town, the city's cultural dilettantes lamented about the woes of consumer culture while eyeing $15 'Plagiarism is Necessary' T-shirts. Despite flirtation with the *idea* of cultural dismemberment, the last thing the ICA and all its fellow institutions want, of course, is the real thing." *Version 90*, Vol. 1 (1990), p. 3. (Available from PMS Cafe Press, 107 Brighton Ave., Allston MA 02134 $13 postpaid.)

3. See, for instance, Guy Debord, *Society of the Spectacle*, Detroit: Black and Red Press, (1976) 1983; Raoul Vaneigem, trans. Donald Nicholson-Smith, *The Revolution of Everyday Life*, London: Aldgate Press, 1983; and Situationist International, *Situationist International Anthology*, trans, Ken Knabb, ed., Berkeley, CA: Bureau of Public Secrets, 1981.

4. Debord, *Society of the Spectacle*, sections 8, 18, 20, 6.

5. *Ibid.*, sections 20, 34.

6. In this and what follows I make parasitic use of sections of an important essay by Jonathan Crary, "Eclipse of the Spectacle," in Brian Wallis, ed., *Art After Modernism: Rethinking Representation*, New York: The New Museum of Contemporary Art, 1984, pp. 283-294. In Situationist terms, this act of *user-friendly* plagiarism is suggestive of a strategic *detournment*, "the fluid language of anti-ideology." See, for instance, Debord, *Society of the Spectacle*, sections 207-209.

7. Herman Melville, "The Confidence Man: His Masquerade", as excerpted in A. David Napier, *Masks, Transformation, and Paradox*, Berkeley: University of California Press, 1986, p. xxi.

8. Napier, *Masks, Transformations and Paradox*, p. 3.

9. Georges Bataille, "Attraction and Repulsion II," in Denis Hollier, ed., *The College of Sociology*, 1937-39, trans. Betsy Wing, Minneapolis: University of Minnesota Press, 1988, pp. 114-15.

10. Avery Gordon, *Ghostly Memories: Feminist Rituals of Writing the Social Text*, Ph.D. Dissertation, Boston College, Chestnut Hill, MA., 1990, p. 17.

11. *Ibid.*

12. D.L. Crockett-Smith, "Cowboy Eating His Children," in *Cowboy Amok*, Oakland, CA: The Black Scholars Press, 1987, p. 3.

13. Zora Neale Hurston, *The Sanctified Church*, Berkeley: Turtle Island, 1983, p. 81.

14. D.L. Crockett-Smith, "Cowboy Eating His Children," p. i.

15. See, for instance, Christic Institute, "The Contra-Drug Connection," in Renee Goldsmith Kasinsky, ed., *Crime, Oppression, and Inequality*, Needham Heights, MA: Ginn Press, 1991, pp. 157-168.

16. Hurston, *The Sanctified Church*, p. 91.

17. Judith Butler, *Gender Troubles: Feminism and the Subversion of Identity*, New York: Routledge, 1990, p. 137.

18. Monica Sjöö and Barbara Mor, *The Great Cosmic Mother: Rediscovering the Religion of the Earth*, San Francisco: Harper and Row, 1987, p. 21.

19. For the most part this passage and its "textual surrounds" represents a reinscription of Zora Neale Hurston, *Mules and Men*, Bloomington: Indiana University Pres, 1978, p. 246.

20. Butler, *Gender Troubles*, p. 120.

21. *Ibid.*, p. 126.

22. *Ibid.*

23. Simpson, *Orphans*, pp. 140-141.

24. Arthur Kroker, Marilouise Kroker and David Cook, *Panic Encyclopedia: the Definitive Guide to the Postmodern Scene*, New York: St. Martin's Press, 1989, p. 58.

25. Jean Baudrillard, *The Ecstasy of Communication*, trans. Bernard and Caroline Schutze, New York: Semiotext(e), 1988, pp. 17-18.

26. Jean Baudrillard, *Seduction*, trans. Brian Singer, New York: St. Martin's Press, 1990, pp. 88-89.

27. Ishmael Reed, *Mumbo Jumbo*, New York: Bantam Books, 1972, p. 87.

28. Simpson, *Orphans*, pp. 220, 221.

29. Alan Moore and Alan Davis, *Miracleman, No. 4*, Guerneville, CA: Eclipse Comics, November 1985.

30. *Ibid.*

31. Jean Baudrillard, *Simulations*, trans. Paul Foss, Paul Patton and Phillip Beitchman, New York: Semiotext(e), 1983, p. 115.

list of visual references

Part One. Still from the video text. *Bored to Death/War TV,* Jeremy Grainger and Stephen Pfohl. Source: remix of CNN & C₃I.

Chapter 1. "Fascism: byte by byte." Still from video-text *Death at the Parasite Cafe.* Source: remix of John Heartfield photomontage, contemporary advertising. S. Pfohl.

Chapter 2. "Cold Face Fingered." Still from video-text *Death at the Parasite Cafe.* Source: remix of Fendi advertisement. S. Pfohl.

Chapter 3. "Seven Hearts and a Jack." Still from video-text *Death at the Parasite Cafe.* Source: *Prison Notebooks of Jack O. Lantern.* S. Pfohl.

Chapter 4. "First Doll." Still from video-text *Death at the Parasite Cafe.* Source: remix of Barbie doll with words. S. Pfohl.

Chapter 5. "The Ecstasy of Communication." Still from video-text *Death at the Parasite Cafe.* Source: remix of John Heartfield photomontage, contemporary advertising. S. Pfohl.

Part Two. Still from the video text. *Bored to Death/War TV,* Jeremy Grainger and Stephen Pfohl. Source: remix found television.

Chapter 6. "While Eye/'I' (W)rite." Still from video-text *Death at the Parasite Cafe.* Source: *Prison Notebooks of Jack O. Lantern.* S. Pfohl.

Chapter 7. "White on Black TV." Still from video-text *Death at the Parasite Cafe.* Source: remix of prison scenes, Max Headroom. S. Pfohl.

Chapter 8. "Butcher Block Bush." Still from video-text *Death at the Parasite Cafe.* Source: remix John Heartfield photomontage. S. Pfohl.

Chapter 9. "And Behind My Back in HIStory." Still from video-text *Death at the Parasite Cafe.* Source: remix Joseph LaMantia, Stephen Pfohl (detail), photocollage. S. Pfohl.

Chapter 10. "College of Sociology, Osage Avenue." Still from video-text *Death at the Parasite Cafe.* Source: remix "Fantomas," Cinémathèque francaise and Cobbs Creek Park neighborhood, Philadephia after May 13, 1985 police bombing. S. Pfohl.

Part Three. Still from the video text *Criminological Displacements,* Stephen Pfohl and Avery Gordon. Boston: Parasite Cafe Productions, 1985. Source: remix Post-Attica Prison Riot Round-up, Bentham's Panopticon.

Chapter 11. "War Machine Face." Still from video-text *Death at the Parasite Cafe.* Source: night-vision goggles, Force 160, U.S. Army special-forces aviation unit. S. Pfohl.

Chapter 12. "Voodoo Metamorphosis." Still from video-text *Death at the Parasite Cafe.* Source: Remix of Jackie Orr photocollage, "Psycho-geographies, 1990"; Nell Dor photo, "Study in Black and White"; D'Ora Studios, Josephine Baker photo; Hannah Hoch photomontage; and David Henry, Boston building implosion photo. S. Pfohl.

Chapter 13. "Orphan Cats in Car." Still from video-text *Death at the Parasite Cafe."* Source: Jackie Orr photocollage. S. Pfohl.

Cover, Back, Front and End Pages. Source: remix of BOSTON GLOBE, CNN & C₃I. Jeremy Grainger.

acknowledgements

What parasitic connections engender this text? And what contradictions? The first time I was exposed to the term postmodernity was during a seven week institute on "Marxism and the Interpretation of Culture" at the University of Illinois. It was the summer of 1983 and the teachers who influenced me most were Gayatri Chakravorty Spivak, Stuart Hall and my fellow students. Between that time and this (w)riting there have been many others. I wish to give particular thanks to Jeremy Grainger for collaborating in the artistry, design and production of these pages and to Jackie Orr and Avery Gordon for countless moments of dialogue, critical engagement and sustaining friendship. And to Arthur and Marilouise Kroker, my CultureTexts editors and friends, for continuous support, encouragement and inspiration. And to Simon Winder, my editor at St. Martin's, and Amy Agigian, Charles Sarno and Fido Rodenbeck for assistance in editing this text.

And thanks to all of you who have at different times provided responses to the multiplicity of thoughts, words and parasitic fragments that constitute this (w)riting; but especially to Marc Driscoll, Andrew Herman, Victoria Burke, Pelle Lowe, Sandra Joshel, Janet Wirth-Cauchon, William Bogard, Susan Wildman, Paul Breines, Gisela Hinkle, Carel Rowe, Larry Zaborski, Alex Wirth-Cauchon, Tracey Stark, Stephanie Kulick, Maureen Whalen, Eric Mendelson, David Crockett Smith, Bill Coughlin, T. R. Young, Peg Bortner, Kathy Acker, Nettie & Celie, Stanley Aronowitz, Kathleen Ferraro, Ray Michalowski, Dorothy Smith, Warren Niesluchowski, Sev Bruyn, Josef Mendoza, Donna Heinley, Emily Kearns, Diane Nelson, Malcolm Murray, Glyn Hughes, Joseph Schneider, Michael Petrunik, Winifred Breines, Judith Butler, Michael Ryan, Hope Kurtz, Monique Brinson, Tim Norris, Eric Mendleson, Tres Pyle, Kim Sawchuk, Charles Derber, Donna Gaines, Drew Humphries, Ron Kramer, Diane Vaughan, Kristen Koptiuch, Wellington Bowler, Maria del Mar, Cheryl Boudreaux, Gail Faurschou, Doug Kellner, Eric Steinhart, Gale Miller, Tom Moylan, Jim Holstein, Teresa Podlesney, Andrew Haase, Herman Gray, Steve Best, María Milagros López, Ian Parker, Paul Smith, Chris Sharrett, Kate Stout, Andrew Ross, Richard Dello Bono, Heidi Figueroa, Christine Braunberger, Leigh Anthony, John Broughton, Ann Margaret Shy, David Ashley, David Crouteau, Holly Mason, Cristina Favretta, Laure Liverman, David Mayer, Sean Hayes, David Smagalla, Stuart Wamsley, KDN DLX, Damon Smith, Deb Furey, Lia Gagiatano, David Lach, Kathy Brady, Leah Blesoff, Reto Muller, Kelly Fitzgerald, Tony Vogt, Lisa Fuentes, Patricia Mellencamp, Susan Willis, Lisa Gonzales, Michael Lowe, Ben Davidson, Louis Kantos, Joseph LaMantia, Paul Gray, David Lach, Sandy Tarrant, Catherine Hollander, Sharlene Hess-Biber, Linda Paone, Emily Zakin, David Karp, Colleen Nagel, Lauren Leja, Bill Gamson, Steve LeBanc, Eunice Dougherty, Catherine John, Paul Cheevers, Paul Stein, George McLean, John Donovan, John Williamson, Paul Shervish, Ashley Barr, and Harry Mika. And to Boston College, the Audio-Visual Department of Boston College, WZBC-FM, the Center for Justice Studies at Arizona State University and Sit Com International for various sorts of institutional support.

Stephen Pfohl is an Associate Professor of Sociology at Boston College where he teaches courses on social theory, postmodern culture, deviance and social control, images and power, and social psychoanalysis. He is the author of *Predicting Dangerousness: the social construction of psychiatric reality*; *Images of Deviance and Social Control: a sociological history*; and the forthcoming *Venus in Video: cybernetics, male mas(s)ochism and the parasitism of ultramodern power*. A video maker, performing artist, and member of Sit Com International, Pfohl is also 1991-92 President of the Society for the Study of Social Problems.

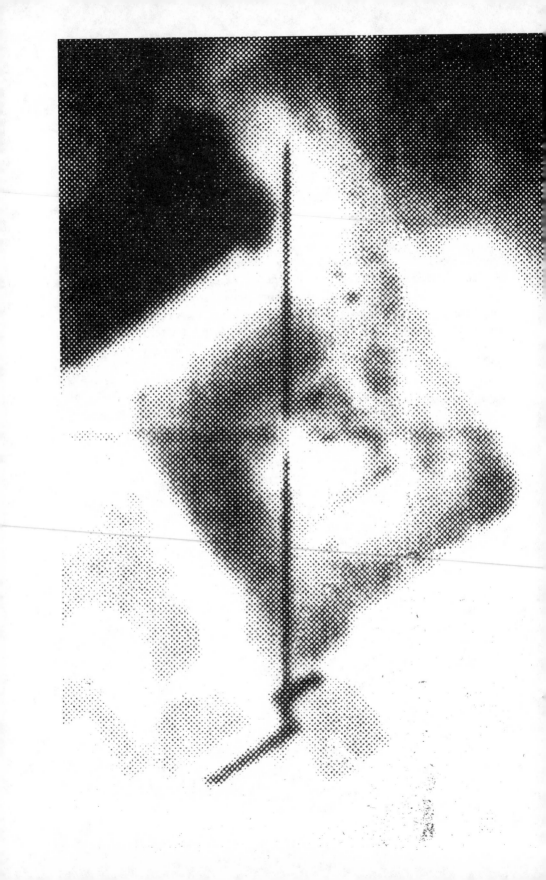